T0223165

Lecture Notes in Artificial Intelligence 1359

Subseries of Lecture Notes in Computer Science
Edited by J. G. Carbonell and J. Siekmann

Lecture Notes in Computer Science

Edited by G. Goos, J. Hartmanis and J. van Leeuwen

Springer

Berlin
Heidelberg
New York
Barcelona
Budapest
Hong Kong
London
Milan
Paris
Santa Clara
Singapore
Tokyo

Grigoris Antoniou   Aditya K. Ghose
Mirosław Truszczyński (Eds.)

Learning and Reasoning with Complex Representations

PRICAI'96 Workshops
on Reasoning with Incomplete
and Changing Information
and on Inducing Complex Representations
Cairns, Australia, August 26-30, 1996
Selected Papers

 Springer

Series Editors
Jaime G. Carbonell, Carnegie Mellon University, Pittsburgh, PA, USA
Jörg Siekmann, University of Saarland, Saarbrücken, Germany

Volume Editors

Grigoris Antoniou
School of Computing and Information Technology, Griffith University
Nathan, QLD 4111, Australia
E-mail: ga@cit.gu.edu.au

Aditya K. Ghose
Department of Business Systems, University of Wollongong
Wollongong, NSW 2522, Australia
E-mail: aditya@uow.edu.au

Mirosław Truszczyński
Computer Science Department, University of Kentucky
773C Anderson Hall, Lexington, KY 40506-0046, USA
E-mail: mirek@cs.engr.uky.edu

Cataloging-in-Publication Data applied for

Die Deutsche Bibliothek - CIP-Einheitsaufnahme

Learning and Reasoning with complex representations : selected
papers / PRICAI'96, Workshops on Reasoning with Incomplete and
Changing Information and on Inducing Complex Representations,
Cairns, Australia, August 26 - 30, 1996. Grigoris Antoniou ... (ed.). -
Berlin ; Heidelberg ; New York ; Barcelona ; Budapest ; Hong Kong
; London ; Milan ; Paris ; Santa Clara ; Singapore ; Tokyo : Springer,
1998
    (Lecture notes in computer science ; Vol. 1359 : Lecture notes in
    artificial intelligence)
    ISBN 3-540-64413-X

CR Subject Classification (1991): I.2

ISSN 0302-9743
ISBN 3-540-64413-X Springer-Verlag Berlin Heidelberg New York

© Springer-Verlag Berlin Heidelberg 1998
Printed in Germany

Typesetting: Camera ready by author
SPIN 10631772   06/3142 – 5 4 3 2 1 0   Printed on acid-free paper

Preface

The Pacific Rim International Conference on Artificial Intelligence (PRI-CAI) was set up to facilitate and stimulate the exchange of AI research, information, and technology in the Pacific Rim, and serves as a sister conference to its North American and European counterparts, AAAI and ECAI. This volume is based on two workshops that took place at PRI-CAI'96 in Cairns, Australia:

- The Workshop on Reasoning with Incomplete and Changing Information, and

- The Workshop on Inducing Complex Representations.

Reasoning with incomplete information deals with a central problem in AI, namely the imperfect nature of knowledge in most problems. Incomplete information refers to situations where the information actually required for a decision to be made is not available. In such cases intelligent systems need to make plausible conjectures. Another source of imperfect knowledge is that intelligent systems usually don't operate in a static world, rather their environment changes over time. Thus intelligent systems need to reason with changing information. This volume includes papers which describe a variety of methods, including nonmonotonic reasoning, belief networks and belief revision.

The Workshop on Inducing Complex Representations was motivated by the development, over the past few years, of several complex inductive paradigms where the underlying knowledge representation is more complex than that of the conventional propositional concept-learning systems and hence potentially more useful in real-life applications. Much of this activity has focused on the induction of logic programs or Horn clause theories, giving rise to the area of Inductive Logic Programming. More recently, there has been growing interest in the problem of inducing theories in a variety of distinct but related formalisms. These include constraint-based representations, including constraint logic programs, nonmonotonic theories, spatial representations and equational representations. This workshop set out to bring together researchers from all of these areas, to identify commonalities in the methods utilised and to encourage cross-fertilization of ideas. The response to the idea of such a forum was quite encouraging. This volume contains papers representing all of the areas mentioned above.

The idea of reasoning with non-standard representations, such as those required for dealing with incomplete information, cannot be divorced from the problem of learning using such representations, and vice versa. What we have attempted to do in this volume is highlight the common underlying threads by placing research in both areas in juxtaposition. To our knowledge, this is the first time an attempt such as this has been made. We wish to encourage, through this volume, an emerging trend that involves greater synergy between learning and reasoning with novel, complex, non-standard representations. The volume contains extended versions of selected papers presented at the two workshops. Each of them was scrutinized by three referees from the program committees.

We are particularly happy to include two invited papers by internationally recognized researchers. Henry Kyburg's paper on "Approximate Validity" derives from the theme of the first workshop, while the paper entitled "Curried Least General Generalization: a framework for higher order concept learning", by Srinivas Padmanabhuni, Randy Goebel and Koichi Furukawa derives from the theme of the second workshop. We have also included two tutorial papers which give introductions to selected aspects of the theme of this volume.

This volume would not have been completed without the active support of many persons. First we thank the authors of the contributions since they delivered the backbone of this volume. Our thanks go also to the workshop participants for interesting discussions. The members of the program committees assisted us greatly in improving the quality of the volume. We believe that they represent the high standard of AI researchers in the region, and the diversity of the Pacific Rim.

Finally our thanks go to Joerg Siekmann for his interest in our book proposal, and to Springer-Verlag for its efficient assistance in publishing this volume in its Lecture Notes in Artificial Intelligence series.

October 1997
Grigoris Antoniou, Aditya Ghose, and Mirek Truszczynski

Program Committee: Reasoning with Incomplete and Changing Information

Grigoris Antoniou, Griffith University
David Billington, Griffith University
Phan Minh Dung, Asian Institute of Technology
Boon Toh Low, Chinese University of Hong Kong
C. Kym MacNish, University of Western Auatralia
Javier Pinto, Pontifical Catholic University of Chile
Mirek Truszczynski, University of Kentucky
Mary-Anne Williams, University of Newcastle

Program Committee: Inducing Complex Representations

Koichi Furukawa, Keio University
Aditya Ghose, University of Wollongong
Randy Goebel, University of Alberta
Fumio Mizoguchi, Science University of Tokyo
Srinivas Padmanabhuni, University of Alberta

Table of Contents

Inductive Constraint Logic Programming: An Overview

Srinivas Padmanabhuni
Department of Computing Science
University of Alberta
Edmonton, Canada, T6G 2H1
srinivas@cs.ualberta.ca

Aditya K. Ghose
Decision Systems Lab
Dept. of Business Systems
University of Wollongong
Wollongong, NSW 2522 Australia
aditya@uow.edu.au

Abstract. This paper provides a brief introduction and overview of the emerging area of Inductive Constraint Logic Programming (ICLP). It discusses some of the existing work in the area and presents some of the research issues and open questions that need to be addressed.

1   Introduction

Inductive Logic Programming (ILP) refers to a class of machine learning algorithms where the agent learns a first-order theory from examples and background knowledge. The ILP framework in machine learning is perhaps the most general of all because of the complexity of the concepts learned. The use of first-order logic programs as the underlying representation makes ILP systems more powerful and useful than the conventional empirical machine learning systems. ILP systems have been successfully used in a variety of real life domains including mesh design, protein synthesis, games and fault diagnosis. Most of the first-order representations used in ILP systems are variants of horn-clause based clausal logic of Prolog.

ILP systems have been weak in handling numerical knowledge. Although some existing ILP systems are capable of handling numerical knowledge, the approach in most cases is ad-hoc. Given the obvious utility of extending the power of the logic programming framework to computational domains other than than Herbrand terms (such as sets, strings, integers, reals etc.) and the well-known success of various constraint logic programming languages such as languages like CLP(R), CHIP etc. in various real life applications [1], there is a clear need for developing an inductive framework similar to that of ILP but based on constraint logic programming schemes.

2 Existing work in ICLP

Given that this is a relatively new area, there only a small number of frameworks that attempt a solution to the ICLP problem.

2.1 Kawamura and Furukawa

Furukawa and Kawamura [2] adopted the dominant paradigm in ILP, namely the paradigm of *inverse resolution* for generalizing constraints. As is well known in ILP literature, inverse resolution methods are essentially based on the inversion of the process involved in deduction using resolution. In resolution, given a pair of clauses, called resolvents, a third clause is deduced. In contrast, the process of inverse resolution seeks to invent one of the resolvents, given one of the resolvents and the solved clause. The process basically revolves around three operations, truncation, absorption and intra-construction of two logic program rules.

Truncation Let P1 and P2 be two clauses whose bodies are empty. Then the truncation of P1 and P2 yields a clause which is more general than both P1 and P2.

Absorption Suppose two clauses R1 and R2 on resolution yield the clause R3. Absorption refers to the operation of guessing R2 given R3 and R1.

Intra-Construction Given two clauses C1 and C2, intra-construction refers to the process of generating three clauses R1, R2, and R3 such that R1 and R2 on resolution yield C1 and R2, R3 yield C2 respectively.

In this sense the process of inverse resolution inverts the deduction involved in resolution process.

The ILP frameworks are based on algorithms which are variants of the above-mentioned basic inverse resolution algorithm. The model of θ-subsumption used in ILP cannot be extended to ICLP because of the universal generalization rule adopted in ILP systems, namely, of replacing constants by variables, to yield a generalized formula. But this method is bound to fail with constraint logic programs because of the constraints involved. For instance, the generalization of two equations $\{x = 7, x = 2\}$ is $x = y$ by θ-subsumption. This type of generalization is meaningless, and necessitates the development of domain specific mechanisms to generalize constraint logic programs based on the domain of the constraint s involved.

Kawamura and Furukawa generalize the concepts of least general generalization for general logic programs to constraint logic program generalization, by considering the logic program components and generalization of constraints components separately and merging them. This raises the question of whether there always exists a least general generalization for a given set of constraints. Even if on exists there should be a method to compute the greatest lower bound of all possible constraint generalizations.

In their framework, Kawamura and Furukawa devise methods to compute the inverse resolution based generalizations for linear algebra based constraints.

Consider the development of an absorption algorithm for linear algebra. If c and c2 are two linear algebra constraints, and we need to devise a c1 such that $c1 \cup c2 \vdash c$. Given $c = \{x = 1\}$, and $c1 = \{y = 2, z \geq 2\}$, we get the equation of c_2 as $\{a_1 x + b_1 y = a_1 + 2b_1, a_2 x + b_2 x \geq a_2 + 2b_2\}$. This satisfies $c1 \cup c2 \vdash c$.

2.2 Mizoguchi and Ohwada

Mizoguchi and Ohwada [5][6], extend ideas from ILP based on Plotkin's framework [8] of Relative Least General Generalization(RLGG) to induce constraint logic programs. They consider the spatial layout problem, and devise methods to automatically acquire geometric constraints. The objective in RLGG is to construct a minimum clause that covers a set of positive examples yet maintaining consistency with the negative examples in the presence of background knowledge. RLGG is essentially the minimal clause which in conjunction with background knowledge yields the above satisfiability criterion (with respect to positive and negative examples).

To construct an RLGG, the concepts of constraint subsumption, and constrained LGG need to be explained in detail. A constraint C_1 is said to $C-$ subsume C_2 if for the two sets of constraints C_1 and C_2, there exists a constraint C such that the solution set of $C_1 \cup C$ is same as the solution set of C_2. Let $C_1 = \{p(X) \leftarrow \{X + 3 \leq Y\}, p(Y)\}$ and $C_2 = \{p(X) \leftarrow X + 4 \leq Y, p(Y)\}$. Here C_1 C-subsumes C_2.

Consider two constrained clauses CC_1 and CC_2. The notion of C-subsumption is extended to constrained clauses on the following lines. Let the two constrained clauses CC_1 and CC_2 be:

$$CC_1 = B_0 \leftarrow C_1, B_1, \ldots, B_n$$
and
$$CC_2 = A_0 \leftarrow C_2, A_1, \ldots, A_m$$

where C_1 and C_2 are conjunctions of constraints and each A_i and B_i is a nonconstraint atom. After renaming variables such that A_0 is exactly identical to B_0, and $\{B_1, \ldots, B_n\} \subseteq \{A_1, \ldots, A_n\}$, CC_1 C-subsumes CC_2 if and only if C_1 C-subsumes C_2.

Based on this notion of $C-subsumption$, the *least general constraint set* D of a set of constraints $C_i(i = 1, n)$, is defined such that D C-subsumes all constraints $C_1, \ldots, C_n$. Moreover any constraint set R which C-subsumes all members $C_1, \ldots, C_n$, C-subsumes D too because it is the least general constraint set subsuming the set of constraints $C_1 \ldots C_n$.

A generalization of the concept of the least general generalization of a set of constraints, is the concept of *relative least general generalization* of a set of constraint logic programs in presence of background knowledge. Formally the RLGG for constrained clauses can be defined as the least general constrained clause which in combination with the background knowledge subsumes the set of all input constrained clauses.

Mizoguchi et al. [6] apply the framework of constrained RLGG to the problem of floor planning. The non-overlap conditions of any two rooms in a floor layout is encoded as a set of constrained clauses. Ultimately the solution desired here is the set of position and size values of the rooms.

In practice there is no finite or tractable RLGG as it contains an intractably large number of atoms and constraints. But suitable practical language restrictions have been shown to yield a computationally feasible RLGG algorithm which can be the basis of learning clauses in ICLP. These restrictions are collectively referred to as *bias*.

A variety of types of bias have been proposed by the authors to regulate the size of RLGG. Some of the common types of biases are based on semantic notions such as *mode* and *type* of constraint. Other types are based on functional dependencies between variables of a constrained clause.

2.3 Page and Frisch

Page and Frisch [7] extend the concepts involved in the generalization of atoms, to more general forms of atoms, especially atoms with constraints attached to them. The constraint is a logical expression built of specialized predicates called *constraint predicates* and represents a form of restriction on the atom to which the constraint is involved. Some examples are:

$eats(x, y)/COW(x) \wedge GRASS(y) \wedge GREEN(y)$,
$eats(x, onland(y))/COW(x) \wedge GREEN(y) \wedge TASTY(onland(y))$

The restriction imposed on the generalization of these atoms in Frisch's paper was that the term, present in the constraint part had to be present in the atom part of the constrained atom.

In their work, Frisch and Page identified generalization in terms of background knowledge. The background theory is termed as *constraint theory* and it is a first-order theory whose only predicates are constraint predicates. In addition to the constrained generalization, they also describe sorted generalization, as a special case where the following restrictions apply in addition to the normal constraint restrictions: Only monadic constraint predicates may be used and only variables are constrained and a given variable may occur in only one atomic formula of the constraint. Thus *sorted generalization* is a specialized case of *constrained generalizations*.

For generalization of constrained atoms, the three factors taken into account are the background theory, the language of atoms and the constraints on the atoms. In general a constrained atom e_1 is considered to be more general than another constrained atom e_2 iff there is a substitution θ such that θ maps the head of e_1 to the head of e_2 and θ respects the constraints.

Based on this notion of generalization, the least general constrained atom is defined as the constrained atom that is more general than a given set of constrained atoms and is less general than any other constrained atom which is more general than any member of the given set of constraints. However in many cases, it is not possible to define least generalization exactly. In such a case a set of minimal non-comparable generalization of the given set of constrained atoms is found. Such a set of generalizations is called a *complete set of incomparable generalizations* (CIG).

It is shown that *a set of constrained atoms built from the same ordinary predicate has a singleton CIG*. This conjecture is true because constrained atoms allow for use of generalized terms rather than just sorts in the constrained atoms.

Consider the following example to illustrate computation of the CIG of a set of constrained atoms.

Example 1. Consider the following set of constraints forming the background theory:

$\{LARGER(succ(brown), succ(tom)), LARGER(succ(mary), succ(lisa)),$
$LARGER(brown, tom), LARGER(mary, lisa), MALE(brown),$
$MALE(tom), FEMALE(lisa), FEMALE(mary),$
$\forall x \forall y MALE(x) \land FEMALE(y) \rightarrow LARGER(x, y)\}.$

With reference to the above background knowledge, if we were to compute the CIG of the set of constrained atoms $\{BULLIES(tom, x)/FEMALE(x),$ $BULLIES(y, mary)/MALE(y)\}$. the answer would be:
$\{BULLIES(x, y)/LARGER(x, y) \land MALE(x) \land FEMALE(y)\}.$

With reference to the same background knowledge, if we we were to compute the CIG of the set of constrained atoms $\{BULLIES(succ(brown), succ(tom)),$ $BULLIES(succ(mary), succ(lisa))\}$, then the answer would be
$\{BULLIES(succ(x), succ(y))/LARGER(x, y) \land LARGER(succ(x), succ(y))\}.$

It is thus clear that background knowledge had a role in deriving the CIG of the input constrained atoms.

2.4 Sebag et al.

Sebag et al. (see [9] [10] and their chapter in this volume) propose a framework for learning clauses which can discriminate between positive and negative examples expressed as constrained clauses. They conjecture that only a subset of the entire set of discriminating clauses need to be determined fully in order to explicitly represent the learned concept. The remaining clauses of the concept can be derived from these basic set of clauses. Thus they use a two step induction process in learning constrained clauses. The first step called small induction gives a computational characterization of the sufficient discriminating clauses. In the second step of exhaustive induction, the entire set of discriminating clauses is constructed.

2.5 Martin and Vrain

In their study of induction of constraint logic programs, Martin and Vrain [4] conjecture that instead of interpreting function symbols in constraints symbolically, if we interpret them by more semantic means, there is scope for development of better algorithms for generalizing and inducing constraint logic programs. They propose a method to learn logic programs containing function symbols other than mere constants. They are able to use the interpretation of functions not as mere symbols but as semantic entities based on consideration of their domains. They rely not on a syntactic notion of function terms as is usually the case in ILP, but consider the semantics of functions in terms of the domain values and interpretations. They use the domain values of the functions, and develop a model for learning constraint logic programs based on the domain values of a function in the program and its role in discriminating between positive and negative examples. In their work they do not concentrate on generating complete and consistent logic programs from the given positive and negative examples. Instead they develop a notion of coverage of the input positive and negative examples based on a concept called *D-coverage*[4]. The notion of *D-coverage* is not shown to be sufficient for learning complete and consistent logic programs but has been shown to be successfully employable for useful classes of constraint logic programs.

D-coverage: A *D-atom* refers to a predicate of form $p(d_1, d_2, .., d_n)$ where p belongs to the set of allowed predicates in the CLP signature. and each of the d_i's belong to the domain of CLP. A D-atom e is covered by a constrained clause, with respect to the background knowledge (BK^+) and the set of positive examples (E^+) if there is a valuation which makes the head of the clause to be e and makes the body of the constrained clause to be true including the constraint part of the clause. Thus, the notion of D-coverage is based on a semantic notion of functions and is not a symbolic notion.

Example 2. Consider the example specification, where $D = N$, the set of positive integers. Let *pred* be the function involved, and let it be interpreted as predecessor function of natural numbers. The basic predicate *even* is defined by $BK^+ = \{even(0), even(2), even(4)\}$ and the target predicate *odd* is given by $E^+ = \{odd(1), odd(3), odd(5)\}$, and $E^- = \{odd(2), odd(4)\}$. In this example a possible solution is then:

$\{odd(X) \leftarrow X = 1.odd(X) \leftarrow pred(pred(X)), odd(Y).\}$

The idea is to build constrained clauses by adding iteratively to the body of the clause either a constrained atom or a constraint, until no negative example is *D-covered*.

The different steps involved in building D-linked constrained clauses are as follows:

1. Choose a random example e belonging to the set of target examples belonging to E^+.
2. Build a relevant clause which D-covers e.
3. Build a set of possible constraints or constrained atoms which can be added to the body of the clause.
4. Use an entropy measure to choose the best constraint which is added to the body of the clause so that as many positive D-uncovered examples are covered.

Because of the complexity of the problem of finding constrained clause due to the infinite number of the possible terms, the generalization needs to be controlled by use of a suitable form of *bias*. Different restrictions on the structure of the possible generalizations are imposed. Some of the biases used here are:

1. Limitation on the depth of terms
2. Limitation on the number of constraints
3. Limiting use of other functions inside a top level function. e.g. pred is not allowed inside the succ function, otherwise it can lead to an infinite computation.

This work in the direction of generalization of constraint logic programs illustrates some important factors which need to be taken into consideration when generalizing constraints and constraint logic programs.

3 Research issues and open questions

It is clear that the ICLP area is well-motivated, with possible applications including robot motion planning,spatial reasoning, temporal reasoning, graphical layout problems and computer aided publishing, amongst others. It is also clear that several outstanding research issues remain. We shall consider, now, some of the basic questions that need to be addressed by ICLP researchers.

1. *Constraint induction:* Much needs to be done in defining techniques for inducing constraints in the well-known constraint domains. Of interest as well is the issue of integrating domain-specific constraint induction methods to obtain techniques for inducing constraint logic programs which operate on multiple domains. One interesting approach to this problem is the work of Padmanabhuni, You and Ghose that appears in this volume.
2. *Adaptation of ILP techniques to ICLP:* It is important to consider which of the existing ILP techniques may be adapted for ICLP. In the previous section we saw the ICLP version of inverse resolution and RLGG frameworks. It would be interesting to observe if inverse unification, inverse entailment, generalized subsumption and other models of generalization which have been used in ILP can be extended to ICLP. The work of Martin and Vrain [4] mentioned in the previous section stresses the need to interpret functions and predicates in a more semantic sense than is done in the usual ILP case. In our opinion the biggest stumbling block in the direction of adaptation of ILP techniques to ICLP based systems is the syntactic interpretation of the functions and predicates involved in the CLP. The most commonly used technique in the process of induction in ILP, the replacing of a constant by a variable, is inapplicable to generalize in CLP's because it is based on a syntactic interpretation of functions and predicates.
3. *Semantics:* Even though the study of ICLP is driven more by applications, a comprehensive and accessible semantic basis is still needed to foster growth of the field.

4. *Bias:* A major area of research motivated by all the ICLP systems discussed in the previous section involves the question of developing appropriate notions of bias and language restrictions as a means of managing the time and space complexity inherent in the problem.

5. *Novel applications:* New application domains where automatic acquisition of constraints may be helpful, such as computer aided publishing [3], need to be studied.

6. *Learnability studies:* The other aspect of the interest involves studies on learnability issues from computational learning theory.

References

1. J. Jaffar and M.J.Maher. Constraint logic programming: a survey. *Journal of Logic Programming*, pages 503–581, 1994.

2. T. Kawamura and K. Furukawa. Towards inductive generalization in constraint logic programs. In *Proceedings of the IJCAI-93 workshop on inductive logic programming*, pages 93–104, Chamberry, France, August 1993. Academic Press.

3. F. Jacquenet M. Bernard and C. Nicolini. Induction of constraint logic programs for computer-aided publishing. In *Proceedings of the International Conference on Artificial Intelligence and Soft Computing*, Banff, Canada, 1997.

4. Lionel Martin and Christel Vrain. Induction of constraint logic programs. In *Proceedings of Algorithms and Learning Theory (ALT) - 1996*, Sydney, Australia, 1996. Springer Verlag.

5. F. Mizoguchi and H. Ohwada. Constraint-directed generalization for learning spatial relations. In *Proc. Second international workshop on ILP*, Tokyo, Japan, 1992.

6. F. Mizoguchi and H. Ohwada. Constrained relative least general generalization for inducing constraint logic programs". *New Generation Computing*, 13:335–368, 1995.

7. C.D. Page and A.M. Frisch. Generalizing atoms in constraint logic. In *Proc. Second international conference on knowledge representaion and reasoning*, pages 429–440, 1991.

8. G.D. Plotkin. A note on inductive generalization. *Machine Intelligence*, 5:101–124, 1971.

9. M. Sebag and C. Rouveirol. *Constraint inductive logic programming*, pages 277–294. Advances in ILP. IOS Press, 1996.

10. Michele Sebag and Celine Rouveirol. Induction of maximally general clauses compatible with integrity constraints. In Stefan Wrobel, editor, *Proc. of Fourth International workshop on Inductive Logic Programming*, 1994.

Some Approaches to Reasoning with Incomplete and Changing Information

Grigoris Antoniou

CIT, Griffith University

Nathan, QLD 4111, Australia

ga@cit.gu.edu.au

Mary-Anne Williams

Department of Management

The University of Newcastle

Callaghan, NSW 2308, Australia

maryanne@u2.newcastle.edu.au

1 Incomplete and changing information

Humans are constantly faced with the necessity of making decisions. Some may affect everyday situations (such as "How am I going to work?"), others may be of a long term nature ("What should I study?"). In the ideal case, we would have all the relevant information about the problem at hand, and then would apply logical reasoning to draw a conclusion.

Unfortunately, this is not usually the case. Instead we must decide based on *incomplete information* only. For example, imagine a doctor in an emergency case. She has to begin immediately with the treatment even without knowing the exact cause of the symptoms; in this case she has to make some assumptions about the most plausible or most dangerous possible causes. Obviously it would be completely inappropriate to await all the necessary test results before making a diagnosis and beginning with the correct treatment – probably by then the patient would be dead (An additional difficulty may be that sometimes all the tests don't single out a cause, perhaps because something cannot be tested for).

Another area where incomplete information prevails is law. A fundamental legal principle of Western societies is that somebody is assumed innocent unless their guilt has been proven.

When our decisions are based on conjectures due to the incompleteness of the information at hand, they may turn out to be wrong. Consider the following piece of text:

Smith entered the office of his boss. He was nervous.

I claim that most people have a rather clear idea who the word "he" refers to (Smith). Let's continue with the text.

After all, he didn't want to lose his best employee.

Now most people would have to revise their assumption. After all, "he" referred to the boss. The previous assumption was based on the default rule that typically employees are nervous when confronted with their boss. But in the presence of the additional information, the assumption turned out to be wrong.

In fact, even complete information may not be sufficient to make a decision that will be correct forever. This would be true in a static environment, but not in a changing world. In other words, *changing information* may be an alternative cause why we may have to revise a previously drawn conclusion.

Note that up to now we have been talking about humans. The examples and arguments above carry over to intelligent information systems in a natural way. After all, these systems are supposed to exhibit human–like behaviour.

The purpose of this tutorial paper is not to give a complete overview of the vast area of reasoning with incomplete and changing information. Rather we intend to discuss in some depth some basic approaches that have emerged.

2   Nonmonotonic reasoning

Nonmonotonic reasoning comprises a collection of reasoning methods based on logic. The name stems from the following observation. In classical logic, if the number of given premises is increased, then so does the set of conclusions. More formally:

If $M \models \varphi$ and $M \subseteq M'$, then $M' \models \varphi$.

In other words, the set of conclusions grows monotonically with the set of premises. This behaviour is perfectly acceptable in areas such as mathematics: once a theorem is proven, there is no way it will be shown to be wrong when other theorems are derived.

But in everyday situations reasoning isn't monotonic, precisely due to the problem of incomplete information. When assumptions are used to make plausible conclusions, some of these conclusions may turn out to be wrong in the face of new (more secure) evidence to the contrary.

The main three classical approaches to nonmonotonic reasoning are Default Logic [51], Autoepistemic Logic [46] and Circumscription [44]. Recently research has also focused on an abstract study of nonmonotonicity, rather than the study of single approaches [33, 40].

Nonmonotonic reasoning has proven to be fruitful in the study of negation in logic programming. Currently the most prominent (and in a sense extreme) nonmonotonic semantics of logic programs are the stable model semantics [23] and well-founded semantics [59].

Rather than try to give an overview of the broad field of nonmonotonic reasoning, in the following we selected to present the basic ideas and concepts of three nonmonotonic approaches: autoepistemic logic, default logic, and the stable model semantics of logic programs.

2.1   Autoepistemic logic

One of the most prominent methods for nonmonotonic reasoning is autoepistemic logic, a formalism that was developed by Moore [47]. Its main idea is to give a formal account of an agent reasoning about his own knowledge or beliefs. Consider the following dialog:

Are the Rolling Stones giving a concert in Brisbane next week?
No, because else I would have heard of it.

We can illustrate some interesting points using this example. First, it is clear that I have no definite knowledge that the Rolling Stones are not giving a concert in Brisbane next week. In this sense, my knowledge is incomplete, and, by giving a negative answer, I am making a conjecture. This conjecture is based on reflection upon the knowledge I have (if something so important is happening in my city, then I will know).

To proceed with the example, suppose that I buy the Courier Mail the morning after the conversation took place, and read the headlines:

The concert of the century: The Rolling Stones in Brisbane next week!

Now situation has changed. I know that the Stones *are* giving the concert, so my answer to the question above would now be "Yes". This means that the old conclusion I had drawn from introspection is no longer valid and must be revised. In this sense, my reasoning is nonmonotonic (new information has invalidated a previous conclusion).

Autoepistemic logic formalizes this kind of reasoning. The approach it takes is to introduce a so-called modal operator L that is applied to first order sentences (i.e. formulae without free variables). $L\varphi$ has the meaning

I know φ (or I believe that φ).

Our concert example is formulated as follows:

concert $\to$ Lconcert ("If a concert takes place then I know it")
$\neg$Lconcert ("I don't know that a concert will take place")

The first rule is equivalent to $\neg Lconcert \to \neg concert$, which says that I conclude *not concert* if I do not explicitly know *concert*. This is similar to the idea of negation as failure, in that my failing to find a proof for *concert* based on my current knowledge leads to the conclusion that *concert* is wrong.

The L-operator may be applied in a nested way in the sense that, for example, I may know that I don't know something. Thus, we may write down LLp, $L\neg Lq$, $\neg LL(\neg p \vee Lr)$ etc.

2.1.1 Syntax of AEL

Autoepistemic formulae (AE–formulae) are defined as the smallest set satisfying the following:

- Each closed first–order formula is an AE–formula.

- If φ is an AE–formula, then $L\varphi$ is also an AE–formula.

- If φ and ψ are AE–formulae, then so are the following: $\neg\varphi$, $(\varphi\vee\psi)$, $(\varphi\wedge\psi)$, $(\varphi \to \psi)$.

The set of all AE–formulae is denoted by *For*. An *autoepistemic theory (AE–theory)* is a set of AE–formulae.

We will also need the following syntactical concepts. The *kernel* T_0 of an AE-theory T is defined as the set of all first order formulae that are members of T.

Given an AE-theory T, $sub(T)$ is the union of $sub(\varphi)$, for all $\varphi \in T$, where $sub(\varphi)$ is defined as follows:

- $sub(\varphi) = \emptyset$ for first order formulae φ

- $sub(\neg\varphi) = sub(\varphi)$

- $sub(\varphi \vee \psi) = sub(\varphi \wedge \psi) = sub(\varphi \rightarrow \psi) = sub(\varphi) \cup sub(\psi)$

- $sub(L\varphi) = \{\varphi\}$.

2.1.2 Expansions of autoepistemic theories

What is the knowledge an agent with introspection would have, given a set of facts (AE-formulae) T? It will be a set E of AE-formulae that (i) includes T, (ii) allows introspection, in the sense that I may reason about what I know and what I don't know, and (iii) is grounded in T in the sense that the knowledge in E must be reconstructible using T, belief in (knowledge of) E, and non-belief in (non-knowledge of) E^C. That means, given T, knowledge of E, and non-knowledge of E^C (the complement of E), it must be possible to logically derive all the information included in the expansion E.

The semantics of autoepistemic logic is given in terms of so-called *expansions*, pieces of knowledge defining a sort of "world views" compatible with and based on the given knowledge.

Definition 2.1 Let T and E be sets of AE-formulae. We denote the set $\{L\varphi|\varphi \in E\}$ as LE, and the set $\{\neg L\psi|\psi \notin E\}$ as $\neg LE^C$. $\models$ denotes the usual first order entailment. Define $\Omega_T(E) := \{\varphi|T \cup LE \cup \neg LE^C \models \varphi\}$. E is an *expansion* of T iff $E = \Omega_T(E)$.

The only thing we must additionally say is that each AE-formula $L\varphi$ is considered as a new atom of the logical language, and it is not necessary or allowed to go into the structure of φ. So, it is impossible to use logical reasoning *within* the scope of an L-operator. Here are some simple examples:

$$\{p \rightarrow Lp, p\} \models Lp$$

$$\{(p \vee q) \rightarrow Lq, p\} \models Lq$$

$$\{L(p \vee q) \rightarrow Lq, Lp\} \not\models Lq$$

One of the main properties of expansions is stability: a set E is called *stable* if the following conditions hold:

- $\varphi \in E \Rightarrow L\varphi \in E$

- $\varphi \notin E \Rightarrow \neg L\varphi \in E.$

The concept of stability clearly reflects introspection, i.e. autoepistemic reasoning: if A is in my knowledge, then I know A, I know that I know A etc. On the other hand, if I do not know B, then I know that I do not know B etc.

Let us look at the definition of an expansion. What it essentially says is the following: imagine that you decide to believe (include in your knowledge) a set of AE-formulae T. Given this decision, a set of AE-formulae can be deduced from the given theory T and the belief we adopted (represented as $LE \cup \neg LE^C$). If in this way we turn out to obtain the belief set E we adopted ("Truth implies belief (knowledge)"), and only E ("Belief (knowledge) implies truth"), then E is an expansion of T.

There is a close relationship between expansions (and more generally stable sets) and kernels (first order portions of AE-theories). Indeed, the following theorem should not be surprising, if one looks carefully at the properties of stability.

Theorem 2.2 If, for two stable sets E and F, $E_0 = F_0$, then $E = F$. Conversely, for each deductively closed first order theory T there is a stable set F such that $F_0 = T$.

For example, consider the following AE-theory (borrowed from [12]).

$(german \wedge \neg L\neg drinks\text{-}beer) \to drinks\text{-}beer$
$german$

There is only one expansion of this theory. There is no possibility of deriving $\neg drinks\text{-}beer$, therefore $\neg L\neg drinks\text{-}beer$ is contained in the expansion. Thus, the first rule is applicable and derives $drinks\text{-}beer$. The only expansion of this theory has the kernel $Th(\{german, drinks\text{-}beer\})$. But if we extend the theory by adding

$(eats\text{-}pizza \wedge \neg Ldrinks\text{-}beer) \to \neg drinks\text{-}beer$
$eats\text{-}pizza$

then the extended theory has two expansions: as before we may conclude *drinks-beer*, so the kernel of one expansion contains *german, eats-pizza*, and *drinks-beer*. Alternatively we may decide to use the new rule regarding pizza eaters; since we do not know *drinks-beer*, we may conclude *¬drinks-beer*, so the kernel of the other expansion contains *german, eats-pizza* and *¬drinks-beer*.

2.1.3 An operational interpretation of autoepistemic logic

The following approach to determining expansions of AE-theories can be summarized as follows:

- Partition $sub(T)$ into a part $E(+)$ you believe in, and a part $E(-)$ you do not believe in.

- Compute the corresponding kernel $E(0)$ of a potential expansion, using T, belief in $E(+)$, and non-belief in $E(-)$.

- Check whether the stable set determined by $E(0)$ is indeed an expansion (this test is carried out in a simpler way; see the following description for details).

Example 2.3

Consider the autoepistemic theory $T = \{Lp \to p\}$. There are two possible decompositions of $sub(T) = \{p\}$: either we decide to believe in p or not. These two possibilities correspond exactly to the two lines of the following table. The tests carried out succeed, and we have as result that T has exactly two expansions, one with kernel $Th(\emptyset)$ ($Th(S)$ denotes the deductive closure of S) and one with kernel $Th(\{p\})$ (it is the information on the third column). The general method will be described in a moment, where the approach of this table is formally introduced and informally explained.

$E(+)$	$E(-)$	$E(0)$	$E(+) \subseteq E(0)$	$E(-) \cap E(0) = \emptyset$	expansion
$\{p\}$	$\emptyset$	$Th(\{p\})$	yes	yes	yes
$\emptyset$	$\{p\}$	$Th(\emptyset)$	yes	yes	yes

To simplify the situation, we treat first autoepistemic theories without nested occurrences of the L-operator. In this case, $sub(T)$ consists, by definition, only of first order formulae.

Procedure for AE-theories without L-nesting

$Expansions := \emptyset$
FORALL partitions $E(+)$ and $E(-)$ of $sub(T)$ DO
    BEGIN
        $E(0) := \{\varphi \in For_0 | T \cup LE(+) \cup \neg LE(-) \models \varphi\}$
        IF $E(+) \subseteq E(0)$ AND $E(-) \cap E(0) = \emptyset$
        THEN $Expansions := Expansions \cup \{E(0)\}$
        END
    END

Some short comments on this procedure: $E(0)$ is the set of first order formulae that follows from T, belief in $E(+)$ and non-belief in $E(-)$. The condition $E(+) \subseteq E(0)$ tests whether $E(0)$ includes what we decided to believe in, while the condition $E(-) \cap E(0) = \emptyset$ tests whether $E(0)$ excludes everything we decided not to believe in. If both conditions are passed, then we have determined an expansion (more precisely, the kernel of an expansion). Finally, we turn to the general case, in which $sub(T)$, and thus also $E(+)$ and $E(-)$ need not be first order.

Procedure for general autoepistemic theories

$Expansions := \emptyset$
FORALL partitions $E(+)$ and $E(-)$ of $sub(T)$ DO
    BEGIN
        $E(0) := \{\varphi \in For_0 | T \cup LE(+) \cup \neg LE(-) \models \varphi\}$

Let E be the unique stable set with kernel $E(0)$
IF $E(+) \subseteq E$ AND $E(-) \cap E = \emptyset$
THEN *Expansions* := *Expansions* $\cup \{E\}$
END
END

Example 2.4

Consider the theory $T = \{p \to L\neg p\}$. The following table shows that none of the decompositions of $sub(T) = \{\neg p\}$ passes both tests. Therefore, this theory does not possess any expansions.

$E(+)$	$E(-)$	$E(0)$	$E(+) \subseteq E(0)$	$E(-) \cap E(0) = \emptyset$	expansion
$\{\neg p\}$	$\emptyset$	$Th(\emptyset)$	no	yes	?
$\emptyset$	$\{\neg p\}$	$Th(\{\neg p\})$	yes	no	?

The reader may ask why we have used "?" in the last column instead of "no". The reason is the following: all we obtain from a failed test is that *this decomposition of $sub(T)$* (represented by the current line in the table) is not successful and does not justify that $E(0)$ is the kernel of an expansion. It may be the case, though, that *another decomposition yields exactly the same set $E(0)$ and passes both tests in columns 4 and 5*. Example 2.5 illustrates this. But, what we are sure about is the following: for each expansion E of T there is a line in the table such that the tests are passed and the computed set $E(0)$ is the kernel of E. So, after completing the whole table, question marks are interpreted as negative answers if there is not another line with the same $E(0)$ which passes the tests.

Example 2.5

Let $T = \{\neg Lp \to q, Lq \to p, Lq \to q\}$; $sub(T) = \{p, q\}$. The following table shows that $Th(\{p, q\})$ is the kernel of the only expansion of T. Note that this set occurs twice in the table below, in line 1 and in line 3. Line 3 fails, but we write "?" and not "no" which would be wrong: $E(0)$ *is* the kernel of an expansion, obtained from line 1!

$E(+)$	$E(-)$	$E(0)$	$E(+) \subseteq E(0)$	$E(-) \cap E(0) = \emptyset$	expansion
$\{p, q\}$	$\emptyset$	$Th(\{p, q\})$	yes	yes	yes
$\{p\}$	$\{q\}$	$Th(\emptyset)$	no	yes	?
$\{q\}$	$\{p\}$	$Th(\{p, q\})$	yes	no	?
$\emptyset$	$\{p, q\}$	$Th(\{q\})$	yes	no	?

2.1.4 Historical and bibliographical remarks

Developed by Moore [46, 47], Autoepistemic Logic is one of the main non-monotonic formalisms, and is treated in books like [12, 43]. AE-logic has been extensively studied in literature, e.g. [22, 41, 24]. A thorough presentation of the mathematical properties is found in [26].

One interesting question is the relationship between autoepistemic and default logic [51]. In general, autoepistemic logic allows more freedom in that expansions are more loosely grounded in the given theory than default extensions. Thus, the two methods are not equivalent. [30] shows that default theory T can be represented as an AE-theory T' such that the kernels of the so-called *strongly grounded expansions* of T' correspond exactly to the extensions of T; see also [42].

One of the main limitations of autoepistemic logic is that quantification into the scope of the L-operator is not allowed. [32] extends the logic in this direction. The same author developed the Hierarchic Autoepistemic Logic [31] to deal with some deficiencies of AEL: to allow priorities among formulae, and to increase computational efficiency. The main idea is to consider a collection of subtheories linked together in a hierarchy, and to use a set of L-operators with restricted applicational scope. Though new representational problems arise, [6] shows an interesting application.

2.2 Default Logic

2.2.1 The notion of a default

Suppose I am asked in the morning how I intend to go to work. My answer is "By bus" because usually I go to work by bus. This rule of thumb is represented by the default

$$\frac{goToWork : useBus}{useBus}$$

which is read as follows: "If I have to go to work, and if I may assume that I can use the bus (meaning that nothing to the contrary is known), then I decide to use the bus". So I leave home, walk to the bus station and read a notice saying "No buses today because we are on strike!". Now I definitely know that I cannot use the bus to go to work, therefore the default is no longer applicable (now I cannot assume that I may use the bus). I have to take back my previous conclusion, so my behaviour is nonmonotonic.

Defaults can be used to model *prototypical reasoning* which means that most instances of a concept have some property. One example is the statement "Typically, children have (living) parents" which may be expressed by the default

$$\frac{child(X) : hasParents(X)}{hasParents(X)}.$$

Defaults naturally occur in many application domains. Let us give an example from legal reasoning. According to German law, a foreigner is usually expelled if they have committed a crime. One of the exceptions to this rule concerns political refugees. This information is expressed by the default

$$\frac{criminal(X) \land foreigner(X) : expel(X)}{expel(X)}$$

in combination with the rule

$$political Refugee(X) \rightarrow \neg expel(X).$$

Defaults can be used naturally to model the *Closed World Assumption* which is used in database theory, algebraic specification, and logic programming. According to this assumption, an application domain is described by certain axioms (in form of relational facts, equations, rules etc.) with the following understanding: a ground fact (that is, a non–parameterized statement about single objects) is taken to be false in the problem domain if it does not follow from the axioms. The closed world assumption has the simple default representation

$$\frac{true : \neg \varphi}{\neg \varphi}$$

for each ground atom φ. The explanation of the default is: if it is consistent to assume $\neg \varphi$ (which is equivalent to not having a proof for φ) then conclude $\neg \varphi$.

Further examples of defaults can be found in, say, [9, 17, 38, 50].

2.2.2 The syntax of default logic

A *default theory* T is a pair (W, D) consisting of a set W of predicate logic formulae (called the *facts* or *axioms* of T) and a countable set D of defaults. A *default* δ has the form

$$\frac{\varphi : \psi_1, \ldots, \psi_n}{\chi}$$

where $\varphi, \psi_1, \ldots, \psi_n, \chi$ are closed predicate logic formulae, and $n > 0$. The formula φ is called the *prerequisite*, $\psi_1, \ldots, \psi_n$ the *justifications*, and χ the *consequent* of δ. For a set D of defaults, $cons(D)$ denotes the set of consequents of the defaults in D. A default is called *normal* iff it has the form $\frac{\varphi : \psi}{\psi}$.

2.2.3 An operational definition of extensions

For a given default theory $T = (W, D)$ let $\Pi = (\delta_0, \delta_1, \ldots)$ be a finite or infinite sequence of defaults from D without multiple occurrences. Think of Π as a possible order in which we apply some defaults from D. Of course, we don't want to apply a default more than once within such a reasoning chain because no additional information would be gained by doing so. We denote the initial segment of Π of length k by $\Pi[k]$, provided the length of Π is at least k (from now on, this assumption is always made when referring to $\Pi[k]$). With each such sequence Π we associate two sets of first–order formulae, $In(\Pi)$ and $Out(\Pi)$:

- $In(\Pi)$ is $Th(W \cup \{cons(\delta) \mid \delta$ occurs in $\Pi\})$[1]. So, $In(\Pi)$ collects the information gained by the application of the defaults in Π and represents the *current knowledge base* after the defaults in Π have been applied.

---

[1]$Th(M)$ denotes the deductive closure of M in classical logic.

- $Out(\Pi) = \{\neg\psi \mid \psi \in just(\delta)$ for some δ occurring in $\Pi\}$. So, $Out(\Pi)$ collects formulae that should not turn out to be true, i.e. that should not become part of the current knowledge base even after subsequent application of other defaults.

- Π is called a *process of* T iff δ_k is applicable to $In(\Pi[k])$, for every k such that δ_k occurs in Π.

Given a process Π of T we define the following:

- Π is *successful* iff $In(\Pi) \cap Out(\Pi) = \emptyset$, otherwise it is *failed*.

- Π is *closed* iff every $\delta \in D$ that is applicable to $In(\Pi)$ already occurs in Π. Closed processes correspond to the desired property of an extension E being closed under application of defaults in D.

Consider the default theory $T = (W, D)$ with $W = \{a\}$ and D containing the following defaults:

$$\delta_1 = \frac{a : \neg b}{d}, \quad \delta_2 = \frac{true : c}{b}.$$

$\Pi_1 = (\delta_1)$ is successful but not closed since δ_2 may be applied to $In(\Pi_1) = Th(\{a, d\})$. $\Pi_2 = (\delta_1, \delta_2)$ is closed but not successful: both $In(\Pi_2) = Th(\{a, d, b\})$ and $Out(\Pi_2) = \{b, \neg c\}$ contain b. On the other hand, $\Pi_3 = (\delta_2)$ is a closed and successful process of T. According to the following definition, which was first introduced in [4], $In(\Pi_3) = Th(\{a, b\})$ is an extension of T, in fact its single extension.

Definition 2.6 *A set of formulae E is an* extension of *the default theory T iff there is some closed and successful process Π of T such that $E = In(\Pi)$.*

Let $T = (W, D)$ be the default theory with $W = \emptyset$ and $D = \{\delta_1, \delta_2\}$ with

$$\delta_1 = \frac{true : p}{\neg q}, \quad \delta_2 = \frac{true : q}{r}.$$

The only closed and successful process is (δ_1), so T has exactly one extension, namely $Th(\{\neg q\})$. The right path of the tree shows an example where application of a default destroys the applicability of a previous default: δ_1 can be applied after δ_2, but then $\neg q$ becomes part of the In-set, whilst it is also included in the Out-set (as the negation of the justification of δ_2).

Let $T = (W, D)$ with $W = \{green, aaaMember\}$ and $D = \{\delta_1, \delta_2\}$ with

$$\delta_1 = \frac{green : \neg likesCars}{\neg likesCars}, \quad \delta_2 = \frac{aaaMember : likesCars}{likesCars}.$$

T has exactly two extensions, $Th(\{green, aaaMember, likesCars\})$ and $Th(\{green, aaaMember, \neg likesCars\})$.

2.2.4 Existence of extensions

We saw that a default theory may not have any extensions. Is this a shortcoming of default logic? One might hold the view that if the default theory includes "nonsense" (for example $\frac{true:p}{\neg p}$), then the logic should indeed be allowed to provide no answer. According to this view, it is up to the user to provide meaningful information in the form of meaningful facts and defaults; after all, if a program contains an error, we don't blame the programming language.

The opposite view regards nonexistence of extensions as a drawback, and would prefer a more "fault–tolerant" logic; one which works even if some pieces of information are deficient. This viewpoint is supported by the trend towards heterogeneous information sources, where it is not easy to identify which source is responsible for the deficiency, or where the single pieces of information are meaningful, but lead to problems when put together.

A more technical argument in favour of the second view is the concept of *semi–monotonicity*. Default logic is a method for performing nonmonotonic reasoning, so we cannot expect it to be monotonic when new knowledge is added to the set of facts. However we would expect that the addition of new defaults would yield more, and not less information[2]. Formally, semi–monotonicity means the following:

> Let $T = (W, D)$ and $T' = (W, D')$ be default theories such that $D \subseteq D'$. Then for every extension E of T there is an extension E' of T' such that $E \subseteq E'$.

Default logic violates this property. For example, $T = (\emptyset, \{\frac{true:p}{p}\})$ has the single extension $E = Th(\{p\})$, but $T' = (\emptyset, \{\frac{true:p}{p}, \frac{true:q}{\neg q}\})$ has no extension. So nonexistence of extensions leads to the violation of semi–monotonicity. Even though the concept of semi–monotonicity is not equivalent to the existence of extensions, these two properties usually come together.

If we adopt the view that the possible nonexistence of extensions is a problem, then there are two alternative solutions. The first one consists in restricting attention to those classes of default theories for which the existence of extensions is guaranteed. Already in his classical paper [51] Reiter showed that if all defaults in a theory T are normal (in which case T is called a *normal default theory*), then T has at least one extension. Essentially this is because all processes are successful, as can be easily seen.

Theorem 2.7 *Normal default theories always have extensions. Furthermore they satisfy semi–monotonicity.*

One problem with the restriction to normal default theories is that their expresiveness is limited. In general, normal default theories are strictly more expressive than general default theories. Normal defaults have limitations particularly regarding the interaction among defaults. Consider the example:

---

[2]Some researchers would disagree with this view and regard semi–monotonicity as not desirable; see, for example, [12].

Bill is a high school dropout.
Typically, high school dropouts are adults.
Typically, adults are employed.

These facts are naturally represented by the normal default theory
$T = (\{dropout(bill)\}, \{\frac{dropout(X):adult(X)}{adult(X)}, \frac{adult(X):employed(X)}{employed(X)}\})$. T has the single extension $Th(\{dropout(bill), adult(bill), employed(bill)\})$. It is acceptable to assume that Bill is adult, but it is counterintuitive to assume that Bill is employed! That is, whereas the second default *on its own* is accurate, we want to prevent its application in case the adult X is a high school dropout. This can be achieved if we change the second default to

$$\frac{adult(X) : employed(X) \wedge \neg dropout(X)}{employed(X)}.$$

But this default is not normal. Defaults of this form are called *semi-normal*; [16] studied this class of default theories, and gave a sufficient condition for the existence of extensions. Another way of expressing interactions among defaults is the use of explicit priorities; see, for example, [13].

Instead of imposing restrictions on the form of defaults in order to guarantee the existence of extensions, the other principle way is to modify the concept of an extension in such a way that all default theories have at least an extension, and that semi–monotonicity is guaranteed. Two important default logic variants in this direction are Justified Default Logic [37] and Constrained Default Logic [14].

2.2.5 Joint consistency of justifications

It is easy to see that the default theory consisting of the defaults $\frac{true:p}{q}$ and $\frac{true:\neg p}{r}$ has the single extension $Th(\{q, r\})$. This shows that the *joint consistency* of justifications is not required. Justifications are *not* supposed to form a set of beliefs, rather they are used to sanction "jumping" into some conclusions.

This design decision is natural and makes sense for many cases, but can also lead to unintuitive results. As an example consider the default theory, due to Poole, which says that, by default, a robot's arm (say a or b) is usable unless it is broken; further we know that either a or b is broken. Given this information, we would not expect both a and b to be usable.

Let us see how default logic treats this example. Consider the default theory $T = (W, D)$ with $W = \{broken(a) \vee broken(b)\}$ and D consisting of the defaults

$$\frac{true : usable(a) \wedge \neg broken(a)}{usable(a)}, \quad \frac{true : usable(b) \wedge \neg broken(b)}{usable(b)}.$$

Since we do not have definite information that a is broken we may apply the first default and obtain $E' = Th(W \cup \{usable(a)\})$. Since E' does not include $broken(b)$ we may apply the second default and get $Th(W \cup \{usable(a), usable(b)\})$

as an extension of T. This result is undesirable, as we know that either a or b is broken.

Two important default logics which adopt the idea of joint consistency are Constrained Default Logic [14] and Rational Default Logic [45].

The joint consistency property gives up part of the expressive power of default theories: under this property any default with several justifications $\frac{\varphi:\psi_1,...,\psi_n}{\chi}$ is equivalent to the modified default $\frac{\varphi:\psi_1\wedge...\wedge\psi_n}{\chi}$ which has one justification. This is in contrast to a result in [9] which shows that in Reiter's Default Logic, defaults with several justifications are strictly more expressive than defaults with just one justification. Essentially, in default logics adopting joint consistency it is impossible to express default rules of the form "In case I am ignorant about p (meaning that I know neither p nor $\neg p$) I conclude q". The natural representation in default form would be $\frac{true:p,\neg p}{q}$, but this default can never be applied if joint consistency is required, because its justifications contradict one another; on the other hand it can be applicable in the sense of Reiter's Default Logic.

Another example for which joint consistency of justifications is undesirable is the following. When I prepare for a trip then I use the following default rules:

If I may assume that the weather will be bad I'll take my sweater.
If I may assume that the weather will be good then I'll take my swimsuit.

In the absence of any reliable information about the weather I am cautious enough to take both with me. But note that I am not building a consistent belief set upon which I make these decisions; obviously the assumptions of the default rules contradict each other. So Reiter's default logic will treat this example in the intended way whereas joint consistency of justifications will prevent me from taking both my sweater and my swimsuit with me.

2.3 Stable models of logic programs

Sometimes it is convenient to express information in the form of logic programs. The treatment of negation in logic programming is closely related to nonmonotonicity – in fact *negation as failure* was an early formalism with nonmonotonic flavour.

2.3.1 Basics of logic programming

A *logic program clause* is an expression of the form

$$A \leftarrow B_1,\ldots,B_n, not\ C_1,\ldots, not\ C_m,$$

where $A, B_1,\ldots,B_n, C_1,\ldots,C_m$ are atomic formulae, and $n, m \geq 0$. A is called the *head* of the clause, and $B_1,\ldots,B_n, not\ C_1,\ldots, not\ C_m$ form the *body*. If all formulae involved in the clause are ground then the clause is called *ground*. If $m = 0$ then the clause is called *definite*. If $n = m = 0$, then the clause is called a *fact*, otherwise a *rule*.

A *logic program* P is a set of program clauses. A *definite logic program* (or *Horn logic program*) is a logic program which consists of definite program clauses only.

Now we give an interpretation of logic programs based on predicate logic; it is determined by considering the following representation of a program clause in first–order logic:

$$\forall(A \leftarrow B_1 \wedge \ldots \wedge B_n \wedge \neg C_1 \wedge \ldots \wedge \neg C_m).$$

The *predicate logic interpretation* of a logic program P is denoted by $pc(P)$, and is the first–order theory which consists of the predicate logic interpretation of all program clauses in P.

Let P be a logic program. Every model of the first–order theory $pc(P)$ is called a *model of P*. Every Herbrand model of $pc(P)$ is called a *Herbrand model of P*. The following theorem holds.

Theorem 2.8 *Every logic program possesses at least one minimal (w.r.t. set inclusion) Herbrand model.*

In general, a logic program may possess several minimal Herbrand models. For example, the logic program consisting of the clause

$$p \leftarrow not\ q$$

possesses two minimal Herbrand models, $\{p\}$ and $\{q\}$. But if we restrict attention to *definite* program clauses, then there is a uniquely determined *least* Herbrand model.

Theorem 2.9 *A definite logic program P has a unique least Herbrand model, denoted by $\mathcal{M}_P$.*

In the definition of stable models to follow we make use of the set of ground instances of a logic program P, resulting in a ground logic program which is denoted by $ground(P)$. It can be shown that for a logic program P, the (predicate logic) models of $pc(ground(P))$ are exactly the Herbrand models of P.

2.3.2 Stable models of logic programs

Given a program clause

$$A \leftarrow B_1, \ldots, B_n, not\ C_1, \ldots, not\ C_m,$$

the predicate logic interpretation treats the negation symbol *not* as classical negation: in order to conclude A, we have to know (or prove) that $\neg C_i$ is true, for all $i \in \{1, \ldots, m\}$.

What is "wrong" with this interpretation? Well, in many cases we may wish to interpret *not* in a different way. For example, we may wish to interpret (or assume) *not connection(newcastle, sydney, 12pm)* to be "true" if we look up the timetable and do not find this train connection (as opposed to actually *knowing* that there is no such connection). This type of negation is called *negation as failure*, and its nonmonotonic character is obvious: a change in the timetable may invalidate a previous conclusion which was based on the absence of some information. A first approximation of the meaning of a program clause is the following:

> If $B_1, \ldots, B_n$ are currently provable,
> and if none of $C_1, \ldots, C_n$ is currently provable,
> then conclude A.

Of course, this interpretation is still vague in that it does not specify what "is currently known" actually means. Nevertheless, it resembles the intuitive interpretation of a default in Default Logic. The stable semantics uses this observation to assign meaning to logic programs. In particular, it uses the following translation of logic programs into default theories.

The Default Logic interpretation of a ground program clause Cl

$$A \leftarrow B_1, \ldots, B_n, not\ C_1, \ldots, not\ C_m$$

is given by the default

$$df(Cl) = \frac{B_1 \wedge \ldots \wedge B_n : \neg\, C_1, \ldots, \neg\, C_m}{A}\,{}_3.$$

We define $df(P)$, the *default logic interpretation* of the logic program P, to be the default theory (W, D) with $W = \emptyset$ and $D = \{df(Cl) \mid Cl \in ground(P)\}$.

- Let M be a subset of the Herbrand base. M is a *stable model* of the logic program P iff $Th(M)$ is an extension of $df(P)$.

For example, the following program has only the stable model $\{p(1,2), q(1)\}$:

$p(1,2)$
$q(X) \leftarrow p(X, Y), not\ q(Y).$

As another example, let P be the program

$p \leftarrow q, not\ r$
$q \leftarrow r, not\ p$
$r \leftarrow p, not\ q.$

Its only stable model is the empty set. Notice that both examples have a unique stable model. This is not necessarily the case, since default theories may have none, one, or several extensions. The reader is asked to give a logic program with more than one stable model.

Further note that in both cases above, the stable set is also a minimal Herbrand model of the logic program. This is not coincidental, as shown by the following result.

---

[3] In case $n = 0$ or $m = 0$, the prerequisite resp. justification of $df(Cl)$ is the formula *true*.

Theorem 2.10 *Let P be a logic program. A stable model of P is a minimal Herbrand model of P. In particular, if P is a definite logic program, then $\mathcal{M}_P$ is the unique stable model of P.*

The converse of this result is not true, which means that not every minimal Herbrand model of P is a stable model of P. To see this, consider the logic program consisting of the single clause $p \leftarrow not\ p$. P has the minimal Herbrand model $\{p\}$, but the corresponding default theory $(\emptyset, \{\frac{true:\neg p}{p}\})$ has no extension, so P has no stable model.

2.3.3 The original definition

In this section we give the original definition of stable models of Gelfond and Lifschitz, and show that it is equivalent to that used in the previous section. Let M be a subset of the Herbrand base. We call a ground program clause

$$A \leftarrow B_1, \ldots, B_n, not\ C_1, \ldots, not\ C_m$$

irrelevant w.r.t. M if at least one C_i is included in M. Given a logic program P, we define the *reduct of P w.r.t.* M, denoted by P^M, to be the logic program obtained from $ground(P)$ by

1. removing all clauses that are irrelevant w.r.t. M, and

2. removing all premises $not\ C_i$ from all remaining program clauses.

Note that the reduct P^M is a definite logic program, and we are no longer faced with the problem of assigning semantics to negation, but can use the least Herbrand model instead. The (historically) original definition went along the lines that M is a stable model of P iff $M = \mathcal{M}_{P^M}$. The following result shows that this definition is equivalent to the one given previously.

Theorem 2.11 *Let P be a logic program, and M a subset of the Herbrand base. M is a stable model of P (in the sense of subsection 2.3.3) iff M is the least Herbrand model of P^M.*

2.3.4 Historical and bibliographical remarks

The classical paper on logic programming is [7], and the classical textbook on the field is [36]. The study of the meaning of negation in logic programming using nonmonotonic semantics has exploded since the late 80s. Stable model semantics was introduced by Gelfond and Lifschitz in [23]. The relationship between stable models and Default Logic was discovered by Bidoit and Froidevaux [10], and Marek and Truszczynski [42]. Logic programs with classical negation were introduced and studied by Gelfond and Lifschitz [25]. An in–depth comparison between stable model semantics and Default Logic can be found in Marek and Truszczynski's book [43], from which theorem 18.5 was taken.

The well–founded semantics was introduced by van Gelder, Ross and Schlipf in [59]. There is a procedural mechanism for WFS called *SLS–resolution* [52], and an implementation in Prolog, the so–called *OLDT–algorithm* [58, 60]. For a recent book on reasoning with logic programming see [2].

3 Belief revision

Nonmonotonic reasoning is a process that allows a reasoner to make plausible conjectures in the absence of complete information. Belief Revision, on the other hand, provides mechanisms for changing information in the light of new information. These mechanisms can be used to incorporate new information into a knowledge base without leading to inconsistency.

Belief revision is a process that can be used to modify a knowledge base when new information is acquired. If the new information is consistent with the knowledge base then this process is straightforward; simply add the new information. On the other hand, if the new information contradicts the knowledge base then great care must be exercised, otherwise the introduction of inconsistency will comprise the integrity of the knowledge base.

In order to incorporate new information which is inconsistent with the knowledge base, the system or agent must *decide* what information it is prepared to give up. Belief revision attempts to model rational decisions concerning modifications to a knowledge base.

Let us say that we currently believe that *all birds have feathers* and that our friend Zigmund has a bird called *Suzie*; consequently we also believe that *Suzie has feathers*. One day we actually meet *Suzie*, and are somewhat surprised to learn that she does not have feathers. How should we modify our knowledge in view of this new fact. Not only must we retract the inferred information that *Suzie has feathers*, but we must also remove other beliefs which are also in conflict with the new information. We appear to have several possible courses of action to follow in this regard: (i) retract the information that *Suzie is a bird*, (ii) retract that *all birds have feathers*, or (iii) retract both. The choice we make will depend upon the relative importance we attribute to our background information. If we are rational and have less confidence that *Suzie is a bird* than *all birds have feathers* we would probably prefer the solution that (i) offers, conversely if we believe *Suzie is a bird* more strongly than *all birds have feathers* then we might prefer (ii). If we cannot decide which to prefer, or if they are causally linked then we might relinquish both beliefs to make way for the acceptance of the new information. ¿From this intuitive discussion we see how a preference ordering of our knowledge base might help resolve the nontrivial problem of choosing what information to surrender in order to avoid inconsistency.

The belief revision framework restricts itself to modeling changes to logical theories that involve the addition and removal of facts. Therefore, we do not consider the possibility of explicitly modifying individual facts, such as transforming *all birds have feathers* to *all birds except Suzie have feathers*, as a primitive operation. Modifying individual facts is often seen in machine learning for example, and can be modelled in the belief revision framework by observing that *all birds have feathers* entails *all birds except Suzie have feathers*, therefore removing *all birds have feathers* and retaining *all birds except Suzie have feathers* achieves the same result.

Belief revision models *rational modifications* to knowledge bases guided by the principle of *Minimal Change*; sadly though, the notions of *rationality* and *minimality*, in the sense we would like to capture, defy explicit definition. Intuitively, by rational we mean things like: the reasoner realises that inconsistency is problematical and thus actively seeks to avoid it, and that given our example it is not sufficient to retract only the fact that *Suzie has feathers* because it is derivable from the remaining information. The principle of Minimal Change says that, as much information should be conserved as is possible in accordance with an underlying preference relation. The underlying preference relation is used to capture the information *content* of the knowledge base, the reasoning agent's *commitment* to this information, and how the information should behave under *change*.

It has often been incorrectly argued that the choices (i) and (ii) are more minimal than (iii), because only *two* basic facts are jettisoned as opposed to *three*. The problem with this argument is that the interdependencies among our beliefs might force us to discard more than the minimal *number* of beliefs. The web of *causal* interdependencies is enmeshed in the preference relation, and cardinality measures are not the only, nor necessarily the most appropriate, when it comes to measuring the *magnitude of change*. For instance, to take our example a little further, it might have been that the only reason for believing that *all birds have feathers* is that *Suzie has feathers*, so if we contract *Suzie has feathers* then it should be permissible to retract *all birds have feathers* in the process. Clearly, then cardinality is not the only allowable measure of change. Sometimes the most rational response is to forfeit more than the minimal number of beliefs. For instance, it may be better remove a single strongly held belief rather than several weakly held beliefs?

The framework for belief revision developed herein is known as the AGM paradigm, so-called after its founders Carlos Alchourrón, Peter Gärdenfors and David Makinson [1]. It is a formal framework for modeling ideal and rational changes to repositories of information under the principle of Minimal Change. In particular, it provides mechanisms for modeling the coherent retraction and incorporation of information.

Technically, the framework models corpora of information as logical theories, and changes in information content as functions that take a theory (the current knowledge base) and a logical sentence (the new information) to another theory (the new knowledge base). There are several types of change functions, and we focus on: *contraction, withdrawal [39], expansion*, and *revision*. Contraction and withdrawal functions model the retraction of information, whilst expansion and revision model various ways of incorporating information. All four functions are interrelated.

Change functions can be described either *axiomatically* using rationality postulates, or *constructively* using certain preference relations. The rationality postulates are properties that we would expect rational change functions to satisfy and they characterise various classes of change functions. Moreover they may be satisfied by more than one function. An individual function can be singled out using a preference relation such as an *epistemic entrenchment ordering* which provides the extralogical information required to make necessary choices concerning what information should be given up.

3.1 Expansion

Expansion models the simplest change to a knowledge base, it involves the acceptance of information without the removal of any previously accepted information, and as a consequence it may lead to an inconsistent knowledge base.

The *expansion* of a theory T[4] with respect to a sentence φ is the logical closure of T and φ. The set of all theories of a language $\mathcal{L}$. is denoted by $\mathcal{K_L}$, and formally, an expansion function $^+$ is a function from $\mathcal{K_L} \times \mathcal{L}$ to $\mathcal{K_L}$, mapping (T, φ) to T_φ^+ where $T_\varphi^+ = \text{Th}(T \cup \{\varphi\})$.

Clearly, expansion is a monotonic operation, that is, $T \subseteq T_\varphi^+$, and if $\neg\varphi \in T$, then T_φ^+ is inconsistent. Certainly if $\neg\varphi \notin T$, then we can accept that the Principle of Minimal Change is at work, since T_φ^+ would be the *smallest* change we can logically make to T in order to incorporate φ.

In contradistinction to expansion, it turns out that both contraction and revision are nonunique operations and cannot be realised using logical and set theoretical notions alone.

3.2 Contraction

Contraction of a knowledge base involves the retraction of information, the difficulty, as we noted in the introduction, is in determining those sentences that should be given up. We are usually presented with a choice. For example, perhaps our reasoner erroneously believed that *Suzie is a sulphur-crested cockatoo* and subsequently wished to retract it, this may or may not involve the removal of other beliefs, such as *Suzie has yellow and white feathers*, depending on how he views the causal dependencies, etc.

A *contraction* of T with respect to φ involves the removal of a set of sentences from T so that φ is no longer implied, provided φ is not a tautology. Formally, a contraction function $^-$ is any function from $\mathcal{K_L} \times \mathcal{L}$ to $\mathcal{K_L}$, mapping (T, φ) to T_φ^- which satisfies the following postulates. For any $\varphi, \psi \in \mathcal{L}$ and any $T \in \mathcal{K_L}$:

($^-$1) $T_\varphi^- \in \mathcal{K_L}$

($^-$2) $T_\varphi^- \subseteq T$

($^-$3) If $\varphi \notin T$ then $T \subseteq T_\varphi^-$

($^-$4) If $\nvdash \varphi$ then $\varphi \notin T_\varphi^-$

($^-$5) $T \subseteq (T_\varphi^-)_\varphi^+$ (*recovery*)

---

[4]Not to be confused with expansions of autoepistemic theories!

($^-$6) If $\vdash \varphi \leftrightarrow \psi$ then $T_\varphi^- = T_\psi^-$

($^-$7) $T_\varphi^- \cap T_\psi^- \subseteq T_{\varphi \wedge \psi}^-$

($^-$8) If $\varphi \notin T_{\varphi \wedge \psi}^-$ then $T_{\varphi \wedge \psi}^- \subseteq T_\varphi^-$

The postulates embody the principle of *Minimal Change*, and act as integrity constraints for change functions. They do not uniquely determine a change function, rather their purpose is to identify the set of possible new knowledge bases that might reasonably result when information is retracted from the current knowledge base, T. The postulates themselves are explained in various works by Gärdenfors [19] and are motivated via the criterion of informational economy.

The first postulate ($^-$1) simply says that the result of a contraction is a theory, so that contracting information results in a theory, i.e. the new knowledge base is logically closed. Essentially the change functions described in the AGM paradigm model the processes of an ideal reasoning agent. Since theories are typically infinite structures the first postulate will not usually be satisfied by a computer-based implementation. Postulate ($^-$2) says that contracting a theory only involves the removal of old information and never the incorporation of new information, therefore when information is contracted no spurious information is added. Postulate ($^-$3) says when the information φ is not accepted then taking it away should have no effect, indeed ($^-$2) and ($^-$3) considered together say that if φ is not in T, then $T_\varphi^- = T$. Postulate ($^-$4), says if φ is not a tautology then it must be removed in the contraction T_φ^-. Postulate ($^-$5) together with the previous four, says if $\varphi \in T$ then $T = (T_\varphi^-)_\varphi^+$. In other words, no more information is lost than can be reincorporated by an expansion with respect to the explicit information contracted, that is, if we contract φ and then immediately replace it using expansion then we obtain the theory we started with. Intuitively then, this postulate forces a *minimal* amount of information to be lost during a contraction. Postulate ($^-$6) says that the same result is obtained whenever we contract with respect to equivalent logical sentences, that is, contraction is not dependent on the syntax of the information to be contracted. The last two postulates deal with the association of contracting a conjunction $\varphi \wedge \psi$ and the contraction of each conjunct, φ and ψ, individually. In order to contract $\varphi \wedge \psi$ we *must* at the very least contract either φ or ψ, and we might also consider contracting both of them depending on the mechanism we adopt to help us make the choice. Postulate ($^-$7) says that the theory that results from contracting with respect to $\varphi \wedge \psi$ should never be *smaller* than taking the intersection of T_φ^- and T_ψ^-. That is to say, beliefs in both T_φ^- and T_ψ^- should always be contained in $T_{\varphi \wedge \psi}^-$. Postulate ($^-$8) says that if φ is not contained in the contraction with respect to the conjunction $\varphi \wedge \psi$ then the contraction with respect to this conjunction cannot be larger that the theory obtained by contraction φ alone. Given postulates ($^-$1) and ($^-$6), postulates ($^-$7) and ($^-$8) together imply that $T_{\varphi \wedge \psi}^-$ is equivalent to either T_φ^-, T_ψ^- or $T_\varphi^- \cap T_\psi^-$.

The postulates for contraction identify a class of functions for a knowledge base and for each one of these functions Gärdenfors and Makinson showed that there is a preference criterion that can be used to construct it.

The most controversial of these postulates is *recovery*, (⁻5), because one can argue that it is not always an appropriate requirement, especially for a limited reasoning agent. A withdrawal function is similar to a contraction function with the exception that it may not satisfy recovery. In particular, a *withdrawal function* satisfies (⁻1) – (⁻4) and (⁻6) – (⁻8), but not necessarily (⁻5). Withdrawal functions will play an important role in section 3.5.3.

3.3 Revision

Revision attempts to change a knowledge base as *little as possible* in order to incorporate newly acquired information. This new information may be inconsistent with the knowledge base. In order to maintain consistency some old information may need to be retracted. Thus revision functions are nonmonotonic in nature, and related to withdrawal and contraction functions.

The process of revision was discussed in the introduction where our reasoner, if you recall, was mistaken about Suzie's possession of feathers, and had to revise his knowledge by accepting that *Suzie is featherless*.

Formally, a revision function * is any function from $\mathcal{K}_\mathcal{L} \times \mathcal{L}$ to $\mathcal{K}_\mathcal{L}$, mapping (T, φ) to T_φ^* which satisfies the following postulates. For any φ, $\psi \in \mathcal{L}$ and any $T \in \mathcal{K}_\mathcal{L}$:

(*1) $T_\varphi^* \in \mathcal{K}_\mathcal{L}$

(*2) $\varphi \in T_\varphi^*$

(*3) $T_\varphi^* \subseteq T_\varphi^+$

(*4) If $\neg\varphi \notin T$ then $T_\varphi^+ \subseteq T_\varphi^*$

(*5) If $T_\varphi^* = \bot$ then $\vdash \neg\varphi$

(*6) If $\vdash \varphi \leftrightarrow \psi$ then $T_\varphi^* = T_\psi^*$

(*7) $T_{\varphi \wedge \psi}^* \subseteq (T_\varphi^*)_\psi^+$

(*8) If $\neg\psi \notin T_\varphi^*$ then $(T_\varphi^*)_\psi^+ \subseteq T_{\varphi \wedge \psi}^*$

The revision postulates also attempt to encapsulate the Principle of Minimal Change. According to (*1) revising a theory results in a theory. Postulate (*2) says that the information to be added by a revision is always successfully incorporated. Postulate (*3) tells us that revising a theory can never incorporate more information than an expansion operation. Postulate (*4), says if $\neg\varphi$ is not in T then the expansion of T with respect to φ is contained in the revision with respect to φ. This postulate is written in its weakest form, and the main point for our purposes is that the postulates (*3) and (*4) together say that if φ is consistent with T, then $T_\varphi^* = T_\varphi^+$. Postulate (*5) tells us that the only way to obtain an inconsistent theory is to revise with an inconsistent sentence φ. Postulate (*6) says that revision functions are syntax independent. Postulate

(*7) says that the theory that results from revising with respect to $\varphi \wedge \psi$ should never contain more than the revision with respect to φ followed by the expansion with respect to ψ. According to (*8) if $\neg\psi$ is not contained in the revision with respect to φ then the revision with respect to φ followed by the expansion with respect to ψ should not contain more information than the theory that results from revising with respect to $\varphi \wedge \psi$. If the revision function * satisfies the first six postulates, then the postulates (*7) and (*8) considered together imply that $T^*_{\varphi\vee\psi}$ is equivalent to T^*_φ, T^*_ψ or $T^*_\varphi \cap T^*_\psi$.

Several explicit relationships exist between the various change functions. In the theorems below Alchourron, Gärdenfors and Makinson demonstrated that contraction and revision functions are interdefinable.

Theorem 3.1 *If $^-$ is a contraction function and $^+$ the expansion function, then * defined by the* Levi *Identity below defines a revision function.*

$$T^*_\varphi = (T^-_{\neg\varphi})^+_\varphi$$

Theorem 3.2 *If * is a revision function, then $^-$ defined by the* Harper *Identity below defines a contraction function.*

$$T^-_\varphi = T \cap T^*_{\neg\varphi}$$

3.4 Epistemic entrenchment orderings

As noted earlier the rationality postulates for contraction and revision merely describe classes of functions; they do not provide a mechanism for defining a particular function. For any theory there might be a vast number of functions that satisfy the postulates for contraction and revision. So in order to single out a unique one, additional structure is necessary; this usually takes the form of a preference relation such as an epistemic entrenchment ordering.

According to Stalnaker, it is necessary "to impose additional structure on our notion of a belief state before we can say very much about the way beliefs change", and when it comes to deciding those beliefs to discard, "the choice will depend on assumptions about epistemic and causal dependence and independence of the reasons one has for one's beliefs as well as on the beliefs themselves".

Gärdenfors' epistemic entrenchment orderings [19] are based on a relative ranking of information according to its importance in the face of change. This ordering can be used to uniquely determine a change function by providing a selection criteria that can be used to identify those sentences to be retracted, those to be retained, and those to be acquired during changes. Intuitively, when faced with a choice, sentences having the lowest degree of epistemic entrenchment are shed.

Definition *Given a theory T of $\mathcal{L}$, an* epistemic entrenchment related to T *is any binary relation $\leq$ on $\mathcal{L}$ satisfying the conditions below:*

(EE1) If $\varphi \leq \psi$ and $\psi \leq \chi$, then $\varphi \leq \chi$.

(EE2) For all φ, $\psi \in \mathcal{L}$, if $\varphi \vdash \psi$ then $\varphi \leq \psi$.

(EE3) For all φ, $\psi \in \mathcal{L}$, $\varphi \leq \varphi \wedge \psi$ or $\psi \leq \varphi \wedge \psi$.

(EE4) When $T \neq \bot$, $\varphi \notin T$ iff $\varphi \leq \psi$ for all $\psi \in \mathcal{L}$.

(EE5) If $\psi \leq \varphi$ for all $\psi \in \mathcal{L}$, then $\vdash \varphi$.

If $\varphi \leq \psi$, then we say ψ is *at least as entrenched as* φ. We define $\varphi < \psi$, as $\varphi \leq \psi$ and not $\psi \leq \varphi$. If $\varphi \leq \psi$ and $\psi \leq \varphi$, then we say φ and ψ are *equally entrenched*.

The condition (EE1) requires that an epistemic entrenchment ordering be transitive. (EE2) says that if φ is logically stronger than ψ, then ψ is at least as entrenched as φ. For example the sentence $\varphi \vee \psi$ is entailed by φ, and (EE2) tells us that $\varphi \vee \psi$ is at least as entrenched as φ, in other words we believe in $\varphi \vee \psi$ at least as much as φ. It certainly would not make any sense to believe in φ *more* strongly than $\varphi \vee \psi$; a rational agent could hardy be less certain of $\varphi \vee \psi$ than it is of φ. The condition (EE3) together with (EE1) and (EE2) implies that a conjunction is ranked at the same level as its least ranked conjunct. For example, if $\varphi \leq \psi$ then $\varphi \wedge \psi \leq \varphi$ and $\varphi \leq \varphi \wedge \psi$, so $\varphi \wedge \psi = \varphi$. The condition (EE4) tells us that sentences not in the theory T are minimal, and (EE5) says that the tautologies are maximal.

Definition *For an epistemic entrenchment ordering $\leq$ and a sentence φ, define $\mathrm{cut}_{\leq}(\varphi) = \{\psi : \varphi \leq \psi\}$.*

The set $\mathrm{cut}_{\leq}(\varphi)$ contains all those sentences that are at least as entrenched as φ. An important property of an epistemic entrenchment is that it is a total preorder of the sentences in $\mathcal{L}$ such that the following theorem holds.

Theorem 3.3 *If $\leq$ is an epistemic entrenchment, then for any sentence φ, $\mathrm{cut}_{\leq}(\varphi)$ is a theory.*

Since a subtheory of a finitely axiomatizable theory may not be finitely axiomatizable we give the following result concerning a *finite description* of an epistemic entrenchment ordering. In the next section we develop a computational model for change functions using a finite description of an epistemic entrenchment ordering, and the following theorem provides the theoretical basis for the one we adopt.

Theorem 3.4 *An epistemic entrenchment ordering $\leq$ is finitely representable if and only if it has a finite number of natural partitions, and for all $\varphi \in \mathcal{L}$, $\mathrm{cut}_{\leq}(\varphi)$ is finitely axiomatizable.*

The following results of Gärdenfors and Makinson [20] provide us with a constructive method for building change functions from an epistemic entrenchment ordering. Theorem 3.5 gives a condition that can be used for constructing a contraction function, and Theorem 3.6 provides a similar one for constructing a revision function.

Theorem 3.5 *Let T be a theory of $\mathcal{L}$. For every contraction function $^-$ for T there exists an epistemic entrenchment $\leq$ related to T such that (E^-) is true for every $\varphi \in \mathcal{L}$. Conversely, for every epistemic entrenchment $\leq$ related to T, there exists a contraction function $^-$ such that (E^-) is true for every $\varphi \in \mathcal{L}$.*

$$(E^-) \qquad T_\varphi^- = \begin{cases} \{\psi \in T : \varphi < \varphi \vee \psi\} & \text{if } \nvdash \varphi \\ T & \text{otherwise} \end{cases}$$

Given an epistemic entrenchment related to T, the condition (E^-) explicitly determines the information to be retained, and retracted in a contraction operation. Furthermore, every contraction function can be constructed from some epistemic entrenchment ordering.

Returning to our example, if *Suzie has feathers $\vee$ all birds have feathers* is strictly more entrenched than *Suzie has feathers*, then *all birds have feathers* will remain after the contraction of *Suzie has feathers*. Conversely, if *Suzie has feathers $\vee$ all birds have feathers* and *Suzie has feathers* are equally entrenched, then *all birds fly* will be retracted.

It is easy to show using (E^-) that if ψ is at least as entrenched as φ then under the contraction with respect to $\varphi \wedge \psi$, the conjunct φ is removed, and if φ and ψ are equally entrenched then both are retracted. This mirrors our intuition that sentences with the lowest epistemic entrenchment are given up.

An analogous result for revision is provided in the theorem below.

Theorem 3.6 *Let T be a theory of $\mathcal{L}$. For every revision function * for T there exists an epistemic entrenchment $\leq$ related to T such that (E^*), below, is true for every $\varphi \in \mathcal{L}$. Conversely, for every epistemic entrenchment $\leq$ related to T, there exists a revision function * for T such that (E^*) is true for every $\varphi \in \mathcal{L}$.*

$$(E^*) \qquad T_\varphi^* = \begin{cases} \{\psi \in \mathcal{L} : \neg\varphi < \neg\varphi \vee \psi\} & \text{if } \nvdash \neg\varphi \\ \bot & \text{otherwise} \end{cases}$$

Gärdenfors and Makinson [20] showed that for a finite language, an epistemic entrenchment related to T is determined by the ordering of the dual atoms (maximal disjunctions) in T. They also showed that there is a one-to-one correspondence between epistemic entrenchment orderings and revision (and contraction) functions, consequently the number of revision (and contraction) functions for T is equal to the number of epistemic entrenchment orderings on the dual atoms[5] in T. Therefore, finding the number of possible revision (and contraction) functions for T amounts to calculating the number of ways we can

---

[5]If the language consists of the atoms $p_1, \ldots, p_n$, then a dual atom is a formula $L_1 \vee \ldots \vee L_n$, where for each i, L_i is either p_i or $\neg p_i$.

place a total preorder on the dual atoms in T. But first note that if there are k atoms in the language, then there are 2^k dual atoms. For instance, if the only atoms are φ and ψ then the set of dual atoms is $\{\varphi \vee \psi, \varphi \vee \neg\psi, \neg\varphi \vee \psi, \neg\varphi \vee \neg\psi\}$.

Theorem 3.7 *For a theory T in a finite language, if n is the number of dual atoms in T, then the number of revisions (and contraction) functions is given by:*

$$p(n) = \Sigma_{m=1}^{n} m! S(m, n)$$

where $S(m, n)$, are Stirling numbers of the second kind, that is, the number of partitions of an $n-element$ set into m parts.

The growth of $p(n)$ is more rapid than exponential; $p(1) = 1$, $p(2) = 3$, $p(3) = 13$, $p(4) = 75$, $p(5) = 541 \cdots$, hence the class of change functions described by the rationality postulates is colossal in n, the number of dual atoms!

Finally, an epistemic entrenchment ordering is a *total* preorder. It is possible to relax many of the definitions to allow *partial* orderings, discussing the ramifications of doing so is outside the scope of this tutorial paper. Instead we'll mention some work in this direction. Katsuno and Mendelzon [29] introduced a revision function based on a partial preordering of models and identified a weaker version of (*8) that is satisfied by revision functions constructed from a partial preorder on models.

3.5 Implementing belief revision

Several problems arise when one attempts to implement the process of belief revision. First, because AGM change functions take an epistemic entrenchment ordering together with a sentence, to be contracted or accepted, and produce a theory, the entrenchment ordering is lost. Consequently, iterated revision is not naturally supported. Most applications where belief revision capabilities would be most valuable require iterated revision capabilities. So from a practical perspective modeling the iteration of change is essential. Second, because epistemic entrenchment orderings typically rank an infinite number of sentences in a logical language, there is a serious *representation* problem for computer-based implementations.

In this section we define a *finite partial entrenchment ranking* which can be used to generate a finitely representable epistemic entrenchment ordering. Then we describe a simple computational model that adjusts this ranking using an *absolute measure of minimal change*. Any theorem prover can be used to realise it. The adjustment of a finite partial entrenchment ranking is a mechanical procedure that can be used to support the iteration of change functions. Finally, we demonstrate the explicit relationships between change functions constructed from partial entrenchment rankings, and epistemic entrenchment orderings. Somewhat surprisingly it turns out that standard AGM revision and contraction functions can be constructed from partial entrenchment rankings.

3.5.1 Finite Partial Entrenchment Rankings

A *finite partial entrenchment ranking* grades the content of a finite knowledge base according to its epistemic importance, and as such it can be used to specify a finitely representable epistemic entrenchment ordering. Formally defined below, this ranking maps a finite set of sentences to rational numbers. Intuitively, the higher the value assigned to a sentence the more firmly held it is, or the more entrenched it is.

Definition *A finite partial entrenchment ranking is a function* **B** *from a finite subset of sentences into the interval* $[0, 1]$ *such that the following conditions are satisfied for all* $\varphi \in \text{dom}(\mathbf{B})$:

(PER1) $\{\psi \in \text{dom}(\mathbf{B}) : \mathbf{B}(\varphi) < \mathbf{B}(\psi)\} \nvdash \varphi$.

(PER2) *If* $\vdash \neg\varphi$, *then* $\mathbf{B}(\varphi) = 0$.

(PER3) $\mathbf{B}(\varphi) = 1$ *if and only if* $\vdash \varphi$.

(PER1) says sentences assigned a value higher than an arbitrary sentence φ, do not entail φ, (PER2) says inconsistent sentences are assigned zero, and (PER3) says that tautologies are assigned 1. An example of a finite partial entrenchment ranking is given below. Convince yourself that it satisfies the property (PER1).

Example Let **B** be given by

$$\mathbf{B}(bird(suzie) \vee \neg bird(suzie)) = 1,$$
$$\mathbf{B}(\forall X(bird(X) \rightarrow feathers(X))) = 0.3,$$
$$\mathbf{B}(bird(tweety)) = 0.2,$$
$$\mathbf{B}(\forall X(bird(X) \rightarrow wings(X))) = 0.1,$$
$$\mathbf{B}(bird(suzie) \wedge \neg bird(suzie)) = 0.$$

A finite partial entrenchment ranking can be used to represent a finitely representable epistemic entrenchment ordering. Of course, a finite ranking does *not* imply that the language is finite.

The numerical assignment can be viewed in two distinct ways: (i) *qualitatively*, where the relative ordering of sentences is used, or (ii) *quantitatively*, where the numerical value assigned to sentences possesses some extra meaning, such as probability, and a calculus based on their numerical value adopted.

The intended interpretation of a finite partial entrenchment ranking is that sentences mapped to numbers greater than zero represent the *explicit* beliefs, and their logical closure represents its *implicit* beliefs.

Definition *Define the* explicit information content *represented by* **B** *a finite partial entrenchment ranking to be* $\{\varphi \in \text{dom}(\mathbf{B}) : \mathbf{B}(\varphi) > 0\}$, *and denote it by* $\exp(\mathbf{B})$. *Similarly, define the* implicit information content *represented by* $\mathbf{B} \in \mathcal{B}$ *to be* $Th(\exp(\mathbf{B}))$, *and denote it by* content(**B**).

A finite partial entrenchment ranking usually represents an *incomplete specification* of an agent's preferences from which an epistemic entrenchment ordering can be generated. Note there is no unique way of generating an epistemic entrenchment ordering from a partial specification in general. For example, if $\mathbf{B}(\varphi) = 0.2$ and $\mathbf{B}(\psi) = 0.4$ then all compatible epistemic entrenchment orderings will have $\varphi < \psi$, however one compatible epistemic entrenchment ordering will have $\psi < \varphi \vee \psi$, whilst another will have $\psi = \varphi \vee \psi$. The epistemic entrenchment ordering we generate for our computational model gives sentences the *minimum* possible degree of entrenchment. For the example above, the generated epistemic entrenchment ordering would have $\psi = \varphi \vee \psi$ because $\varphi \vee \psi$ must be at least as entrenched as ψ by (EE2) but need not be strictly more entrenched.

In order to describe epistemic entrenchment orderings generated from a ranking it will be necessary to rank implicit information. In the definition below we assign a minimal degree of acceptance to implicit information under the constraint of (PER1).

Definition *Let φ be a nontautological sentence. Let $\mathbf{B}$ be a finite partial entrenchment ranking. We define the* degree of acceptance *of φ to be*

$$
\text{degree}(\mathbf{B}, \varphi) = \begin{cases} \text{largest } j \text{ such that } \{\psi \in \exp(\mathbf{B}) : \mathbf{B}(\psi) \geq j\} \vdash \varphi \\ \qquad \qquad \qquad \qquad \qquad \qquad \text{if } \varphi \in \text{content}(\mathbf{B}) \\ 0 \qquad \qquad \qquad \qquad \qquad \qquad \text{otherwise} \end{cases}
$$

You should be able to see that one could design a simple procedural algorithm to calculate the degree of acceptance of a sentence φ given the information encoded in a finite partial entrenchment ranking. Tautologies have degree 1, and to determine the degree of a nontautological sentence φ we can adopt a straightforward top down procedure. Attempt to prove φ using the sentences assigned the largest value in the range of $\mathbf{B}$, say n, if we are successful then φ is assigned degree n, otherwise try to prove it using sentences assigned the next largest degree, say m, and those assigned n, if φ is successfully proven then it is assigned degree m, etc. Try this procedure with the following example. A bottom-up procedure could also be used, or indeed a procedure based on a binary search. For further discussion see [LANGXXX].

Example Let $\mathbf{B}$ be given by

$\mathbf{B}(bird(suzie) \vee \neg(bird(suzie))) = 1,$
$\mathbf{B}(\forall X(bird(X) \rightarrow feathers(X))) = 0.3,$
$\mathbf{B}(bird(suzie)) = 0.2,$
$\mathbf{B}(\forall X(bird(X) \rightarrow wings(X))) = 0.1,$
$\mathbf{B}(bird(suzie) \wedge \neg bird(suzie)) = 0.$

Using $\mathbf{B}$ we calculate the minimal degree of acceptance of the following implicit information.

$\text{degree}(\mathbf{B}, feathers(suzie)) = 0.2,$

degree($\mathbf{B}$, $(\forall X(bird(X) \rightarrow feathers(X))) \wedge bird(tweety)) = 0.2$,
degree($\mathbf{B}$, $wings(suzie)) = 0.1$,
degree($\mathbf{B}$, $feathers(suzie) \wedge wings(suzie)) = 0.1$,
degree($\mathbf{B}$, $\neg bird(suzie)) = 0$,
degree($\mathbf{B}$, $\neg feathers(suzie)) = 0$.
degree($\mathbf{B}$, $feathers(suzie) \wedge \neg feathers(suzie)) = 0$.

Theorem 3.8, below, shows how a finite partial entrenchment ranking can generate an epistemic entrenchment ordering using degrees of acceptance.

Theorem 3.8 *Let $\mathbf{B}$ be a finite partial entrenchment ranking, and φ, ψ be sentences. Define $\leq_{\mathbf{B}}$ by $\varphi \leq_{\mathbf{B}} \psi$ iff $\vdash \psi$, or* degree($\mathbf{B}, \varphi$) $\leq$ degree($\mathbf{B}, \psi$). *Then $\leq_{\mathbf{B}}$ is an epistemic entrenchment ordering related to* content($\mathbf{B}$).

We refer to $\leq_{\mathbf{B}}$ as *the minimal epistemic entrenchment ordering generated from* $\mathbf{B}$. ¿From Theorem 3.8 we see that the tautologies are maximal, and sentences not in content($\mathbf{B}$) are minimal with respect to $\leq_{\mathbf{B}}$. Since dom($\mathbf{B}$) is finite, the minimal epistemic entrenchment ordering generated is finite, that is, $\leq_{\mathbf{B}}$ possesses a finite number of natural partitions.

Back to our simple example, if $\mathbf{B}(\varphi) = 0.2$ and $\mathbf{B}(\psi) = 0.4$ then the minimal epistemic entrenchment ordering generated by $\mathbf{B}$ is given by the following ordering on dual atoms: $\neg\varphi \vee \neg\psi <_{\mathbf{B}} \varphi \vee \neg\psi <_{\mathbf{B}} \neg\varphi \vee \psi =_{\mathbf{B}} \varphi \vee \psi$. ¿From this ordering we can derive $\varphi \wedge \psi =_{\mathbf{B}} \varphi <_{\mathbf{B}} \psi =_{\mathbf{B}} \varphi \vee \psi$

Recall that an epistemic entrenchment ordering, $\leq$, is *finitely representable* if and only if every cut$_{\leq}(\varphi)$ is finitely axiomatizable. Consequently, $\leq$ is finitely representable if and only if there exists a finite partial entrenchment ranking $\mathbf{B}$ such that $\leq = \leq_{\mathbf{B}}$.

It is not hard to show that given a finitely representable epistemic entrenchment ordering there exists a finite partial entrenchment ranking that can generate it. In fact, a partial entrenchment ranking can be considered to be a (possibly minimal) specification of a finite epistemic entrenchment ordering. However, going from a finitely representable epistemic entrenchment to a finite partial entrenchment ranking is a nonunique process. For example, consider the epistemic entrenchment ordering: $\neg\varphi \vee \neg\psi < \varphi \vee \neg\psi < \neg\varphi \vee \psi = \varphi \vee \psi$. Any of the following three finite partial entrenchment rankings could be used to generate it using the function degree, that is, $\leq = \leq_{\mathbf{B}_1} = \leq_{\mathbf{B}_2} = \leq_{\mathbf{B}_3}$.

(a) $\mathbf{B}_1(\neg\varphi \vee \neg\psi) = 0, \mathbf{B}_1(\varphi \vee \neg\psi) = 0.2, \mathbf{B}_1(\neg\varphi \vee \psi) = 0.4, \mathbf{B}_1(\varphi \vee \psi) = 0.4$.
(b) $\mathbf{B}_2(\neg\varphi \wedge \neg\psi) = 0, \mathbf{B}_2(\varphi \vee \neg\psi) = 0.2, \mathbf{B}_2(\psi) = 0.4$.
(c) $\mathbf{B}_3(\varphi) = 0.2, \mathbf{B}_3(\psi) = 0.4$.

We call finite partial entrenchment rankings *equivalent* if they generate the same minimal epistemic entrenchment ordering. In this sense the rankings $\mathbf{B}_1$, $\mathbf{B}_2$ and $\mathbf{B}_3$ above are equivalent.

3.5.2 Iterated Revision

¿From a practical perspective the AGM paradigm does not provide a policy to support the iteration of its theory change functions. This property is attractive in a theoretical context because it allows the resultant theory to adopt any of many possible epistemic entrenchment orderings depending on the desired dynamic behaviour. In practice, however, a *policy for change* is necessary.

In this subsection we describe a procedure for *adjusting* a finite partial entrenchment ranking. This procedure governs the dynamic behaviour of the system.

The information input for the standard AGM change functions is a sentence. If our aim is to modify a ranking then not only do we need a sentence but we also need a degree of acceptance to assign it in the adjusted ranking. In other words, we need to know where in the new ranking the sentence should reside.

We define the *adjustment of a partial entrenchment ranking*, below, the new information is a contingent sentence φ and a number $0 \leq i < 1$ where φ is the information to be accepted, and i is the degree of acceptance φ is to be assigned in the adjusted ranking.

Adjustments use a *policy for change* based on an *absolute minimal measure*; they transmute a finite partial entrenchment ranking so as to incorporate the desired new information using an absolute minimal measure of change. The set of contingent sentences is denoted $\mathcal{L}^{\bowtie}$.

Definition *Let $\varphi \in \mathcal{L}^{\bowtie}$ and $0 \leq i < 1$. We define the adjustment of a finite partial entrenchment ranking $\mathbf{B}$ to be an function $*$ such that*

$$\mathbf{B}^\star(\varphi, i) = \begin{cases} (\mathbf{B}^-(\varphi, i)) & \text{if } i \leq \text{degree}(\mathbf{B}, \varphi) \\ (\mathbf{B}^-(\neg\varphi, 0))^+(\varphi, i) & \text{otherwise} \end{cases}$$

where

$$\mathbf{B}^-(\varphi, i)(\psi) = \begin{cases} i & \text{if } \text{degree}(\mathbf{B}, \varphi) = \text{degree}(\mathbf{B}, \varphi \vee \psi) \text{ and } \mathbf{B}(\psi) > i \\ \mathbf{B}(\psi) & \text{otherwise} \end{cases}$$

for all $\psi \in \text{dom}(\mathbf{B})$, and

$$\mathbf{B}^+(\varphi, i)(\psi) = \begin{cases} \mathbf{B}(\psi) & \text{if } \mathbf{B}(\psi) > i \\ i & \text{if } \varphi \leftrightarrow \psi \text{ or } \mathbf{B}(\psi) \leq i < \text{degree}(\mathbf{B}, \varphi \to \psi) \\ \text{degree}(\mathbf{B}, \varphi \to \psi) & \text{otherwise} \end{cases}$$

for all $\psi \in \text{dom}(\mathbf{B}) \cup \{\varphi\}$.

Adjustments define change functions for *theory bases*, rather than logically closed sets of sentences as in the previous section. Note that an adjustment is not defined for inconsistent, or tautological sentences. Accepting inconsistent information will compromise the integrity of the system, and thus ought to be avoided, whilst tautologies must always be assigned 1. So the definition focuses on the principle case, and can easily be extended to include both tautological and inconsistent sentences, if desired.

Intuitively, an (φ, i)–adjustment of $\mathbf{B}$ involves minimal changes to $\mathbf{B}$ such that φ is accepted with degree i. In particular, each sentence $\psi \in \text{dom}(\mathbf{B})$ is reassigned a number closest to $\mathbf{B}(\psi)$ in the adjusted partial entrenchment ranking $\mathbf{B}^*(\varphi, i)$ under the guiding principle that if we reduce the degree of an accepted sentence φ, to i, say, then we also reduce the degree of each sentence that would be retracted in φ's contraction to i as well.

There are essentially two processes at work in an adjustment; sentences migrate *up* or *down* the ranking. Migration downwards is related to contraction, whilst movement upwards is related to expansion; movement upwards must ensure that the new ranking satisfies (PER1).

Adjustments use the *relative ranking* of information encoded in a partial entrenchment ranking, and they *preserve finiteness*; adjusting a finite partial entrenchment ranking results in a finite ranking, and if $\exp(\mathbf{B})$ is finite then $\exp(\mathbf{B}^*(\varphi, i))$ is finite.

The following theorem illustrates the interrelationships between theory base revision and theory base contraction based on adjustments. In particular, Theorem 15.3(i) is analogous to the Harper Identity and it captures the dependence of contraction on the information content of the theory base, that is, $\exp(\mathbf{B})$. Similarly Theorem 3.9(ii) is analogous to the Levi Identity.

Theorem 3.9 *Let* $\mathbf{B} \in \mathcal{B}$, *let* * *be an adjustment, and let* $0 < i < 1$. *Then*

(i) $\exp(\mathbf{B}^*(\varphi, 0)) = \exp(\mathbf{B}^*(\neg\varphi, i)) \cap \exp(\mathbf{B})$, *and*

(ii) $\exp(\mathbf{B}^*(\varphi, i)) = \exp(\mathbf{B}^*(\neg\varphi, 0)) \cup \{\varphi\}$.

We illustrate the adjustment of a theory base in the simple example below.

Example $\mathbf{B}(\varphi \vee \chi) = 0.4, \mathbf{B}(\varphi \rightarrow \psi) = 0.3, \ \mathbf{B}(\varphi) = 0.25, \ \mathbf{B}(\chi) = 0.1$.

(a) Consider the reorganisation of $\mathbf{B}$ where more compelling evidence for φ is acquired, and we decide to increase the degree of acceptance of φ from 0.25 to 0.6. We obtain the following:

$\mathbf{B}^*(\varphi, 0.6)(\varphi) = 0.6$,
$\mathbf{B}^*(\varphi, 0.6)(\varphi \vee \chi) = 0.6$,
$\mathbf{B}^*(\varphi, 0.6)(\varphi \rightarrow \psi) = 0.3$,
$\mathbf{B}^*(\varphi, 0.6)(\chi) = 0.1$,
$\text{degree}(\mathbf{B}^*(\varphi, 0.6), \varphi \vee \psi) = 0.6$,
$\text{degree}(\mathbf{B}^*(\varphi, 0.6), \psi) = 0.3$
$\text{degree}(\mathbf{B}^*(\varphi, 0.6), \varphi \rightarrow \chi) = 0.1$,
$\text{degree}(\mathbf{B}^*(\varphi, 0.6), \neg\varphi) = 0$,
$\text{degree}(\mathbf{B}^*(\varphi, 0.6), \neg\psi) = 0$, and
$\text{degree}(\mathbf{B}^*(\varphi, 0.6), \neg\chi) = 0$.

(b) Now let's consider the contraction of φ, that is, $\mathbf{B}^*(\varphi, 0)$.

$\mathbf{B}^\star(\varphi,0)(\varphi \vee \chi) = 0.4$,
$\mathbf{B}^\star(\varphi,0)(\varphi \rightarrow \psi) = 0.3$,
$\mathbf{B}^\star(\varphi,0)(\chi) = 0.1$,
$\mathbf{B}^\star(\varphi,0)(\varphi) = 0$,
degree($\mathbf{B}^\star(\varphi,0), \varphi \rightarrow \chi) = 0.1$,
degree($\mathbf{B}^\star(\varphi,0), \varphi \vee \psi) = 0$,
degree($\mathbf{B}^\star(\varphi,0), \psi) = 0$
degree($\mathbf{B}^\star(\varphi,0), \neg\varphi) = 0$,
degree($\mathbf{B}^\star(\varphi,0), \neg\psi) = 0$, and
degree($\mathbf{B}^\star(\varphi,0), \neg\chi) = 0$.
%vspace6pt

3.5.3 Connections with theory change

In this section we investigate the behaviour of adjustments by exploring their relationship with standard AGM theory change functions. In particular, the relationship between *theory base change* functions constructed by the adjustment of a finite partial entrenchment ranking, $\mathbf{B}$, and *theory change* functions constructed by the minimal epistemic entrenchment ordering generated from $\mathbf{B}$.

Theorem 3.10, below, is a delightful little result that demonstrates that if $i > 0$ then $\mathbf{B}^\star(\varphi,i)$ embodies a revision. In particular, content($\mathbf{B}$) $\mapsto$ content($\mathbf{B}^\star(\varphi,i)$) defines a revision function.

Theorem 3.10 *Let $\mathbf{B} \in \mathcal{B}$, let $\star$ be an adjustment, and let $0 < i < 1$. Let * be the revision function for* content($\mathbf{B}$) *uniquely determined by (E^*) and $\leq_{\mathbf{B}}$. Then*

(i) $\exp(\mathbf{B}^\star(\varphi,i)) = (\text{content}(\mathbf{B}))^*_\varphi \cap \{\exp(\mathbf{B}) \cup \{\varphi\}\}$, *and*

(ii) $(\text{content}(\mathbf{B}))^*_\varphi = \text{content}(\mathbf{B}^\star(\varphi,i))$.

Theorem 3.11, below, shows that $\mathbf{B}^\star(\varphi,0)$ represents a withdrawal function.

Theorem 3.11 *Let $\mathbf{B} \in \mathcal{B}$, let $\star$ be an adjustment. If $^-$ is defined by* $(\text{content}(\mathbf{B}))^-_\varphi = \text{content}(\mathbf{B}^\star(\varphi,0))$ *then $^-$ is a withdrawal function.*

The adjustment $\mathbf{B}^\star(\varphi,0)$ does not describe a contraction because the recovery postulate, $(^-5)$, is not always satisfied. The underlying reason for this is that adjustments of $\mathbf{B}$ force $\exp(\mathbf{B}^\star(\varphi,0))$ to be a subset of $\exp(\mathbf{B})$. The following example illustrates that recovery is not always satisfied. Consider $\mathbf{B}$ to be given by; $\mathbf{B}(\varphi) = 0.5$ and $\mathbf{B}(\psi) = 0.3$. According to the definition of an adjustment $\exp(\mathbf{B}^\star(\varphi,0))$ is empty, hence $\psi \notin \text{Th}(\exp(\mathbf{B}^\star(\varphi,0)) \cup \{\varphi\})$.

If it is desirable to satisfy recovery then we can adapt an idea of Nebel's, namely assign $\mathbf{B}^\star(\varphi,0)(\varphi \rightarrow \psi) = \mathbf{B}(\psi)$ for all $\psi \in \exp(\mathbf{B})$ reassigned zero in the adjustment. This ensures the satisfaction of recovery because ψ will be reintroduced if φ is reassigned $i > 0$, that is, $\psi \in \text{content}(\mathbf{B}^\star(\varphi,i))$.

Despite the result in Theorem 3.10, the next theorem shows that enough information is retained by adjustment to satisfy recovery if we expand with respect to $\neg\varphi$ and keep those sentences that were part of the original implicit information content. Therefore, somewhat surprisingly, $\exp(\mathbf{B}^*(\varphi, 0))$ contains sufficient information to reconstruct a contraction function.

Theorem 6 *Let* $\mathbf{B} \in \mathcal{B}$, *let* $*$ *be an adjustment. Let* $^-$ *be the contraction function for* content($\mathbf{B}$) *uniquely determined by* (E^-) *and* $\leq_{\mathbf{B}}$. *Then*

(i) $\exp(\mathbf{B}^*(\varphi, 0)) = (\text{content}(\mathbf{B}))_{\varphi}^- \cap \exp(\mathbf{B})$,

(ii) $(\text{content}(\mathbf{B}))_{\varphi}^- = Th(\exp(\mathbf{B}^*(\varphi, 0)) \cup \{\neg\varphi\}) \cap \text{content}(\mathbf{B})$, *and*

(iii) if $\exp(\mathbf{B})$ *is a theory then* $(\text{content}(\mathbf{B}))_{\varphi}^- = \text{content}(\mathbf{B}^*(\varphi, 0))$.

Theorems 3.10(i) and 3.12(i) highlight the syntax sensitivity of revision and contraction. It is generally conceded that the sensitivity to syntax should simply reflect a higher level of commitment to explicit information than the implicit information.

The problem of syntax dependence stems from the inherent property that, there may be a maximal subset of content($\mathbf{B}$), say X, which might be the result of an AGM contraction however there may not be a subset of $\exp(\mathbf{B})$, say Γ, such that $Th(\Gamma) = X$. As a consequence the syntactical description of $\exp(\mathbf{B})$ *constrains* the way a finite partial entrenchment ranking can be naturally modified. For instance, consider a ranking given by: $\mathbf{B}_1(\varphi \vee \psi) = 0.8$ and $\mathbf{B}_1(\varphi \wedge \psi) = 0.6$. Observe that $\psi \notin \text{content}(\mathbf{B}_1{}^*(\varphi, 0))$ since ψ is lost in the contraction of φ. This happens because in order to contract φ the conjunction $\varphi \wedge \psi$ must be retracted, hence ψ is lost as a side-effect. However if the *equivalent* ranking $\mathbf{B}_2(\varphi \vee \psi) = 0.8$, $\mathbf{B}_2(\varphi) = 0.6$ and $\mathbf{B}_2(\psi) = 0.6$ had been used instead, then $\psi \in \text{content}(\mathbf{B}_2^*(\varphi, 0))$.

Theorem 3.12(i) succintly captures the dependence of a contraction on the explicit information content of the theory base, $\exp(\mathbf{B})$. In particular, a sentence is retained if and only if it is explicit information, and it would have been retained by corresponding contraction function on the theory content($\mathbf{B}$) using the construction based on $\leq_{\mathbf{B}}$. Theorem 3.12(i) establishes a similar result for revision. Hence, adjustments retain as much explicit information as possible.

Theorems 3.10(ii) and 3.12(ii) show that theory change functions can be formulated in terms of adjustments. Furthermore, Theorem 3.12(iii) reassuringly tells us that if the explicit and implicit information content are identical then adjustment of the ranking corresponds to a contraction function for content($\mathbf{B}$).

We conclude that the connections between the adjustment of partial entrenchment rankings and the standard AGM change functions established in this section provide strong support for the adjustment procedure. However, it suffers from two main problems: (i) the user must specify the independence of information with respect to change, and (ii) the ranking may be degraded over time because the ranks have an inherent tendency to merge. A related more promising, though computationally expensive procedure, called *maxi-adjustment* can be found in [[62], [63]].

The main challenge then, is the design of the appropriate syntactical form of the partial entrenchment ranking, that is, determining the explicit information in a ranking that reflects the desired behaviour of the system. The results in this section tell us that important information should be explicit and the independence of information must also be explicit.

3.6 Historical and bibliographical remarks

An epistemic entrenchment ordering is not the only preference relation from which change functions can be constructed. Some alternative constructions are based on a systems of spheres [27], and selection functions [1]. Dubois and Prade have demonstrated that there are close connections between epistemic entrenchment orderings and certain orderings in possibilistic logic [15]. A discussion of the postulates can be found in [20], and Gärdenfors and Rott give a recent detailed survey of belief revision in [21]. Another change function, called *update*, was identified by Winslett [64], and explored by Katsuno and Mendelzon [29].

The study of change for theory bases has been conducted by authors such as Fuhrmann [18], Hansson [28], Makinson [39], Nebel [49] Rott[53] and Williams [61]. Iterated change has been addressed from the constructive perspective by Spohn [56], Boutilier [11] and Nayak [48]. Lehmann [35] has proposed postulates for iterated revision.

References

[1] C. Alchourrón, P. Gärdenfors and D. Makinson. On the Logic of Theory Change: Partial Meet Functions for Contraction and Revision, *Journal of Symbolic Logic*, 50(1985): 510-530.

[2] J. Alferes and L.M. Pereira (1996). *Reasoning with Logic Programming*, LNAI 1111, Springer.

[3] G. Antoniou and V. Sperschneider (1993). Computing Extensions of Nonmonotonic Logics. In *Proc. 4th Scandinavian Conference on Artificial Intelligence*, IOS Press.

[4] G. Antoniou and V. Sperschneider (1994). Operational Concepts of Nonmonotonic Logics – Part 1: Default Logic. *Artificial Intelligence Review* 8: 3–16.

[5] G. Antoniou (1997). *Nonmonotonic Reasoning*. The MIT Press.

[6] D.E. Appelt and K. Konolige (1988). A Nonmonotonic Logic for Reasoning about Speech Acts and Belief Revision. In Reinfrank et. al. (eds.), *Nonmonotonic Reasoning, Proc. 2nd International Workshop*, Springer LNAI 346.

[7] K.R. Apt and M.H. van Emden (1982). Contributions to the theory of logic programming. *Journal of the ACM* 29: 841–862.

[8] K.R. Apt and R.N. Bol (1994). Logic Programming and Negation: A Survey. *Journal of Logic Programming* 19,20: 9–71.

[9] P. Besnard (1989). *An Introduction to Default Logic*. Springer.

[10] N. Bidoit and C. Froidevaux (1991). General logic databases and programs: default logic semantics and stratification. *Information and Computation* 91: 85–112.

[11] C. Boutilier. Revision Sequences and Nested Conditionals. In the *Proceedings of the Thirteenth International Joint Conference on Artificial Intelligence*, Morgan Kaufmann, 519 – 525, 1993.

[12] G. Brewka (1991). *Nonmonotonic Reasoning: Logical Foundations of Commonsense*. Cambridge University Press.

[13] G. Brewka (1994). Reasoning about Priorities in Default Logic. In *Proc. of the 12th National Conference on Artificial Intelligence (AAAI-94)*. AAAI/MIT Press 1994, 940–945.

[14] J.P. Delgrande, T. Schaub and W.K. Jackson (1994). Alternative approaches to default logic. *Artificial Intelligence* 70(1994): 167–237.

[15] D. Dubois and H. Prade. Possibilistic Logic. *Handbook of Logic in Artificial Intelligence and Logic Programming*, Volume3, Nonmonotonic Reasoning and uncertain Reasoning, Gabbay, D., Hogger, C., and Robinson, J. (eds), Claredon Press, Oxford, 1994.

[16] D. Etherington (1987a). Formalizing Nonmonotonic Reasoning Systems. *Artificial Intelligence* 31(1987): 41–85.

[17] D. Etherington (1987b). *Reasoning with Incomplete Information*. Pitman 1987.

[18] A. Fuhrmann. Theory Contraction through Base Contraction. *Journal of Philosophical Logic*, 20(1991): 175 – 203.

[19] P. Gärdenfors. *Knowledge in Flux: Modeling the Dynamics of Epistemic States*, Bradford Books, The MIT Press, Cambridge Massachusetts, 1988.

[20] P. Gärdenfors and D. Makinson. Revisions of Knowledge Systems using Epistemic Entrenchment. In the *Proceedings of the Second Conference on Theoretical Aspects of Reasoning about Knowledge*, 83 – 96, 1988.

[21] P. Gärdenfors and H. Rott. Belief Revision. *Handbook of Logic in Artificial Intelligence and Logic Programming Volume IV: Epistemic and Temporal Reasoning*, Chapter 4.2, Gabbay, D., Hogger, C., and Robinson, J. (eds), Claredon Press, (in press).

[22] M. Gelfond (1987). On Stratified Autoepistemic Theories. In *Proc. American National Conference on Artificial Intelligence*.

[23] M. Gelfond and V. Lifschitz (1988). The stable semantics for logic programs. In *Proceedings of the 5th International Symposium on Logic Programming*. MIT Press.

[24] M. Gelfond and H. Przymusinska (1989). Formalization of Inheritance Reasoning in Autoepistemic Logic. *Fundamenta Informaticae* 13(4): 403–444.

[25] M. Gelfond and V. Lifschitz (1990). Logic programs with classical negation. In *Proceedings 7th International Conference on Logic Programming*. MIT Press.

[26] M. Gelfond and H. Przymusinska (1992). On Consistency and Completeness of Autoepistemic Theories. *Fundamenta Informaticae* 16:59–92.

[27] A. Grove. Two Modellings for Theory Change. *Journal of Philosophical Logic*, 17(1988): 157 – 170.

[28] S.O. Hansson. New Operators for Theory Change. *Theoria*, 55(1989): 115 – 132.

[29] H. Katsuno and A.O. Mendelzon. On the Difference between Updating a Knowledge Database and Revising it. In Belief Revision, Gärdenfors, P. (ed), Cambridge Press, Cambridge, 1992.

[30] K. Konolige (1988a). On the relation between default and autoepistemic logic. *Artificial Intelligence* 35:343–382; see also Errata, *Artificial Intelligence* 41:115, 1989.

[31] K. Konolige (1988b). Hierarchic Autoepistemic Theories for Nonmonotonic Reasoning: Preliminary Report. In Reinfrank et. al. (eds.), *Nonmonotonic Reasoning, Proc. 2nd International Workshop*, Springer LNAI 346.

[32] K. Konolige (1991). Quantifying in Autoepistemic Logic. *Fundamenta Informaticae* 15(3–4).

[33] S. Kraus, D. Lehmann and M. Magidor (1990). Nonmonotonic reasoning, preferential models and cumulative logics. *Artificial Intelligence* 44: 167–207.

[34] J. Lang (1997). Possibilistic Logic: Algorithms and Complexity. in J.Kohlas and S. Moral (eds), Handbook of Algorithms for Uncertainty and Defeasible Reasoning, Kluwer Academic Publishers.

[35] D. Lehmann. Belief Revision, Revised. In the *Proceedings of the Fourteenth International Joint Conference on Artificial Intelligence*, 1995.

[36] J. Lloyd (1987). *Foundations of logic programming*, 2nd ed., Springer.

[37] W. Lukaszewicz (1988). Considerations on Default Logic. *Computational Intelligence* 4(1988): 1–16.

[38] W. Lukaszewicz (1990). *Non-Monotonic Reasoning – Formalization of commonsense reasoning*. Ellis Horwood.

[39] D. Makinson. On the Status of the Postulate of Recovery in the Logic of Theory Change. *Journal of Philosophical Logic*, 16(1987): 383 – 394.

[40] D. Makinson (1994). General patterns in nonmonotonic reasoning. In *Handbook of Logic in Artificial Intelligence and Logic Programming* Vol. 3, Oxford University Press, 35–110.

[41] W. Marek (1989). Stable Theories in Autoepistemic Logic. *Fundamenta Informaticae* 12:243–254.

[42] W. Marek and M. Truszczynski (1989). Relating Autoepistemic Logic and Default Logic. *Proc. 1st International Conference on Knowledge Representation and Reasoning.*

[43] W. Marek and M. Truszczynski (1993). *Nonmonotonic Logic - Context-Dependent Reasoning*, Springer.

[44] J. McCarthy (1980). Circumscription – A Form of Non–Monotonic Reasoning. *Artificial Intelligence* 13: 27–39.

[45] A. Mikitiuk and M. Truszczynski (1995). Constrained and rational default logics. In *Proc. 14th International Joint Conference on Artificial Intelligence*, Morgan Kaufmann, 1509–1515.

[46] R.C. Moore (1984). Possible-world semantics for autoepistemic logic. In *Proc. Non-monotonic reasoning Workshop*, New Paltz.

[47] R.C. Moore (1985). Semantical Considerations on Nonmonotonic Logic. *Artificial Intelligence* 25:75–94.

[48] A. Nayak. Iterated Belief Change Based on Epistemic Entrenchment. *Erkenntnis* 4 (1994): 353 – 390.

[49] B. Nebel. A Knowledge Level Analysis of Belief Revision. In *Principles of Knowledge Representation and Reasoning: Proceedings of the First International Conference*, Morgan Kaufmann, San Mateo, CA, 301 – 311, 1989.

[50] D. Poole (1994). Default Logic. In *Handbook of Logic in Artificial Intelligence and Logic Programming*, Oxford University Press.

[51] R. Reiter (1980). A Logic for Default Reasoning. *Artificial Intelligence* 13:81–132.

[52] K. Ross (1992). A procedural semantics for well–founded negationin logic programs. *Journal of Logic Programming* 13: 1–22.

[53] H. Rott. A Nonmonotonic Conditional Logic for Belief Revision I. In A. Fuhrmann and M. Morreau (eds), *The Logic of Theory Change*, Springer-Verlag, LNAI 465, Berlin, 135 – 183, 1991.

[54] T. Schaub (1992). On Constrained Default Theories. In *Proc. 10th European Conference on Artificial Intelligence*, Wiley 1992, 304–308.

[55] V. Sperschneider and G. Antoniou (1991). *Logic: A Foundation for Computer Science*, Addison-Wesley.

[56] W. Spohn. Ordinal Conditional Functions: A Dynamic Theory of Epistemic States. In Harper, W.L., and Skyrms, B. (eds), *Causation in decision, belief change, and statistics, II*, Kluwer Academic Publishers, p105 – 134, 1988.

[57] R. Stalnaker. A theory of conditionals. in Recher, N. (ed), *Studies in Logical Theory*, Blackwell, Oxford, 98 – 112, 1968.

[58] H. Tamaki and T. Sato (1986). OLD Resolution and Tabulation. In *Proceedings of the Third International Conference on Logic Programming*. Springer.

[59] A. van Gelder, K.A. Ross and J.S. Schlipf (1991). The Well–Founded Semantics for General Logic Programs. *Journal of the ACM* 38,3: 620–650.

[60] D.S. Warren (1991). Computing the Well–Founded Semantics of Logic Programs. *Technical Report 91/12*, Computer Science Department, SUNY at Stony Brook.

[61] M.A. Williams. On the Logic of Theory Base Change. In Logics in Artificial Intelligence, C. MacNish, D. Pearce and L.M. Pereira (eds), LNCS No 835, 86 – 105, Springer Verlag, 1994.

[62] M-A. Williams (1996). *Towards a Practical Approach to Belief Revision: Reason-Based Change*, Luigia Carlucci Aiello and C. Shapiro (eds), Proceedings of the Fifth International Joint Conference on Principles of Knowledge Representation and Reasoning, Morgan Kaufmann Publishers, 412 - 421.

[63] M-A. Williams (1997). *Anytime Belief Revision*, in the Proceedings of the Fifteenth International Joint Conference on Artificial Intelligence, Morgan Kaufmann.

[64] M. Winslett. Reasoning about action using possible models approach. In the *Proceedings of the National Conference on Artificial Intelligence (AAAI)*, 89 – 93, 1988.

Curried Least General Generalization: A Framework for Higher Order Concept Learning

Srinivas Padmanabhuni and Randy Goebel
Department of Computing Science
University of Alberta
Edmonton, Alberta, Canada T6G 2H1
E-mail: {srinivas, goebel}@cs.ualberta.ca
WWW: http://www.cs.ualberta.ca/~{srinivas, goebel}
Voice: +1-403-492-2683
Fax: +1-403-492-1071

Koichi Furukawa
Graduate School of Media and Governance
Keio University
5322 Endo, Fujisawa, Kanagawa 252, Japan
E-mail: furukawa@sfc.keio.ac.jp
WWW: http://www.sfc.keio.ac.jp/~furukawa
Voice: +81-466-47-5111 Ext. 3235 or 3231
Fax: +81-466-47-5350

Abstract. Continued progress with research in inductive logic programming relies on further extensions of their underlying logics. The standard tactics for extending expressivity include a generalization to higher order logics, which immediately forces attention to the computational complexity of higher order reasoning.

A major thread of inductive logic programming research has focussed on the identification of preferred hypothesis sets, initiated by Plotkin's work on least general generalizations (LGGs). Within higher order frameworks, a relevant extension of LGG is Furukawa's hyper least general generalization (HLGG) [FIG97].

We present a relevant higher order extension of Furukawa's HLGG based on currying, which we call Curried Least General Generalization (CLGG). The idea is that the formal difficulties with the reasoning complexity of a higher order language can be controlled by forming new hypothetical terms restricted to those obtainable by Currying. This technique subsumes the inductive generalization power of HLGG, provides a basis for a significant extension of first order ILP, and is theoretically justified within a well understood formal foundation.

1 Motivation and Introduction

First-order logic has been the major focus of research in the field of machine learning, as developed within *inductive logic programming* (ILP) [Mug92, Rae93].

The typical ILP framework uses first-order Horn clauses as the underlying representation language for inductive generalization. The computational difficulty of dealing with general first-order clauses is well acknowledged, which justifies the ILP concentration on the Horn clause restriction, and the development of several induction algorithms [Pop70, Plo70, Plo71a, Plo71b] for clausal representation. This restriction, which makes the clausal language computationally attractive, also makes induction algorithms efficient enough to be practical for real application.

The standard ILP implementation strategy is based on procedural engines for carrying out the inverse of deduction on first order clausal syntax. An important part of the historical development of logic programming are the relatively efficient algorithms for restricted deduction using resolution, which provide the basis for languages like Prolog, and which have been widely used in a variety of artificial intelligence applications over the past two decades. Unlike deduction, induction has multiple possible outcomes, so ILP introduces additional complexity, due to the multiple outcomes possible with the inversion of deduction algorithms. The consequence is the desire to distinguish the "best" of the outcomes, thus the motivation for adopting Plotkin's ideas and their derivatives.

Despite the common first order clausal restriction, there are many situations where the expressivity of higher order logics provides for direct representation of knowledge that is otherwise difficult to express, so the development of reasoning systems that manipulate fragments of higher order languages continues. Some (relatively) efficient deduction algorithms for higher-order logic [NM90] have been successfully developed. This has led to the implementation of higher-order languages like λ-prolog [NM90] and HOL [GM93], which are based on deduction mechanisms in certain *restricted* forms of higher-order logic. These languages have been successfully used for formal reasoning in many different areas, including hardware design and verification, reasoning about security, proofs about real-time systems, semantics of hardware description languages, compiler verification, program correctness, modeling concurrency, and program refinement.

Further, there are certain aspects of inductive and deductive reasoning with first order logic, which provide the motivation for considering higher order extensions to the first order logic based algorithms for ILP.

For efficiency considerations in first order deduction systems, suitable restrictions are required that enable the design of computationally feasible reasoning algorithms. These restrictions are typically cast as higher-order meta-information—and used in even relatively pedestrian language extensions. Consider the case of the language PROLOG, based on deduction of first-order clauses. In Prolog, there are a variety of meta-predicates which are quite often used to guide the "pure deduction" component of the computation. Some of these predicates are not, ! (cut), ;(or), setof, and bagof. So higher-order predicates are a part of the meta-information necessary for implementing deduction systems in first-order logic.

In the induction of first-order clauses in ILP, one use of higher-order meta-information is as a bias to control the complexity of the induction process in generalizing from ground examples to first-order formulae. Some of the examples of such higher-order meta information include information about the mode of arguments of clauses, as well as second-order schema to guide the predicate invention phenomenon in the induction process. These are typical examples of higher-order meta information used in a variety of ILP systems like CIA[RB92] and RDT [KW92].

The above factors provide a strong motivation for research on identifying subsets of higher-order logic which can be efficiently exploited for induction. Keeping the computational costs in mind, one might reason that investigation of higher-order logics is not a worthwhile project to undertake. But the above argument *vis-a-vis* tractable subsets of higher-order logic is a promising research strategy. Moreover development of induction algorithms for higher-order logics is potentially fruitful in generating meta-information for both inductive and deductive reasoning with first-order logic programs. Some recent studies by Muggleton [FM92] [MJ94] suggests potentially important directions of research in the inductive generalization of higher-order clauses. He suggests that the use of higher-order logic in induction might help in improving both efficiency and expressivity in certain induction domains. Feng and Muggleton [FM92] develop an algorithm for generalization in a restricted form of λ-calculus and demonstrate its use in a class of program transformations. But the main problem in [FM92] is the use of a λ-calculus-based abstraction formalism which complicates the development of algorithms for generalization. Complexity issues for such algorithms are not clearly presented in that system.

Here we present a higher-order extension to the LGG (least general generalization) algorithm of Plotkin [Plo70], the ground-breaking work in machine learning which forms the basis of a majority of ILP algorithms [Mug92, Rae93]. We exploit the technique of *currying* [Sch24, Cur30], commonly used in applicative (functional) programming, for inductive logic programming and develop a framework for *Curried least general generalization* (CLGG).

Currying provides a uniform basis for exportability of ideas from first-order logic based induction to higher-order logic induction. Though currying doesn't provide the full power of λ-calculus, we show how many important classes of useful higher-order structures can be obtained by using first-order algorithms on curried forms of first-order expressions. We then discuss the different issues concerned with controlling the complexity of such induction process in a variety of cases, and discuss feasible higher-order generalizations. An interesting outcome is the extendibility of the various forms of bias restrictions used in ILP to higher order induction, which is a key factor in development of a computationally attractive higher-order learning system.

A system based on higher-order induction can be used to capture some potentially useful kinds of higher-order meta information for ILP. In addition there are diverse applications of such a system which can be studied such as classes of program transformations.

We also extend the idea of relative least general generalization (RLGG) [Plo70] to our subset of higher-order logic obtained by using currying on first-order terms and clauses. We present generalizations of the various algorithms in Plotkin's RLGG framework to work for this restricted subset of higher-order logic. We discuss the meaningful higher-order generalizations achievable by these extended algorithms, which are otherwise not achievable in ILP. The issues involved in implementing any such extended algorithm are examined, in particular the exportability of efficiency ideas in ILP, like syntactic bias, to guide higher-order induction. In addition, some important applications of such higher-order induction system are examined. This includes a new interpretation of HLGG [FIG97] by CLGG.

In summary, we discuss a plethora of possible directions in which this work can be extended.

2 Currying as a foundation for CLGG

The most natural language for describing higher-order expressions mathematically is the λ-calculus, whose language consists of structures called λ-terms. A λ-term is either:

1. A variable , e.g.x, is a λ-term;
2. An application MN , where both M and N are λ-terms;
3. An abstraction $\lambda x.M$, where M is a λ-term.

In the form MN, we say that M is applied to N. Similarly we say that $\lambda x.M$ abstracts x in M.

The variable occurrences in a $\lambda-$term are of two types: free or bound. An occurrence of a variable x in a term P is bound iff it is a part of P with the form $\lambda x.M$; otherwise it is free.

For any λ-term M,N and any variable x, M $[N/x]$ is defined to be the result of substituting N for every free occurrence of x in M, and changing bound variables to avoid clashes.

The essential mechanism of manipulating λ-calculus terms is the syntactic process called β-reduction. The β-reduction rule is defined as follows:

$(\lambda x.E)$ M $\longleftrightarrow_\beta$ E $[M/x]$,

where the necessary restrictions for x not being free, apply.

So the language of λ-calculus is very convenient for representing higher-order terms. Implicit in the above representation of function applications is the understanding that we will use only function applications of the form MN, (M applied to N), where M and N are both λ-terms. But in many functional programming languages, function applications are multi-argument in nature, i.e. a function is applied to a multitude of arguments.

The phenomenon of *Currying* [Sch24, Cur30], is used to convert multiple argument functions to a form representable in λ-calculus. *Currying* refers to the process of converting a multi-argument function application of the form M N ... P (where M,N,... P are all λ-terms) to another expression of the form $(((...(MN)...)P)$ which is representable in λ-calculus.

In the framework of inductive logic programming, the underlying language is the language of first-order terms. The domain of first order terms ($T(F,X)$) constructed from the set of functions F, and the set of variables X consists of terms defined recursively as follows:

- A variable is a term
- If f is an *n-ary* function symbol, and $t_1, \ldots, t_n$ are terms, then
  $f(t_1, t_2, \ldots, t_n)$is a term.

A first order term can be converted by *currying* to a λ-term by use of a single binary function called *apply*, to first-order terms pairwise. A first-order variable x is converted to x, and a first-order term of the form $f(t_1)$ is converted to $apply(f, conv(t_1))$, where $conv(t_1)$ denotes the converted form of t_1. Extending this to $f(t_1, t_2, \ldots, t_n)$, we get the form $apply(apply(...apply(f, conv(t_1)), conv(t_2))$ ..., $conv(t_n)$, where $conv(t_i)$ represents the converted form of t_i.

The currying process thus enables us to represent any first-order term as a λ-term.

3 Curried least general generalization

3.1 Language

The advantage of applying *currying* to first-order terms as shown in the previous section is that it has only one function, namely *apply*, and any multi-argument or constant function reduces to a constant in the term. Therefore a binary function constant *plus* will be treated the same as a unary function constant like *successor*, or a zero-ary function constant like 0. This removes any difference between functions of different arity.

Extending the idea, we remove the difference between predicates of different arities, and treat predicates as multi-argument functions returning only true or false. This enables us to use predicates as constants in our language.

In our term structure , a term belonging to $T(F, X, P)$, the set of curried terms, is defined by the following inductive rules:

1. Any first order or higher-order variable x, (a multi-argument function or predicate) is a term.
2. An application apply$(t1, t2)$, where $t1, t2 \in T(F, X, P)$, is a term.

This is the same as the original definition of first-order term except that only one binary function symbol (apply) is used, and the differences between higher-order and first-order terms evaporates. Any term in this superset of first order logic shall be equivalently referred to as a *curried first order term* or simply *curried term*. A *curried clause* is a set of curried terms with appropriate signs.

The set of terms in this language forms a superset of the set of first order terms, and includes additional higher-order terms not representable in first order syntax. We do not concentrate on the full λ-calculus for our language because of complexity considerations and show that even this conservative higher order extension of first order logic terms is capable of providing useful higher-order expressions which are significantly more expressive than first order logic.

Now we present a model for inductive generalization for this language subset of full λ-calculus by extending ideas from Plotkin's RLGG framework to this superset of first order logic.

3.2 θ-subsumption under the new representation

In ILP, the model of induction is based on the relation between pairs of clauses termed as θ-subsumption. We extend the notion of θ-subsumption for curried first order terms, defined as follows:

Definition 1 (Curried θ-subsumption) *A curried clause P is said to θ-subsume another curried clause Q, iff there exists a substitution θ such that $P\theta \subseteq Q$.*

This definition induces a generality relation between any two curried clauses.

For example, the clause containing only the term $apply(f, X)$ θ-subsumes the clause $\{apply(f, 1), apply(g, 2)\}$. This relation induces a lattice on the clauses in our language, similar to the ILP case.

3.3 The LGG algorithm for clauses under the new representation

Here we show that when we apply the LGG algorithm for first order clauses to the clauses in our representation scheme, we get a higher order concept. We call the output of this algorithm a curried least general generalization (CLGG). The LGG algorithm, when applied to the curried representation, will extract the higher-order predicates from the set of input first order predicates.

The steps in our algorithm for obtaining the CLGG are as follows:

(1) Convert any function from the form $f(t_1 \ldots t_n)$
   to $app(app(\ldots app(f, t_1), t_2) \ldots, t_n)$.
(2) Then apply the LGG algorithm which runs as follows:

  1. The LGG of terms $f(s_1, s_2, \ldots, s_n)$ and $f(t_1, t_2, \ldots, t_n)$ is $f(LGG(s_1, t_1), \ldots, LGG(s_n, t_n))$. The LGG of terms $f(s_1, \ldots, s_n)$ and $g(t_1, \ldots, t_n)$, where $f \neq g$ is the variable v where v represents this pair of terms throughout.
  2. The LGG of two terms $p(s_1, s_2, .., s_n)$ and $p(t_1, t_2, \ldots, t_n)$ is $p(LGG(s_1, t_1), \ldots, LGG(s_n, t_n))$,
  3. LGG is undefined when the sign or predicate symbols are unequal.
  4. The LGG of two clauses C_1 and C_2 is $\{l : l_1 \in C_1$ and $l_2 \in C_2$ and l_1 has the same sign and predicate symbol as l_2 and $l = lgg(l_1, l_2)\}$.

Consider, for example, the two clauses $\{apply(f, 1)\}$ and $\{apply(g, 1).\}$. The CLGG of these two clauses is $\{apply(X, 1)\}$.

3.4   CRLGG: Curried relative least general generalization of clauses

The advantage of ILP systems over other learning systems is in their ease of using background knowledge in guiding the induction process. In Plotkin's learning framework, the LGG definition is generalised to include generalizations in the presence of background knowledge. This generalization in the presence of background knowledge is called relative least general generalization (RLGG).

Let P be a set of clauses in our language, i.e., P is a set of curried first order clauses. Let C and D be two curried first order clauses. The curried relative least general generalization $CRLGG_P(C, D)$ of C and D relative to P, is the least general clause within the θ-subsumption lattice for which $P \wedge CRLGG_P(C, D) \rightarrow C \wedge D$.

Similar to the RLGG of ILP, the CRLGG of a pair of clauses in our system can also be pretty large, thus requiring suitable restrictions for achieving feasible higher-order generalizations.

4   Some meaningful higher-order generalizations achievable by CLGG

By removing the distinction between the unary and n-ary functions, we are able to represent higher order terms. Here we show that this representation in CLGG is able to capture some elementary higher order properties which cannot be captured in first order logic, without recourse to λ-calculus.

Example 1 Transitivity. Consider the first order predicates brighter-than and lighter-than. We know that if lighter-than(X,U) and lighter-than(U,Z) are both true, then lighter-than(X,Z) is also true for any X,U and Z. Similar property holds true for brighter-than. If we were to capture this generic higher-order property of **transitivity** of predicates, it is impossible to capture this notion in one first order clause. But in our curried syntax, such a property can be captured by a clause $\{apply(apply(P, X), Z) \leftarrow apply(apply(P, X), Y), apply(apply(P, Y), Z).\}$. We can obtain instantiations of the clause for the predicate constants lighter-than and brighter-than respectively.

Example 2 Sortedness. Consider a list of integers. For convenience we shall represent a list in the prolog syntax as opposed to the curried constructor based notation for lists. Say we have a list $[X|Y]$, we know that the predicate ascending-order-sorted(L), where L is a list, can be represented by the set of clauses, $\{ascending - order - sorted([X]), ascending - order - sorted([X|[Y|Z]]) \leftarrow X <= Y, ascending-order-sorted([Y|Z])\}$. Similar set of clauses for descending-order can be shown. But if we can capture the underlying relation in either case which is the generic property of **sortedness**, we can represent it conveniently in the curried syntax: $\{sorted([X]), sorted([X|[Y|Z]]) \leftarrow X <= Y, sorted([Y|Z])\}$. This notion of the higher order property of sortedness cannot be captured in first order logic.

Example 3 Inverse & Identity . Consider the generic mathematical operation of inverse. If we were to define the property of inverse and identity for each mathematical operation we would have to define individual inverse and identity predicates for each mathematical operation. Consider addition(Plus) where we assume 0 to be the additive identity. The inverse predicate would be defined by plus(inv-plus(x),x)=0. And analogously for multiplication we would have mult(inv-mult(x),x)=1. We can generalize the two operations of inverse and identity for any algebraic operation, and represent these generic versions of inverse and identity in the curried syntax. The generic higher-order predicates of **inverse** and **identity** can be defined by the equality relation $apply(apply(P, apply(apply(inverse, P), x)), x) = apply(identity, P)$. Here we can substitute add or multiply for P, and get the unary minus and reciprocal operations for the inverse respectively and 0, 1 for identities, respectively.

Example 4 Program transformations. Many examples representing similarities in structure between different logic programs can also be be captured in our curried syntax. This justifies the use of our generalization algorithms in program transformations. For example, a clause like $apply(P, apply(f, X)) \leftarrow apply(f, apply(P, X))$ represents a generic structure for programs of the type $addtwo(s(x)) \leftarrow s(addtwo(x))$, where addtwo represents addition by two and s represents the successor function. So program transformations is one high potential area where our generalization model has promising applications.

5 Issues in the use of CLGG algorithm to build a feasible higher order learning system

The advantage of using CLGG is in the fact that the algorithm is a direct application of the first order LGG algorithm. Hence this enables us to export ideas used in reducing the complexity of the generalization process in first order LGG-based systems like GOLEM [MF90], to our higher order CLGG system.

The extension of the features used to control the explosion of choices in GOLEM needs to be studied with reference to the modified curried syntax. In this context the first question that needs to be examined is the capability of GOLEM to generalize in the new modified syntax. In the following subsection, we show some examples, executed in GOLEM [MF90], which show the feasibility of using restrictions analogous to GOLEM for curried terms. This provides a basis for an implementable higher order generalization system based on LGG.

5.1 Experiments with GOLEM

In GOLEM, the underlying bias restrictions to the language of clauses are both semantic and syntactic. Here we show the achievability of generalization of certain classes of curried higher order terms and also curried first order terms using GOLEM. We present two sample runs from GOLEM for curried representation each showing generalization capabilities of first order and higher order curried terms respectively.

Example 1

```
% Background Knowledge
apply(milk,a1).
apply(milk,a2).
apply(milk,a3).
apply(milk,a4).
apply(aquatic,a5).
apply(aquatic,a6).
apply(aquatic,a7).
apply(aquatic,a8).
apply(apply(class,a1),mammal).
apply(apply(class,a2),mammal).
apply(apply(class,a3),mammal).
apply(apply(class,a4),mammal).
apply(apply(class,a5),fish).
apply(apply(class,a6),fish).
apply(apply(class,a7),fish).
apply(apply(class,a8),fish).

%  Positive Examples

apply(apply(class,a1),mammal).
apply(apply(class,a2),mammal).
apply(apply(class,a3),mammal).
apply(apply(class,a4),mammal).

apply(apply(class,a5),fish).
apply(apply(class,a6),fish).
apply(apply(class,a7),fish).
apply(apply(class,a8),fish).
% Negative Examples

apply(apply(class,a5),mammal).
apply(apply(class,a6),mammal).
apply(apply(class,a7),mammal).
apply(apply(class,a8),mammal).
apply(apply(class,a1),fish).
apply(apply(class,a2),fish).
apply(apply(class,a3),fish).
apply(apply(class,a4),fish).
apply(milk,a5).
```

```
% GOLEM output

apply(apply(class,A),mammal) :- apply(milk,A).
apply(apply(class,A),fish) :- apply(aquatic,A).
```

This example shows how the terms in the first order component of curried terms are still generalizable in GOLEM under the curried representation.

Example 2

```
% Background Knowledge

!- randseed.

apply(apply(mem,0),[0]).
apply(apply(mem,1),[1]).
apply(apply(mem,2),[2]).
apply(apply(mem,3),[3]).
apply(apply(mem,4),[4]).
apply(apply(mem,0),[0,0]).
apply(apply(mem,1),[0,1]).
apply(apply(mem,0),[1,0]).
apply(apply(mem,0),[2,0]).
apply(apply(mem,1),[1,1]).
apply(apply(mem,1),[2,1]).
apply(apply(mem,2),[2,2]).
apply(apply(mem,2),[3,2]).
apply(apply(mem,3),[2,3]).
apply(apply(mem,3),[4,2,3]).
apply(nat,0).
apply(nat,1).
apply(nat,2).
apply(nat,3).
apply(nat,4).
apply(apply(memb,0),[0]).
apply(apply(memb,1),[1]).
apply(apply(memb,2),[2]).
apply(apply(memb,3),[3]).
apply(apply(memb,4),[4]).
apply(apply(memb,0),[0,0]).
apply(apply(memb,1),[0,1]).
apply(apply(memb,0),[1,0]).
apply(apply(memb,0),[2,0]).
apply(apply(memb,1),[1,1]).
apply(apply(memb,1),[2,1]).
```

```
apply(apply(memb,2),[2,2]).
apply(apply(memb,2),[3,2]).
apply(apply(memb,3),[2,3]).
apply(apply(memb,3),[4,2,3]).
```

%Positive Examples

```
apply(apply(mem,0),[0]).
apply(apply(mem,1),[1]).
apply(apply(mem,2),[2]).
apply(apply(mem,3),[3]).
apply(apply(mem,4),[4]).
apply(apply(mem,0),[0,0]).
apply(apply(mem,1),[0,1]).
apply(apply(mem,0),[1,0]).
apply(apply(mem,0),[2,0]).
apply(apply(mem,1),[1,1]).
apply(apply(mem,1),[2,1]).
apply(apply(mem,2),[2,2]).
apply(apply(mem,2),[3,2]).
apply(apply(mem,3),[2,3]).
apply(apply(mem,3),[4,2,3]).
apply(apply(memb,0),[0]).
apply(apply(memb,1),[1]).
apply(apply(memb,2),[2]).
apply(apply(memb,3),[3]).
apply(apply(memb,4),[4]).
apply(apply(memb,0),[0,0]).
apply(apply(memb,1),[0,1]).
apply(apply(memb,0),[1,0]).
apply(apply(memb,0),[2,0]).
apply(apply(memb,1),[1,1]).
apply(apply(memb,1),[2,1]).
apply(apply(memb,2),[2,2]).
apply(apply(memb,2),[3,2]).
apply(apply(memb,3),[2,3]).
apply(apply(memb,3),[4,2,3]).
```

% Negative examples

```
apply(apply(mem,0),[1,2]).
apply(apply(mem,3),[]).
apply(apply(mem,0),[1]).
apply(apply(memb,0),[1,2]).
apply(apply(memb,3),[]).
```

```
apply(apply(memb,0),[1]).
apply(nat,[]).
```

```
% GOLEM output
```

```
apply(apply(A,B),[B|C]).
apply(apply(A,B),[C,D|E]) :- apply(apply(A,B),[D|E]).
```

This example illustrates the higher order capabilities of the LGG algorithm under our curried syntax. Both predicates *mem* and *memb* have the same structure within the output program representable by the curried outcome returned above. Therefore we can conclude that currying added to GOLEM has higher order capabilities not captured in the original GOLEM.

Additional observations The two examples in the previous section, show the applicability of semantic and syntactic bias restrictions used by GOLEM even in the curried representation. But GOLEM has certain other kinds of meta information too, e.g. modes of predicates, which is provided by the user to restrain the size of the RLGG obtained, and to control the explosion of possible alternatives. Such type of meta information needs to be incorporated in computation of CRLGG in order to gain similar efficiency. Some first order examples in GOLEM were not generalizable in a controlled manner in the curried form, due to the lack of the appropriate meta-information for curried terms. But a suitable change in the appropriate component of GOLEM (for dealing with mode information for curried representation of the terms) should help us achieve the full power of GOLEM for our curried representation.

5.2 Efficiency Issues

In the previous subsection it was shown that currying provides the capability of generalizing certain kinds of higher order information in GOLEM. It was shown that simple first order terms generalizable under GOLEM are also generalizable under the curried syntax. This leads to the conclusion that the bias restrictions on the clauses in GOLEM, which make the task of generalizing with RLGG achievable, are also applicable to the curried first order terms. In this context the observations made in the previous subsection stress the need for a change in the part of the procedural engine of GOLEM which deals with the mode information of arguments of predicates. A systematic study of the restricted subset of curried first order terms needs to be done as to what the bias restrictions imposed in GOLEM mean in the curried context. More precisely, the bias restrictions like generative clauses, determinacy and functional dependencies need to be studied in the curried context.

6 Applications of CLGG

As seen above, there are a variety of different higher order predicates that can be characterized by curried first order terms. So CLGG can be exploited in a variety of application domains where higher-order information is used. We briefly describe two such classes of applications.

6.1 Program transformations

Some restrictions of the CLGG can be used to generate transformations equivalent to certain program transformations. As shown above, CLGG can be used to capture similar programs into one common structure. This enables us to reason about equivalence of different programs based on templates of programs written in curried form which are obtained by generalization. In the following, we consider a special case of CLGG, which again resembles a class of program transformation algorithms.

Hyper Least General Generalization: a special case of CLGG If we restrict our curried generalization to generalization of two predicates at a time, along with generalization of variables but not involving any function generalization, we get a restricted form of generalization. We can call this new form of generalization after Furukawa's term hyper least general generalization (HLGG) [FIG97]. HLGG is defined for two literals like

$$p(g(a), a)$$
$$q(g(b), b)$$

The generalization of two literals that have *different* predicate symbols causes the invention of a new predicate. Let the two clauses to be generalized by HLGG [FIG97] be $C1$ and $C2$, and the two literals chosen from $C1$ and $C2$ be $p(T1)$ and $q(T2)$, respectively. During the HLGG process on $C1$ and $C2$, assume that $p(T1)$ and $q(T2)$ are generalized by HLGG and the result $gen\_p\_q(T)$ is obtained. This new predicate $gen\_p\_q(T)$ is defined by

$$gen\_p\_q(T) : - p(T1). \tag{1}$$
$$gen\_p\_q(T) : - q(T2).$$

where T, $T1$ and $T2$ are terms and $T = LGG(T1, T2)$. The new predicate $gen\_p\_q(T)$ represents $p \vee q$, or a superconcept of p and q.

The generalized procedure induced via generalization in HLGG is equivalent to an application of the program transformation **folding** operation [BD77] to the original clauses, using the newly invented predicate. That is, the folding of clauses $C1$ and $C2$ by definition (1) yields the same effect as applying HLGG to $C1$ and $C2$.

This folding operation can also be considered as a kind of relative generalization. That is, performing LGG relative to the definitions of newly invented predicates will produce the HLGG C of $C1$ and $C2$. This follows because

$$BK \cup \{C\} \models C1 \wedge C2$$

where BK denotes background knowledge. This suggests an efficient implementation of clause-HLGG by first introducing new predicates using literal-HLGG and then performing RLGG.

HLGG can be formulated as a special case of CLGG, involving a two step process. In the first step, we compute the CLGG of the two terms which are generalizable by HLGG. Let the two terms involved in the HLGG computation be $p(T1)$ and $q(T2)$. The CLGG of the two terms is of the form app(X,T), where T is the curried translation of LGG of T1 and T2, and X is a new variable not found in either T1 or T2. We then replace the X in $app(X, T)$ by a predicate constant gen_p_q. On translation of this curried expression into normal form and addition of the two clauses as in the HLGG definition above, we have the required expression for HLGG.

The equivalence of the HLGG, shown above to be a restricted application of CLGG, and the program transformation technique of folding, suggests that CLGG can be used for more complex program transformations.

6.2 Bias Generator for ILP systems

As indicated in the introduction, higher order templates are commonly used in specifying bias for induction of logic programs. In particular second order clauses form the basis for bias to control the induction in the ILP systems CIA [RB92] and RDT [KW92]. For example, if the bias is the clause $\{P(X) \leftarrow Q(X), R(X)\}$ then the available vocabulary for the induction is the set of instances of the above clause.

Given ground positive examples with suitable background examples together with negative examples, the generalized algorithm based on currying can generate curried higher order clauses like the above clause used as bias in RDT [KW92]. So CLGG provides a tool for automating the process of generating biases in ILP. The biases generated from curried generalization of ground examples can be used to form the appropriate bias needed to guide the induction process in ILP systems which use higher-order schema as the syntactic bias. This idea provides a useful tool for experimenting with suitable biases based upon ground example inputs.

7 Conclusions and Scope for future work

This paper introduces a novel concept in first order induction algorithms endowing them with the capability of generalizing higher-order clauses which are otherwise not representable in first order logic. The important difference from an earlier work [FM92] is the non-reliance on λ-calculus as the higher order representation language. In [FM92], λ-calculus is used as the underlying paradigm and generalization algorithms involved are complex due to this representation.

In our presentation, we have exported the notion of *currying* from functional programming to induction of first order logic expressions. This resulted in a superset of first order logic in which some key higher-order functions can be represented without taking recourse to λ-calculus. The generalization algorithms applied to first order logic in ILP have been used to generate higher-order clauses without recourse to λ-calculus. Extensions of first order generalization algorithms in ILP to curried first order logic have been presented. The GOLEM examples show the feasibility of inducing higher-order clauses within this framework. Additionally, at least two important application areas of CLGG based generalization, namely program transformations and bias generation for ILP, have been outlined.

Further studies is underway on the following extensions of the framework presented:

1. A theoretical characterization of semantic and syntactic restrictions used in GOLEM, when applied to curried terms. This also includes the study of different classes of restrictions of the curried first order logic and generation of meaningful clauses corresponding to such restrictions.
2. Use of CLGG as a program transformation tool.
3. Use of the CLGG as a tool for automating the process of selection of biases for certain first order induction algorithms like RDT.
4. Incorporation of mode based semantic information into the curried generalization algorithm in extended GOLEM.

Acknowledgements

This work has been supported by the Natural Sciences and Engineering Research Council of Canada, and by the Canadian Federal Networks of Centres of Excellence Institute for Robotics and Intelligent Systems.

References

[BD77]   R.M. Burstall and J. Darlington. A transformation system for developing recursive programts. *Journal of the ACM*, 24(1):44–67, 1977.

[Cur30] Haskell B. Curry. Grundlagender kombinatorischen logik. *Am. J. Math.*, 52:509–536, 1930.

[FIG97] K. Furukawa, M. Imai, and R. Goebel. Hyper least general generalization and its application to higher-order concept learning. Reserach Memo IEI-RM 97001, SFC Research Institute, Keio University, 5322 Endo, Fujisawa-shi, Kanagawa 252, Japan, 1997.

[FM92]   C. Feng and S. Muggleton. Towards inductive generalisation in higher order logic. In D. Sleeman and P. Edwards, editors, *Proceedings of the Ninth International Workshop on Machine Learning*, San Mateo, California, 1992. Morgan Kaufman.

[GM93]   M.J.C. Gordon and T.F. Melham. *Introduction to HOL: A theorem proving environment for higher order logic.* Cambridge University Press, 1993.

[KW92]   J. Kietz and S. Wrobel. *Controlling the Complexity of Learning in Logic through Syntactic and Task-Oriented Models.* Inductive Logic Programming. Academic Press, 1992.

[MF90]   S. Muggleton and C. Feng. Efficient induction of logic programs. In *Proceedings of the First Conference on Algorithmic Learning Theory*, Tokyo, Japan, 1990.

[MJ94]   Stephen Muggleton and C.David Page Jr. Beyond first-order learning : Inductive learning with higher-order logic. Technical Report PRG-TR-13-94, Oxford University, UK, 1994.

[Mug92] S. Muggleton, editor. *Inductive logic programming.* Academic Press, New York, 1992.

[NM90]   G. Nadathur and D. Miller. Higher-order horn clauses. *Journal of the ACM*, 37(4):777–814, 1990.

[Plo70] G.D. Plotkin. A note on inductive generalization. In B. Meltzer and D. Michie, editors, *Machine Intelligence*, volume 6, pages 153–163. Edinburgh University Press, Edinburgh, 1970.

[Plo71a] G.D. Plotkin. Automatic methods of inductive inference. Ph.d. dissertation, University of Edinburgh, Edinburgh, Scotland, 1971.

[Plo71b] G.D. Plotkin. A further note on inductive generalization. In B. Meltzer and D. Michie, editors, *Machine Intelligence*, volume 6, pages 101–124. Edinburgh University Press, Edinburgh, 1971.

[Pop70] R.J. Popplestone. An experiment in automatic deduction. In B. Meltzer and D. Michie, editors, *Machine Intelligence*, volume 5, pages ???—??? Edinburgh University Press, Edinburgh, 1970.

[Rae93] Luc De Raedt. A brief introduction to inductive logic programming. In *Proceedings of the 1993 International Symposium on Logic Programming*, pages 45–51, Vancouver, Canada, October 26-29 1993.

[RB92]   L. De Raedt and M. Bruynooghe. Interactive theory revision: an inductive logic programming approach. *Machine Learning*, 8(2), 1992.

[Sch24] M. Schonfinkel. Uber die baustine der matematischen logik. *Math. Annalen*, 92:305–316, 1924.

Approximate Validity

Henry E. Kyburg, Jr.
Computer Science and Philosophy
University of Rochester, Rochester, NY 14627, USA *

Abstract. We discuss the nature of argument. We look more closely at the two main forms of nonmonotonic inference. We present a simple semantics for them, due to Teng. We show how this natural semantics leads to a characterization of approximate validity in terms of sets of models. Various of Lifschitz's benchmarks are discussed in this framework.

1 Introduction

Let us begin with a distinction between argument and inference. I take inference to be a psychological phenomenon. As such, it is, in a sense, private. An individual, an agent, infers one proposition from another. Perhaps one could sometimes say that an agent infers a proposition (I think the result of inferring is always propositional) from non-propositional entities—observations, attitudes, sensations, impulses, or what have you. In many cases of inference there is a corresponding formal object which we call an argument. An argument, as distinct from an inference, is a public, social, entity. This is not to say that we can't, as an aid to our inferring, formulate arguments privately, for our own purposes. It is rather that even such private arguments conform, or are intended to conform, to the standards of public argument.

So what is an argument? While the degree to which inference is dependent on language is unclear, it is certainly the case that arguments proceed in a public linguistic framework. There is a language in which the argument is expressed. Typically an argument has premises, statements in the canonical language; rules of inference that are applied; and a conclusion.

The kinds of arguments we know most about are those that can be expressed in first order logic. These are the arguments we mainly encounter in mathematics. To be sure, there are controversies concerning the principles that should govern such arguments (for example *tertium non datur*, or the principle of the excluded middle), but for the most part we all agree that the paradigm cases of validity are indeed valid.

What is validity? As we all know for the case of standard first order logic, an argument is valid just in case every model of the premises is also a model of the conclusion. A model in this case is a structure consisting of a domain D of objects, and an interpretation function I that assigns to every name in the language an individual in the domain, to every k-place predicate in the language

* Research for this work was supported by the National Science Foundation, grant IRI-9411267

a set of k-tuples of objects in the domain (a subset of $\mathcal{D}^k$), and to every n-place functor in the language, a function from $\mathcal{D}^n$ to $\mathcal{D}$. (If we have primitive sentences, they can be construed as 0-place predicates, whose interpretation is the empty set (for false) or $\mathcal{D}$ (for true).) Tarski showed us how to define truth in such a model.

There are arguments that involve more than first order logic. The best understood among these are modal arguments: arguments whose sentences include such terms as 'possibly' or 'necessarily'. Of course what we want is a notion of truth that will allow us to say that a valid modal argument is an argument whose conclusion is true in every model of the premises. But now we must expand the notion of a model. Following Kripke, we take a model to consist of a domain D, an interpretation m, and an accessibility relation $\mathcal{R}$. We say that $\Box S$ is true in a model $\mathcal{M}$ just in case S is true in every model $\mathcal{M}'$ that is accessible from $\mathcal{M}$ by $\mathcal{R}$ i.e, every model $\mathcal{M}'$ such that $\mathcal{R}(\mathcal{M}, \mathcal{M}')$.

Modal logic is more complicated than ordinary first order logic because we have the parameter $\mathcal{R}$ to take account of in specifying models. We may take $\mathcal{R}$ to be universal (yielding a counterpart to validity), reflexive (yielding **T**), reflexive and transitive (yielding **S4**), or reflexive, symmetric, and transitive (for **S5**), and so on.

Let us now consider inductive and nonmonotonic logic. It has long been known (if not always fully internalized) that inductive inference is not intended to be valid: the premises (the data) may be true, but the conclusion (the hypothesis we infer from the data) may be false. Those are the chances we take. As Hume pointed out, there is no contradiction in supposing that all the billiard balls we've looked at move on impact, and yet that the next billiard ball (or all future billiard balls, for that matter) may behave differently. This is no more than to say that induction (and we include here statistical inference) is not deduction.

One response that has been made by many respectable philosophers has been to seek premises that "if assumed, will serve to render our inferences probable." A major theme of *Human Knowledge: Its Scope and Limits*, is to find such premises. "What must we be supposed to know, in addition to particular observed facts, if scientific inferences are to be valid?" [Rus48, p. 494] The idea is the following: While a scientific generalization G (All crows are black; the melting point of phosphorus is $27.4 \pm .1$ degrees centigrade;...) may not deductively follow from the evidence provided by a large sample of crows, or a careful determination of the melting point of phosphorus, it will do so with the help of supplementary premises. For example, we might assume that all species of birds are monochromatic, or that every chemical element has a single melting point (both of which are false; but both of which hold for the most part). No one would supposes that we could know these generalities a priori, even if they were true, but it has been hoped that there are very broad and general empirical principles that can be used to shore up scientific inference in general.

This view has largely disappeared from philosophy. A certain form of the view that we should seek general empirical assumptions which would render our common sense inferences valid, seems, however, to have found new life in computer science. The point of nonmonotonic logic is to derive conclusions from premises that do not imply those conclusions. The general idea in nonmonotonic logic, as in the treatment of inductive logic just alluded to, is to add premises that, together with the initial premise set, do imply those conclusions. These premises are only added tentatively: they are subject to withdrawal, if it appears that they are false.

Suppose we have a finite set of object language statements S, and we feel that we should ordinarily be able to infer T from S, even though we can imagine circumstances C under which S might be true and T false. One (relatively uninformative) way of handling this situation would be to say that we should add the conditional $\text{Adj}S \to T$ to the set of statements S (where $\text{Adj}S$ is the adjunction of the statements in S), unless C turns out to be implied by what we know. Thus if S does not entail C, the inference goes through; if S is expanded so that it does entail C, the inference must be withdrawn. Hence "nonmonotonic".

Thus default logic allows us to infer γ from α, provided $\beta_1, \ldots, \beta_k$ are consistent with everything else we know. This is equivalent to adding the conditional, $\alpha \to \gamma$ to the premises, so long as the β's are all possible. Show me a β, of course, and I'll have to withdraw that premise. Similar things can be said about autoepistemic logic, circumscription, and other formalisms for nonmonotonic argument. A nonmonotonic inference is acceptable if S permits the inference to T, where S permits the inference provided it entails no countervailing facts. Often this notion of validity can be spelled out with the help of modal constructs (thus "if $\beta_1, \ldots, \beta_k$ are all *possible*, relative to S," in the case of default logic).

In classical logic, we evaluate deductive arguments not only by their validity, but also in terms of their soundness. That is, we require not only that the conclusion be true in every model in which the premises are true, but also that the premises in fact be true.

It can be argued that this is not quite the form in which the requirement of soundness should be put. In order for you and I to agree that the conclusion C is warranted, we need both to agree on the validity of the argument for it (remember that an argument is a public entity, and validity an objective notion), and also to agree that the premises are acceptable. "Truth" is not quite to the point. If the premises are true, but I don't know it, or have no warrant for accepting it, I need not (should not) accept the conclusion. If the premises are false, but I have every reason to think that they are true (and the argument is valid) then I should accept the conclusion.

Using the term I've used elsewhere[Kyb96], let us say that a standard first order argument is "objectively sound" if it is valid, and if the premises are objectively warranted. Of course this means that "objective soundness" is relative to a body of information. (I reluctantly withhold the term "knowledge" in view of the fact that many people think that truth is part of knowledge.) I say "objectively" since I want something more than subjective belief: whether you *believe* that masses attract each other with a force approximately inversely proportional to their distance apart, you *ought* to, and you ought to accept the conclusion of a deductive argument that takes that and similar well established facts as its premises.

Similar considerations apply to modal arguments. Soundness requires that the premises be true, but the truth of a modal premise requires a specific interpretation of the modal operators: we must have in mind a particular relation $\mathcal{R}$ of accessibility. Even then objective soundness seems to be more germane to our human concerns: we should require the premises to be well established rather than true. It is less clear how to tell when a statement of necessity is well established, and in fact this is the subject of considerable philosophical argument; in the case of most nonmonotonic systems, 'necessity' corresponds to deducibility which, if not decidable, is at least a precise notion.

When we turn to inductive argument it becomes reasonably clear that the attempt to find a grand inductive premise that will serve to turn induction into deduction has been a failure. First, nobody has come up with a premise (say, concerning the uniformity of nature) that actually can serve that function. Second, if we had such a premise that could serve to render inductive argument deductively valid, it is very unlikely that it could be considered well established in the sense that it is incumbent upon the ordinary person to accept it.

The program of nonmonotonic logic is far less ambitious. The premises we call on to turn plausible arguments into tentative deductive arguments (tentative, because new information can block the arguments) are far less ambitious and broad reaching. These premises are now called "assumptions"; the idea sometimes appears to be that by calling something an "assumption" one is relieved of the obligation to justify it or to ensure that it is (reasonably) accepted. Of course from the point of view of pure logic anything goes. From this point of view we are interested in the *relation* between the assumptions (premises) and the conclusion. But from this pure point of view, soundness is irrelevant. If we are interested in the question of whether the argument makes the acceptance of the conclusion rationally obligatory, both premises and "assumptions" must be rationally obligatory, and the distinction between assumptions and premises disappears.

When it comes to incorporating uncertain inference in the intelligent systems that underly our artificial agents, the question of soundness is crucial. We may want our systems to learn about the world, in the sense that the constraints within which they behave are appropriate or *reasonable*. The models for uncertain inference introduced by Teng provide a way of exploring these desiderata that is quite independent of the particular formalism adopted.

2   Teng Models

We begin by introducing Teng's partition sequences of possible worlds [Ten96], or as I will call them, Teng models. Consider a set $\mathcal{W}$ of models of a first order language. A partition sequence is a sequence of disjoint subsets of $\mathcal{W}$, such that their union is $\mathcal{W}$—i.e., the non-empty elements of the sequence form a partition of the set of all models. Teng has shown that partition sequences can be taken as a common semantics for nonmonotonic inference in the form of autoepistemic logic, in the form of default logic, in terms of possibility theory, and in terms of probabilistic threshholding and conditionalization.

For present purposes what is important is that the transition from one element of the possible world sequence to the next, in the case of default logic follows a default rule, and in the case of autoepistemic logic, follows from a conditional corresponding to the normal form (as characterized by Konolige either case, the particular extension we end up with depends on the order of the rules (statements) we apply. We consider these two cases in turn.

We need to intepret possibility and necessity in terms of partition sequences. The accessibility relation is simple: $\mathcal{R}$ holds between models v and w, $\mathcal{R}(v, w)$ just in case the equivalence class to which v belongs is at least as early in the sequence as the equivalence class to which w belongs. As usual, $\Box\phi$ is true in v just in case ϕ is true in every model w such that $\mathcal{R}(v, w)$, and $\Diamond\phi$ is true in v just in case ϕ is true in some model w such that $\mathcal{R}(v, w)$.

2.1 Default Logic

A default partition sequence for $\Delta = \langle D, F \rangle$ is partition sequence satisfying the following conditions:

1. W_0 consists of the models ruled out by the factual premises F of the default theory $\langle D, F \rangle$.

2. For $0 < i < n$, there exists a default rule $\alpha : M\beta_1, \ldots, M\beta_m / \gamma$ in D such that

   (a) $\Box\alpha$ is true in all the models from i to n,

   (b) $\Diamond\beta_1, \ldots, \Diamond\beta_m$ are true in some model in the set W_n, and

   (c) W_i consists of those models, not among those in W_0 to W_{i-1}, in which γ is false.

3. Any default rule that can be applied to models in W_n has been applied. (I.e., if α is true in all the models in W_n, and each of the β's is true in some model in W_n, then γ is true in every model in W_n.)

Theorem 9 (Teng): A set of formulas E is an extension of a default theory $\Delta = \langle D, F \rangle$ if and only if there is a default partition sequence $P = \langle W_0, \ldots, W_n \rangle$ for Δ, such that E is the set of non-modal formulas true in every model in W_n.

It has often been remarked that default inferences often go through, intuitively, even when there is no statistical basis for them. "Typicality" or "propensity" or "presumption" can replace statistics. On the other hand, informal descriptions of defaults often include such expressions as "frequently" or "for the most part," or "ordinarily". I would like to propose that the standard of default validity lies in *model* frequency: we want the conclusion to be true in most (or almost all) of the models in which the premises are true, or which are "picked out" by the premises. This need not correspond to an empirical frequency in the world. Let us see how this idea fits in with Teng models of default inference.

Informally, what occurs in a default partition sequence is that, first, we rule out those models that are not consistent with our factual data F (the models thus ruled out constitute W_0). Second, at each level i, we apply a default rule, and rule out all the models (not already ruled out) in which the consequent γ of the rule is false. For a rule with prerequisite α to be applicable in the set of models W_i requires that α be true not only in all the models in W_i, but also in all the models in W_{i+1}, and so on down to W_n, since all of these models are accessible from any model in W_i. For a rule with justifications $\beta_1, \ldots, \beta_m$ to be applicable requires that each β_i be true in some model that is not ever ruled out by the rules we are considering. That there be models in W_n in which each of the β_i's is true clearly assures this.

Consider an explicitly statistical example. Suppose that α is the sentence "tom is a red-toed warblesinger and almost all red-toed warblesingers build their nests in poplars," and γ is the sentence "tom builds his nest in a poplar." A first stab at a default rule would be: $\alpha : /\gamma$. It is quite clear that of the models in which α is true, almost all of them are also models in which γ is true (tom may denote any entity in the domain that falls into the interpretation of 'red-toed warblesingers.'

But a little reflection would suggest that this is not the whole story. We know enough about birds to know that (most of them) will build nests in substitute trees, if their preferred trees are not available. So a natural constraint for the inference is that it be possible for tom to build in a poplar tree. That is, it must not be part of our knowledge that "tom does not have access to poplar trees." That includes, of course, default knowledge.

Of course we can think of other constraints. For example, it is possible that we know "tom is a male, and that among warblesingers only females build nests." A natural constraint is that this, too, not be part of our knowledge.

The picture that emerges is that we face a reference class problem: the β's are exactly the sentences that, were their negations to be known, would interfere with the application of the statistical knowledge embodied in α. The sentence α picks out a set $\mathcal{M}(\alpha)$ of models. The sentence γ is true in almost all (most, many) of those models. The inference to γ would not be plausible, however, if the negations of any of $\beta_1, \ldots, \beta_m$ were true. If the negation of β_i were true, then γ would not be true in almost all (most, many) of the models.

What constitutes "Almost all" depends on context, of course. In statistics, it corresponds to the problem of choosing significance levels or confidence coefficients. How does a body of knowledge "pick out" a set of models relevant to a given sentence? Suppose that

α: "Oscar is a Bird."

γ: "Oscar can fly."

d: $\alpha : /\gamma$

The default d, in this case, is plausibly thought of as depending on the fact that almost all birds fly, but this is not ordinarily construed as a "fact" in the same sense that "Oscar is a bird" is construed as a fact. Let us, however, rule out, i.e., include in W_0 those models in which it is not true that almost all birds fly. Thus W_0 consists of models in which α is false, and in which the *fact* that almost all birds fly is false. Consider one of the remaining models; the following two constraints must hold:

$$\mathcal{I}(Bird) = \{d_1, \ldots, d_k\}$$

$$\mathcal{I}(Oscar) = d_1 \text{ or } \mathcal{I}(Oscar) = d_2, \ldots \text{ or } \mathcal{I}(Oscar) = d_k$$

However many models there are satisfying the first constraint, they may be divided into k kinds, corresponding to the k possibilities allowed by the second constraint. In "almost all" of these models, $\mathcal{I}(Oscar) \in \mathcal{I}(Can\,fly)$. Since this is true whatever the interpretation of "Bird", it is true in general: the set of models picked out by α ("Oscar is a bird") is the set of all models in which that is true and in which the default d is appropriate. Almost all of them make γ true as well.

In general the set of models picked out by α need NOT be the set of all those models compatible with our information in which α is true. Example: Suppose we have:

α: "Jane is a resident of Rochester who lives at 110 East Main Street, and almost all residents of Rochester own umbrellas."

β_1: "Jane does not belong to any class of residents who reject the use of umbrellas on moral grounds."

γ: "Jane owns an umbrella."

The set of models picked out by α includes those in which most people who live at 110 East Main Street fail to own umbrellas, as well as those in which most people who live at 110 East Main Street do own umbrellas. In this set of models, the interpretation of "Jane" is a member of the interpretation of "people who live at 110 East Main Street," and the proportion of those models in which Jane owns an umbrella may vary from 0 to 1. To get a sensible result, we must look at a larger class of models—all of those in which "Jane is a resident of Rochester" is true. Since the interpretation of "Jane" may be any member of the interpretation of "resident of Rochester", in almost all models in the broader class will be models in which "Jane owns an umbrella" is true.

The problem of determining how α picks out models in general is non-trivial: it is the problem of how to choose the correct reference class given a rich background of statistical information. Efforts have been made to contribute to this problem in [Kyb83, Kyb97].

2.2 Autoepistemic logic

An autoepistemic partition sequence for A in ML is a sequence satisfying the following conditions on Teng models:

1. $W_0 = \emptyset$.

2. For each W_i, $0 < i < n$, there exists a formula $L\alpha \land \neg L\beta_1 \land \ldots \land \neg L\beta_m \rightarrow \gamma \in A$ such that

   (a) α is true in all models w in W_n,

   (b) $(\exists w_1, \ldots, w_m \in W_n)(\neg\beta_1 \text{is true in} w_1, \ldots, \neg\beta_m \text{is true in} w_m$, and

   (c) $W_i = \{w : w \notin \bigcup_{j=0}^{i-1} W_j \land \gamma \text{is false in} w\}$

3. For all formulas $L\alpha \land \neg L\beta_1 \land \ldots \land \neg L\beta_m \rightarrow \gamma \in A$, if α is true in w for all $w \in W_n$, and $\exists w_1, \ldots, w_m \in W_n$ such that β_1 is true in $w_1, \ldots, \beta_m$ is true in w_m, then γ is true in w for all models w in W_n.

Theorem 13 (Teng): An autoepistemic theory T is a consistent stable expansion of a set of premises A iff there is an autoepistemic partition sequence $P = \langle W_0, \ldots, W_n \rangle$ for A such that $W_n \neq \emptyset$ and T is the stable set characterized by the kernel $\{\phi : \phi$ is true in w for all $w \in W_n\}$.

Again what we have is a sequence of sets of models. Each set of models in the sequence, other than the first and last, is ruled out by an application of an axiom in the autoepistemic theory A. Although modal locutions are involved in the statement of the theory A, the theory is in fact determined by its non-modal statements—its kernel. The final member of the sequence of sets of models is the set of models in which the statements of the kernel of the theory A are satisfied.

3 Lifschitz' benchmarks

Vladimir Lifschitz [Lif89] has provided us with a long list of benchmark problems on which to test nonmonotonic arguments. They include arguments for which default reasoning seems most appropriate as well as arguments concerning inheritance, as well as some other argument forms. We will look at the default examples and the inheritance examples. Lifschitz claims that "In most cases there is a general consensus in the nonmonotonic community about the validity of the patters of reasoning exemplified in these problems..." [Lif89, p. 202] but it is arguable that not all of these patterns should represent rational inferences. Our approach may throw some light on this matter.

3.1 Benchmark A-1

1. Blocks A and B are heavy.

2. Heavy blocks are normally on the table.

3. A is not on the table.

4. therefore B is on the table.

Put in terms of defaults, (1) and (3) are 'Facts', and (2) represents the default: $heavy(x) : Mon - table(x)/on - table(x)$. The force of "normally" is that almost all models in which "$heavy(\tau)$" is true are models in which "$on - table(\tau)$" is also true. If we know otherewise, that's another matter. In this case, when $\tau = A$ we know otherwise; when $\tau = B$ we don't.

3.2 Benchmark A-2

1. Blocks A and B are heavy.

2. Heavy blocks are normally on the table.

3. A is not on the table.

4. B is red.

5. Therefore B is on the table.

We have an extra fact now, which, intuitively we should regard as irrelevant to our conclusion. The previous reconstruction still goes through: Most models—the normal models—of (1) and (3), will be models in which "B is on the table" is true. Notice that this is similar to the case of umbrella-owning we considered before. The proportion of models of (1), (3), and (4) in which "B is on the table" is true may be anywhere from 0 to 1, depending on the proportion of red *and* heavy blocks that are on the table. We don't know this proportion, so, as in the case of umbrella-owning, we look at a class of models broader than that in which all our premises are true.

3.3 Benchmark A-3

1. Blocks A and B are heavy.

2. Heavy blocks are normally red.

3. Heavy blocks are normally on the table.

4. A is not on the table.

5. B is not red.

6. Therefore B is on the table.

7. Therefore A is red.

Here the facts are represented by (1), (4), and (5); we have two defaults, represented by (2) and (3). To obtain (6), we look at models of (1) and (4); to obtain (7) we look at models of (1) and (5).

Now we encounter an interesting issue. Does it follow from (2) and (3) that heavy blocks are normally *both* red and on the table? It is surely easy to imagine circumstances under which one would want to deny this. If you construe "normally" as "more often than not", it is easy to see that defaults (2) and (3) can be true while the joint default is false. Thus it is not clear that the conjunction of (6) and (7) should be obtainable.

Of course we don't know that we are in the circumstance in which the joint default is wrong. Suppose that the two defaults are "conditionally independent" in a fairly plain sense, then will we obtain the conjunction of (6) and (7)? Not necessarily, because the corresponding conjunctive default may still be under threshhold in force.

Teng models show us what is going on. We obtain (6) from (1), (4), and (5) by looking at models of (1) and (4). Now the models we want are those in which (1), (4), (5), and (6) are true. To infer (7), we must look at the set of models in which (1) and (5) are true. But now we must take into account *both* (4) and (6). While (4) could be disregarded (by the umbrella argument) when we did not have to take (6) into account, the situation may be changed when we do have to take (6) into account. The appropriate reference class of models may no longer support the default expressed by (3).

If the two defaults are minimally persuasive, they will interfere with each other, and we will be lead to two extensions: one with (6) and not (7), and one with (7) and not (6).

Can we ensure that the conjunction does hold by default? A minimal adjustment to ensure this is to replace (2) by (2'):

$$heavy(x) : \mathrm{Mred}(x), \mathrm{M} \neg \mathrm{on} - \mathrm{table}(x)/\mathrm{red}(x)$$

. Then we are assured of the applicability of (3), even after (2) has been applied.

In general, let $\beta_1, \ldots, \beta_m$ pick out models of α in which γ *fails* to be true normally. We include among the β's the consequences of previous nonmonotonic inferences. We have here R. A Fisher's "recognizable subsets" [Fis56, pp. 109–110] applied to the statistics of sets of models.

3.4 Benchmark A-4

1. Blocks A and B are heavy.

2. Heavy blocks are normally on the table.

3. A is possibly an exception.

4. Therefore B is on the table.

This seems to be a very weak inference, and does not appear to introduce anything new. On the construction that we have been looking at, the premises might even support the conclusion "Therefore A is on the table." It seems clear, in any event, that the premises are consistent with "A is on the table."

3.5 Benchmark A-5

1. Block A is heavy.

2. Heavy blocks are normally on the table.

3. A is not on the table.

4. Therefore All heavy blocks other than A are on the table.

Intuitions vary with regard to this inference. Those who see nonmonotonic inference as being governed by an overarching metaprinciple that exceptions to our general knowledge are to be minimized regard it as correct. Others find the conclusion too strong; Lifschitz [Lif89, p. 214] cites Ginsberg to this effect.

The inference is related to that in Benchmark A-3. Suppose that A, B_1, B_2, $\ldots B_m$ are all the blocks. We certainly seem to be in a position to infer that B_1 is on the table, that B_2 is on the table, and so on. What is required by the conclusion, however, is the *conjunction* of all these particular conclusions. Let β_i be the statement "block B_i is on the table." What we need to draw the general conclusion is a sequence of defaults of the form

$$\frac{heavy(B_i) : \text{Mon} - \text{table}(B_i) \wedge \text{M}\neg\text{on} - \text{table}(B_1) \wedge \ldots \wedge \text{M}\neg\text{on} - \text{table}(B_{i-1})}{on - table(B_i)}$$

Whether such a sequence of defaults can be made plausible or not is another question. It is in any event useful to observe the connection between the conclusion in this case, which Lifschitz seems to regard as justified, and the lottery paradox, or Sorites. Poole [Poo91] has noticed this connection and discussed it. One must be aware of the progressive weakening of the strength of the argument, even when each of the conclusions depends on the same statistical constraints on models.

3.6 Benchmark A-6

1. Blocks A, B, and C are heavy.

2. Heavy blocks are normally on the table.

3. At least one of A and B is not on the table.

4. Therefore C is on the table.

5. Therefore exactly one of A and B is not on the table.

The conclusion (4) follows as before; that one of A and B is not on the table should not be taken as interfering with the inference based on the fact that most models of(1), "C is on the table" is true. Lifschitz expresses some doubt about the desirability of being able to infer the second conclusion [Lif89, p. 215].

On our construction (5) does not follow at all. If (1) and (3) are true, the only models that are admissible are those in which 50% of $\{A, B\}$ are not on the table, and those in which 100% of $\{A, B\}$ are not on the table. To infer "$on - table(A)$" we would have to disregard (3) and look at models of (1) (compare the umbrella story).

But we can't do this, since (contrary to the umbrella case) the proportion of models of (1),(3) in which "$on - table(A)$" is true is *less* (0 or 1/2) than the proportion of models of (1) in which "$on - table(A)$" is true.

The guiding intuition is that while we can appropriately disregrd *vaguer* information, we cannot disregard *conflicting* information.

Thus

We cannot infer "$on - table(A)$"

We cannot infer "$on - table(B)$"

We cannot infer "Exactly one of A, B is on the table."

3.7 Benchmark A-7

1. Heavy blocks are normally on the table.

2. At least one heavy block is not on the table.

3. Therefore exactly one heavy block is not on the table.

This is an odd benchmark since surely we would not want an inference procedure to justify the conclusion. It is a conclusion that would follow from an approach which minimizes exceptions; so much the worse, I should think, for such approaches. We have no reason to suppose that (3) holds in most models of (2). Note that there is no conflict here with other premises.

3.8 Benchmark A-8

1. Block A is heavy.

2. Heavy blocks are normally on the table.

3. At least one heavy block is not on the table.

4. Therefore A is on the table.

The conclusion (4) is true in almost all the models of (1) and (3). We might note that the ordinary language use of "normally" would *entail* (3), so that A-8 is really not different from A-1.

3.9 Benchmarks A-9 – A-11

1. Jack asserts that block A is on the table.

2. Mary asserts that block A is not on the table.

3. Jack is ordinarily right.

4. Mary is ordinarily right.

5. Mary is more reliable than Jack.

6. Therefore A is not on the table.

From (1) and the default expressed by (3), we could conclude that A is on the table. From (2) and the default expressed by (4) we could conclude that A is not on the table. But, as the existence of the priority (5) shows, these defaults are not independent. It makes no sense to say that Mary is more reliable than Jack, unless their testimonies can conflict. But if their testimonies can conflict, and when they do Mary is more reliable, then we should express the default (3) as (1):M"A is on the table" $\land$ M¬(2)/"A is on the table." In the presence of (2), then, default (3) does not apply.

Whether we want the conclusion (6) is another question. The defaults (2) and (3) go over naturally into the assertions:

In almost all models in which "Jack asserts that block A is on the table" is true, "block A is on the table" is true.

In almost all models in which "Mary asserts that block A is on the table" is true, "block A is on the table" is true.

These claims can both be true, but not in the presence of (1) and (2). What we can conclude in presence of (1) and (2), even taking into account (5) is unclear. Perhaps Mary's claims are veridical 90% of the time, and Jack's are veridical 80% of the time, but in the models in which they contradict each other, each is wrong 50% of the time. What we need in order to derive the advertised conclusion is

In almost all models in which "Mary asserts that block A is not on the table" is true, and in which "Jack asserts that block A is on the table" is true, block A is not on the table.

but this represents a much stronger claim, intuitively, than 5.

3.10 Benchmark B-1

1. Animals normally do not fly.

2. Birds are animals.

3. Birds normally fly.

4. Ostriches are birds.

5. Ostriches normally do not fly.

6. Therefore animals other than birds do not fly.

7. Therefore birds other than ostriches fly.

8. Therefore ostriches do not fly.

Conclusions (6) and (7) seem wrong; conclusion (8) seems bizarre: The natural implicature of "F's ordinarily do not X" is that there are F's that X, and there are F's that don't X, but the typical F doesn't X.

What does make sense is that in place of these conclusions we could justify conclusions about individuals when there are premises that put these individuals into the right spot in the hierarchy. Thus

Add the premise "Charles is an animal," and conclude "Charles does not fly."

Add the premise "Charles is an animal and not a bird," and conclude "Charles does not fly."

Add the premise "Jane is an ostrich," and conclude "Jane does not fly."

Add the premise "Susan is a bird and not an ostrich," and conclude "Susan flies."

And so on.

There is no problem, as suggested by Lifschitz [Lif89, p. 215] about combining universalities and normalities. What is important in each case is the proportion of models picked out by the premises in which the conclusion holds.

3.11 Benchmark B-2

1. Animals normally do not fly.

2. Birds are animals.

3. Birds normally fly.

4. Bats are animals.

5. Bats normally fly.

6. Ostriches are birds.

7. Ostriches normally do not fly.

8. Therefore birds other than ostriches fly.

9. Therefore bats fly.

10. Therefore ostriches do not fly.

For the reasons adduced in the previous section, the juxtaposition of (5) and (9) and of (7) and (10) seem very strange. The conclusion (8) also seems too strong, and I would be suspicious of a nonmonotonic logic that yielded it. Of course particular instances would make sense: Tom the bat flies; Sally the ostrich does not fly; Peter the non-ostrich bird flies.

3.12 Benchmark B-3

1. Quakers are normally pacifists.

2. Republicans are not normally pacifists.

3. Therefore Quakers who are not Republicans are pacifists.

4. Therefore Republicans who are not Quakers are not pacifists.

Again the conclusions seem excessively strong. What does seem suggested are derived rules, from which conclusions could be drawn in particular cases. Thus the possibility of Republican Quakers suggests the two rules:

$Q(x) :MP(x),M\neg R(x)/P(x)$

$R(x) :M\neg P(x),M\neg Q(x)/\neg P(x)$

3.13 Benchmark B-4

1. Quakers are normally pacifists.

2. Republicans are not normally hawks.

3. Pacifists are normally politically active.

4. Hawks are normally politically active.

5. Therefore Quakers who are not republicans are pacifists.

6. Therefore Republicans who are not Quakers are hawks.

7. Therefore Quakers, Republicans, pacifists and hawks are politically active.

With the addition of the implicit and presumably intended premise "Pacifists are not Hawks and Hawks are not Pacifists" we should get (5) and (6) in the modified form of normality rules.

Can we get the conclusion (7) in the same modified form: e.g., Quakers are normally politically active? It depends. If our criterion of "normally" is 95%, the warrant for (1) will be that in 95% of the models in which "$Quaker(\tau)$" holds, so does "$Pacifist(\tau)$" hold. Similarly, the warrant for (2) will be that in 95% of the models in which "$Pacifist(\tau)$" holds, so does "$politically - active(\tau)$" hold, where in each case τ is an arbitrary variable-free term like "Sam." But now it is clear that it may not be the case (or, of course it may be—we just don't know) that in 95% of the models in which "$Quaker(\tau)$"holds, so does "$politically - active(\tau)$" hold.

4 Conclusion

Teng models of nonmonotonic inference embody the idea that what is going on in nonmonotonic inference is that we are step by step peeling away incredibilities from a set of models. If γ is a reasonable default conclusion from α so long as $\beta_1, \ldots, \beta_m$ are each possible, then we peel away the models in which γ is false, if the β's are true in some models of our final extension.

If we construe incredibility as rarity among the set of models that are picked out by our premises, then we are led to focus on statistics concerning models. These statistics may or may not reflect frequencies in the world. If almost all birds in the world fly, then that high frequency will be reflected in the models in which Tweety is interpreted as a bird. But we may also construe "Birds normally fly" in a way that does not reflect a frequency in the world. Nevertheless, if it is to be a basis for reasonable inference, it should be the case that among the models in which Tweety is interpreted as a bird almost all should be models in which "Tweety flies" is true.

We get some new insights into nonmonotonic arguments from this construal alone. In addition, however, we make a connection to the statistical problem of the reference class: to what base population do we refer x in order to get the most useful guidance as to whether x is F? A useful form of default rule, for example, is the following:

$$\frac{\alpha(\tau) : M\gamma(\tau), M\neg\beta_1(\tau), \ldots, M\neg\beta_m(\tau)}{\gamma(\tau)}$$

What this comes to is this: that $\gamma(\tau)$ is almost always true in models in which $\alpha(\tau)$ is known, and in which $\neg\gamma(\tau)$ is not known, and in which none of $\beta_1(\tau)$, $\ldots, \beta_m(\tau)$ are known. The $\beta_i(\tau)$ pick out models in which $\gamma(\tau)$ is not usually true. Mere vaguenesss (where we simply do not know how often β_i's are γ's is no problem).

In statistical terms, the β_i's correspond to the recognizable subsets of models about which we have conflicting information. Absent this conflicting information, we can draw a nonmonotonic conclusion.

Looking at the frequencies in which a sentence is true in a class of models picked out by a set of premises has a number of virtues to recommend it.

- It corresponds intuitively to the demand that reasonable conclusions be true "for the most part."

- It fits in well with the simple Teng models where monotonic inference is construed as elmininating the incredible, step by step.

- It throws some light on the standard examples of nonmonotonic inference.

- It makes use of principles explored in detail in connection with probabilistic inference—in particluar the principles behind picking out an appropriate reference class.

– It does not require, what a number of commentators have objected to, frequencies in the world. Normality may be construed in terms of propensities, or tendencies, or degrees of entailment, without required that we have statistical knowledge about frequencies in the world.

References

[Fis56] Ronald A. Fisher. *Statistical Methods and Scientific Inference*. Hafner Publishing Co., New York, 1956.

[Kyb83] Henry E. Jr. Kyburg. The reference class. *Philosophy of Science*, 50:374–397., 1983.

[Kyb96] Henry E. Kyburg. Induction and bayesian inference and indu tive inference. In David Dowe, Kevin Korb, and Jonathan Oliver, editors, *ISIS*, page p 6. World Scientific, Singapore, 1996.

[Kyb97] Henry E. Jr. Kyburg. Combinatorial semantics: the semantics of frequent validity. *Computational Intelligence*, forthcoming, 1997.

[Lif89] Vladimir Lifschitz. Benchmark problems for formal nonmonotonic reasoning. In M. Reinfrank, J. deKleer, M.L. Ginsberg, and E. Sandewall, editors, *Non-Monotonic Reasoning*, pages 202–219. Springer-Verlag, 1989.

[Poo91] David Poole. The effect of knowledge on belief: Conditioning, specificity and thelottery paradox in default reasoning. *Artificial Intelligence*, 49:281–307, 1991.

[Rus48] Bertrand Russell. *Human Knowledge:Its Scope and Limits,*, volume New York. Simon and Schuster, 1948.

[Ten96] Choh Man Teng. Possible world partition sequences: A unifying framework for uncertain reasoning. In Eric Hlorvitz and Finn Jensen, editors, *Uncertainty in Artificial Ingelligence*, pages 517–524. Morgan Kaufman, San Francisco, 1996.

Inductive Theories from Equational Systems

Michael Bulmer

Department of Mathematics, University of Tasmania,
GPO Box 252-37, Hobart, 7001, Australia
Michael.Bulmer@utas.edu.au

Abstract. We present a procedure for generating inductive theories from systems of equational data. An analysis of the consistency of the resulting conjectures is used to generate experiments and to select between competing theories. An application to a blocks world is given.

1   Introduction

As part of a general automated reasoning system based on term rewriting, we have developed a procedure for generating inductive theories from an equational system. We have in mind a reasoner whose knowledge (or *belief basis*) is this equational system and whose beliefs are generated by (deductive) equational proof. Augmenting this with the inductive procedure empowers the reasoner to make conjectures from its knowledge.

In this paper we briefly present the procedure and then look at what can be said about changes in inductive belief caused by changes in the reasoner's knowledge.

In this first section we describe the language used. Section 2 defines the notion of a conjecture and presents the procedure for generating conjectures from an equational system. We then have an empirical belief dynamics for the inductive reasoning, observing changes in the conjectures as the reasoner's knowledge changes. These conjectures as a whole may not be consistent with the knowledge. In Section 3 we look at breaking such an inconsistent system into consistent subsets, each giving a different theory to explain the data. This may then suggest experiments to perform in order to obtain a single consistent theory. The problem of deciding which of these theories to adopt as an interim working theory is examined in Section 4, making use of Popper's notion of falsifiability. Finally, in Section 5 we give a graphical example of this reasoning process using a blocks world.

Language

Our language is that of a many-sorted and variable-free term algebra T_Σ generated by a signature Σ. A signature can be viewed as a graph with labelled edges and vertices, as in Figure 1, with the elements of T_Σ generated by "following the arrows" to build terms. The vertices of the graph are called *sorts*, and the edges *morphisms*. For example, father Alice : Ground → Person and male father :

Person → Sentence are terms for the signature in Figure 1. The number of morphisms in a term f is the *length*, $\delta(f)$, of f. Thus $\delta(\text{father Alice}) = 2$.

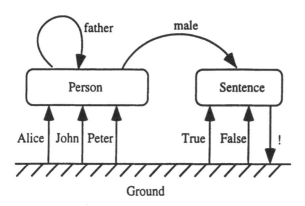

Fig. 1. Family Signature

If $f : \sigma \to \tau$ is a term then we say f has *domain* dom$(f) = \sigma$, and *codomain* cod$(f) = \tau$. For a *grounded* term $f :$ Ground $\to \tau$ we will usually write $f \in \tau$. A term f with domain other than Ground is called a *Σ-function*.

For each sort σ a signature automatically contains the *identity* morphism $i : \sigma \to \sigma$ and the *erasing* morphism $! : \sigma \to$ Ground. For any terms f and g we have the structural rules $fi \to f$, $if \to f$, and

$$f \,! \, g \to \begin{cases} f, & \text{if dom}(g) = \text{Ground}; \\ f\,!, & \text{if dom}(g) \neq \text{Ground} \end{cases}$$

For a given signature Σ, we define the set of *Σ-equations* by

$$\mathcal{E}_\Sigma = \{s = t : s, t \in T_\Sigma, s, t : \sigma \to \tau\}.$$

For each equation $s = t$ we have a corresponding inequation $\neg(s = t)$, or $s \neq t$, and define the set of all inequations by $\neg\mathcal{E}_\Sigma = \{s \neq t : (s = t) \in \mathcal{E}_\Sigma\}$. We write $\mathcal{F}_\Sigma = \mathcal{E}_\Sigma \cup \neg\mathcal{E}_\Sigma$, and call a subset $F \subseteq \mathcal{F}_\Sigma$ a *Σ-system*.

If f arises from a single morphism in Σ, i.e. $\delta(f) = 1$, then f is called a *Σ-word*. Grounded Σ-words may be declared to represent an *entity* in the modelled world. For example, we represent the two classical notions of truth as the grounded words True, False $\in$ Sentence, or three different people as Alice, John, Paul $\in$ Person. We call such declared words the *Σ-entities* of Σ.

The important idea is that these entities are distinct. Having declared a collection of Σ-entities we implicitly require that any Σ-system F contains the inequation $a \neq b$ for all distinct Σ-entities a and b. Thus if we declare True and False to be Σ-entities then every Σ-system will contain True $\neq$ False. We will usually declare ground words to be entities by writing them with an uppercase letter (reflecting the similarity with a proper noun).

This language extends to an algebra with additional constructors, such as products and sets. Sets in particular are important for capturing multi-valued functions and recursive definitions [1]. The general use of such constructors is beyond the scope of this paper, but we will make use of the *empty set* $\phi : \sigma \to \tau$ which acts as a two-sided erasing morphism (so that $f\phi = \phi = \phi g$).

Equational Proof

Fundamental to our purpose is the theory of equational reasoning, as described in [6], [3], [2]. If $F \subseteq \mathcal{F}_\Sigma$ and $e \in \mathcal{E}_\Sigma$ then we write $F \Rightarrow e$ if there is an equational proof of e from the equations in F.

Definition 1. A Σ-system F is *consistent* if there is no inequation $(s \neq t) \in F$ such that $F \Rightarrow (s = t)$. If F is not consistent we say it is *inconsistent*.

Inconsistency will primarily arise when the predictions of a conjectured system contradict the enforced entity inequations, as discussed in Sections 3 and 4.

2   Induction

We call an equation between two Σ-functions a *function equation*. A *grounded equation*, such as father Alice = John, typically gives information about the result of applying a function to an entity. We will usually refer to a collection of grounded equations as a *database*.

If a Σ-system F contains the function equation $f = g$ then for any $x \in$ dom(f) we immediately have $F \Rightarrow (fx = gx)$. (Note that $x \in$ dom(f) is equivalent to $x \in$ dom(g) since we must have dom$(f) =$ dom(g) to form $f = g$.) Thus the inclusion of $f = g$ in F captures the universally quantified statement $\forall x(fx = gx)$. The inverse of this observation, captured in the following definitions, is the basis of our induction.

Definition 2. A *fact* from a system Δ is a function equation $f = g$ such that $\Delta \not\Rightarrow (f = g)$ and $\Delta \Rightarrow (fx = gx)$ for all $x \in$ dom(f).

Definition 3. A *conjecture* from a system Δ is a function equation $f \simeq g$ such that $\Delta \not\Rightarrow (f = g)$, $\Delta \not\Rightarrow (f \neq g)$, $\Delta \Rightarrow (fx = gx)$ for at least one $x \in$ dom(f) and there is no $y \in dom(f)$ such that $\Delta \Rightarrow (fy \neq gy)$.

A fact is a function equation which holds universally when applied to any entity of appropriate type, and is not already a consequence of the system Δ. A conjecture does not hold universally, but has at least one supporting case and is not contradicted by other information in Δ. We use the notation $\simeq$ to indicate the lack of universal support.

Proof by consistency [7] has been used to show that the universal facts are inductive *theorems* of Δ, in the sense of *mathematical induction*. Conjectures are of more interest to us since they instead capture the process of *scientific* induction.

The induction procedure follows simply from these definitions, generating function equations which have support in Δ. Let $\mathrm{IND}(\Delta, n)$ be the conjectures thus generated involving functions of length at most n. As n increases the number of functions to be considered grows exponentially. To work with this we apply the process iteratively. Starting with $\Delta_1 = \mathrm{IND}(\Delta, 1)$, we evaluate

$$\Delta_{j+1} = \Delta_j \cup \mathrm{IND}(\Delta \cup \Delta_j, j+1),$$

the conjectures arising from the result of induction for length j being used to eliminate candidates of length $j+1$. We have proved elsewhere [1] that the result, Δ_∞, of this process is finite.

Example

Consider the signature

$$\Sigma = \left\{ \begin{array}{l} \text{True, False} \in \text{sentence,} \\ \text{John, Peter, Alice, Paul} \in \text{person,} \\ \text{male : person} \to \text{sentence,} \\ \text{father : person} \to \text{person} \end{array} \right\}$$

and the database

$$\Delta = \left\{ \begin{array}{l} \text{father Paul} = \text{Peter,} \\ \text{father Alice} = \text{John,} \\ \text{male Peter} = \text{True,} \\ \text{male John} = \text{True} \end{array} \right\}.$$

Applying IND to Δ gives the two conjectures

$$\Delta_2 = \mathrm{IND}(\Delta, 2) = \left\{ \begin{array}{l} \text{male} \simeq \text{True !,} \\ \text{male father} \simeq \text{True !} \end{array} \right\}.$$

Viewing this externally, the first of these is false in the world we want to model, while the second is true. The first appears simply because the only people whose gender is mentioned in the database are male, giving no counter-examples to refute the conjecture. As the breadth of data increases, fewer such extreme conjectures will be made. For example, consider the larger database

$$\Delta' = \Delta \cup \{\text{male Alice} = \text{False}\}$$

where now

$$\Delta'_2 = \mathrm{IND}(\Delta', 2) = \{\text{male father} \simeq \text{True !}\}.$$

We would then expect this remaining conjecture to persist as further data is added.

There are two types of changing belief involved here. Firstly is that of the belief the reasoner has in the knowledge Δ. We are working with the assumption that there is no noise in the data, so that anything supplied to the reasoner is true for some world. However we need not have a static world, and the *belief revision* of [4] may be necessary if Δ were to become inconsistent. We refer to this as *deductive* belief dynamics since it is based on consistency, in turn dependent on the deductive proof operator $\Rightarrow$.

With this simple example we see that we also have an *inductive* belief dynamics. This is brought about by the functional dependence of our conjectured knowledge on the underlying knowledge Δ. As we expand or revise Δ we have a corresponding change in $\text{IND}(\Delta)$. We then have some control over our inductive beliefs, provided by the *experiments* we choose to perform to augment Δ. This is discussed in the following section.

3 Consistency

While, by definition, a single conjecture must be consistent with the original data, it is common that an inductive theory of two or more conjectures may not. In this case we cannot extend belief to the full set of conjectures and must instead seek a subset which is consistent.

With the database

$$\Delta = \left\{ \begin{array}{l} \text{male Paul} = \text{True,} \\ \text{male Alice} = \text{False,} \\ \text{female Paul} = \text{False,} \\ \text{not False} = \text{True, not True} = \text{False} \end{array} \right\}$$

we obtain the conjectures

$$\Delta_2 = \left\{ \begin{array}{l} \text{female} \simeq \text{False !,} \\ \text{not female} \simeq \text{True !,} \\ \text{female} \simeq \text{not male,} \\ \text{not female} \simeq \text{male,} \\ \text{not not} = \text{i} \end{array} \right\} .$$

Combining the second and fourth conjectures gives male $\simeq$ True !, which then implies male Alice = True, contradicting the information in Δ. We say that Δ_2 is *inconsistent with respect to* Δ.

Definition 4. A subset $C' \subseteq C$ is *maximally consistent* in C with respect to Δ if C' is consistent with respect to Δ and there is no $e \in C \setminus C'$ such that $C' \cup e$ is consistent with respect to Δ.

When the Δ is clear we will say simply that C' is a maximally consistent subset of C.

Lemma 5. *Suppose C is the result of induction on Δ. Then if C is inconsistent with respect to Δ, C contains at least two maximally consistent subsets.*

Proof By definition, any single conjecture $c_1 \in C$ is consistent with respect to Δ. We can successively add conjectures to the set $\{c_1\}$ to give a larger consistent set until no longer possible. This gives a maximally consistent $C_1 \subset C$ containing c_1. Since the whole of C is not consistent there exists another $c_2 \in C \setminus C_1$, and similarly there must be a maximally consistent $C_2 \subset C$ containing c_2. Since $c_2 \notin C_1$, C_1 and C_2 are two distinct maximally consistent subsets of C. □

Hence if a set of induced beliefs are inconsistent, there are at least two smaller belief sets which are consistent and maximal. We can view these smaller sets as *competing theories* for explaining the data. For the above example, we have the maximally consistent subsets

$$
C_1 = \left\{ \begin{array}{l} \text{female} \simeq \text{False !,} \\ \text{not female} \simeq \text{True !,} \\ \text{not not} = i \end{array} \right\},
$$

$$
C_2 = \left\{ \begin{array}{l} \text{female} \simeq \text{not male,} \\ \text{not female} \simeq \text{male,} \\ \text{not not} = i \end{array} \right\}.
$$

C_1 and C_2 correspond to two differing theories about the function **female**. One theory says that every person is female, while the other says that to be female is not to be male. A reasoner must choose one of these as a *working theory*.

If a set of conjectures C is consistent with respect to a database Δ, then we define the *predictions*, $P_C(\Delta)$, of C with respect to Δ to be the set of all data f such that $\Delta \cup C \Rightarrow f$ and $\Delta \not\Rightarrow f$.

In the above example we have

$$
P_{C_1}(\Delta) = \{\text{female Alice} = \text{False}\} \text{ and}
$$
$$
P_{C_2}(\Delta) = \{\text{female Alice} = \text{True}\}.
$$

The obvious experiment for the reasoner to perform is to find the value of **female Alice**. We capture this in the following definitions.

Definition 6. An *experiment* is a composition of a function term $f : \sigma \to \tau$ and an entity $a \in \sigma$. The *result* of an experiment fa is an equation $fa = b$ for some entity $b \in \tau$.

Definition 7. Suppose Δ gives rise to competing theories $C_1, \ldots, C_n$. If there is some experiment fa such that $(fa = b) \in P_{C_j}(\Delta)$ and $(fa = c) \in P_{C_k}(\Delta)$ for some b distinct from c, then fa is a *crucial* experiment for Δ.

The motivation for this definition is obvious. If $C_j \cup \Delta \Rightarrow fa = b$ and $C_k \cup \Delta \Rightarrow fa = c$ then the result of fa must contradict C_j or C_k, or possibly both. The intrinsic belief dynamics of applying IND to the new database will then revise C_j and C_k, finding a maximal subset of each which is consistent with the result of fa. Both will decrease in size and ultimately one or both will disappear.

The crucial experiment for our example is female Alice. However, a database need not give crucial experiments, even if inconsistency is present. Furthermore, experimentation is about the future and we are still left with the problem of which maximally consistent system to take as a working theory.

4 Falsifiability

One well known approach to this question is to look at the *falsifiability* of each theory [8]. A theory is then stronger if it is more likely to be falsified. Einstein's theory of gravitation, the standard example of this, made many bold and observable predictions, opening it to being easily falsified were it incorrect. Here, unlike standard physics, our term signature is finite, and we use this to make various assumptions which allow us to quantify falsifiability.

We also have a pragmatic use for the notion of a falsifiable theory. If our reasoner is faced with a number of competing theories then we would like to carry out experiments to decide between them, ultimately falsifying all but one. By taking the theory which is most falsifiable as a working theory we in a sense maximise the chance of this happening.

Definition 8. Let C be a set consistent with respect to a database Δ. If $(fa = b) \in P_C(\Delta)$ and the result of the experiment fa is $fa = c$, for some c distinct from b, then we say that C is *falsified*.

Without any additional information about the domain, the chance of a theory being falsified according to this definition is thus proportional to the number of predictions it makes, and the quality of those predictions. A theory which makes no predictions can never be falsified and so is less useful than one which does make predictions and so can be tested. Furthermore a theory which makes, for example, a prediction about the result of a Sentence-valued experiment is more likely to be right, and less likely to be falsified, than one making a prediction for a Person-valued experiment. We capture these ideas in the following definition.

Definition 9. The *falsifiability*, $F_C(\Delta)$, of a theory C for a database Δ is

$$F_C(\Delta) = 1 - \prod_{e \in P_{C_1}(\Delta)} \frac{1}{|\text{cod}(e)|}.$$

Popper's notion of theory strength is then given by the following defintion:

Definition 10. Let C_1 and C_2 be two theories for a database Δ. Then C_1 is *a stronger theory* than C_2 if

$$F_{C_1}(\Delta) > F_{C_2}(\Delta).$$

We frequently have conjectures only between predicates, in which case the the codomain consists of True and False and so has constant size 2. The above condition then becomes

$$\left(1 - \prod_{e \in P_{C_1}(\Delta)} 1/2\right) > \left(1 - \prod_{e \in P_{C_2}(\Delta)} 1/2\right),$$

$$\text{or} \quad (1/2)^{|P_{C_1}(\Delta)|} < (1/2)^{|P_{C_2}(\Delta)|},$$

giving the following simple result:

Lemma 11. *Let C_1 and C_2 be two theories for a database Δ with every element of C_1 and C_2 a predicate. Then C_1 is a stronger theory than C_2 if*

$$|P_{C_1}(\Delta)| > |P_{C_2}(\Delta)|.$$

Our definition of theory strength is based on probabilities but there is one situation where we can be certain that a theory is stronger than another, captured in the following definition.

Definition 12. *A theory C_1 is strictly stronger than theory C_2 if any prediction of C_2 is also a prediction of C_1, and not conversely.*

That is if C_1 is strictly stronger than C_2 then $P_{C_2}(\Delta) \subset P_{C_1}(\Delta)$ so that

$$\prod_{e \in P_{C_2}(\Delta)} \frac{1}{|cod(e)|} < \prod_{e \in P_{C_1}(\Delta)} \frac{1}{|cod(e)|},$$

giving the natural relationship between 'stronger' and 'strictly stronger':

Lemma 13. *Let C_1 and C_2 be two theories for a database Δ. If C_1 is strictly stronger than C_2 then C_1 is stronger then C_2.*

The following example illustrates the calculation of falsifiability and shows that the converse to this lemma does not hold.

Example

Consider the following signature:

$$\Sigma = \left\{ \begin{array}{l} \text{Alice, John, Jill, Jenny, Kelly,} \\ \text{Paul, Peter, Mary} \in \text{person,} \\ \text{Blue, Brown, Green} \in \text{colour,} \\ \text{eyeColour : person} \to \text{colour,} \\ \text{father, mother,} \\ \text{wife, sister : person} \to \text{person} \end{array} \right\}.$$

We make the observations Δ about our families:

$$\Delta = \left\{ \begin{array}{l} \text{father Alice = John, father Paul = Peter,} \\ \text{wife John = Jill, wife Peter = Mary,} \\ \text{mother Alice = Jill, sister John = Jenny,} \\ \text{sister Jill = Mary, sister Mary = Kelly,} \\ \text{eyeColour Alice = Blue, eyeColour John = Brown,} \\ \text{eyeColour Jill = Blue, eyeColour Paul = Green,} \\ \text{eyeColour Jenny = Brown} \end{array} \right\} .$$

We have three maximally consistent sets of conjectures

$$C_1 = \left\{ \begin{array}{l} \text{eyeColour mother} \simeq \text{eyeColour,} \\ \text{wife father} \simeq \text{mother} \end{array} \right\},$$

$$C_2 = \left\{ \begin{array}{l} \text{eyeColour sister} \simeq \text{eyeColour,} \\ \text{wife father} \simeq \text{mother} \end{array} \right\},$$

$$C_3 = \left\{ \begin{array}{l} \text{eyeColour mother} \simeq \text{eyeColour,} \\ \text{eyeColour sister} \simeq \text{eyeColour} \end{array} \right\},$$

with corresponding predictions

$$P_{C_1}(\Delta) = \left\{ \begin{array}{l} \text{eyeColour Mary = Green,} \\ \text{mother Paul = Mary} \end{array} \right\},$$

$$P_{C_2}(\Delta) = \left\{ \begin{array}{l} \text{eyeColour Mary = Blue,} \\ \text{eyeColour Kelly = Blue,} \\ \text{mother Paul = Mary} \end{array} \right\},$$

$$P_{C_3}(\Delta) = \left\{ \begin{array}{l} \text{eyeColour Kelly = Blue,} \\ \text{eyeColour Mary = Blue} \end{array} \right\} .$$

With three elements in colour, the probability of C_3 being falsified is $1 - (\frac{1}{3})^2 = 0.889$. Eight elements in person gives the probability of C_1 being falsified as $1 - (\frac{1}{3})(\frac{1}{8}) = 0.958$ and of C_2 being falsified as $1 - (\frac{1}{3})^2(\frac{1}{8}) = 0.986$. We thus take C_2 as the strongest theory.

Note that C_2 is in fact strictly stronger than C_3, though only stronger than C_1.

Finally, note that the problem of finding the theory of an arbitrary set of conjectures is likely to be computationally hard. Our present interest is in the reasoning itself, rather than in the practicalities of efficient implementation. However, obtaining a single maximally consistent set is a linear process since any conjecture can be extended to a maximal set by successively adding conjectures which retain consistency until all conjectures have been tried. Thus for large systems of conjectures we can also make use of our falsifiability criterion by taking a small sample of maximally consistent sets, generated by extending each of a collection of conjectures, and selecting the strongest of those as the working theory. Choosing the conjectures to extend from those not already in a generated maximal set can result in a good approximation to the full theory of the conjectures.

5   Blocks World

The well-known blocks world ([9], [5]) provides us with a graphical illustration of our reasoner's inductive beliefs. At each stage of learning the reasoner draws a picture of its beliefs to show what it thinks.

We represent the blocks world by the signature

$$\Sigma = \left\{ \begin{array}{l} \text{A, B, C, D, E} \in \text{block,} \\ \text{below, above : block} \rightarrow \text{block,} \\ \text{table : block} \rightarrow \text{sentence} \end{array} \right\}.$$

For example, we use below B = A to say that A is below B and table A = True to say that A is on the table.

The reasoner uses values of table and below to draw a picture of its beliefs. (We have deliberately not used above since it leaves the reasoner to figure out below values from given information about above.) For each block A, ..., E, the reasoner first consults its declared knowledge to determine if the block is on the table or on a block which it knows the location of. If successful it draws a block in its place in the world. If the declared knowledge is not sufficient then it tries to determine the same information using its inductive conjectures. If this is successful the block is also drawn, but is shaded to indicate it is based on conjectured information. If no information is available then the block is not shown.

The following details a sample session with an implementation of this system. The reasoner begins with no knowledge about the position of the blocks, giving the empty table in Figure 2(a). The remaining arrangements are the result of the following statements.

(b) 'A is on the table.' The reasoner makes the conjecture table $\simeq$ True !, guessing that this property holds for all blocks. A is drawn with certainty on the table, with the remaining blocks also positioned on the table but shaded to indicate that their position is only conjectured.

(c) 'A is below B.' The reasoner makes the additional conjecture table below $\simeq$ True !, that everything below something is on the table. However, this conjecture doesn't provide any new predictions.

(d) 'B is not on the table.' The initial conjecture that everything is on the table is falsified and blocks C, D, and E are removed.

(e) 'B is above A.' The four conjectures generated are inconsistent, resulting in the maximally consistent subsets given in Table 1. None give any predictions and so each is unfalsifiable, leaving us unable to choose a strongest theory. We arbitrarily choose the first as a working theory. In our blocks world this is in fact redundant: with no predictions we will not see any results of the reasoner's conjectures.

(f) 'C is below D.' Here we have the same maximally consistent sets but this time with associated predictions, as shown in Table 2. The third theory is most falsifiable and so we choose it as a working theory.

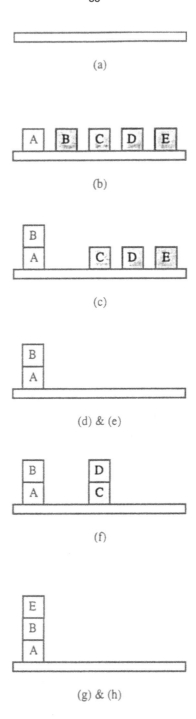

Fig. 2. Blocks world with multiple theories.

Conjectures	$\mathcal{P}_C$	$\mathcal{F}_C$
below above $\simeq$ i	ϕ	0.0
above below $\simeq$ i		
below above $\simeq$ i	ϕ	0.0
table above $\simeq$ False !		
above below $\simeq$ True !	ϕ	0.0
table below $\simeq$ True !		
table below $\simeq$ True !	ϕ	0.0
table above $\simeq$ False !		

Table 1. Maximally consistent sets for Figure 2(e)

Conjectures	$\mathcal{P}_C$	$\mathcal{F}_C$
below above $\simeq$ i	above C = D	0.8
above below $\simeq$ i		
below above $\simeq$ i	ϕ	0.0
table above $\simeq$ False !		
above below $\simeq$ True !	table C = True	0.9
table below $\simeq$ True !	above C = D	
table below $\simeq$ True !	table C = True	0.5
table above $\simeq$ False !		

Table 2. Maximally consistent sets for Figure 2(f)

The approximate equivalence between falsifiability and the number of predictions has an obvious practical meaning here. If more predictions are made then the reasoner will be able to describe the location of more of the blocks so that the strongest theory will be the best at completing the reasoner's picture.

(g) 'B is below E.' This falsifies two of the previous competing theories. The remaining two and their predictions are given in Table 3.

(h) The remaining dilemma here is quite subtle. The three conjectures generated all seem natural and so it is strange that there is an inconsistency. The problem lies in the equation above below $\simeq$ i which in fact is *not* valid in the physical world we are modelling. Applying below to A can never give a block and so we can never obtain the right-hand identity. To capture this we add that 'There is nothing below A,' encoded in the equation below A = ϕ. We then have the unique maximal theory given in Table 4.

Conjectures	$\mathcal{P}_C$	F_C
below above $\simeq$ i	above B = E	0.96
above below $\simeq$ i	above C = D	
below above $\simeq$ i	ϕ	0.0
table above $\simeq$ False !		

Table 3. Maximally consistent sets for Figure 2(g)

Conjectures	$\mathcal{P}_C$	F_C
below above $\simeq$ i	ϕ	0.0
table above $\simeq$ False !		

Table 4. The unique maximally consistent set for Figure 2(h)

Concluding Remarks

The approach presented here is part of a larger system which includes equational methods for deductive and abductive reasoning [1]. The implmentation of this system has given a concrete model to explore the relationships between the various kinds of reasoning. For example, here we have used the deductive results of believing conjectures, their predictions, to give a measure of theory strength. We anticipate other benefits will similarly arise from this unified approach.

To this end we have restricted our attention to a *linear* term language, where all functions are unary or nullary. As seen in the examples, even with this restricted language we can examine some interesting problems. However, to approach more realistic examples we need the richer language. So far, only a few such problems have been examined [1].

Acknowledgments

The fundamental idea of an entity and its role in variable-free reasoning is due to Desmond Fearnley-Sander. I would like to also thank Simon Wotherspoon for his observations which greatly improved the efficiency of the IND implementation.

References

1. M. Bulmer. *Reasoning by Term Rewriting.* PhD thesis, University of Tasmania, 1995. To appear.
2. P. Le Chenadec. *Canonical forms in finitely presented algebras.* Pitman, London, 1986.

3. N. Dershowitz. Completion and its Applications. In H. Aït Kaci and M. Nivat, editors, *Resolution of Equations in Algebraic Structures*, volume 2, pages 31–85. Academic Press, London, 1989.

4. P. Gärdenfors. *Knowledge in Flux: Modelling the Dynamics of Epistemic States*. MIT Press, 1988.

5. M. Genesereth and N. Nilsson. *Logical Foundations of Artificial Intelligence*. Morgan Kaufmann, Palo Alto, 1988.

6. G. Huet and D. C. Oppen. Equations and Rewrite Rules: A Survey. In R. Book, editor, *Formal Language Theory: Perspectives and Open Problems*, pages 349–405. Academic Press, 1980.

7. D. Kapur and D. R. Musser. Proof by Consistency. *Artificial Intelligence*, 31:125–157, 1987.

8. K. Popper. *Conjectures and Refutations - The Growth of Scientific Knowledge*. Routledge and Kegan Paul, London, 1974.

9. E. Rich. *Artificial Intelligence*. McGraw-Hill, Singapore, 1986.

The Role of Default Representations in Incremental Learning

Aditya K. Ghose[1], Srinivas Padmanabhuni[2], Randy Goebel[2]

[1] Decision Systems Lab
Department of Business Systems
University of Wollongong
NSW 2522 Australia
aditya@uow.edu.au
[2] Department of Computing Science
University of Alberta, Edmonton
Alberta, Canada, T6G 2H1
{srinivas, goebel}@cs.ualberta.ca

1 Introduction

Inductive Logic Programming refers to a class of machine learning algorithms where the agent learns a first-order theory from examples and background knowledge. The ILP framework in machine learning is perhaps the most general of all because of the complexity of the concepts learned. The use of first-order logic programs as the underlying representation makes ILP systems more powerful and useful than the conventional empirical machine learning systems. ILP systems have been successfully used in a variety of real life domains including mesh design, protein synthesis, games and fault diagnosis.

An incremental ILP system is basically an ILP system but instead of being provided with all the negative and positive examples in a monolithic fashion, the examples are provided to the system incrementally. The learned concept is then revised (specialized or generalized) depending upon the input example. If the input example is positive and is not explained by the learned concept, the concept needs to be generalized. On the contrary if the input example is negative, and the learned concept is not consistent with the negative example, the concept needs to be specialized.

In a somewhat independent strand of research, reasoning with incomplete information has emerged as a crucial component of intelligent systems. Default reasoning focusses on reasoning with defeasible assertions, or assumptions, and has found application in areas as diverse as formalizations of common-sense inference, implemented knowledge based systems, database query languages and requirements specifications. A wide variety of formalisms for default reasoning have been reported in the literature. In this paper, we bring together these two separate strands of research.

This paper asks two seemingly unrelated questions:

- Can default representations play a role in the process of incrementally learning classical theories ?

– Can incremental learning approaches be used to learn default theories ?

The answers to both questions turn out to be yes, and the solutions generated turn out to be closely inter-related. In answering the first question, we show how default representations can improve specialization procedures by providing an intensional representation for the multiple possible outcomes of the specialization process. This permits us to define lazy evaluation procedures for iterated sequences of specialization steps, thereby deferring premature commitment to a specific outcome and enabling us to generate provably minimal outcomes. Deferring commitment also permits us to respond rationally to dynamically changing contexts.

A crucial requirement for specialization operations is that the change made to a theory must be minimal. To provide a sound semantic basis to the notion of minimal change to a theory, we draw on yet another strand of research, that of belief revision. Belief revision research looks at how agents can minimally change their beliefs in the light of inputs from the environment. One of the central results from the area of belief revision is a set of conditions that define minimal change to a theory. We use the conditions relevant to the process of retracting or withdrawing a belief to establish that our approach to specialization is indeed minimal. To put our approach in perspective, we compare it with another approach to specialization which has been evaluated against the yardstick of minimal change provided by the belief revision area: Wrobel's MBR operator [10]. We identify conditions under which our operators coincide and show how our work improves on that of Wrobel.

We then consider the second problem, that of incrementally learning default theories. We establish the semantics of inducing default theories and present an incremental learning procedure for default theories which is correct with respect to these semantics. The procedure draws on our approach to minimal specialization of classical theories in many different ways. It uses the same approach to handling negative examples as our minimal specialization operator: augmenting the set of constraints in the default theory. Elsewhere in the procedure, we apply our minimal specialization operator directly to specialize the set of constraints in the default theory when it blocks the derivation of positive examples. Here too, our approach enjoys the benefits of lazy evaluation and deferred choice.

The paper is organized as follows. Section 2 presents the formal preliminaries of belief revision, default reasoning and Wrobel's MBR operator. Section 3 presents the minimal specialization operator. Section 4 presents the semantic setting for inducing default theories. Section 5 presents an incremental learning algorithm for default theories. We present concluding remarks in Section 6.

2 Preliminaries

2.1 Belief revision

Alchourrón, Gärdenfors and Makinson have undertaken a systematic study of the dynamics of belief change, resulting in what is currently popularly known as the

AGM framework for belief change [1], [5], [4]. In the AGM framework, the belief state of an agent is represented by a deductively closed, logically consistent set of propositional sentences called a *belief set*. They define three kinds of belief change operations: *expansion*, in which the new belief being added is guaranteed to be consistent with the existing body of beliefs; *contraction*, in which an existing belief is retracted; and *revision*, in which a new belief, which may possibly be inconsistent with existing beliefs, is added. The operations of contraction and revision can be defined in terms of each other, as shown by the *Levi identity* below (here, K_A^*, K_A^- and K_A^+ denote, respectively, the revision, contraction and expansion of K with A):

$$K_A^* = (K_{\neg A}^-)_A^+$$

The *Harper identity* [6] ($K_A^- = K_{\neg A}^* \cap K$) similarly defines contraction in terms of revision. We describe only contraction operators in this section, since the corresponding revision operators follow via the Levi identity. Alchourrón, Gärdenfors and Makinson define a set of rationality postulates for each of the operations of expansion, revision and contraction. The postulates for contraction are listed below.

1- For any sentence A and any belief set K, K_A^- is a belief set.
2- $K_A^- \subseteq K$.
3- If $A \notin K$, then $K_A^- = K$.
4- If $\not\models A$, then $A \notin K_A^-$.
5- If $A \in K$, then $K \subseteq (K_A^-)_A^+$.
6- If $\models A \leftrightarrow B$, then $K_A^- = K_B^-$.
7- $K_A^- \cap K_B^- \subseteq K_{A \wedge B}^-$.
8- If $A \notin K_{A \wedge B}^-$, then $K_{A \wedge B}^- \subseteq K_A^-$.

Postulate (1-) requires that beliefs be represented in the same form before and after a belief change step. (2-) requires that no new beliefs be held as a result of a contraction. (3-) requires that if the belief to be contracted is not held, then no change should be made. (4-) requires that every contraction operation succeed, unless the belief being contracted is a logical truth. (5-) is the principle of recovery, which requires that if a belief held in a given belief state is retracted and then added back to the belief state, the outcome contains the initial belief state, i.e., the initial belief state is recovered. (6-) is the principle of irrelevance of syntax, which requires that the outcome of a contraction operation be independent of the syntactic form of the beliefs being contracted. (7-) requires that the retraction of a conjunction of beliefs should not retire any beliefs that are common to the retraction of the same belief set with each individual conjunct. (8-) requires that, when retracting the conjunct of two beliefs A and B forces us to give up A, then in retracting A, we do not give up any more than in retracting the conjunction of A and B.

2.2 Default reasoning

Reasoning with incomplete information is a crucial component of intelligent systems. Default reasoning focusses on reasoning with defeasible assertions, or assumptions, and has found application in areas as diverse as formalizations of common-sense inference, implemented knowledge based systems, database query languages and requirements specifications. A wide variety of formalisms for default reasoning have been reported in the literature. For the purposes of this paper, we shall focus on what might be the simplest of these formalisms to ease exposition. We should note, however, that our results are not limited to this formalism alone, but apply to several others as well.

We shall consider default reasoning in the style of the THEORIST system [8] [7] (formalisms inspired by the THEORIST system have been variously categorized as hypothetical reasoning, expectation-based reasoning or the preferred subtheories approach).

Definition 1 [Default theory] *A default theory is a triple* (F, H, C) *where each of F, H and C are sets of first-order sentences (assumed to be written in clausal form) such that* $F \cup C$ *is satisfiable.*

Definition 2 [Default extension] *An* extension *of a default theory* (F, H, C) *is any set* $F \cup h$ *where* $h \subseteq H$ *such that* $F \cup h \cup C$ *is satisfiable and for any* h' *such that* $h \subset h' \subseteq H$, $F \cup h' \cup C$ *is not satisfiable.*

Notice that the definitions above require that the sets F and C be satisfiable, while there is no such restriction on H. The intuition is that F represents the set of *facts* that hold in every extension. C represents the set of *constraints*, which can be used to ensure that extensions do not contain certain assertions. In particular, one should note that for every extension $e \in E(\Delta)$, where $E(\Delta)$ denotes the set of extensions of the default theory Δ, $e \not\models \neg C$ (treating C as the conjunction of its elements). Thus the negations of the assertions in C (as well as their consequences) are not contained in any extension of the corresponding default theory. H denotes the set of *hypotheses* or defaults, which may potentially hold. As such, H is a possibly inconsistent set of assertions. Subsets of this default representation language have been shown to be equivalent to *normal default theories* in Reiter's default logic [9] in [7], and to a default logic variant called Prerequisite-free Constrained Default Logic [2] in [2].

While we shall assume that the first-order assertions in F and C are written in the standard clausal form, sentences with free variables in H will be treated as sentence schemas representing all possible ground instances of the sentence (thus, if $p(X) \in H$, then we shall treat H as containing all possible ground instances of $p(X)$.

2.3 Wrobel's minimal base revision operator

Wrobel has proposed a new specialization operator called the MBR (or minimal base revision) operator. We shall briefly outline this operator(and its supporting definitions) below. Note that we shall use $Cn(X)$ to denote the closure of X under logical consequence.

Definition 3 [10][Derivation] *Let Γ be a theory, and $f \in Cn(\Gamma)$ a query finitely refutable from Γ via resolution. The* derivation *of f in Γ, $\Delta(f, \Gamma)$ is the pair:*

$$\Delta(f, \Gamma) := (f, S)$$

where S, the set of supports *of f, is a set of triples of the form (C, σ, A) where C is a clause in Γ and $\exists g_1, g_2, \ldots g_n \in Cn(\Gamma)$ such that C resolves with $\{g_1, g_2, \ldots g_n\}$ using substitution σ to produce f. A, the set of* antecedents *of S, is recursively defined as follows:*

$$A := \{\Delta(g_1, \Gamma), \ldots, \Delta(g_n, \Gamma)\}$$

Definition 4 [10][Application set] *Let Γ be a theory and $f \in Cn(\Gamma)$. The* application set *of Γ with respect to f is defined as:*

$$\Pi(f, \Gamma) := \{(C, \sigma) \mid \exists S \equiv (C, \sigma, A) \text{ somewhere in } \Delta(f, \Gamma)\}$$

Definition 5 [10][Substitution set] *Let C be a clause in a theory Γ, with variables $vars(C) = \{X_1, \ldots, X_n\}$, let $f \in Cn(\Gamma)$ and $P \subseteq \Pi(f, \Gamma)$. A substitution σ_1 will be deemed to be* more general *than a substitution σ_2. $\sigma_1 \geq_g \sigma_2$ iff there is a substitution θ such that $\sigma_1\theta = \sigma_2$. Let $\Sigma_0(C, P) := \{\sigma \mid (C, \sigma) \in P\}$ denote all substitutions used with C in P. Then, the* substitution set *of C with respect to P is any set $\Sigma(C, P) \subseteq \Sigma_0(C, P)$ such that :*

- *for any $\sigma \in \Sigma_0(C, P)$, there is a a $\sigma' \in \Sigma(C, P)$ such that $\sigma' \geq_g \sigma$.*
- *for no $\sigma \in \Sigma(C, P)$, is there a $\sigma' \in \Sigma(C, P)$ such that $\sigma' \geq_g \sigma$.*

Definition 6 [10][Instance set] *For any non-ground clause C, the* instance set *of C with respect to P is defined as:*

$$I(C, P) := \{(X_1, \ldots, X_n)\sigma \mid \sigma \in \Sigma(C, P), vars(C) = \{X_1, \ldots, X_n\}, n \geq 1\}$$

Definition 7 [10][Corresponding theory] *Let Γ be a theory, $f \in Cn(\Gamma)$ and $P \subseteq \Pi(f, \Gamma)$. The set of clauses occurring in P is defined as:*

$$C(P) := \{C \mid (C, \sigma) \in P\}$$

Then, the theory corresponding to P *is defined as:*

$$\Gamma_\Pi(P) := (\Gamma - C(P)) \cup \{vars(C) \notin I(C, P) \diamond C \mid C \in C(P) \text{ and } C \text{ is non-ground}\} \cup \{C\sigma \mid (C, \sigma) \in P\}$$

Here, $L_0 \diamond C$ is shorthand for the addition of an additional premise L_0 to the body of a clause C. Thus, if C is $L_1, L_2, \ldots, L_n \to L_{n+1}$, then:

$$L_0 \diamond C := L_0, L_1, \ldots, L_n \to L_{n+1}$$

Definition 8 [10][Maximal application, minimal removal sets] *Let f be the assertion to be removed from theory Γ. The set of* maximal application sets *of Γ with respect to f is defined as:*

$\Gamma \downarrow_\Pi f := \Pi(f, \Gamma) \downarrow f := \{P \subseteq \Pi(f, \Gamma) \mid f \notin Cn(\Gamma_\Pi(P)) \text{ and for all } P', \text{ if } P \subset P' \subseteq \Pi(f, \Gamma), \text{ then } f \in Cn(\Gamma_\Pi(P'))\}$

The complement of $\Gamma \downarrow_\Pi f$ *is called the set of* minimal removal sets, *and is defined by:*

$\overline{\Gamma} \downarrow_\Pi f := \overline{\Pi}(f, \Gamma) \downarrow f := \{\Pi(f, \Gamma) - P \mid P \in \Gamma \downarrow_\Pi f\}$

Definition 9 [10][**Add set**] *For a clause* C *with variables* $vars(C) = \{X_1, \ldots, X_n\}$, $n \geq 1$, *in a theory* Γ, *with* f *to be removed and* $P \subseteq \Pi(f, \Gamma)$ *such that* $C \in C(P)$, *we define the* add set *to be:*

$add(C, f, P) := \{(X_1, \ldots, X_n) \notin I(C, P) \diamond C\} \cup \{(f \diamond C)\sigma \mid \sigma \in \Sigma(C, P)\}$

If $n = 0$, *i.e.,* C *is ground,* $\Sigma(C, P) = \{\emptyset\}$, *hence the add set is defined as:*

$add(C, f, P) := \{f \diamond C\}$

Definition 10 [10][**MBR operator**] *Let* f *be the assertion to be removed from theory* Γ. *Let* γ *be a selection function on* $\Gamma \downarrow_\Pi f$. *If* $P' := \gamma(\Gamma \downarrow_\Pi f)$ *denotes the chosen maximally correct application subset of* $\Pi(f, \Gamma)$, *and* $\overline{P} := \Pi(f, \Gamma) - P'$ *is its complement, we can define the* minimal base revision (MBR) *operator* $-'$ *as follows:*

$$\Gamma -' f := \begin{cases} \Gamma - C(\overline{P}) \cup \bigcup_{C \in C(\overline{P})} add(C, f, \overline{P}) & \text{if } f \in Cn(\Gamma) \\ \Gamma & \text{otherwise} \end{cases}$$

We shall now present some examples to illustrate Wrobel's MBR operator. We shall use the notation of the clausal form throughout, i.e., the universal quantifier will be assumed to be implicit.

Example 1. [10] *If* $\Gamma = \{p(a), p(X) \rightarrow q(X)\}$
then $\Gamma -' q(a) = \{p(a), (X) \notin \{(a)\} \wedge p(X) \rightarrow q(X), q(a) \wedge p(a) \rightarrow q(a)\} = \{p(a), (X) \notin \{(a)\} \wedge p(X) \rightarrow q(X)\}$ □

Example 2. [10] *Let* $\Gamma = \{p(X), p(X) \rightarrow q(X), q(X) \rightarrow r(X)\}$. *Then the two possible outcomes of* $\Gamma -' q(f(Y))$, *corresponding to the two choices available to the selection function* γ *are:*

$\{p(X), X \notin \{f(Y)\} \wedge p(X) \rightarrow q(X), q(f(Y)) \wedge p(f(Y)) \rightarrow q(f(Y)), q(X) \rightarrow r(X)\}$
and
$\{X \notin \{f(Y)\} \rightarrow p(X), q(f(Y)) \rightarrow p(f(Y)), p(X) \rightarrow q(X), q(X) \rightarrow r(X)\}$ □

Example 3. [10] *Let* $\Gamma = \{p(X), p(a) \wedge p(b) \rightarrow r(a)\}$. *Then, the two possible outcomes of* $\Gamma -' r(a)$, *corresponding to the two choices available to the selection function* γ *are:*

$$\{(X) \notin \{(a)\} \to p(X), r(a) \to p(a), p(a) \wedge p(b) \to r(a)\}$$
and
$$\{(X) \notin \{(b)\} \to p(X), r(a) \to p(b), p(a) \wedge p(b) \to r(a)\} \quad \Box$$

Wrobel shows that the MBR operator satisfies the first six of the AGM rationality postulates for contraction (the last two are ignored, presumably because they refer to contraction in the iterated case, while the focus of his work is on specialization as a single step operation), reformulated somewhat to reflect the fact that belief states are now non-closed first-order theories.

3 A default-based specialization operator

In this section, we shall define what might be treated as a lazy evaluation approach to provably minimal specialization in the spirit of Wrobel's MBR operator. In its most general form, our operator maps between default theories (in the sense of our definition in Section 2.2). The intuition is that every learned assertion in an incremental learning system is potentially defeasible; subsequent specialization steps may, in fact, bring parts of the hypothesized theory into question. We shall call our operator the *minimal specialization* operator.

Definition 11 [**Minimal specialization operator**] *The* minimal specialization operator $\sim$ *is defined as follows:*

$$(F, H, C) \sim f := (F, H, C \cup \{\neg f\})$$

if $\not\models f$. *If* $\models f$ *then* $(F, H, C) \sim f := (F, H, C)$.

In order to use this operator in the classical specialization setting, where one starts with a theory Γ and an assertion f to be retracted, we set up a default theory $(\emptyset, \Gamma, \emptyset)$. Thus we treat every assertion in the theory Γ as a hypothesis. As well, every universally quantified variable is treated as a free variable, and the resulting sentences are treated as sentence schemas. First, we note that the default theory $(\emptyset, \Gamma, \emptyset)$ generates a single extension which is logically equivalent to the original theory Γ.

Theorem 1 *If* Γ *is satisfiable,* $E((\emptyset, \Gamma, \emptyset)) = \{e\}$ *where* $e \equiv \Gamma$.

The following result establishes that the operator satisfies two essential requirements: first, that it succeed, and second, that it do so by making minimal perturbation to the theory.

Theorem 2 *Let* Γ *be a theory, and let* f *be an assertion to be retracted.*

Success: $e \not\models f$ *for every* $e \in E((\emptyset, \Gamma, \emptyset) \sim f)$.
Minimality: *For any* $e \subseteq Cn(\Gamma)$, *if* $e \in E((\emptyset, \Gamma, \emptyset) \sim f)$, *then there exists no* e' *such that* $e \subset e' \subseteq Cn(\Gamma)$ *and* $e' \not\models f$.

We can now establish that, starting with the default theory $(\emptyset, \Gamma, \emptyset)$, every extension of the default theory obtained as a result of applying the minimal specialization operator to retract the assertion f corresponds to a candidate outcome (modulo the application of the selection function) if Wrobel's MBR operator were to be applied to remove f from Γ. To understand the result below, note that Wrobel's definition of the MBR operator actually defines a class of operators, parameterized by the selection function γ. A specific choice of selection function γ gives us a specific MBR operator $-'_\gamma$.

Theorem 3 *If $e \in E((\emptyset, \Gamma, \emptyset))$, then there exists an MBR operator $-'_\gamma$ such that $e \equiv \Gamma -'_\gamma f$.*

The minimal specialization operator may be viewed as a lazy evaluation version of Wrobel's MBR operator. At each specialization step, an MBR operator generates all candidate outcomes, commits to one of these outcomes and moves on to the next step. The minimal specialization operator, on the other hand, returns a default theory such that the set of candidate outcomes of the MBR operator constitute the set of default extensions. The minimal specialization operator does not require any form of theory preference amongst the default extensions, i.e., commitment to a specific candidate outcome is not required. The operator does not even require that these candidate outcomes be explicitly generated; an intensional representation of the set of candidate outcomes in the form of a default theory is sufficient. Computation of outcomes is deferred until it becomes necessary.

The distinction between the two operators is less obvious over a single specialization step, but becomes more pronounced over iterated specialization steps. There are two major reasons which make the minimal specialization operator more appropriate for the iterated case than the MBR operator.

First, the MBR operator does not perform minimal perturbation to the theory in the iterated case, as the following example will illustrate.

Example 4. Consider Example 3 in the previous section. Assume that the application of an MBR operator selects the second of the two outcomes. Let the next step involve retraction of $p(a)$. An MBR operator would now generate a single candidate outcome:

$$\Gamma' = \{(X) \notin \{(a), (b)\} \to p(X), r(a) \to p(b), p(a) \land p(b) \to r(a)\}$$

However, this is not a minimal outcome. Note that $\Gamma' \not\models p(b)$ in addition to $p(a)$, where mere removal of $p(a)$ would have sufficed. In fact, the first of the two candidate outcomes in the retraction of $r(a)$:

$$\Gamma'' = \{(X) \notin \{(a)\} \to p(X), r(a) \to p(a), p(a) \land p(b) \to r(a)\}$$

represents the minimal outcome of retracting both $r(a)$ and $p(a)$ from Γ. The default theory obtained after successively specializing with $r(a)$ and $p(a)$ using the minimal specialization operator has a single extension which is equivalent to this outcome. $\square$

MBR operators return potentially non-minimal outcomes on account of the requirement that a choice be made immediately to select amongst the multiple candidate outcomes. Subsequent specialization steps may show that an earlier choice was a bad one, if one had the facility to reason retrospectively, but such a facility does not exist in Wrobel's framework, and choices once made cannot be undone. Thus, in the previous example, a choice of Γ' at the first specialization step results in both $p(a)$ and $p(b)$ being removed from the theory at the end of second specialization step. If, on the other hand, Γ''' had been chosen at the first step, no further change would have to be made for the second specialization step. Our minimal specialization operator does not force choice at every step, and is thus able to return minimal outcomes. It is possible to establish formally that the minimal specialization operator necessarily selects the minimal perturbation outcome in the case of iterated specialization.

Theorem 4 *If for any $e \subseteq Cn(\Gamma)$, $e \in E(((\emptyset, \Gamma, \emptyset) \sim f) \sim f')$, then there exists no e' such that $e \subset e' \subseteq Cn(\Gamma)$ and $e' \not\models f \vee f'$.*

The second reason for preferring the minimal specialization operator for iterated specialization is the ability to generate outcomes in a rational manner in the face of dynamic selection criteria. In most practical situations, selection criteria are determined by the context. Contexts change - what might have been a good choice in one context may turn out to be a bad one in another. The MBR operator is ill-equipped to handle dynamic selection criteria. Consider, for instance, a scenario where the selection function is based on the relative priorities between sentences in the theory (i.e., a candidate outcome is selected if it retains sentences of higher priority). ¿From a set of candidate outcomes $\{A, B\}$, let an MBR operator select outcome A on account of the fact that $x \in A - B, y \in B - A$ and $x > y$ (i.e., x takes priority over y). Now, if the next step involves further specializing the theory and the context changes in the meantime so that $y > x$, then an MBR operator would still proceed from the premise that the operative theory is outcome B. MBR operators thus lack the ability to revise previous choices in the light of changed selection criteria driven by context shifts. The minimal specialization operator avoids this problem by deferring choice until it becomes essential.

A crucial question to ask is: when does choice become essential ? In its most general form, our model visualizes specialization as a mapping between default theories. Even when we start with a classical theory, we construct a default theory based on it and obtain a default theory as a result of the specialization process. The process iterates in a straightforward manner. If the next input is a negative example x and there exists an extension e of the current default theory such that $e \models \neg x$, then we need to specialize again. Our model applies well to sequences of consecutive specialization steps. At each step, the assertion to be retracted is added to the set of constraints and no choice is made from amongst the multiple possible default extensions. A choice becomes necessary, however, when a generalization operation must be performed. Intuitively, given a default theory Δ, a generalization step is required if the input is a positive example x

and there exists $e \in E(\Delta)$ such that $e \not\models x$. In a generalization step, one of the multiple possible extensions of the default theory must be selected and a generalization operation must be performed on it. If the next step also involves generalization, we trivially take the outcome of the previous generalization step as the base theory on which the generalization operator is applied. If, on the other hand, the next step involves specialization, we set up a default theory $(\emptyset, \Gamma, \emptyset)$ as before (here Γ is the outcome of the previous generalization step) and apply the minimal specialization operator. Notice that when a choice is forced in a generalization step, all the problems associated with Wrobel's operator return. The advantages of lazy evaluation only accrue in the case of sequences of consecutive specializations.

In the preceding account of incremental learning, our focus has been the traditional one, namely mappings between classical theories. We have used default theories to represent, in an intensional form, the multiple outcomes of the specialization process in order to delay choice for as long as possible. An alternative is to shift the primary focus to the problem of learning default theories. We shall consider this in detail in the next section. We shall see that this approach allows us to better capitalize on the advantages of lazy evaluation and deferred choice that we have discussed earlier.

Our final task in this section is to establish the correctness of the minimal specialization operator with respect to the AGM postulates for contraction. However, unlike Wrobel, we cannot apply the AGM conditions in a straightforward way. This is because the AGM postulates concern mappings between classical theories. Our task, on the other hand, is to establish the properties of a mapping between default theories, or, equivalently, between sets of theories (if one were to treat a default theory as its set of extensions). We therefore reformulate the AGM postulates in order to account for the shift in the representation scheme, while still retaining their intent. Informally, the reformulation looks like this: for every assertion of the form $K \subseteq K'$, we use an assertion of the form *for every extension $e \in \Delta$, there exists an extension $e' \in \Delta'$ such that $e \subseteq e'$ (where Δ plays the role of K and Δ' that of K').*

Theorem 5 *For any default theory Δ and sentences A and B:*

1. *$\forall e' \in E(\Delta \sim A)$, there exists some $e \in E(\Delta)$ s.t. $e' \subseteq e$.*
2. *If $\forall e : (e \in E(\Delta)) \rightarrow (e \not\models A)$, then $E(\Delta \sim A) = E(\Delta)$.*
3. *If $\not\models A$, then $\forall e : (e \in E(\Delta \sim A) \rightarrow (e \not\models A)$.*
4. *If $\forall e : (e \in E(\Delta)) \rightarrow (e \models A)$ then for every $e \in E((W, D))$, there exists some $e' \in E(\Delta \sim A)$ s.t. $e \subseteq e' \cup \{A\}$.*
5. *If $\models A \leftrightarrow B$ then $E(\Delta \sim A) = E(\Delta \sim B)$.*
6. *If $\forall e : (e \in E(\Delta \sim A \wedge B)) \rightarrow (e \not\models A)$ then $E(\Delta \sim A \wedge B) = E(\Delta \sim A)$.*

We ignore the first AGM postulate here, since it only requires that the belief state be represented in the same language before and after a belief change step. This is trivially true with the minimal specialization operator. Result 3 above is a restatement of our earlier success result; we have included it here only to make a complete statement of an AGM-like result. Result 7 above is a stronger result than the last two AGM postulates for contraction. Taken together, these results establish that the minimal specialization operator achieves minimal change in the sense of the AGM postulates as well.

4 Learning default theories: Semantics

Given the ubiquity of knowledge bases that rely on some form of nonmonotonic inference, learning nonmonotonic theories can be potentially very useful. We have also seen in the previous section that using nonmonotonic theories to represent the candidate outcomes of specialization can provide us with significant advantages in terms of lazy evaluation and deferred choice. In this section, we shall establish formally what it means to learn nonmonotonic theories. We shall then use this as the basis for a semantics for learning default theories.

As with semantic settings for ILP, we start with a background theory, a set of positive example E^+ and a set of negative examples E_-. In our case, the background theory Θ_B is a theory in any nonmonotonic reasoning formalism. We assume that we learn a theory Θ_I in the same nonmonotonic representation language as Θ_B. We shall assume that the nonmonotonic reasoning formalism supports two notions of nonmonotonic consequence: *weak* and *strong*. We shall represent these two entailment operators by $\mid\sim_{weak}$ and $\mid\sim_{strong}$ respectively. It is well-recognized that nonmonotonic inference typically gives rise to multiple, possibly mutually incompatible views of the world. The $\mid\sim_{weak}$ operator captures the notion of credulous inference; if an assertion is true in at least one of the multiple possible views of the world, then it is entailed by the $\mid\sim_{weak}$ operator. The $\mid\sim_{strong}$ operator captures the notion of sceptical inference; if an assertion is true in every one of the multiple possible views of the world, then it is entailed by the $\mid\sim_{strong}$ operator.

Definition 12 [NM-Learn Semantics]

Prior satisfiability: $\Theta_B \not\mid\sim_{weak} \neg e$ *for any* $e \in E^-$.
Prior necessity: $\Theta_B \not\mid\sim_{strong} E^+$.
Posterior satisfiability: $\Theta_I \not\mid\sim_{weak} \neg e$ *for any* $e \in E^-$.
Posterior sufficiency: $\Theta_I \mid\sim_{strong} E^+$.

We shall use these semantics to define the setting for learning default theories. As with the setting for general nonmonotonic theories, we shall start with a background default theory Δ_B and induce a default theory Δ_I using a set of positive examples E^+ and a set of negative examples E^-.

Definition 13 [Def-Learn Semantics]

Prior satisfiability: $\forall e : e \in E(\Delta_B), e \wedge E^-$ *is satisfiable.*
Prior necessity: $\exists e : e \in E(\Delta_B), e \not\models E^+$.
Posterior satisfiability: $\forall e : e \in E(\Delta_I), e \wedge E^-$ *is satisfiable.*
Posterior sufficiency: $\forall e : e \in E(\Delta_I), e \models E^+$.

5 An incremental learning algorithm for default theories

A somewhat surprising result of this research is that a simple incremental learning algorithm for default theories exists, following the semantics defined in the previous section. We shall present this algorithm in this section. The algorithm relies on a generalization procedure $Gen(Back, Init, Ex)$ which uses the background theory $Back$ and example Ex to generalize the initial theory $Init$, and returns a theory $Final$ such that $Back \wedge Final \models Ex$. Note that $Back$, $Init$ and $Final$ are not default theories, but classical ones. A wide variety of approaches to generalization in the ILP literature could be used for this purpose. The algorithm also relies on a selection function γ which takes a set of theories and returns a single preferred one. The algorithm uses the $\sim$ operator defined earlier.

Algorithm 1 [Def-Learn]
INPUT:

1. A default theory $\Delta_{init} = (F_{init}, H_{init}, C_{init})$.
2. An input example IN which may be a positive example x^+ or a negative example x^-.

OUTPUT: A default theory $\Delta_{final} = (F_{final}, H_{final}, C_{final})$.

if $IN = x^+$ then
   if $C_{init} \models \neg x^+$ then
      $C_{final} := \gamma(C_{init} \sim x^+)$
   $H_{inter} := H_{init}$
   do for all $e \in E(\Delta_{init})$
      if $e \not\models x^+$ then $H_{inter} := H_{inter} \cup Gen(F_{init}, e, x^+)$
   $\Delta_{final} := (F_{final}, H_{inter}, C_{final})$
elseif $IN = x^-$ then
   if $\exists e : (e \in E(\Delta_{init})) \wedge (e \models x^-)$ then
      $\Delta_{final} = (F_{final}, H_{final}, C_{init} \cup \{x^-\})$

A brief explanation of this algorithm is as follows. If the input is a positive example x^+, we first check if the current set of constraints block the derivation of x^+. If this is the case, we specialize using the $\sim$ operator. Then, for every extension of the current default theory which does not imply x^+, we generalize the extension with the Gen procedure using the initial set of facts as the background theory so that the resulting theory, together with the set of facts, implies x^+. We add the resulting theory to the set of defaults. When all possible extensions have been processed in this fashion, we have a guarantee that every extension of the resulting default theory has x^+ as a consequence. If the input example is negative, we take an approach that is closely related to the $\sim$ operator. We augment the set of constraints to include the negative example, thereby preventing inconsistency with the negative example in any of the extensions.

Notice that a choice is required in this procedure only when the set of constraints is specialized to prevent it from blocking the derivation of a positive example. Otherwise, no choice is required, and all the benefits of lazy evaluation and deferred choice discussed in the previous section accrue. Notice also that set of facts remains unchanged throughout the process. Whatever is learned via generalization is treated as potentially defeasible and hence added to the set of hypotheses.

The following result formally establishes that the procedure *Def-Learn* is sound with respect to the semantics presented in the previous section.

Theorem 6 *Procedure* Def-Learn *satisfies conditions* **posterior satisfiability** *and* **posterior sufficiency** *of* **Def-Learn Semantics**.

It is also possible to show, in a manner similar to the results on the $\sim$ operator, that specialization operations performed by procedure *Def-Learn* satisfy reformulated versions of the AGM postulates for contraction. We ommit these results here for brevity.

6 Conclusions

This paper contributes to the state-of-the-art in two major ways. First, it improves on Wrobel's work on provably minimal specializations by presenting an operator which is provably minimal even in the case of iterated sequences of specializations. The operator also benefits from the advantages of lazy evaluation and deferred choice. Second, it provides a semantic basis for inducing default theories and presents an incremental learning algorithm which is sound with respect to these semantics. The only other approach to learning default theories that we are aware of is that of Dimopoulos and Kakas [3]. Our work differs significantly from their's because our setting is incremental while their's is not. The underlying default logic in their work also differs significantly from ours. We believe that our work will provide the starting point for implemented systems that learn default theories and thence, fielded practical applications.

References

1. Carlos E. Alchourrón, Peter Gärdenfors, and David Makinson. On the logic of theory change: partial meet contraction and revision functions. *Journal of Symbolic Logic*, 50:510–530, 1985.
2. J. P. Delgrande, T. Schaub, and W. K. Jackson. Alternative approaches to default logic. *Artificial Intelligence*, 70(1-2), 1994.
3. Yannis Dimopooulos and Antonis Kakas. Learning non-monotonic logic programs: Learning exceptions. In *Proc. of ECML-95*, pages 122–137, 1995.
4. Peter Gärdenfors. *Knowledge in Flux: Modeling the Dynamics of Epistemic States.* MIT Press, Cambridge, MA, 1988.
5. Peter Gärdenfors and David Makinson. Revisions of knowledge systems using epistemic entrenchment. In *Proc. of the Second Conference on Theoretical Aspects of Reasoning about Knowledge*, pages 83–95, 1988.

6. W. L. Harper. Rational belief change, popper functions and counterfactuals. *Synthese*, (30):221–262, 1975.

7. David Poole. A logical framework for default reasoning. *Artificial Intelligence*, 36:27–47, 1988.

8. David Poole, Randy Goebel, and Romas Aleliunas. Theorist: a logical reasoning system for defaults and diagnosis. In N.J. Cercone and G. McCalla, editors, *The Knowledge Frontier: Essays in the Representation of Knowledge*, pages 331–352. Springer Verlag, 1987.

9. Raymond Reiter. A logic for default reasoning. *Artificial Intelligence*, 13(1 and 2):81–132, 1980.

10. Stefan Wrobel. On the proper definition of minimality in specialization and theory revision. In *Proc. of ECML-93*, pages 65–82, 1993.

Learning Stable Concepts in a Changing World

Michael Harries[1]* and Kim Horn[2]

[1] Department of Artificial Intelligence
School of Computer Science and Engineering
University of NSW, Australia
mbh@cse.unsw.edu.au
[2] Predictive Strategies Unit
Australian Gilt Securities Limited
Australia
kim@ags.com.au

Abstract. Concept drift due to hidden changes in context complicates learning in many domains including financial prediction, medical diagnosis, and network performance. Existing machine learning approaches to this problem use an incremental learning, on-line paradigm. Batch, off-line learners tend to be ineffective in domains with hidden changes in context as they assume that the training set is homogeneous.

We present an off-line method for identifying hidden context. This method uses an existing batch learner to identify likely context boundaries then performs a form of clustering called *contextual* clustering. The resulting data sets can then be used to produce context specific, locally stable concepts. The method is evaluated in a simple domain with hidden changes in context.

1 Introduction

Prediction in real world domains is complicated by potentially unstable underlying phenomena. In the financial domain, for example, market behaviour can change dramatically with changes in contract prices, interest rates, inflation rates, budget announcements, and political and world events. This *concept drift* is due to changes in context, and is often directly reflected by one or more attributes. When changes in context are not reflected by any attribute they can be said to be hidden. Hidden changes in context cause problems for any predictive approach that assumes concept stability.

The most common approach to learning in domains with hidden changes in context is to generalise from a window that moves over recently past instances and use the learnt concepts for prediction only in the immediate future. Such an approach was initially suggested in [5]. Examples of this approach include [13], [6], [4], and an adaptation in [9]. In domains of this nature, quick adaption to new contexts is the primary requirement for learning systems. The Flora family of algorithms [13] directly address fast adaptation to new, previously unseen,

---

* Michael Harries was supported by an Australian Postgraduate Award (Industrial).

contexts by dynamically adjusting the window size in response to changes in accuracy and concept complexity.

There are a large number of domains in which context can be expected to repeat. In these domains, it would be valuable to store existing knowledge about past contexts for re-use. Flora 3 [12] addresses domains in which contexts recur, and does so as a secondary consideration to the adaptive learner. This is achieved by storing and retrieving concepts that appear stable as the learner traverses the series.

An alternative to the windowing approach is to examine the data *en masse* and attempt to directly identify concepts associated with stable, hidden contexts.

In this paper we present Splice, a meta-learning system that implements such an approach. The Splice algorithm has three stages:

1. Use an existing batch machine learner to identify possible changes in context as partitions on the time attribute.
2. Refine the identified changes in context by clustering the intervals according to apparent similarity of context. We call this *contextual* clustering.
3. Use the clustered, context specific data sets to learn stable concepts. These concepts are referred to as *local* concepts and together form a description of the whole domain, known as a *global* concept.

Splice is evaluated on a simple domain drawn from the literature using C4.5 [8] as the underlying batch learner. We use this domain and learning system only to demonstrate that the method is viable. The approach is applicable to more complex domains and other learning paradigms such as ILP.

1.1 Representing Time

In the domains we are examining in this paper time plays an important role. Time allows us to differentiate between different contexts when the changes in context are hidden. Windowing and other existing approaches to these domains do not explicitly represent time as an attribute. The reason for this exclusion is that using time as an attribute causes problems for prediction. For example, an attempt to build a system to predict political parties from past data, may induce the following decision tree.

```
Country = America
    Year < 1992:  Government = Republican
    Year >= 1992:
        Public Wants Change = yes: Government = Democrat
        Public Wants Change = no:  Government = Unknown
```

This decision tree is of limited use in predicting future governments as all future values of year must be greater than 1992. Hence, if such a tree were used directly for prediction, only the post 1992 fragment of the tree would be used.[1]

---

[1] Such a tree could be used directly for prediction in an iterative sense. This approach has the advantage that no window size need be set or adjusted as the tree incorporates segmentation on time. It is also, unfortunately, susceptible to very small contexts being incorrectly identified at the most recent interval of time.

Such a decision tree is, however, useful for understanding the past and implies that time is important in delineating two contexts, pre 1992 and post 1992. The post 1992 section of the tree contains a local, or context specific, concept in which the importance of 'Public Wants Change' is evident.

1.2 Identifying Context Change

Despite the problems introduced by using time in predictive problems, the decision tree in the example above does contains useful information about changes in context. The ability of decision trees to capture context is associated with the fact that decision tree algorithms use a form of context-sensitive feature selection (CSFS) [2]. A number of machine learning algorithms can be regarded as using CSFS including decision tree algorithms [8], rule induction algorithms [1] and ILP systems [7]. All of these systems produce concepts containing information about context.

The problem faced in domains with hidden changes in context is that the context is not explicitly available. Context is, however, often reflected as contiguous intervals of some attribute, in this case it is time. When time has this property, we call it the *environmental* attribute.[2]

Given an *environmental* attribute, we can utilise a CSFS machine learning algorithm to gain information on hidden changes in context.[3] In order to represent hidden changes in context as partitions on the environmental attribute, we restrict the machine learning algorithm to one that is able to provide splits on that attribute.

The likelihood of such a system correctly identifying partitions on the environmental attribute will be a function of, at least, context duration, the number of different contexts, the complexity of each local concept, and noise.

The partitions initially identified can be expected to contain errors of two types:

- Noise or serial correlation errors. These would take the form of random splits on time.
- Errors due to repetition of tests on time in different parts of the concept. These would take the form of a group of values clustered around the actual point where the context changed.

The initial partitioning of time into stable intervals can be refined by contextual clustering. This process combines similar intervals of the dataset, where the similarity of two intervals is based upon the degree to which a partial model is accurate on both intervals.

---

[2] The *environmental* attribute could be any ordinal attribute over which instances of a hidden context are liable to be contiguous. There is also no restriction, in principle, of the environmental attribute to one dimension. Some alternative environmental attributes are one or more dimensions of space, and space-time combinations.

[3] Windowing approaches also assume that hidden context is liable to be contiguous in time. This assumption is made implicitly and is necessary as a window is useful only if its instances are primarily from a single context.

1.3 Incremental 'vs' Batch Approaches

Machine learning techniques can be broadly categorised as either batch or incremental. Batch systems learn by examining a large collection of instances en masse and forming a single concept. Incremental systems evolve and change a classification scheme as new observations are processed [10]. The window based systems, described above, could all be described as incremental in approach.

In many situations, there is no constraint to learn incrementally. For example, many organisations maintain large data bases of historical data that are prime targets for data mining. These data bases may hold instances that belong to a number of contexts but do not have this context explicitly recorded. Many of these data bases may incorporate time as an essential attribute, for example, financial records and stock market price data. Interest in mining datasets of this nature suggest the need for systems that can learn global concepts and are sensitive to a changing and hidden context.

The likely advantages of employing this method on domains with hidden changes in context are:

- A global concept can be learnt that partitions the data based on context rather than on an arbitrary window of most recent cases.
- After producing a set of local concepts and associated contexts, it should be possible to identify repeating contexts and to reason about expected context duration and sequence.
- Local concepts can be verified by experts.
- Some form of cross-validation over time can be applied for local concept verification.
- Local concepts can be used for prediction.

2 Splice

Splice uses time as an environmental attribute to learn a set of local concepts. Local concepts identified by Splice can be used both for understanding the target domain and for prediction.

Splice is a meta-level algorithm that incorporates an existing batch learner. In this study we employed C4.5 [8], with no modifications, as the underlying learning system. The underlying learner for Splice could, in principle, be replaced by any other CSFS machine learner that can provide explicit splits on time. As we expect the underlying learner to deal with noise, Splice does not have (or need) a mechanism to deal with noise directly.

The Splice algorithm is detailed in Figure 1. It consists of three stages:

1. Partition Dataset
2. Perform Contextual Clustering
3. Learn Local Concepts

We examine each of these in turn.

Input required:

  – Data set with an environmental attribute
  – Threshold accuracy parameter θ with a possible range of 0 to 100

Algorithm:

  – Stage 1: Partition Dataset
     • Use batch learner to classify the initial data set and produce an initial concept.
     • Extract tests on the time identified in the initial concept.
     • Tests on time are used to partition the dataset into *intervals*.
     • Tests on time also used to partition the initial concept into *partial* concepts. Partial concepts are fragments of the the initial concept associated with a particular interval of time.
  – Stage 2: Perform Contextual Clustering
     • Evaluate the accuracy of each *partial* concept on each *interval* of data.
     • Rate each *partial* concept by coverage of the data set. Coverage is the total number of examples in *intervals* classified by the *partial* concept at better than the threshold accuracy θ.
     • Create an ordered set X of partial concepts.
     • While X is not empty:
        * Select best partial concept from X.
        * Create a new cluster from covered *intervals*.
        * For all *intervals* used in the cluster, remove the associated *partial* concept from X.
  – Stage 3: Learn Local Concepts
     • Apply the batch learner to each contextual cluster in order to learn a new local concept. Context is delineated in time by the boundaries of the cluster.

The Splice output consists of all local concepts produced.

Fig. 1. The Splice Algorithm

2.1   Partition Dataset

Splice first uses the underlying batch learner to build an initial concept from the whole data set. As C4.5 as the underlying learner, the initial concept is a decision tree. By learning a concept description of the whole domain including time, we can expect to identify the significant tests on time. Each test on time provides a split, identifying a possible change in context. The splits on time are extracted from the initial concept and used to define both *intervals* of the dataset and *partial* concepts.

2.2 Perform Contextual Clustering

In this stage, we attempt to cluster the *intervals* identified above.

Splice determines the accuracy of each partial concept by classifying the individuals in each *interval*. This process is simplified by shifting each *interval* into the relevant time values for each partial concept. This allows us to re-use the initial concept. We may need, for instance, to classify an *interval* with time values from i to j using a candidate concept defined by a partition of time from k to l in the initial concept. This is achieved by replacing the time value for each instance of the *interval* with the time k.[4] The *interval* is then classified using the initial concept. This substitution is repeated for each combination of *partial* concept and *interval*. The error rate is recorded in a Local Accuracy Matrix.

A *partial* concept is considered to cover an *interval* of the data set if the error rate (as a percentage) when classifying that *interval* is less than the accuracy threshold parameter θ. The default setting for θ is 10%. We expect that adjusting this parameter will be useful in different domains. Each *partial* concept is rated in terms of data set coverage. This is the number of instances in all the *intervals* of the data set that it covers. An ordered set X of *partial* concepts is created.

The actual clustering procedure proceeds as follows. The best *partial* concept is selected from the set X. All the *intervals* that it covers are used to form a new cluster. The *partial* concepts associated with the *intervals* used are removed from the set X. This step is then repeated with the next best candidate concept until set X is empty.

The contextual clustering step could conceivably be replaced by an algorithm that directly post-processed the initial C4.5 tree. Preliminary investigations into such an algorithm suggest that it could be viable in an environment with simple concepts and low noise, but is likely to fail with more complex and noisy environments. The Splice contextual clustering algorithm was designed to identify and combine similar intervals of the data set under a broad range of conditions including those of substantial noise and complex concepts.

2.3 Learn Local Concepts

The underlying learner, C4.5, is used to learn a *local* concept from each contextual cluster from the previous stage. It is important to note that at this stage the environmental attribute, time, is not included in the attribute set.

Splice is able to exploit recurring contexts by building larger combined data sets. Using larger combined data sets can improve the quality of the local concepts produced by C4.5.

---

[4] The value used in replacing time values in the *interval* could be any in the partition defining the partial concept, in this case it could be any value from k to l.

3   Experimental Results

The following experiments were primarily designed to demonstrate the viability of the Splice approach. The first experiment applies Splice to a single dataset with recurring contexts. It serves to both confirm that Splice will work on domains with recurrent concepts and as an illustration of the execution of Splice. The second experiment compares the classification accuracy of Splice and C4.5 in a domain with hidden changes in context. The third experiment investigates the effect of noise and training duration on Splice's ability to correctly report target local concepts.

3.1   Data Sets

The data sets used in the following experiments are based on those used in Stagger [10] and subsequently used by [13]. While our approach and underlying philosophy are substantially different, this allows some comparison of results.

The domain chosen is artificial and a program was used to generate the data. This program allows us to control recurrence of contexts and other factors such as noise[5] and duration. The domain has four attributes, time, size, colour and shape. Time is treated as a continuous attribute. Size has three possible values: small, medium and large. Colour has three possible values: red, green and blue. Shape also has three possible values: circular, triangular, and square.

The program randomly generates a series of examples from the above attribute space. Each example is given a unique time stamp and classified according to the currently active target concept. In this study, we employed three simple target concepts:

1. (size = small) ∧ (colour = red)
2. (colour = green) ∨ (shape = circular)
3. (size = medium) ∨ (size = large)

Artificial contexts were defined by changing the currently active target concepts at predetermined intervals. In this study, the intervals were over a count of cases generated by the program.

3.2   Experiment 1 - Applying Splice to Temporal data

This experiment applies Splice to a dataset with recurring concepts. It serves both to confirm that Splice is able to extract target local concepts from a dataset with recurring concepts and as an illustration of the execution of Splice[6].

---

[5] In the following experiments, $n\%$ noise implies that the class was randomly selected with a probability of $n\%$. This method for generating noise was chosen to be consistent with [13].

[6] In all experiments reported Splice was run with the threshold accuracy parameter θ set to a default of 10%. The underlying learner, C4.5, was run with default pruning parameters and with subsetting.

The training set consists of concepts (1) for 40 instances, (2) for 40 instances, (3) for 40 instances, and repeating (1) for 40 instances, (2) for 40 instances, and (3) for 40 instances. No noise was applied to the data set.

Results. The sequence followed by Splice in learning local concepts from the data set described above is illustrated in Figure 2, Table 1 and Figure 3. Figure 2 contains the initial concept built by C4.5 over the entire data set. Table 1 shows the Local Accuracy Matrix built in stage 2 of the algorithm. Figure 3 shows the local concepts learnt from this particular data set.

```
Size = small:
|   Time > 188 : no (22.0/1.3)
|   Time <= 188 :
|   |   Colour = blue: no (19.0/2.5)
|   |   Colour = red:
|   |   |   Time <= 52 : yes (9.0/1.3)
|   |   |   Time > 52 :
|   |   |   |   Time <= 126 : no (8.0/1.3)
|   |   |   |   Time > 126 : yes (4.0/2.2)
|   |   Colour = green:
|   |   |   Time > 159 : yes (6.0/1.2)
|   |   |   Time <= 159 :
|   |   |   |   Shape = square: no (3.0/1.1)
|   |   |   |   Shape in {circular,triangular}:
|   |   |   |   |   Time > 91 : no (7.0/1.3)
|   |   |   |   |   Time <= 91 :
|   |   |   |   |   |   Time <= 38 : no (5.0/1.2)
|   |   |   |   |   |   Time > 38 : yes (4.0/1.2)
Size in {medium,large}:
|   Time <= 39 : no (21.0/1.3)
|   Time > 39 :
|   |   Time > 202 : yes (20.0/1.3)
|   |   Time <= 202 :
|   |   |   Time <= 119 :
|   |   |   |   Colour = green: yes (26.0/1.3)
|   |   |   |   Colour in {red,blue}:
|   |   |   |   |   Time > 77 : yes (19.0/1.3)
|   |   |   |   |   Time <= 77 :
|   |   |   |   |   |   Shape in {square,triangular}: no (10.0/1.3)
|   |   |   |   |   |   Shape = circular: yes (3.0/1.1)
|   |   |   Time > 119 :
|   |   |   |   Time <= 158 : no (27.0/1.4)
|   |   |   |   Time > 158 :
|   |   |   |   |   Colour = green: yes (11.0/1.3)
|   |   |   |   |   Colour in {red,blue}:
|   |   |   |   |   |   Shape in {square,triangular}: no (13.0/1.3)
|   |   |   |   |   |   Shape = circular: yes (3.0/1.1)
```

Fig. 2. C4.5 decision tree (using time)

Table 1. Local Accuracy Matrix: Partial concept error on individual data sets (%).

Data set	Range	Partial concepts											
		0	1	2	3	4	5	6	7	8	9	10	11
0	0-38	0	13	44	65	88	75	21	0	31	47	52	75
1	39-39	0	0	0	100	100	100	100	0	0	0	100	100
2	40-52	70	54	8	8	39	54	70	70	24	8	24	54
3	53-77	68	64	12	0	24	28	56	68	16	12	4	28
4	78-91	86	79	58	43	0	8	72	86	65	72	50	8
5	92-119	83	90	43	33	8	0	72	83	36	43	25	0
6	120-126	0	15	58	58	100	86	0	0	43	58	43	86
7	127-158	0	13	41	47	85	72	7	0	29	41	35	72
8	159-159	0	0	0	0	0	0	0	0	0	0	0	0
9	160-188	59	45	11	11	38	52	59	59	25	4	25	52
10	189-202	58	58	29	0	36	36	29	58	29	29	0	36
11	203-239	71	84	55	38	14	0	55	71	41	57	25	0

The initial concept decision tree in Figure 2, as generated by C4.5, is not succinct nor is it easy to interpret. If applied directly to the prediction of future instances, only a small fragment of the tree would be used.

The decision tree contains a substantial amount of information on past contexts. Splits identified on time in the initial concept are used to define both partial concepts and *intervals* of the data set. Each partial concept is evaluated on all *intervals* of the data set. The results of this evaluation form the Local Accuracy Matrix (LAM), Table 1. It should be noted that some of the ranges shown in the LAM are due to spurious splits on time in the initial concept.

The LAM is used as input for the contextual clustering operation. As shown in Figure 3, the contextual clusters are then used to produce local concepts. For the first two local concepts generated, Splice was able to successfully identify and combine all non-contiguous intervals of the same context. The results for this run were that all target concepts were successfully identified and that one additional incorrect local concept was identified.

The twin tasks for Splice are to correctly identify target concepts and minimise the number of incorrectly identified concepts. On the same task, Splice correctly identified concept one 97 times out of 100 trials, concept two 96 times out of 100 trials, and concept three 100 times out of 100 trials. Splice also identified, on average, 0.8 incorrect or spurious concepts per trial. We anticipate that a substantial proportion of these spurious concepts could be identified by restricting contextual clustering to a minimum required coverage and a maximum permitted fragmentation. This has not yet been investigated. In the case presented, neither of these strategies would have been effective.

Although spurious local concepts are not desirable, their effect is minimal in prediction tasks. When local concepts are used for prediction, a secondary system must be used to select the currently active local concept for use in prediction

```
Current best partial concept is 0 with 80 data items covered
        context 0     0-38
        context 1     39-39
        context 6     120-126
        context 7     127-158
        context 8     159-159
Local concept learnt:
        Colour in {green,blue}: no (52.0)
        Colour = red:
        |    Size = small: yes (11.0)
        |    Size in {medium,large}: no (17.0)
**** equals target concept 1: (size = small) & (colour = red)


Current best partial concept is 5 with 80 data items covered
        context 4     78-91
        context 5     92-119
        context 8     159-159
        context 11    203-239
Local concept learnt:
        Size = small: no (31.0/1.0)
        Size in {medium,large}: yes (49.0)
**** equals target concept 3: (size = medium) | (size = large)


Current best partial concept is 3 with 53 data items covered
        context 2     40-52
        context 3     53-77
        context 8     159-159
        context 10    189-202
Local concept learnt:
        Colour = green: yes (22.0)
        Colour in {red,blue}:
        |    Shape in {square,triangular}: no (24.0)
        |    Shape = circular:
        |    |    Size = small: no (3.0/1.0)
        |    |    Size in {medium,large}: yes (4.0)
**** close to target concept 2 but not correct


Current best partial concept is 9 with 44 data items covered
        context 1     39-39
        context 2     40-52
        context 8     159-159
        context 9     160-188
Local concept learnt:
        Colour = green: yes (20.0)
        Colour in {red,blue}:
        |    Shape in {square,triangular}: no (17.0/1.0)
        |    Shape = circular: yes (7.0/1.0)
**** equals target concept 2: (colour = green) | (shape = circular)
```

Fig. 3. Annotated extract from splice log

of the next item[7]. The task of selecting the correct local concept from a set of local concepts valid in different contexts is not altered by that set containing a concept that is not valid in any context[8]. Hence, if the secondary system is competent in selecting the current concept with no spurious concepts, it should be able to avoid selecting spurious concepts in most cases.

This experiment demonstrates that Splice can be used to improve our understanding of the domain and to generate succinct and accurate local concepts.

3.3 Experiment 2 - Direct Comparison with C4.5

This experiment compares the accuracy of Splice to C4.5 when trained on a data set containing hidden context shifts. After training, the resulting concepts are fixed and used for prediction on a similar data set. C4.5 is employed to provide a baseline performance for this task and was trained without the attribute time. This comparison is not altogether fair on C4.5, as it was not designed for use in domains with hidden changes in context.

The training set consists of concepts (1) for 50 instances, (2) for 50 instances, and (3) for 50 instances. The test set consists of concepts (1) for 50 instances, (2) for 50 instances, (3) for 50 instances, and repeated (1) for 50 instances, (2) for 50 instances, and (3) for 50 instances.

To apply the local concepts identified by Splice for prediction purposes, it was necessary to devise a method for selecting relevant local concepts. This is not a trivial problem, hence, for the purposes of this experiment we chose a simple method. The classification accuracy of each local concept over the last five examples was recorded. The most accurate concept was used in predicting the class of the next example. Any ties in accuracy were solved by randomly selecting between local concepts. The first case was classified by randomly selecting a local concept. Future work will investigate alternate local concept selection methods.

The results, presented below, show the average classification success rates at several levels of noise for both Splice and C4.5 over 100 randomly generated training and test sets. For this experiment, noise was only generated in the training set.

Results. Figure 4 shows that Splice successfully identified the local concepts from the training set and that the correct local concept can be successfully selected for prediction purposes in better than 95% of cases. The extreme dips in accuracy when contexts change are an effect of the local concept selection method. C4.5 seems to do relatively well on concept 2 with an accuracy of approximately 70%. C4.5 on concepts 1 and 3 correctly classifies between 50% and 60% of cases.

---

[7] See experiment 2.

[8] With the exception of possible effects due to the number of concepts from which to select.

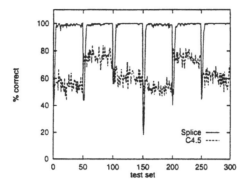

Fig. 4. C4.5 comparison, trained with no noise

Figures 5,6 and 7 show a gradual decline in the classification accuracy achieved by Splice as noise increases. At 30% noise, the worst result achieved by Splice is an 85% classification accuracy on concept 2. C4.5 on the other hand is still classifying with approximately the same accuracy as it achieved in figure 4. C4.5 predictive stability over a range of noise of between 0 and 30% is testament to its stability in adverse situations.

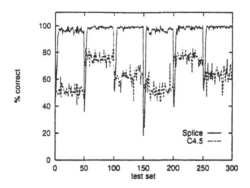

Fig. 5. C4.5 comparison, trained with 10% noise

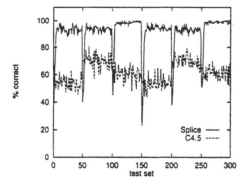

Fig. 6. C4.5 comparison, trained with 20% noise

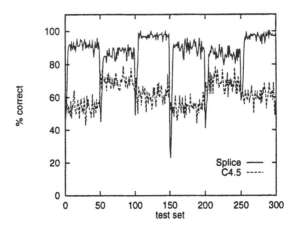

Fig. 7. C4.5 comparison, trained with 30% noise

3.4 Experiment 3 - The Effects of Noise and Duration

This experiment investigates the performance of Splice under varying levels of noise and duration. Splice was first trained on a randomly generated training set containing examples of each of the Stagger concepts. The set of local concepts learnt by Splice were then assessed for correctness against each target concept. The results show the proportion of correct local concept identifications achieved, and the average number of incorrect local concepts identified.

Training sets were generated using a range of concept duration and noise. Concept duration corresponds to the number of instances for which a concept is active. Duration ranges from 10 instances to 150 instances. Noise ranges from 0% to 30%. Each training set consists of concept (1) for D instances, concept (2) for D instances, and concept (3) for D instances, for some duration D.

Each result reported is based on 100 randomly generated training sets.

Results. Figures 8, 9 and 10 show the success levels of Splice in correctly identifying each target concept under varying levels of both concept duration and noise. In this domain, Splice is well behaved, with a graceful degradation of performance as noise levels increase. Concept duration reduces the negative effect of noise. Figure 11 shows the number of incorrect concepts learnt by Splice for different levels of noise and training concept duration. In this too, Splice is well behaved, showing both graceful degradation of performance with increased noise, and well bounded numbers of incorrect concepts learnt.

4 Discussion

Experiment 1 demonstrated that Splice can reconstruct the original concepts used in the generation of a dataset with recurring contexts.

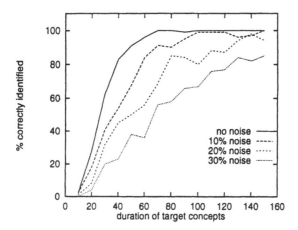

Fig. 8. Identification of concept 1

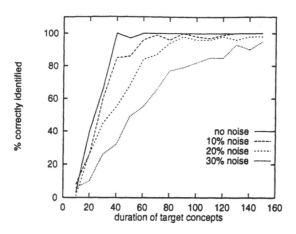

Fig. 9. Identification of concept 2

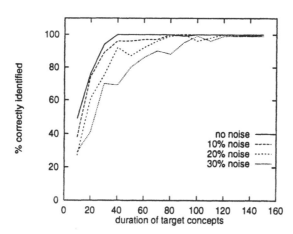

Fig. 10. Identification of concept 3

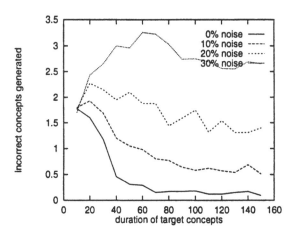

Fig. 11. Incorrect concepts identified

In experiment 2, Splice was shown to perform well on a task similar to that approached by both Flora [13] and Stagger [10]. The combination of Splice with a simple strategy for selection of the current local concept was demonstrated to be effective on a prediction task. As the selection mechanism assumes that at least one of the local concepts will be correct, Splice almost immediately moves to its maximum accuracy on each new local concept. In published results on a similar domain the Flora family of on–line learners [13] (in particular Flora 3, the learner designed to exploit recurring context) appear to reach much the same level of accuracy as Splice. As expected for an on–line learning approach, however, they require some time to fully reflect changes in context.

This comparison is problematic for a number of reasons. Splice has the advantage of first seeing a training set containing 50 instances of each context before beginning to classify and of being able to assume that all possible contexts had at least been seen. The iterative learners have the advantage of continuous feedback with an unconstrained updating of concepts. Splice does have feedback, but can only select from amongst its current local concepts in adaptation to the feedback. Once Splice misses a local concept, there is no second chance. If Splice can be shown to be effective on more complex domains, it may be possible and desirable to use some combination of Splice with an adaptive learner.

Experiment 3 demonstrates that on this domain, Splice is well behaved with changing levels of noise and duration of target concept. Splice was able to take advantage of additional concept duration in order to minimise the effect of noise. At all noise levels, the number of spurious concepts identified by Splice fell within reasonable bounds. This is particularly promising, given that no heuristics were added to disqualify poor candidate local concepts.

The reason that Splice has been able to perform well is that it is able to identify stable concepts under a range of concept duration and noise. We conjecture that its ability to deal with noise is enhanced by the ability to combine similar intervals of the data set. It can use all the data set at one time and benefit from the accuracy achieved by the underlying learner. The potential for combining similar contexts and hence building more accurate concepts is substantial.

We see the main application for Splice, not in direct prediction, but rather as the first stage in identifying and reasoning about context in domains when context is hidden.

4.1 Application of Splice to Prediction Tasks

The above experiments demonstrate that Splice can successfully learn local concepts from hidden contexts in a simple domain. A number of issues arise in the possible application of Splice to more complex domains and real world problems. Two of these are re-training and identification of the relevant local concept.

In a real world predictive application, we anticipate that new training could be triggered by poor predictive performance or by recognising that new cases fall in previously unseen areas of attribute space [3]. Re-training could either employ all past cases or employ a window overlapping the previous training set. If the second of these options were used, any new local concepts thus identified by re-training could be added to the set of previously identified local concepts. This scheme avoids the need to maintain a full history of seen examples.

In Experiment 2, a very simple heuristic was used to select the relevant local concept employed for prediction. More complex domains will require more complex methods to identify the relevant local concept. One approach may be to reason about duration and likely sequences of the identified contexts as suggested in [11].

Some on-line learners can use the proceeding concept to seed the development of new concepts. Splice is unable to share structure across contexts. It is possible that this limitation will reduce the effectiveness of Splice in situations with slow drift. On the other hand, this characteristic is an advantage in situations with sudden drift. This is also a problem in situations where concepts are disjunctive and drift occurs only in one part of the concept.

Another exciting prospect is to use Splice with an underlying relational learner.

5 Conclusion

A new meta-learning algorithm, Splice, enables an underlying machine learning system to learn local concepts from domains with hidden changes in context. We demonstrated that the Splice approach is viable in at least a simple domain and is robust in the presence of noise in the domain presented.

The results indicate that Splice works well on the sample domain. It is essential that scaling issues be investigated in future work. We expect to apply additional heuristics to rate the viability of local concepts and to minimise time complexity.

We also aim to investigate methods for utilising local concepts in predictive applications, and methods for reasoning about the local concepts and contexts identified.

The meta-learning approach will allow us to investigate the application of Splice to problems that require a more complex inductive paradigm. Our only requirement is that we are able to extract information about context change in order to partition the data set by context. Initially, we will investigate relational learners such as FOIL. Other ILP systems and more complex inductive systems will then be considered.

References

1. P. Clark and T. Niblett. The CN2 induction algorithm. *Machine Learning*, 3:261–283, 1989.
2. Pedro Domingos. Context-sensitive feature selection for lazy learners. *Artificial Intelligence Review*, 11:227–253, 1997. Special issue on lazy learning, edited by David Aha.
3. M. Harries and K. Horn. Detecting concept drift in financial time series prediction using symbolic machine learning. In Xin Yao, editor, *Eighth Australian Joint Conference on Artificial Intelligence*, pages 91–98, Singapore, 1995. World Scientific Publishing.
4. F. Kilander and C. G. Jansson. COBBIT - a control procedure for COBWEB in the presence of concept drift. In Pavel B. Brazdil, editor, *European Conference on Machine Learning*, pages 244–261, Berlin, 1993. Springer-Verlag.
5. M. Kubat. Floating approximation in time-varying knowledge bases. *Pattern Recognition Letters*, 10:223–227, 1989.
6. M. Kubat and G. Widmer. Adapting to drift in continuous domains. In *Proceedings of the 8th European Conference on Machine Learning*, pages 307–310, Berlin, 1995. Springer.
7. J. R. Quinlan. Learning logical definitions from relations. *Machine Learning*, 5:239–266, 1990.
8. J. R. Quinlan. *C4.5: Programs for Machine Learning*. Morgan Kaufmann Publishers Inc., San Mateo, California, 1993.
9. M. Salganicoff. Density adaptive learning and forgetting. In *Machine Learning: Proceedings of the Tenth International Conference*, pages 276–283, San Mateo, California, 1993. Morgan Kaufmann Publishers.
10. Jeffory Schlimmer and Richard Granger, Jr. Incremental learning from noisy data. *Machine Learning*, 1(3):317–354, 1986.
11. G. Widmer. Recognition and exploitation of contextual clues via incremental meta-learning. Technical Report oefai-96-01, Austrian Research Institute for Artificial Intelligence, 1996.
12. G. Widmer and M. Kubat. Effective learning in dynamic environments by explicit concept tracking. In Pavel B. Brazdil, editor, *European Conference on Machine Learning*, pages 227–243, Berlin, 1993. Springer-Verlag.
13. G. Widmer and M. Kubat. Learning in the presence of concept drift and hidden contexts. *Machine Learning*, 23:69–101, 1996.

Inducing Complex Spatial Descriptions in Two Dimensional Scenes

Brendan McCane[1], Terry Caelli[2], and Olivier de Vel[3]

[1] Department of Computer Science, University of Otago, Dunedin, New Zealand.
[2] Department of Computer Science Curtin University of Technology GPO Box U
1987 Perth, W.A. Australia.
[3] Department of Computer Science James Cook University of North Queensland
Townsville, Qld, 4811, Australia.

1 Introduction

Very few object recognition systems attempt to learn the representations of the objects which they are to recognise. Some common techniques include evidence based systems ([4] and [3]) and neural network approaches ([7]). However, evidence based systems decouple the unary and relational attributes and therefore expose themselves to the label compatibility problem (where two distinct objects have the same unary and relational relationships, but are structurally different). Consider Figure 1 with circles representing parts (unary attribute: shading value of part) and lines representing relationships between parts (relational attribute: distance between parts). Both objects have 2 black, 1 grey and 1 white circle, and all relational attributes between the parts are the same. For example, both objects have: a distance of 4 between a black and grey circle, a distance of 2 between a black and grey circle etc. It is impossible to distinguish these objects unless more complex structural information is used. The systems descibed in [4] and [3], could not discriminate between the two objects. Of course, higher order attributes (eg ternary) could be used, but these are difficult to accurately extract in the presence of noise and/or occlusion. The neural network approaches of Poggio and Edelman ([7]) attempt to recognise 3D objects from 2D images, but only in a very restricted domain (wireframe objects) so the techniques described there are not generally applicable.

More recently, Bischof and Caelli ([1, 2]) have described a technique called Conditional Rule Generation (CRG) which resolves the problems of label compatibility by coupling unary and relational attributes in a manner somewhat related to FOIL ([8]). In this paper we describe an extension to CRG, called FCRG (Fuzzy Conditional Rule Generation), how it learns complex spatial relationships and the implications of the label compatibility problem with respect to 3D object recognition.

2 The FCRG Learning Algorithm

Objects in a 2D scene can be considered as consisting of a number of parts, $p_i, (i = 1, 2, ..., N)$. Each part can be represented as an n-tuple of unary at-

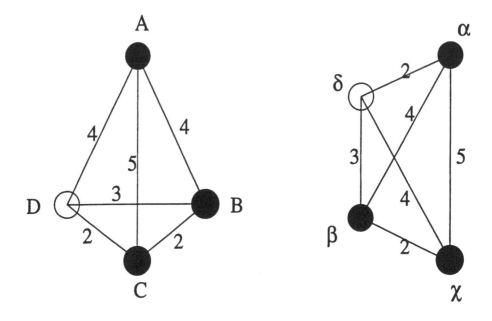

Fig. 1. The label compatibility problem: the two objects shown are obviously distinct, yet the possess the same unary (shading value of part) and relational attributes (distance between parts). This is a problem for learning systems which decouple the two attribute sets into separate attribute spaces.

tributes $u(p_i)$, and each relationship between the parts can be represented as an n-tuple of relational attributes $b(p_i, p_j), (i, j = 1, 2, ..., N; i \neq j)$.

In the learning phase it is assumed that each object is presented separately as a number of training views. All training views are presented serially, but not necessarily in any order. The training views are in the form of intensity images from which regions are extracted. The regions are used as the object parts from which unary and relational attributes are extracted.

The FCRG technique works by grouping unary attributes from all parts, of all views of all objects into a unary attribute space U. Each point in the unary attribute space is representative of a single part. The attribute space U is then partitioned into a number of fuzzy clusters (rules), U_i. Some clusters may be unique with respect to class membership, and these clusters uniquely define which class the corresponding part belongs to. Other clusters will contain multiple classes and these need to be examined further. For the non-unique clusters, the relational attributes between a part and other parts in the view, are calculated to form a relational attribute space, UB_i. The relational attribute space, UB_i, is clustered into a number of clusters UB_{ij}. Again, some clusters will be unique while others will not. The unary attributes of the second part, p_s, are used to form another unary attribute space UBU_{ij}, which is again clustered to form clusters UBU_{ijk}. This process can continue until all clusters are unique, resulting in clusters at the $UBUB, UBUBU, UBUBUB, ...$ levels, but, in some cases, clusters may be unresolvable at any level. In this case, the clusters need to be refined at some level, either by reclustering a particular attribute space into more clusters, or by splitting clusters ([1]).

The FCRG learning algorithm is not unlike the FOIL algorithm in that it maximises class separation by adding predicates to the (item) clauses that cover the maximum number of positive training examples and the minimum number of negative training examples. The FCRG tree can also be represented in clause form, by following each possible path from the root to the leaves, resulting in clauses of the form:

$$C_n \leftarrow U(x), B(x,y), U(y), B(y,z), U(z), ... \tag{1}$$

where C_n is the nth class, and x, y, and z are object parts, and the U's and B's are fuzzy clusters in unary and relational attribute spaces respectively. However, the two algorithms differ in that FCRG constrains the ordering of the object parts (ie literals - $UBUB...$), uses continuous attributes, allows backtracking by cluster refinement, and uses fuzzy decision boundaries. Furthermore, due to the fuzzy nature of the rules induced, it is possible to traverse the decision tree more than one branch at a time during the object recognition phase, thereby enabling the evaluation of the amount of membership of the path in each class.

3 Results

3.1 Handling the Label Compatibility Problem

Figure 2 displays how the FCRG tree is created when learning to distinguish between the two classes shown in Figure 1. Since this is an artificial example, fuzzy clustering is not used. At the U level, 3 clusters (U_1, U_2, U_3) are formed at shading values of 1 (white), 2 (grey), and 3 (black) respectively. Each cluster containing more than one class needs to be expanded. In this case, all clusters must be expanded, but the figure shows the expansion of cluster U_1 only, for clarity. From the parts in cluster U_1, we extract all the possible relational attributes and perform clustering at the UB level. Here again three clusters are formed with relational distance values of 2, 4, and 5. Again, each cluster with more than one class (all of them in this case) requires expanding. In the figure, we show the expansion of clusters $U_1 B_1$ and $U_1 B_3$. At the next level of clustering (UBU), we form an attribute space consisting of unary attributes of the second parts involved in the relational attributes of the parent cluster (eg parts ξ and C from cluster $U_1 B_3$). This UBU attribute space is again clustered, and this process continues creating clusters at the UBU, $UBUB$, $UBUBU$, ... levels, until all clusters contain a single class, or the maximum height of the tree is reached. An example rule can be extracted from the FCRG tree of Figure 2:

$$C_2 \leftarrow U(x) == 1, B(x,y) == 5, U(y) == 1, B(y,z) == 4$$

Where $U(x)$ refers to the unary attributes of part x (in this case, shading value), and $B(x,y)$ refers to the relational attributes between parts x and y (in this case, the distance between the parts). Similar rules can be created for all other paths from root to leaves of the FCRG tree.

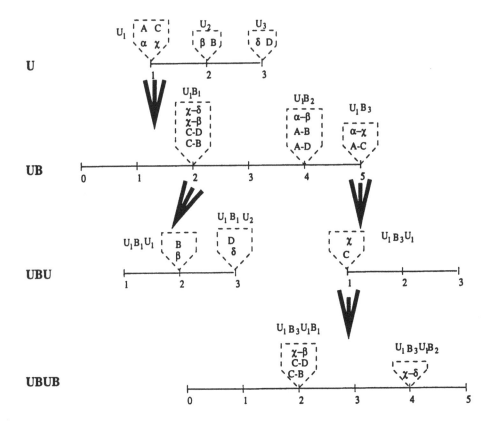

Fig. 2. Solving the Label Compatibility Problem: the unary and relational attribute spaces are both 1-dimensional, hence the clusters actually fall on a single point. The figure shows part of the tree formed by FCRG.

At recognition time, for the example above, we need only examine chains (lists of connected parts) until one of the rules gives a definitive answer (some rules may be unresolvable at any level). However, this is true only if the input is perfect (which is never true for computer vision applications). In practice, all the chains generated from the test object should be followed down the tree, and a final decision on the appropriate class of the test object can be made by a maximum frequency decision.

3.2 A Practical Example

We shall demonstrate the usefulness of the technique and the impact of the label compatibility problem in trying to learn 3D machine components (also referred to as "objects") from 2D intensity images (also see [5]). In this example, there are 10 different machine components which are to be learnt from numerous 2D intensity images. Figure 3 shows all the objects used in the experiment. The unary attributes which were used in this example are: aspect ratio, a symmetry measure (higher values mean less symmetric), compactness ($perimeter^2/area$), convex deficiency, and the mean and variance of the intensity across the region. The binary attributes used were: relative position of one region with respect to the other; relative orientation of the major axes; relative size of the two regions; maximum distance between the two regions; percentage overlap of the boundaries of the two regions; and the maximum and minimum depth difference between the two regions obtained from a depth-from-stereo algorithm ([6]). To evaluate the performance of FCRG, the image database was split into two sets - a training set and a test set - both of which consist of three different views from each of the stable resting positions of each object. FCRG is then tested on the training objects to give a measure of accuracy, and on the test objects to give a measure of the generalisation ability of the system.

Firstly, let us examine the parts which cluster together (and should be of similar shape). Figure 4 displays all the object parts which are closest to cluster U0. As can be seen from the figure, the majority of parts are very similar in shape, and the clustering has worked quite well in this case. Similarly, Figure 5 shows some of the object parts which are closest to cluster U10. These parts are more compact, more symmetric (in terms of centre-line symmetries), and are mostly convex, compared to the parts given in cluster U0. Clearly, the current clustering of the object parts, whilst appropriate, does not separate the classes. Hence the reason for expanding the clusters to make use of relational attributes (between parts).

It is also useful to examine the extent to which the label compatibility problem affects recognition results. As the depth of the tree increases, the recognition algorithm employs longer part chains, and is thus able to handle more complex label compatibility problems. Figure 6 shows the accuracy and generalisation results (as discussed above) for increasing depth of the FCRG tree. In both cases, there is little or no improvement in performance at depths greater than two (two part chains - UB), and in fact the performance drops off at depths greater than three (UBU). This indicates that, in practice, the label compatibility problem is limited to two part chains which further indicates that techniques based on more complete matching schemes (such as graph matching) are perhaps unnecessary. A further advantage of restricting the FCRG tree to depths of two are three is that the size of the tree is significantly smaller than at larger depths as indicated in Figure 7. Learning and recognition times are also significantly reduced at smaller depths.

4 Discussion

Given the difficulty of the problem, the FCRG classifier performs remarkably well, recognising objects with an accuracy of over 90% for seen samples, although

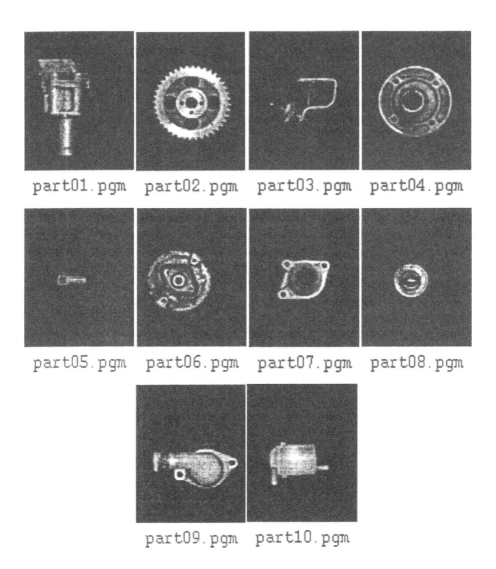

part01.pgm   part02.pgm   part03.pgm   part04.pgm

part05.pgm   part06.pgm   part07.pgm   part08.pgm

part09.pgm   part10.pgm

Fig. 3. All objects: intensity images of all objects used in the experiments.

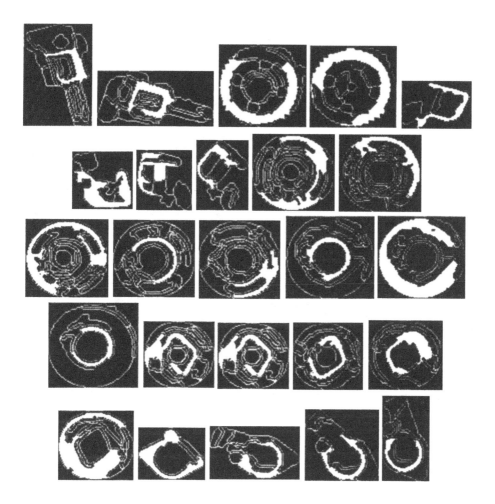

Fig. 4. Object Parts in Cluster 0: the object part is highlighted and the outline of the remainder of the object is also given.

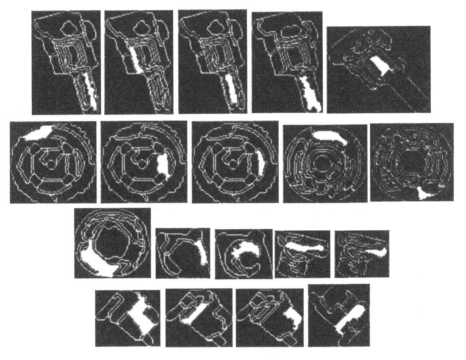

Fig. 5. Object Parts in Cluster 10: the object part is highlighted and the outline of the remainder of the object is also given.

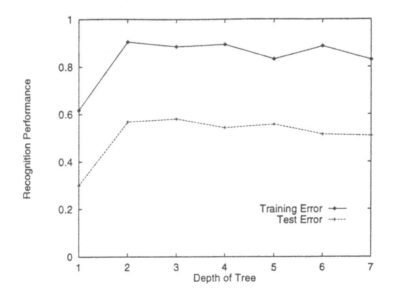

Fig. 6. Recognition Performance for Varying Depth: the figure shows the accuracy (training set) and generalisation (test set) performance as the depth of the tree is increased.

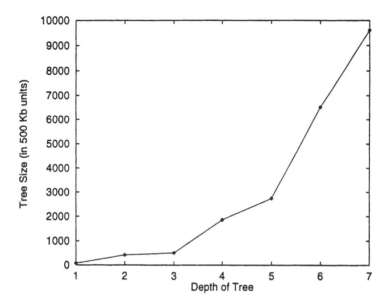

Fig. 7. Size of the FCRG Tree for Varying Depth: the figure shows the relationship between the final size of the FCRG tree and the maximum depth of the tree.

the accuracy is less for unseen samples (at 55%). It has been noted, however, that FCRG would be useful as the hypothesis component in a complete object recognition system where a back-end testing component should improve the recognition performance dramatically.

The major result shown in this paper involves the impact of the label compatibility problem. We believe that unary and relational attributes should not be decoupled and thus introduce the label compatibility problem. Nevertheless, the results shown here, indicate that, in practice, only two part chains are required to distinguish between most objects. This indicates that accounting completely for the label compatibility problem (such as using full graph matching schemes) is not required, allowing for possible performance improvements in terms of time and size requirements, without sacrificing recognition performance. Still, further experimentation is required on differing data sets to undeniably establish this result.

There are clearly many problems yet to overcome in this domain. Learning systems are only as good as the data they are trained and tested on. The major challenge appears to be generating good segmentation of images (whether 2D or 3D) and using an appropriate attribute set for the problem at hand ([5] explore this last problem in more detail).

References

1. Walter Bischof and Terry Caelli. Learning structural descriptions: a new technique for conditional clustering and rule generation. *Pattern Recognition*, pages 689–697, May 1994.
2. Walter F. Bischof and Terry Caelli. Visual learning of patterns and objects. *IEEE Transactions System, Man and Cybernetics*. In Press.
3. Terry Caelli and Ashley Dreier. Variations on the evidence-based object recognition theme. *Pattern Recognition*, 27(2):185–204, 1994.
4. Anil K. Jain and Richard Hoffman. Evidence-based recognition of 3D objects. *IEEE Transactions on Pattern Analysis and Machine Intelligence*, 10(6):783–802, November, 1988.
5. Brendan McCane, Terry Caelli, and Olivier de Vel. Recognising 3D machine objects using a fuzzy machine learning approach. In *Pacific Rim International Conference on Artificial Intelligence 96 Poster Proceedings*, pages 77–85, Cairns, 1996. Poster Proceedings.
6. Brendan J. McCane and Olivier de Vel. A stereo matching algorithm using curve segments and cluster analysis. Technical Report 94/5, Dept. Computer Science, James Cook University, 1994. http://www.cs.jcu.edu.au/ftp/web/research/techreports/ftp94.html#94-5.
7. T Poggio and S Edelman. A network that learns to recognise 3D objects. *Nature*, 343:263–266, 18th January 1990.
8. J.R. Quinlan. Learning logical definitions from relations. *Machine Learning*, 5:239–266, 1990.

A Framework for Learning Constraints: Preliminary Report

Srinivas Padmanabhuni,Jia-Huai You
Department of Computing Science,
University of Alberta, Canada T6G 2H1.
e-mail: srinivas,you@cs.ualberta.ca

Aditya Ghose
Decision Systems Lab
Dept. of Business Systems
University of Wollongong
NSW 2522 Australia
e-mail: aditya@uow.edu.au

Abstract. Constraints represent a powerful way of specifying knowledge in any problem solving domain. Typically the appropriate constraints for a given problem need to be fully specified. In general it is difficult to describe the appropriate constraints in every problem setting. Hence automatic constraint acquisition is an important problem.

In this paper we develop a model for automatic constraint acquisition. We show that a universal scheme for generalizing constraints specified on variables across any domain, whether continuous or discrete, is not feasible. Here we provide a generalization model for constraints specified in the form of relations with explicit enumeration of allowed tuples. We provide a scheme to generalize the constraints expressed in this form in our model. We discuss the properties of the generalized constraint obtained from input constraints.

We also show that this scheme provides a uniform method of generalization for any type of constraint on variables with finite and discrete domain. In the end we elaborate upon the different applications of our scheme. We show how learning in our scheme can help improve the search efficiency in a CSP,

Keywords: Constraint Programming, Learning.

1 Motivation and Introduction

Machine Learning [Shavlik and Dietterich 90] is the subfield of artificial intelligence that studies the automated acquisition of knowledge as a result of experience. Learning is studied for a wide variety of reasons: to discover general principles of intelligence , to get a better understanding of human learning and to acquire domain-specific knowledge for performing a task better.

Machine learning research can be classified on various dimensions depending upon the context. The primary dimensions of learning we need to consider are representation of knowledge, the technique employed in learning and the domain of application.

We shall study the machine learning systems keeping in view one particular application domain, i.e. constraints. Before we look at the role of learning in constraints, we shall explore the area of constraints.

A *constraint* [Mackworth 92] refers to *relation that must be satisfied*. For example, the relation that all bodies falling under gravity must have the same acceleration is a *constraint*.

Since there exist a variety of real world problems, the variables being used in a problem can be from diverse domains. Similarly the constraints being used in the problem can also be of diverse types, e.g. integer variables with interval domains, real variables with continuous domain etc. Again diverse types of constraints involving the above variables are used in practice like arithmetic and order constraints, set constraints etc.

Constraint programming refers to process of solving the problems specified as sets of constraints. The most common method of specifying constraints in constraint programming applications is as a constraint satisfaction problem(CSP). A CSP [Mackworth 92]is defined by a set of variables, each of which have a set of possible values (their domain), and a set of constraints (relations) between these variables. The solution to a CSP is a set of variable-value assignments which satisfy the constraints.

As described earlier the domains can be of diverse types as can be constraints. But the predominant type of specification of CSP involves variables with discrete and finite domains. The CSP is then solved by use of certain techniques called *consistency* techniques in conjunction with backtracking.

Another common way of specification of constraints is the form of a *constraint logic program*. A *constraint logic program* is a generalization of a logic program, in the sense that the clauses can contain constraints in the body. A constraint logic program is a set of clauses with predicates in the head, but may contain constraints along with predicate symbols in the body of the clause. e.g. The CLP P = {p(Y) :- Y < 2, q(Y). ; a(Z) :- Z > 1 } is a two clause CLP. The semantics of a constraint logic program is similar to a logic program except that the process of unification as in logic programs is replaced by the process of constraint satisfaction to solve the constraints involved in the clauses.

There are situations in real life warranting the need for development of machine learning systems for constraints. Typically in any problem solving domain, the constraints are fully specified before a solution to the problem is attempted. But there are certain application domains where it might be difficult to obtain an explicit set of appropriate constraints to define a problem. In such a case a mechanism for automatically acquiring constraints becomes necessary.

Automatic constraint acquisition calls for development of learning mechanisms for constraints. As the constraint representations vary in the type of domain, a variety of machine learning systems can be developed for constraints.

Thus in this paper we develop a model for automatic constraint acquisition.

2 Constraints and learning

Empirical learning has been the principal source of systems capable of learning symbolic knowledge, the common form of knowledge in constraints. In these systems, inductive reasoning is performed on externally supplied examples to produce general rules. In any such system, the learner is fed a series of characterizing examples classified into two sets of instances: positive and negative examples. The objective is to produce a generalized description which is able to explain all the positive instances and yet not explain any of the negative instances. Based on the methods involved in the obtaining of the generalized description, the inductive learning systems[Wu 95] are broadly classified into the following four categories:

Attribute based induction The purpose of such systems is to produce a generalized description as decision trees or control rules from a set of positive and negative relational tuples as input so that all the input positive examples are covered and is consistent with the negative examples. The correctness of the learned description is tested by a sample *test set* from among the same relational base.

Incremental Generalization and Specialization Here background knowledge is specified as a hierarchy to choose between different descriptions. The descriptions are generalized and specialized according to this hierarchy to decide the final form of the learned description.

Unsupervised Concept Formation The learner finds a generalized description from the input examples by use of clustering similar data into a concept, and giving in the end a concept a description satisfying certain description like Minimum description Length or some similar measure. This technique is most popular in data mining systems.

Inductive Logic Programming [Muggleton 92] The most recent class of machine learning algorithms based on use of first-order logic as underlying knowledge representation to generate descriptions. Inductive Logic programming systems use a combination of all the above three techniques in conjunction with background knowledge in the learning process. Inductive Logic programming systems use a combination of all t he three systems above in the learning process.

As seen from above the most recent work in the area of learning is in learning first-order clauses or logic programs to give the stream of "Inductive Logic Programming". Logic programs are more expressive than any propositional knowledge representation scheme. Hence the field of Inductive Logic Programming has been applied in a variety of daily life applications. Also as seen from the definition in the earlier section, we find that constraint logic programs are even more expressive than logic programs because of incorporation of the concept of constraints in them. Thus it would be worthwhile to explore if ideas from inductive logic programming can be exported or extended to Constraint Logic Programs.

But in a constraint logic program, the process of deductive inference of logic programs is replaced by a more generalized notion of constraint solving. Thus if any learning scheme were to be developed for constraint logic programs, the first step in that direction would be to develop models for learning simple constraints which can then be combined with the Inductive Logic programming techniques to get the notion of *Inductive Constraint Logic Programming*.

This is a strong motivation for us to develop frameworks for automatic constraint acquisition or constraint learning.

Before proceeding with the illustration of our model of learning constraints, we shall review existing work related to constraint learning . Because the field of constraints is relatively nascent, there are relatively fewer systems which apply machine learning to constraint based applications.

2.1 Earlier work in Constraint Learning

Mizoguchi and Ohwada[Mizoguchi and Ohwada 92] developed the notion of *constraint-directed generalization* in constraint logic programs to acquire spatial layout information. They propose a mechanism to learn generalized spatial constraint given a set of input spatial constraints so that each of the input spatial constraint is satisfied by the generalized spatial constraint. In physical terms the generalized constraint represents a region which satisfies all input spatial constraints.

Zweben et al.[Zweben et al. 1992] describe an explanation-based learning variant to capture the notion of analytic learning in the domain of constraint based schedules. The idea is to learn search control knowledge for a constraint based scheduling system. The learned knowledge is used for improving the performance in future occasions especially to depth-first backtracking through the space of partial schedules.

Furukawa et al.[Kawamura and Furukawa 93] describe a generic learning model for constraints based on exporting ideas from Inductive Logic Programming to Constraint Logic Programming. They describe the model for linear algebra, and how more general constraints can be learned from initial linear constraints.

Most of the work reported in automatic constraint acquisition has been in the area of constraints on continuous domains. This motivates us to develop a generic model for automatic constraint acquisition in discrete domains.

3 A framework for learning constraints

As discussed earlier, the best paradigm to implement constraint learning mechanisms is the empirical learning method. Now there is a spectrum of empirical learning paradigms which have been applied in machine learning systems. The fundamental process of learning in empirical learning is "Induction" or "Generalization". To date the vast majority of the inductive empirical learning systems have been based on propositional knowledge representation. The only learning systems based on non-propositional system are based on the Inductive Logic Programming Systems based on clausal representation.

Before we proceed with a generalized framework for learning constraints, we need to identify the type of constraints we shall be concentrating for development of learning schemes. Clearly for constraint systems on variables with continuous domains, there cannot be a uniform representation of all the constraints because of the infinite number of choices for each variable. Thus such type of constraint domains call for learning schemes specific to the application being considered[Kawamura and Furukawa 93][Mizoguchi and Ohwada 92].

On the other hand when we consider constraints on variables with discrete domains, we have a uniform representation as relations for the underlying constraints. This may of course be infeasible if the underlying domain is infinite. But a majority of the work in constraint programming is based on finite domain constraints. Thus we shall be concentrating on the constraints with finite and discrete domains. A major portion of the work in constraint programming is based on such type of constraints. In fact the CSP problem formulation is based on finite domain discrete constraints. *Thus our motivation in this thesis to develop a framework for learning constraints on discrete and finite domains.*

As a starting point we shall develop an inductive generalization mechanism for constraints on finite and discrete domains which are explicitly specified as relations (i.e. sets of allowable tuples). We shall call such a representation of constraints as *ECSP form*, short for Explicit CSP form. To begin with we should see whether existing learning frameworks of empirical learning can be exported to take care of constraints in *ECSP form*. Theoretically any constraint on finite and discrete domain can be converted to *ECSP form* by explicit enumeration of allowed combination of values. Hence any learning scheme on *ECSP form* can be theoretically applied to any finite domain discrete constraint application. In contrast to the highly application specific nature of constraint learning mechanisms to be developed for constraints on continuous domains, this uniformity for finite discrete domains prompted us to develop a comprehensively applicable learning system for *ECSP form* of constraints.

But the existing inductive empirical learning methods are unsuitable for the ECSP form of representation, for the following two reasons:

1. Learning methods based on clausal representation (Inductive Logic Programming) systems [Muggleton 92], when applied to ECSP form, generalize too much, because they replace any set of ground instances of a variable with a variable, e.g. Given the inputs R(1,2), and R(3,4), the algorithm produces R(X,Y), which is too general.

2. Learning methods based on propositional knowledge representation forms cannot be used because of two reasons:
   (a) Intractability of the three stage process: Conversion of ECSP form to the particular knowledge representation , application of the generalizing algorithm in that form and the conversion back to ECSP form.

   (b) Intractable size of the conversion of ECSP form into the native knowledge representation in most of the cases.

This prompts us to look for an alternative form of knowledge representation which is closer to the representation of constraints in order to reduce the complexity of the learning process. We achieve this by using the same relational representation for both the input constraints and the output learned form of constraint. In the next few sections we shall develop the model for learning ECSP form of knowledge. In the end we shall discuss the extensions to the basic models in detail, which will enable us to generalize the model to handle more generic form of finite discrete constraints and will allow us to use existing empirical learning frameworks to that end. We discuss a few applications of this model of learning ECSP form in detail.

4 A framework for learning ECSP form of knowledge

In the previous sections we were motivated as to the need for a generalized learning model for constraints. Existing constraint learning frameworks concentrate on use of domain specific representations, especially continuous domains, for design of learning schemes for constraints. In this section first we shall develop a model for learning constraints on discrete domain. Our model shall be developed for the simplest case where we have constraints on variables with finite and discrete domains. Such constraints shall be called as the ECSP form (Explicit Constraint Satisfaction problem). We shall show how existing learning frameworks cannot be extended to the domain of discrete constraints due to several context-dependent reasons.

First we shall develop the most basic model for empirically learning ECSP form of constraints with just positive examples in the learning context. Then we discuss how we shall generalize and enhance the model in different directions.

5 The model for learning ECSP constraints

In this section, we propose a learning (generalization) scheme for data represented in the ECSP form. We have shown in the preceding section how existing learning algorithms are unsuitable for the ECSP type of knowledge representation. The model for learning constraints in the ECSP form is presented in the subsections below.

5.1 Subsumption Ordering in the *ECSP form*

In this section the mechanism of generalizing predicates in *ECSP form* will be presented.

In *ECSP form*, the predicates are represented by relations on finite domains. The generalization operations in the representation are based on subsumption ordering between the predicates.

Definition 5.1 (Predicate Subsumption) *A relation R subsumes another relation S iff $S \subseteq \prod_{attr(S)}(R)$, where $\prod_{attr(S)}$ denotes the projection operator onto attribute columns of S.*

Consider the following example:

```
R =
        A   B
        ------
        0   1
        1   0
        ------

S  =
        A   B   C
        -----------
        0   1   0
        1   0   0
        1   1   0
        -----------
Here,   S subsumes   R.
```

The abovementioned subsumption relation induces a partial order on the predicates. As with any partial order , the subsumption ordering induces a lattice on the predicates. The lattice has the universal relation $\mathcal{R}$ as the Top of the lattice and the empty relation ϕ as the Bottom of the lattice.

Thus the above subsumption relation defines the notions of "generality" and "specificity" in relation to knowledge represented in the ECSP form. Any constraint higher in the lattice(i.e. more general) than a given constraint C captures all the knowledge contained in the constraint C. Consider the example above, Here R states that A can take the values 0 and 1 only. S also conveys the same information. But S conveys an additional knowledge to the effect that C can take the value 0 only. If we consider the solution space of a CSP represented by the relation R, S is more conservative than R because of the additional constraint on the variable C. But at the same time all the knowledge exhibited by relation R with regard to variables A and B is also contained in S. Hence we have a form of representation of knowledge which generalizes the relevant knowledge in a given constraint and yet is able to reduce the solution space of the problem. The method conveniently combines knowledge in two or more constraints and gives a closer approximation to the solution because of the reduction of solution space. Hence this provides us a mechanism to speedup the process of finding solution in a CSP problem.

6   Learning model in the positive only case

In the most basic case, we shall consider the case of learning in the presence of only positive constraints. In such a model, it is natural to consider as a generalization a point in the subsumption lattice described in the previous section, which is above every input constraint. We introduce the notion of "most specific" generalizations to the most useful among the multiple generalizations possible in this case. In this section, we shall use the term "constraint" to denote a positive constraint.

We start by investigating the generalization of two constraints.

6.1 Most Specific Generalization and its properties

Given any two constraints(relations) we can then define the Most Specific Generalization of the two constraints (relations)as follows:

Definition 6.1 (Most Specific Generalization) *A relation R is called a Most Specific Generalization of relations R_1 and R_2 iff R subsumes both R_1 and R_2, and attrib(R)= attrib(R_1) $\cup$ attrib(R_2), and for any relation R' such that R subsumes R', it is not the case that R' subsumes both R_1 and R_2.*

Projection of R on R1 or R2 should be a minimal superset of R1 or R2 respectively.

Consider the following example:

```
R   =                        S=


    A  B                     B  C
    -----                    ------
    0  0                     1  1
    0  1                     1  0
    ----                     ------
```

The above two relations can have many MSG's some of which are given below:

```
RS= MSG of R and S =

A B   C    A  B C     A B C    A  B C
-------    --------   -------   ------
0 0   1    0  0 0     0 0 1    0  0 0
0 1   1    0  1 1     0 1 1    0  1 1
1 1   0    0  1 0     0 1 0    1  1 0
-------    --------   -------   --------
```

So the general form of the MSG of R and S above is:

```
          RS =    A  B  C
                  -------
                  0  0  X
                  0  1  1
                  Y  1  0
                  --------
```

Here any relation RS of the above form is a MSG of the given constraints R and S. But to have a conservative generalization it is necessary for us to impose further restrictions on the definition of MSG. We can achieve this by a "Maximal Faithfulness" criterion which restricts the unconstrained slots (like X and Y above), to a value which the particular variable is allowed to take by at least one of the subsumed constraints(here R or S). In such a case there is no relaxation or tightening of the constraint on a variable which is not common to both the relations. Thus we can state the following lemma:

Lemma 1. *For any MSG S of two relations R_1 and R_2 , S is maximally faithful iff it is true that $\forall X$ such that X is not a variable common to R_1 and R_2, $\prod_X(S)$ is equal to $\prod_X(R_1)$ or $\prod_X(R_2)$ whichever applicable.*

We now look at the solution space of the MSG S as compared to the solution space of R_1 or R_2. If we impose the condition of "Maximal Faithfulness" on S, it is possible for a solution tuple(vector) to satisfy R_1 and yet not satisfy S, and similarly for R_2. This is not necessarily true with all MSG's But if the MSG is maximally faithful, this situation is avoided because of the restrictions on the values the slots can take. Now we can show that any solution tuple satisfying a *maximally faithful* S, will satisfy at least one of R_1 or R_2 but not necessarily both because in such a case it would be join of both the constraints. We state this result below. The proof is very straight forward.

Theorem 2. *Let R1 and R2 be two constraints and S be a maximally faithful MSG of R1 and R2. Any solution vector satisfying S will satisfy at least one of R1 or R2.*

In the normal circumstances it often is the case that the join of the two relations R and S forms a subset of the MSG as described in the previous paragraphs. The join is trivially a subset of the MSG of two relations except the following g case. The case is described below:

Let R and S represent the two relations. Let colrs=cols(R)∩ cols(S). Let RC=$\prod_{colrs}$(R) and SC=$\prod_{colrs}$(S). The only case when the join is not a subset of the MSG is given by the following rule: Let card(t,R) represent the cardinality of a tuple t in a relation R. The join of R and S, is not a subset iff $\exists t$ such that $t \in RC$ and $t \in SC$, and both card(t,SC) and card(t,RC) are greater than one. In such a case multiple MSG's can be formed by adjoining the appropriate rows. In all other cases, the join is a subset of the MSG. When R and S are not joinable the join, the empty relation, is a subset of the MSG trivially.

We now summarize the properties of the subsumption ordering and MSG as studied above .

- The subsumption ordering induces a partial order on the constraints(relations).
- Any two constraints can have more than one MSG.
- The empty constraint is subsumed by any constraint.
- The Universal constraint (All the possible variables with all possible values) subsumes any constraint.

- The projection of a *maximally faithful* MSG of two constraints on an attribute that is not common to both the constraints, is the same as the projection of the constraint containing the attribute onto the attribute column.
- The solution space allowed by a maximally faithful MSG of any two constraints is tighter than the solution space of at least one of the constraints.
- Any solution of a maximally faithful MSG of two constraint will satisfy at least one of the constraints.
- The join of any two relations is a subset of the MSG except the case described in the previous section.

6.2 Learning model based on MSG

The MSG algorithm shall be the basis of the learning model we shall be considering. In the most basic model, the inputs are a set of positive constraints, each of which is a finite relation on a set of variables with finite domains. In the section we describe the most basic learning model for constraints. In this section we shall consider only positive constraints to be present in the model. In this simplistic model we assume that we have series of positive constraints input to the learner, without any background knowledge. In such a case the idea is to obtain a generalized representation which encompasses all the knowledge contained in each of the constraints in the input model.

Thus we can obtain the generalization of n constraints by applying the MSG algorithm n times. We show a schematic illustration of the algorithm in the following section. We shall study the properties of such an algorithm in a later section.

6.3 Algorithm for the Positive Only model

Input: A set of constraints $C = C_1, C_2, C_3, ..., C_n$.

Required : to output a constraint C' such that for every i such that C_i belongs to C, C' subsumes C_i.

Algorithm:

$R = C_1$; for (i:= 2 to n) do begin t=MSG(R,C_i); R=t; end;

7 Applications of the basic model

The *ECSP form* of knowledge representation is quite useful in a variety of application domains. Some of the applications that we considered are:

- As a mechanism to learn relations and hence use it in any scenario where a learning model for relations is desired.
- As a tool to improve search efficiency in CSP solving techniques.
- As a model for developing methods to improve scheduling techniques.
- To develop specialized methods for spatio-geometrical reasoning.

We shall explore one such application in slight detail below.

7.1 Improving search efficiency in constraint satisfaction problems

Any finite domain CSP, essentially involves a set of relations with a finite set of variables from finite domains. The solution of a CSP corresponds to a relation satisfying all the constituent input relations. Any CSP solving method essentially traverses the solution space, by continually changing the valuations of the variables.

The *ECSP form* gives a handy tool to aid in the search process for solving a CSP. The idea is analogous to the concept of explanation based generalization in Machine learning. Here the knowledge obtained by traversing through a proof tree is encoded and put to use later. Similarly the search control knowledge can be gathered in the process of searching the solution space of the CSP by keeping search paths in the form of a generalized relation by the MSG algorithm. So when searching for the next valuation in the process of solving, the knowledge encoded in the MSG can be put to use as a heuristic. Conversely the knowledge of failed paths can be used to guide as to which paths not to choose. Since the representation scheme of the *ECSP form* coincides with the scheme used by CSP's, the subsumption relation can be used directly to determine if a certain valuation of a variable is desirable or not.

Thus this is a direct application of learning where the *ECSP form* of knowledge representation scheme is used.

8 Extensions of the framework presented

In this section we shall briefly describe the different directions in which we are working in order to extend the basic framework presented in this article. The extensions being considered in logical order are presented in the following subsections.

8.1 Extension of the basic model to handle negative information

One of the immediate extensions being looked at by us is the incorporation of the notion of a *negative constraint* into the model. Before we proceed further we shall define the notion of "Negative Constraint". A negative constraint is a constraint or a relation on a set of variables which must not be explainable by any learned concept obtained by generalization of the input constraints. In the presence of a negative constraint, also commonly known as a *nogood*, we need to define the notions of *consistency* with respect to a nogood, analogous to a negative example in empirical learning.

This extended model with capability of handling negative examples is very useful in a large number of situations. All the applications mentioned in the basic model case, can be dealt with more efficiently and elegantly. Consider, for example, the CSP speedup application. In this application negative constraints can help in reducing unwanted paths while positive constraints can act as heuristics. This dramatically increases the efficiency of the CSP solving procedure. When we extend the learning model presented in the previous section to handle negative constraints alongside the positive constraints, we have a situation where we can have a spectrum of possible constraints depending upon the idea of how general our model needs to be represented.

8.2 Extension of the model to handle clustering

In the basic model of learning constraints presented, we do not have a difference in representations of data and information, i.e. learned information from the constraints. The representation scheme chosen for representing the learned constraints is the same as the one of the constraints, i.e. the relational form.

It is a good starting point as a model for incorporating learning into constraints. But from a general case of constraint applications, such a type of learning model needs to be diversified depending upon the application domain.

The simplest way of dissociating information learnt from the data input, is by using clustering techniques to cluster similar data into groups and work with these groups in the learning process. Hence this type of scheme will be generalization of the model presented in the previous section, in the sense that the representation schemes for the information and the data differ. Also a whole set of conceptual clustering techniques used in machine learning literature can be applied to constraints represented in ECSP form.

Ellman [Ellman, 1993] describes a system to incorporate clustering techniques into Constraint Satisfaction. He describes a method of clustering approximately equivalent objects into classes, and then using these classes to develop hierarchical constraint solvers.

We can improve upon our basic model by incorporating conceptual clustering techniques in the constraint generalization algorithm. We need to define a measure by which constraints are compared and found similar or dissimilar. Based on such a measure of classification, we can develop a application specific clustering technique over the constraints and develop learning algorithms using these approximated clusters. Thus this is one of the directions in which the basic model presented in our learning model is being extended.

8.3 Background Knowledge incorporation

The existing framework proposed in the earlier section, has no notion on background knowledge which is a fundamental part of present day learning systems based on Inductive Logic Programming.

Thus one direction in which the work presented in the earlier section needs to be extended is to incorporate inference in the presence of background knowledge.

In Inductive Logic programming, the notion of θ-subsumption which is defined as an absolute generality relation is extended in the presence of background first-order knowledge, to give the notion of "Relative Subsumption". Analogously, we should extend our notion of the constraint subsumption to handle background constraints. In such a case we must have a choice of a representation of background knowledge which gives a reasonable motion of relative subsumption which is not too costly to compute.

In this context research needs to be done as to what form of background knowledge of constraints is the best suitable for a generalized constraint learning paradigm with background knowledge. A relational type representation for the constraints in the background knowledge will be intractable , while on the other hand a first-order clausal form will be a disadvantage in terms of granularity of the data considered. A decision tree or a control rule type of background knowledge might be preferable in terms of computational limitations.

Thus incorporation of background knowledge into the learning system developed in the previous sections, is one of the important extensions which needs to be studied.

8.4 A framework for Inductive Constraint Logic Programming

An immediate extension of the basic model presented in this proposal seeks to incorporate the constraint generalization methods into clausal generalization methods based on Inductive Logic Programming to develop a solid foundation for Inductive Constraint Logic Programming. As a first step we shall consider generalizing the framework to handle discrete domain constraint logic programs like CLP(FD) , CC(FD) etc. Freuder and Wallace [Freuder and Wallace 95] extend the notion of the basic "nogoods" to use high-level abstraction for generalizing the nogoods to higher level concepts, in the solving a CSP.

In such a framework we need to develop a neat way to integrate the constraint learning mechanisms with θ-subsumption of ILP, to give notion of generality between two constraint clauses,i.e. clauses with constraints in the body of the clause. Such a framework will be helpful in developing tools for automatic constraint acquisition in domains where CLP's have been used extensively, e.g. intelligent scheduling.

8.5 Development of Inductive Hierarchical Constraint Logic Programming Framework

The other direction in which the model of previous section should be extended is to investigate if constraint learning techniques can be extended to handle constraint hierarchies. Ideally, we would like to have a learning system which will generate the constraint hierarchies once we provide the input constraints as an input.

This type of system would be very useful in automating applications involving hierarchical constraint solving. More precisely this notion of automatically generating hierarchies can be combined with the hierarchical constraint logic programming techniques to give the notion of inductive hierarchical constraint logic programming.

As a starting point we can generalize our work on constraint generalization to generate constraint hierarchies by importing ideas from data mining. In particular work on Mining Knowledge at multiple knowledge levels by Han et al. [Han 95], is a good starting point for such a system.

8.6 Correctness Results

The most important work in the file of learning has been in the computational learning theory. In particular the theory of PAC learning is a neat way to characterize theoretically a learning system which clearly identifies what is the "new" knowledge learnt in a learning system. In our learning system, we can identify the correctness results for data represented as relations based on the PAC learning system.

9 Conclusions and Scope for Future Work

In this paper, we have outlined a model of learning where the underlying knowledge representation scheme is close to the one used in a majority of constraint programming applications. We have shown how existing learning algorithms based on propositional representations or those based on inductive logic programming paradigm are inadequate for learning in the model. We then discuss the subsumption hierarchy in the model and present the learning algorithm for generalizing in our model. We have studied the properties of the results obtained by learning in this model.

Thus we have outlined a generalized learning model for constraints on finite discrete domains. We are working on extending this model in the directions mentioned in the previous section.

References

[Ellman, 1993] Ellman T., Abstraction via approximate symmetry. In Proceedings of the Thirteenth International Joint Conference on Artificial Intelligence, Chamberry, France, August 1993.

[Freuder and Wallace 95] Freuder E.C. and Wallace R.J., "Generalizing inconsistency learning for constraint satisfaction", Proceedings of IJCAI-95 the Fourteenth International Joint Conference on Artificial Intelligence, C. Mellish, ed., Morgan Kaufmann.

[Han 95] Han J., " Mining Knowledge at Multiple Concept Levels", Proc. 4th Int'l Conf. on Information and Knowledge Management (CIKM'95), Baltimore, Maryland, Nov. 1995, pp. 19-24.

[Kawamura and Furukawa 93] Kawamura T. and Furukawa K., "Towards Inductive Generalization in Constraint Logic Programs", Proceedings of the IJCAI-93 Workshop on Inductive Logic Programming, Chambery ,France(August 93), pp. 93-104.

[Mackworth 92] Mackworth A., Constraint Satisfaction, in S.C.Shapiro,ed.,The Encyclopedia of AI,pp 285-293,Wiley, New York,1992.

[Mizoguchi and Ohwada 92] Mizoguchi F. and Ohwada H., "Constraint-directed generalization for learning spatial relations", Proceedings of the International Workshop on Inductive Logic Programming, ICOT TM-1182, Tokyo ,1992.

[Muggleton 92] Muggleton S., Inductive Logic Programming. Academic Press, 1992.

[Page and Frisch 91] Page C.D., and Frisch A.M., "Generalizing atoms in constraint logic ", Proceedings of the Second International Conference on Knowledge Representation and Reasoning, pp 429-440, 1991.

[Scheix et al 93] Scheix T. et al., "Nogood recording for static and dynamic CSP's", Proc. of International Conference on Tools for AI, 1993.

[Shavlik and Dietterich 90] Shavlik J.W., and Dietterich T.G. (eds.), Readings in machine learning. Morgan Kaufmann Publishers , 1990.

[Wu 95] Wu Xindong, Knowledge Acquisition from Databases. Ablex Publishing Corporation, 1995.

[Zweben et al. 1992] Zweben M., Davis E. , Daun B.,Drascher E.,Deale M. and Eskey M., Learning to improve constraint-based scheduling, Artificial Intelligence 58(1992) 271-296.

Induction of Constraint Logic Programs

Michèle Sebag[1] and Céline Rouveirol[2] and Jean-François Puget[3]

(1) LMS – URA CNRS 317
Ecole Polytechnique, 91128 Palaiseau Cedex, France
Michele.Sebag@polytechnique.fr

(2) LRI – URA CNRS 410
Université Paris-XI, 91405 Orsay Cedex, France
Celine.Rouveirol@lri.fr

(3) ILOG, 9 avenue de Verdun, 94253 Gentilly Cedex
jfpuget@ilog.fr

Abstract. Inductive Logic Programming (ILP) is concerned with learning hypotheses from examples, where both examples and hypotheses are represented in the Logic Programming (LP) language. The application of ILP to problems involving numerical information has shown the need for basic numerical background knowledge (e.g. relation "less than"). Our thesis is that one should rather choose Constraint Logic Programming (CLP) as the representation language of hypotheses, since CLP contains the extensions of LP developed in the past decade for handling numerical variables.

This paper deals with learning constrained clauses from positive and negative examples expressed as constrained clauses. A first step, termed *small induction*, gives a computational characterization of the solution clauses, which is sufficient to classify further instances of the problem domain. A second step, termed *exhaustive induction*, explicitly constructs all solution clauses. The algorithms we use are presented in detail, their complexity is given, and they are compared with other prominent ILP approaches.

1 Introduction

Inductive Logic Programming (ILP) is concerned with supervised learning from examples, and it can be considered a a subfield of Logic Programming (LP): it uses a subset of the definite clause language (e.g. used in Prolog) sometimes extended with some form of negation, to represent both the examples and the hypotheses to be learned [14].

The application of ILP to problems involving numerical information, such as chemistry [7], has shown the need for handling basic numerical knowledge, e.g. relation less than. This has often been met by supplying the learner with some ad hoc declarative knowledge [23]. However, one cannot get rid of the inherent limitations of LP regarding numerical variables: functions are not interpreted, i.e. they act as functors in terms. The consequences for that are detailed in section 2.1. Other possibilities are to use built-in numerical procedures [17], or to map the ILP problem at hand onto an attribute-value induction problem [8, 2, 26, 27].

This paper investigates a radically different approach in order to handle numerical information correctly, namely the use of Constraint Logic Programming (CLP) instead of LP as representation language. Indeed, CLP has been developed in the past decade as an extension of LP to other computation domains than Herbrand terms, including e.g. sets, strings, integers, floating point numbers, boolean algebras (see [6] for a survey). We are primarily interested here in the numerical extensions.

This paper extends a previous work devoted to learning constrained clauses from positive and negative examples represented as definite clauses [21]. The extension concerns the formalism of examples, which are thereafter represented as constrained clauses as well; this allows a number of negative examples to be represented via a single constrained clause.

This language of examples and hypotheses constitutes a major difference with other ILP learners, e.g. FOIL [17], ML-Smart [1], PROGOL [13] or REGAL [3] to name a few.

An equally important difference is that our approach is rooted in the Version Space framework [11]. More precisely the set of solution clauses Th here consists of *all* hypotheses partially complete (covering at least one example) and consistent (admitting no exceptions) with respect to the examples [19]. This contrasts with other learners retaining a few hypotheses in Th, optimal or quasi-optimal with regards to some numerical criterion such as the quantity of information for FOIL, or the Minimum Description Length for PROGOL.

This paper presents a 2-step approach. A computable characterization of Th is constructed in a first step, termed *small induction*; this characterization is sufficient for classification purposes. The explicit characterization of Th is obtained in a second step, termed *exhaustive induction*, which is much more computationally expensive than small induction. This 2-step approach allows one to check whether the predictive accuracy of the theory is worth undergoing the expensive process of explicit construction. Further, we show that exhaustive induction can be reformulated as an equivalent constraint solving problem; thereby, the burden of inductive search can be delegated to an external tool, purposely designed for combinatorial exploration of continuous domains or finite sets.

The rest of the paper is organized as follows. Next section briefly presents CLP. Then the induction setting is extended from LP to CLP: the notions of completeness and consistency of constrained clauses are defined. Section 4 is devoted to building constrained clauses consistent with a pair of examples. This is used in section 5, to characterize the set of solution clauses via *small induction*. *Exhaustive induction* is described in section 6, and section 7 is devoted to a complexity analysis of both algorithms. We conclude with some comparison with previous works and directions for future research.

2 Constraint Logic Programming

This section describes the formalism of constraint logic programming, for it both subsumes logic programming [5] and handles clauses that would require an additional background knowledge to be discovered in ILP.

2.1 The need for CLP

As said above, functions are not interpreted in LP; they are only treated as functors for Herbrand terms. It follows that an equation such as X - Y = 0 will never be true in a LP program: as sign '−' is not interpreted, the two sides of the equation cannot be unified.

In practice, Prolog systems offer a limited form of interpreted functions, using the is programming construct. This construct evaluates a ground term built with numerical constants and arithmetic functors, and returns the corresponding numerical value. However, this evaluation only applies to ground terms. Again, the goal Z is X - Y will not succeed unless both X and Y are instantiated with numerical values. Prolog systems also provide some predicates over numerical constants, e.g. =<, which suffer from the same limitations.

Thus, in order to handle numerical variables without extending unification, one must carefully design predicate definitions, and use the interpretation of functions when some ground terms are found. Here is a clever example of such a definition, reported from [23]. The goal is to define the less_than predicate. First thing is to handle the ground case:

    X less_than Y ← number(X), number(Y), !, X =< Y.

    X less_than X ← number(X).

Then, in order to handle the non ground variables, one must introduce explicitly a way to bind the variables. The approach presented in [23] consists in introducing a predicate float, that represents a finite set of numerical constants:

    float(X) ← number(X), !.

    float(X) ← member(X, [0, 0.1, 0.2, 0.4, 0.8, 1.6, 3.2, 6.4]).

The definition of the inequality predicate can then be extended as follows:

    X less_than Y ← float(X), float(Y), X =< Y.

    X less_than Y ← float(X), float(Delta), Y is X + Delta.

Such a clever intensional definition still depends on (and is limited by) an extensional definition of floating point constants.

2.2 Notations and definitions

The key idea of CLP stems from the observation that unification is an algorithm for solving equality constraints between Herbrand terms. Hence, new computation domains can be added to LP if adequate constraint solvers are provided. An alternative to special purpose definitions of predicates and extensional definition of numerical domains, precisely consists of developing an adequate constraint solver, that extends deduction through built-in interpretation of numerical constants and constructs. The CLP scheme thus generalizes the LP scheme as equation solving is a special case of constraint solving.

This requires the introduction of an *algebraic* semantics. Of course, our aim is not to present here an exhaustive state of the art in CLP (see [24]), but rather to define the basic CLP notions with respect to the classical LP and ILP terminology [9, 14].

Let $\mathcal{L} = \mathcal{L}_a \cup \mathcal{L}_c$, be a definite clause language without function symbols other than constants, where $\mathcal{L}_a$ (respectively $\mathcal{L}_c$) defines the set of uninterpreted (resp. interpreted) predicate symbols.

Definition 1. *In the following, a* constraint *denotes a literal built on a predicate symbol in $\mathcal{L}_c$. An* atom *denotes a literal built on a predicate symbol in $\mathcal{L}_a$.*

Definition 2. *A* constrained clause *is a clause of the form:*
$$H \leftarrow B_1 \wedge \ldots \wedge B_m \wedge c_1 \wedge \ldots \wedge c_n$$
where H, $B_1, \ldots, B_m$ are atoms and $c_1, \ldots, c_n$ are constraints. In the following, $c_1 \wedge \ldots \wedge c_n$ is referred to as the constraint part *of the constrained clause, and $H \leftarrow B_1 \wedge \ldots \wedge B_m$ as to the* definite part *of the constrained clause.*

A constrained logic program *is a finite set of constrained clauses.*

A constrained goal *is a clause of the form: $\leftarrow B_1 \wedge \ldots \wedge B_m \wedge c_1 \wedge \ldots \wedge c_n$, where $B_1, \ldots, B_m$ are atoms and $c_1, \ldots, c_n$ are constraints.*

2.3 Operational Semantics of CLP language

In LP, an answer to a query G with respect to a logic program P is a substitution σ (expressed as a set of equalities on variables of G) such that $G\sigma$ belongs to the least Herbrand model of P. An answer to a query G with respect to a CLP program P is not a substitution any more, but a set of consistent constraints such that all atoms in G have been resolved. We refer to [24] for a formal definition of the inference rule used in CLP, as this is beyond the scope of this paper.

Definition 3. *An* answer *to a CLP goal G with respect to program P is a conjunction of constraints $c_1 \wedge \ldots \wedge c_n$ such that*

$$P, \mathcal{T} \models (\forall)(c_1 \wedge \ldots \wedge c_n \rightarrow G), \qquad \text{or equivalently} \qquad P \models_S (\forall)(c_1 \wedge \ldots \wedge c_n \rightarrow G)$$

where P is a constraint logic program, S is a structure, $\mathcal{T}$ is the theory axiomatizing S and $(\forall)F$ denotes the universal closure of F.

The operational semantics of a CLP language can be defined either in terms of logical consequences or in an algebraic way [25] (see [5] for a detailed discussion). From now on, after [24], we use the only notation $\mathcal{D} \models$, which may be read both as the logical or algebraic version of logical entailment.

Definition 4. *A* constraint c *is* consistent *(or* satisfiable*) if there exists at least one instantiation of variables of c in $\mathcal{D}$ such that c is true, noted $\mathcal{D} \models (\exists)c$.*

A constraint c is consistent with *a set (i.e. conjunction) of constraints σ if*
$\mathcal{D} \models (\exists)(\sigma \wedge c)$.
A (set of) constraint(s) σ is inconsistent *if* $\mathcal{D} \models (\forall)(\neg \sigma)$.
Given two (sets of) constraints σ and σ', σ entails σ', noted σ $\prec_c$ σ', if
$\mathcal{D} \models (\forall)(\sigma \rightarrow \sigma')$.

Example: Let variable X have **R** as interpretation domain. Then constraint $(X^2 < 0)$ is unsatisfiable; constraint $(X > 10)$ entails constraint $(X > 5)$.

2.4 Domains of computation

Practically, we require the type of any variable X to be set by a *domain constraint* (equivalent to a *selector* in the Annotated Predicate Calculus terminology [10]). This domain constraint gives the initial domain of instantiation Ω_X of the variable. We restrict ourselves to numerical, hierarchical and nominal variables, where Ω_X respectively is (an interval of) **N** or **R**, a tree, or a (finite or infinite) set.

Domain constraints are of the form $(X \in dom(X))$, where $dom(X)$ denotes a subset of Ω_X. The domain constraints considered throughout this paper are summarized in Table 1.

Type of X	Initial domain Ω_X	Domain constraint $X \in dom(X)$
numerical	(interval of) **R** or **N**	$dom(X)$ interval of **R** or **N**.
hierarchical	tree	$dom(X)$ subtree of Ω_X
nominal	finite or infinite set	$dom(X)$ subset of Ω_X

Table 1: *Domains of computation and domain constraints*

A binary constraint involves a pair of variables X and Y having same domains of instantiation. The advantage of binary constraints is to allow for compact expressions: $(X = Y)$ replaces page-long expression of the form $(X \in \{red\})$ *and* $(Y \in \{red\})$ *or* $(X \in \{blue\})$ *and* $(Y \in \{blue\})$ *or...* The binary constraints considered in this paper are summarized in Table 2.

Type of X and Y	Binary constraints	
numerical	linear inequality	$(X \geq Y + a), (X \leq Y + b)$
hierarchical	generality	$(X \leq Y)$
nominal	equality and inequality	$(X = Y), (X \neq Y)$

Table 2: *Domains of computation and binary constraints*

Our constraint language is restricted to conjunctions of domain constraints and binary constraints as above. Two reasons explain our choice: this language is sufficient to deal with most real world problems, and it is supported by complete constraint solvers [4].

3 Induction setting in CLP

This section briefly recalls the basic induction setting and the Disjunctive Version Space approach. The key definitions of inductive learning, namely completeness and consistency, are then extended from LP to CLP.

3.1 Learning setting and Disjunctive Version Space

Let the positive and negative examples of the concept to be learned be expressed in the language of instances $\mathcal{L}_i$, and let $\mathcal{L}_h$ denote the language of hypotheses. Let two boolean relations of coverage and discrimination be defined on $\mathcal{L}_h \times \mathcal{L}_i$, respectively telling whether a given hypothesis covers or discriminates a given example.

The basic solutions of inductive learning consist of hypotheses that are complete (cover the positive examples) and consistent (discriminate the negative examples).

The Version Space (VS) framework gives a nice theoretical characterization of the set of solutions [11].Unfortunately noisy examples and disjunctive target concepts lead VS to fail, which implies that VS is not applicable to real-world problems[1]. The Disjunctive Version Space (DiVS) algorithm overcomes these limitations via relaxing the completeness requirement [19]. More precisely, DiVS constructs the set Th of all hypotheses that are partially complete (cover at least one example) and consistent. This is done by repeatedly characterizing the set $Th(E)$ of consistent hypotheses covering E, for each training example E.

The elementary step of Disjunctive Version Space actually consists of constructing the set $D(E, F)$ of hypotheses covering E and discriminating some other training example F: if $F_1, F_2, \ldots, F_n$ denote the training examples not belonging to the same target concept as E, termed *counter-examples* to E, then by construction

$$Th(E) = D(E, F_1) \wedge \ldots \wedge D(E, F_n)$$

3.2 From ILP to CLP

When the current training example E is a definite clause, we proposed to express E as $C\theta$, where C is the definite clause built from E by turning every occurrence of a term t_i in E into a distinct variable X_j, and θ is the substitution given by $\{X_j/t_i\}$ [18]:

$$E = C\theta$$

This decomposition allows induction to independently explore the lattice of definite clauses generalizing C, and the lattice of substitutions or constraints over the variables in C, that generalize θ: as a matter of fact, a substitution is a particular case of constraint (a set of equality constraints between Herbrand terms).

When training examples are described by constrained clauses, we must first get rid of the fact that one constrained clause may admit several equivalent expressions.

Definition 5. *Let g be a constrained clause. The canonical form of g is defined as $G\gamma$, where*
* *G is the definite clause built from g by deleting the constraints and turning*

---
[1] Real examples are *always* noisy; real target concepts are usually disjunctive.

every occurrence of a term t_i in g into a distinct variable X_j;
• γ is the maximally specific conjunction of constraints entailed by the constraint part of g and the constraints $(X_j = t_i)$.

Example: Let g be a constrained clause describing some poisonous chemical molecules:

$$g : poisonous(X) \leftarrow atm(X, Y, carbon, T), atm(X, U, carbon, W),$$
$$(Y \neq U), (T > W - 2)$$

The canonical expression of g is $G\gamma$, with

$$G : poisonous(X) \leftarrow atm(X', Y, Z, T), atm(X", U, V, W)$$
$$\gamma : (Y \neq U), (T > W - 2), (X = X'), (X = X"), (X' = X"),$$
$$(Z = carbon), (V = carbon), (Z = V)$$

In the remainder of this paper, "constrained clause" is intended as "constrained clause in canonical form".

Let $E = C\theta$ hereafter denote the constrained clause to generalize. The language of hypotheses $\mathcal{L}_h$ is that of constrained clauses $G\gamma$ where G is a definite clause generalizing C in the sense of θ-subsumption [14], noted $C \prec G$, and γ is a conjunction of constraints set on variables in C, such that θ entails γ (Definition 4):

$$\mathcal{L}_h = \{G\gamma, \text{ such that } C \prec G \text{ and } \theta \prec_c \gamma\}$$

DiVS thus explores a bound logical space with bottom C, and a bound constraint space with bottom θ.

3.3 Completeness and Consistency in CLP

The generality order on constrained clauses is extended from the generalization order on logical clauses defined by θ-subsumption [14], and from the generalization order defined by constraint entailment [6].

Definition 6. *Let $G\gamma$ and $G'\gamma'$ be constrained clauses; $G\gamma$ generalizes $G'\gamma'$, noted $G'\gamma' \prec_h G\gamma$, if there exists a substitution σ on G such that $G\sigma$ is included in G', and $\gamma'\sigma$ entails γ:*

$$G'\gamma' \prec_h G\gamma \quad \text{iff} \quad \text{there exists } \sigma \text{ / } G\sigma \subseteq G' \text{ and } \gamma'\sigma \prec_c \gamma$$

It follows from Definition 6, that any constrained clause $G\gamma$ in the search space $\mathcal{L}_h$, generalizes E (σ being set to the identity substitution on C):

$$G\gamma \in \mathcal{L}_h \quad \text{implies} \quad C\theta = E \prec_h G\gamma$$

Positive examples are represented as constrained clauses concluding to the predicate to be learned tc. Negative examples are also represented as constrained clauses. Indeed, there is no standard semantics for the negation in Logic Programming, and even less for CLP. We therefore explicitly introduce the negation of target predicate tc, noted ^{opp}tc; negative examples are constrained clauses concluding to ^{opp}tc. For instance, if active is the target predicate, we introduce the opposite predicate symbol ^{opp}active (= inactive).

Then, for any constrained clause g, let ^{opp}g be defined as the constrained clause obtained from g by replacing the predicate in the head of g, by the opposite target predicate.

$$^{opp}g : \quad ^{opp}head(g) \leftarrow body(g)$$

The consistency of a constrained clause is defined as follows:

Definition 7. *Let $G\gamma$ and $G'\gamma'$ be constrained clauses. $G\gamma$ is* inconsistent *with respect to $G'\gamma'$ iff there exists a substitution σ on G such that $G\sigma$ is included into $^{opp}G'$ and γ is consistent with $\gamma'\sigma$:*

$$G\gamma \text{ is inconsistent wrt } G'\gamma' \text{ iff } \exists \sigma \text{ such that } G\sigma \subseteq {}^{opp}G' \text{ and } \mathcal{D} \models (\exists)(\gamma \wedge \gamma'\sigma)$$

Such a substitution σ is termed negative substitution *on G derived from $G'\gamma'$.*

$G\gamma$ discriminates $G'\gamma'$, if there exists no negative substitution σ on G derived from $G'\gamma'$.

Example: Let g and g' be two constrained clauses as follows:

$$g : poisonous(X) \leftarrow atm(X, Y, carbon, T), atm(X, U, carbon, W), (T > W - 2)$$
$$g' : {}^{opp}poisonous(X) \leftarrow atm(X, Y, Z, T), atm(X, U, Z, W), (T \leq W)$$

Then, g is inconsistent wrt to g': σ being set to the identity substitution, one sees that a molecule involving two carbon atoms with same valence $(T = W)$ would be considered both *poisonous* according to g, and *non poisonous* according to g'.

4 Building discriminant constrained clauses

This section focuses on the elementary step of Disjunctive Version Space, namely constructing the set $D(E, F)$ of constrained clauses covering E and discriminating F (in the sense of definition 7), where E and F are constrained clauses concluding to opposite target concepts. We assume in this section that E is consistent with respect to F.

Given the chosen hypothesis language, there exists two ways for a candidate hypothesis $G\gamma$ to discriminate F: The first one, examined in section 4.1, operates on the definite clause part of $G\gamma$: $G\gamma$ discriminates F if G involves a predicate that does not occur in F. The second one, examined in sections 4.2 and 4.3, operates on the constraint part of $G\gamma$: $G\gamma$ discriminates F if γ is inconsistent with the constraint part of F.

4.1 Discriminant predicates

Due to the fact that C involves distinct variables only, any clause G subsuming C discriminates F iff it involves a predicate symbol that does not occur in F, termed *discriminant predicate*. Predicate-based discrimination thereby amounts to boolean discrimination (presence/absence of a predicate symbol). More formally,

Proposition 1. *Let $G_{pred}(F)$ be the set of clauses head$(C) \leftarrow p_i()$., for p_i ranging over the set of discriminant predicate symbols. Then, a definite clause that subsumes C discriminates F iff it is subsumed by a clause in $G_{pred}(F)$.*

$G_{pred}(F)$ thereby sets an upper bound on the set of definite clauses that subsume C and discriminate F. Note this set can be empty: e.g. in the chemistry domain, all example molecules are described via the same predicates (*atom* and *bond*), regardless of their class (*poisonous* or *non poisonous*).

4.2 Discriminant domain constraints

Let G be the generalization of C obtained by dropping all discriminant predicates. With no loss of generality, F can be described[2] as $^{opp}G\rho$, with ρ being the constraint part of F.

Hence, G is inconsistent with F; and due to the fact that C (and hence G) involves distinct variables only, any negative substitution on G derived from F (Definition 7) is a permutation of variables in G. Let Σ denote the set of these negative substitutions. Note that constraints on G are trivially embedded onto constraints on C.

One is finally interested in the following constraints on C:

- Constraint θ which is the constraint part of example E,
- Constraint ρ which is the constraint part of example F,
- And the set Σ of negative substitutions derived from F (being reminded that substitutions are particular cases of constraints).

Let us first concentrate on domain constraints, and assume in this subsection that our constraint language is restricted to domain constraints[3]. A constraint γ is thus composed of a conjunction of domain constraints $(X_i \in dom_\gamma(X_i))$, for X_i ranging over the variables in C.

It is straightforward to show that the lattice of constraints on C is equivalent to the lattice $\mathcal{L}_{eq} = \mathcal{P}(\Omega_1) \times \mathcal{P}(\Omega_2) \times \ldots$, where Ω_i denotes the domain of instantiation of X_i, for X_i ranging over the variables of C, and $\mathcal{P}(\Omega_i)$ denotes the power set of Ω_i. An equivalent representation of γ is given by the vector of subsets $dom_\gamma(X_i)$.

---

[2] The predicates appearing in F and not appearing in E can be dropped with no loss of information: given the hypothesis language, they will not be considered in $D(E, F)$.

[3] This restricted language does not include the substitutions, as it does not allow the representation of variable linking. This will be settled in section 4.3.

Building discriminant domain constraints is thus amenable to attribute-value discrimination: two constraints are inconsistent iff they correspond to non overlapping elements in $\mathcal{L}_{eq}$.

Proposition 2. *Let γ be a conjunction of domain constraints $(X_i \in dom_\gamma(X_i))$, and let $\gamma' = (X_{i_0} \in dom_{\gamma'}(X_{i_0})$ be a domain constraint. Constraint γ' is inconsistent with constraint γ iff $dom_\gamma(X_{i_0})$ and $dom_{\gamma'}(X_{i_0})$ are disjoint.*

Let us now characterize the constraints discriminating example F. By definition, $G\gamma$ discriminates F iff γ is inconsistent with $\rho\sigma$ for all σ in Σ.

Definition 8. *An elementary discriminant constraint with respect to a negative substitution σ and a variable X, is a domain constraint on X that is entailed by θ and inconsistent with $\rho\sigma$.*
A maximally general elementary discriminant constraint wrt σ and X is called maximally discriminant.

In the considered domain constraint language (section 2.4), there exists at most one maximally discriminant constraint wrt a negative substitution σ and a variable X, noted $(X \in dom_{\sigma^\bullet}(X))$:

- if X is a numerical variable, such a maximally discriminant constraint exists iff $dom_\theta(X)$ et $dom_\rho(X.\sigma)$ are disjoint, in which case $dom_{\sigma^\bullet}(X)$ is the largest interval including $dom_\theta(X)$ and excluding $dom_\rho(X.\sigma)$.
- if X is a hierarchical variable, such a maximally discriminant constraint exists iff $dom_\theta(X)$ et $dom_\rho(X.\sigma)$ are subtrees which are not comparable, in which case $dom_{\sigma^\bullet}(X)$ is the most general subtree that includes $dom_\theta(X)$ and does not include $dom_\rho(X.\sigma)$.
- if X is a nominal variable, such a maximally discriminant constraint exists iff $dom_\theta(X)$ et $dom_\rho(X.\sigma)$ do not overlap, in which case $dom_{\sigma^\bullet}(X)$ is the complementary in Ω_X of $dom_\rho(X.\sigma)$. For the sake of convenience, domain constraint $(X \in dom_{\sigma^\bullet}(X))$ is noted $(X \notin dom_\rho(X.\sigma))$.

If $dom_{\sigma^\bullet}(X)$ exists, X is said to be σ-*discriminant*.

By construction, a domain constraint on X that is entailed by θ and discriminates $\rho\sigma$ must entail $(X \in dom_{\sigma^\bullet}(X))$. An upper bound on the domain constraints that discriminate $\rho\sigma$ is then given by the disjunction of constraints $(X \in dom_{\sigma^\bullet}(X))$, for X ranging over the σ-discriminant variables in C. More formally,

Proposition 3. *Let $var(C)$ be the set of variables in C, let σ be a substitution in Σ, and let γ_σ be the disjunction of constraints $(X_i \in dom_{\sigma^\bullet}(X_i))$ for X_i ranging over the σ-discriminant variables in $var(C)$. Let γ be a conjunction of domain constraints on variables in C that is entailed by θ. Then,*

$$\gamma \text{ is inconsistent with } \rho\sigma \qquad \text{iff} \qquad \gamma \prec_c \gamma_\sigma$$

Example: Let E and F be as follows:

$E : poisonous(X) \leftarrow atm(X, Y, carbon, T), atm(X, U, carbon, W), T < 24, W \geq 25$

$F : {}^{opp}poisonous(X) \leftarrow atm(X, Y, hydrogen, 18), atm(X, U, carbon, W'), W' \leq 21$

The definite clause C built from E is given below; variables Z and V are nominal, with domain of instantiation $\{carbon, hydrogen, oxygen, \ldots\}$. Variables T and W are continuous, with domain of instantiation $\mathbf{N}$. (Other variables are discarded as they do not convey discriminant information).

$$C : poisonous(X) \leftarrow atm(X', Y, Z, T), atm(X", U, V, W)$$

There is no discriminant predicate $(G = C)$; Σ includes four negative substitutions $\sigma_1, \sigma_2, \sigma_3$ and σ_4 which correspond to the four possible mappings of the two literals atm in C onto the two literals atm in F.

Table 3 shows a tabular representation of the constraints θ and $\rho\sigma_i$, where a case of the matrix is a sub domain of the domain of instantiation of the variable.

	X X' Y	Z	T	X" U	V	W
θ	– – –	carbon	$[0, 24)$	– –	carbon	$[25, \infty)$
$\rho\sigma_1$	– – –	hydrogen	18	– –	carbon	$[0, 21]$
$\rho\sigma_2$	– – –	carbon	$[0, 21]$	– –	hydrogen	18
$\rho\sigma_3$	– – –	hydrogen	18	– –	hydrogen	18
$\rho\sigma_4$	– – –	carbon	$[0, 21]$	– –	carbon	$[0, 21]$

Table 3: Tabular representation of domain constraints

And the (disjunctive) constraint γ_{σ_1} entailed by θ and maximally general such that it is inconsistent with $\rho\sigma_1$ is given as (with $[W \in (21, \infty)]$ written $[W > 21]$ for the sake of readability):

$$\gamma_{\sigma_1} = [Z \notin \{hydrogen\}] \vee [W > 21]$$

4.3 Discriminant binary constraints

We showed that building discriminant binary constraints is amenable to building discriminant domain constraints, via introducing auxiliary constrained variables, termed *relational variables* [21].

As an example, let us consider binary equality or inequality constraints $X = Y$ or $X \neq Y$. One associates to any pair of variables X and Y having same domain of instantiation, the relational variable $(X^=Y)$, interpreted for any substitution σ of C as: $(X^=Y).\sigma = true$ if $X.\sigma = Y.\sigma$, $(X^=Y).\sigma = false$ if $X.\sigma$ and $Y.\sigma$ are distinct constants, and $(X^=Y).\sigma$ is not bound otherwise.

Equality constraint $(X = Y)$ (respectively inequality constraint $(X \neq Y)$) is equivalent to domain constraints on relational variable $(X^=Y)$ given as $((X^=Y) = true)$ (resp. $((X^=Y) = false)$).

Binary arithmetic constraint can be built as domain constraints on relational numerical variables: let (X^-Y) be the constrained variable interpreted as the difference of numerical variables X and Y, the domain constraint $((X^-Y) \in [a, b])$ is equivalent to the binary constraint on X and Y : $(Y + a \leq X \leq Y + b)$.

In the chosen constraint language, all binary constraints can be expressed as domain constraints on such auxiliary variables. Proposition 3 then generalizes as :

Proposition 4. *Let $var^*(C)$ be the set of initial and relational variables in C, let σ be a negative substitution in Σ, and let γ_σ now denote the disjunction of constraints $(X \in dom_\sigma \cdot (X))$ for X ranging over the σ-discriminant variables in $var^*(C)$. Let γ be a conjunction of domain constraints on variables in $var^*(C)$ that is entailed by θ. Then,*

$$\gamma \text{ is inconsistent with } \rho\sigma \quad \text{iff} \quad \gamma \prec_c \gamma_\sigma$$

Constraint γ_σ hence is the upper-bound on the set of constraints on C that are entailed by θ and are inconsistent with $\rho\sigma$.

As an example, the tabular representation (Table 3) is extended to binary constraints as well:

	X	X'	Y	Z	T	X"	U	V	W	Z = U	W - T
θ	–	–	–	carbon	$[0,24)$	–	–	carbon	$[25,\infty)$	false	$[1,\infty)$
$\rho\sigma_1$	–	–	–	hydrogen	18	–	–	carbon	$[0,21]$	false	$[-18,3]$
$\rho\sigma_2$	–	–	–	carbon	$[0,21]$	–	–	hydrogen	18	false	$[-3,18]$
$\rho\sigma_3$	–	–	–	hydrogen	18	–	–	hydrogen	18	true	0
$\rho\sigma_4$	–	–	–	carbon	$[0,21]$	–	–	carbon	$[0,21]$	true	0

Table 4: domain constraints and   binary constraints

And the disjunctive constraint γ_{σ_4} entailed by θ and maximally general such that it is inconsistent with $\rho\sigma_4$ is given as:

$$\gamma_{\sigma_4} = [W > 21] \vee [Z \neq U] \vee [W - T > 0]$$

Last, one considers the conjunction of the constraints γ_σ for σ ranging in Σ:

Proposition 5. *Let G be a generalization of C inconsistent with respect to F, and let γ_F be the conjunction of constraints γ_σ for σ ranging in Σ. Then $G\gamma$ discriminates F iff γ entails γ_F.*

Constraint γ_F thus defines an upper bound on the constraints discriminating F, like $G_{pred}(F)$ is the upper-bound on the set of definite clauses that generalize C and discriminate F. These are combined in the next section in order to characterize all consistent partially complete constrained clauses.

5   Small induction

Our goal is here to characterize the Disjunctive Version Space learned from positive and negative constrained clauses, and to use this characterization to classify further instances of the problem domain.

5.1 Characterizing $Th(E)$

Let all notations be as in the previous section, and let $G\gamma$ be a constrained clause in the hypothesis language. By recollecting results in sections 4.1 and 4.3, $G\gamma$ discriminates F iff either G is subsumed by a clause in $G_{pred}(F)$ or γ entails γ_F:

Proposition 6. *Let $D(E, F)$ be the set of constrained clauses that generalize E and discriminate F, and let $G\gamma$ be a constrained clause generalizing E. Then $G\gamma$ belongs to $D(E, F)$ if and only if*

$$(\exists G' \text{ in } G_{pred}(F) \text{ s.t. } G \prec G') \qquad \text{or} \qquad (\gamma \prec_c \gamma_F) \qquad (1)$$

And the set $Th(E)$ of consistent constrained clauses covering E can be characterized from the set of constrained clauses covering E and discriminating F, for F ranging over the counter-examples $F_1, \ldots F_n$ to E (i.e. the training examples concluding to the concept opposite to that of E); by construction,

$$Th(E) = D(E, F_1) \wedge \ldots \wedge D(E, F_n)$$

In other words, the pairs $(G_{pred}(F_i), \gamma_{F_i})$ constitute a computational characterization of $Th(E)$: they give means to check whether any given constrained clause belongs to $Th(E)$.

The Disjunctive Version Space finally is constructed by iteratively characterizing $Th(E)$, for E ranging over the training set.

However, looking for consistent hypotheses make little sense when dealing with real-world, hence noisy, data. One is therefore more likely interested in hypotheses admitting a limited number of inconsistencies. Let $Th_\varepsilon(E)$ denote the set of hypotheses covering E and admitting at most ε inconsistencies. Then, we show that $Th_\varepsilon(E)$ can be characterized from the pairs $(G_{pred}(F_i), \gamma_{F_i})$, with no additional complexity [19]: a constrained clause $G\gamma$ covering E belongs to $Th_\varepsilon(E)$ iff it satisfies condition (1) above, for all but at most ε counter-examples F_i to E.

The advantage of this approach is to delay the choice of the consistency bias, from induction to classification, at no additional cost [19]:

Induction constructs once and for all the pairs $(G_{pred}(F_i), \gamma_{F_i})$, or a tractable approximation of these [22];

This allows one to tune the degree of consistency of the hypotheses used during classification, at no extra cost[4].

5.2 Classification in Disjunctive Version Space

One major result of this approach is that the computational characterization of the Disjunctive Version Space is sufficient to classify any further instance of the problem domain. In other words, the explicit construction of $Th(E)$, for E ranging over the training examples, gives no extra prediction power.

---

[4] The degree of generality of hypotheses can also be tuned at no extra cost; see [19, 22].

The Disjunctive Version Space includes hypotheses concluding to opposite target concepts, since positive *and* negative examples are generalized. And, though these hypotheses are consistent with the training examples, they usually are inconsistent with one another. Classification therefore does not rely on standard logic, but rather on a nearest-neighbor like approach. The instance I to classify is said to be neighbor of a training example E, if I is generalized by a hypothesis in $Th(E)$; I is thereafter classified in the class of the majority of its neighbors.

One shows that I is generalized by a hypothesis in $Th(E)$ iff it is generalized by a hypothesis in $D(E, F)$, for every counter-example[5] F. And this can be checked from the computational characterization of $D(E, F)$:

Proposition 7. *Let I be an instance of the problem domain, formalized as a conjunction of constrained atoms. Then I is generalized by the body of a clause in $D(E, F)$ iff there exists a generalization G of C and a constraint γ such that the body of $G\gamma$ generalizes I, and either G is subsumed by a clause in $G_{pred}(F)$ or γ entails γ_F.*

The important distinction compared to Prop 6. is that γ is not required to be entailed by θ any more: Prop 7 only requires to consider the substitutions between C and the definite part of I.

5.3   A two-step induction

We thus propose a two step induction scheme. During the first step, called *small induction*, all pairs of training examples (E, F) satisfying opposite target concepts are considered; and for each such pair, we build the set of discriminant definite clauses $G_{pred}(F)$ and the discriminant constraint γ_F (conjunction of disjunctions). As shown above, this is sufficient to address the classification of unseen examples, and characterize the set of consistent partially complete constrained clauses.

During the second step, called *exhaustive induction*, all such consistent constrained clauses are explicitly built, and it is shown in the next section that exhaustive induction can be achieved by constraint solving.

The advantage of this scheme is twofold. First, the burden of explicitly constructing the hypotheses can be delegated to constraint solvers, that is, algorithms external to induction and geared for combinatorial search in discrete and continuous domains.

Second, small induction can be viewed as an on-fly, lazy learning, the complexity of which is much smaller than that of exhaustive induction (section 7): it constructs theories which are not understandable, but yet operational to classify examples. One may then get some idea of the accuracy of a theory, before undergoing the expensive process of making it explicit.

---

[5] Or for all except ε counter-examples, in case the consistency requirement is relaxed.

6 Exhaustive induction

We present here an algorithm called ICP, for *Inductive Constraint Programming*, that constructs the set $Th(E)$ of consistent constrained clauses covering E. In the line of Version Spaces [11], we limit ourselves to construct explicitly the upper bound of $Th(E)$, i.e. the set $G(E)$ of maximally general constrained clauses in $Th(E)$.

ICP proceeds as follows. It first builds the computational characterization of $Th(E)$, i.e. the set of clauses $G_{pred}(F_i)$ and constraint γ_{F_i} for F_i ranging over the counter-examples of E. $G(E)$ is initialized to the empty set and the current constrained clause $G\gamma$ is initialized to the clause $head(C) \leftarrow$.
Then, $G_{pred}(F_i)$ and γ_{F_i} are explored in depth-first, and clause $G\gamma$ is specialized until it discriminates all counter-examples F_i. All consistent constrained clauses are obtained by backtracking on the specialization choices.

Build G(E)
Init
    For $F = F_1, \ldots, F_n$,
        Build $G_{pred}(F)$ and γ_F.
        * Prune γ_F.
    $G(E) = \phi$.
    $G = head(C) \leftarrow$.
    $\gamma = True$.

Main Loop
    For $F = F_1, \ldots, F_n$,
        if G is not subsumed by any clause in $G_{pred}(F)$
        and γ does not entail γ_F, then
            If possible,
                * Specialize $G\gamma$ to discriminate F
            Otherwise,
                Backtrack on the specialization choices
    * If $G\gamma$ is maximally general in $Th(E)$,
        $G(E) = G(E) \bigcup \{G\gamma\}$.
    Backtrack on the specialization choices.

Specialize $G\gamma$ to discriminate F (non deterministic)
    Select a clause G_0 in $G_{pred}(F)$.
        Do $body(G) = body(G) \wedge body(G_0)$
Or,
    For each negative substitution σ_k derived from F
        If γ does not entail γ_{σ_k},
            Select a variable X_j that is σ_k-discriminant
                Do $\gamma = \gamma \wedge (X_j \in dom_{\sigma_k^*}(X_j))$

In this scheme, constraint solving is employed to several tasks (indicated with an asterisk):

It is used to prune γ_F: a partial order noted $<_E$ can be defined on the negative substitutions with respect to the positive substitution [20]. Minimal substitutions with respect to this partial order can be viewed as "near-misses": all substitutions but the minimal ones, can soundly be pruned. This pruning was explicitly dealt with in previous works [18, 20]. It turns out to be a special case of constraint entailment ($\sigma_i <_E \sigma_j$ is equivalent to $\gamma_{\sigma_i} \prec_c \gamma_{\sigma_j}$) and this pruning can therefore be achieved by a constraint solver.

It chiefly allows for building $G\gamma$, through selecting specialization choices, checking whether the current solution $G\gamma$ is subsumed by a clause in $G_{pred}(F_i)$, and backtracking.

Last, it allows for testing whether $G\gamma$ is maximally general[6] in $Th(E)$.

7 Complexity

Assume that the domain of instantiation of any variable can be explored with a bounded cost. Then, the complexity of building the maximally discriminant constraint γ_σ that discriminates a negative substitution σ, is linear in the number of initial and relational variables in C. In our constraint language, this complexity is quadratic in the number $\mathcal{X}$ of variables in C.

If $\mathcal{L}$ denotes an upper bound on the number of negative substitutions derived from a counter-example (the size of Σ), the complexity of building γ_F is then $\mathcal{O}(\mathcal{X}^2 \times \mathcal{L})$. The complexity of building $G_{pred}(F)$ (section 4.1) is negligible compared to that of building γ_F (it is linear in the number of predicate symbols in E, which is upper-bounded by $\mathcal{X}$).

Finally the computational characterization of $D(E, F)$ has complexity $\mathcal{O}(\mathcal{X}^2 \times \mathcal{L})$.

Characterizing the Disjunctive Version Space Th requires all pairs $D(E_i, F_j)$ to be characterized; if N denotes the number of training examples, the computational characterization of Th has complexity $\mathcal{O}(\mathcal{X}^2 \times \mathcal{L} \times N^2)$.

The complexity of classifying an unseen example I from Th (proposition 7) is the size of the implicit characterization of Th times the number of substitutions derived from I, upper bounded by $\mathcal{L}$; the complexity of classification hence is $\mathcal{O}(\mathcal{X}^2 \times \mathcal{L}^2 \times N^2)$.

The complexity of the intentional characterization of Th, via algorithm ICP, is in $\mathcal{O}(N \times (\mathcal{X}^{2 \times \mathcal{L} \times N}))$. Needless to say, the learning and classifying processes based on the computational characterization of Th are much more affordable than those based on the explicit characterization of Th.

The typical complexity of first order logic appears through factor $\mathcal{L}$: if M is an upper bound on the number of literals based on a same predicate symbol that

---

[6] The fact that $G\gamma$ is a maximally general element of $Th(E)$ can be expressed via considering new constraint programs, involving the assertion of all but one elementary constraints satisfied by γ, and the negation of the remaining one. $G\gamma$ is maximally general if such new constraint programs are satisfiable.

occur in an example, and P is the number of predicate symbols, $\mathcal{L}$ is in $M^{M \times P}$. For instance, in the mutagenesis problem [7], examples are molecules involving up to 40 atoms; $\mathcal{L}$ is then 40^{40}.

We therefore used a specifically devised heuristic to overcome this limitation. The exhaustive exploration of the set Σ of negative substitutions, was replaced by a stochastic exploration: we limit ourselves to consider a limited number η of samples in Σ, extracted by a stochastic sampling mechanism [22]. An approximation of $D(E, F)$ was therefore constructed in polynomial time ($\mathcal{O}(\mathcal{X}^2 \times \eta \times N^2)$); to give an order of idea, the number η of samples considered in Σ was limited to 300 (to be compared to 40^{40}). This approach led to outstanding experimental results, compared to the state of the art on the mutagenesis problem [23].

8 Discussion and Perspectives

This section first discusses our choice of a maximally discriminant induction, then situates this work with respect to some previous works devoted to generalization of constraints [16, 12] or reformulation of ILP problems [8, 26, 27].

8.1 Generalization Choices

This work first extends the frame of induction to constraint logic programming; see [22] for an experimental demonstration of the potentialities of this language. Note that this frame does *not allow* to learn clauses that could not be learned by state-of-art learners, supplied with an ad hoc knowledge. Rather, it allows to learn simple numerical relations without requirement for additional knowledge.

A second aspect of this work concerns the tractable characterization of the Disjunctive Version Space of consistent partially complete hypotheses. In opposition, as mentioned earlier, the theories built by either PROGOL or FOIL include only *a few* elements in this set.

Like PROGOL, *ICP* handles non ground examples, in opposition to FOIL [17]; but domain theory (that cannot be put as examples) can be considered only through saturation of the examples: *ICP* cannot use the domain knowledge in order to guide the exploration of the search space, as ML-Smart [1] or PROGOL do.

8.2 Generalization from constraints

As far as we know, the generalization from constraints has only been addressed so far by Page and Frisch [16] and Mizoguchi and Ohwada [12].

In [16], the goal is to generalize constrained atoms. Constrained atoms are handled as definite clauses whose antecedents express the constraints. Constrained generalizations of two atoms are built from the sorted generalizations defined on their arguments. In both [16] and our approach, generalization ultimately proceeds by building constraints. But different issues are addressed. In [16], the main difficulty arises from the possibly multiple generalizations of two terms, which does not occur in our restricted language (section 4.2). In opposition, the main difficulty here comes from the multiple structural matchings among examples (section 7) while such a matching uniquely follows from the unique atom considered in [16].

Another approach of the generalization of constrained clauses is presented by Mizoguchi and Ohwada [12]. This work is nicely motivated by geometrical applications (avoiding the collision between objects and obstacles). The region of safe moves of an object can be 'naturally' described through a set of linear constraints; the goal consists in automatically acquiring such constraints from examples.

[12] first extend the definition of some typical induction operators (minimal generalization, absorption, lgg) to constrained clauses. Then, an *ad hoc* domain theory being given, examples are described by constrained atoms which are generalized through absorption and lgg, in the line of [15].

In what regards the roles respectively devoted to ILP and CLP, the essential differences can be summarized as follows: the induction of constrained clauses is done (a) by incorporating the structure of constraints into ILP, in [16]; (b) by extending the inverse resolution approach to CLP in [12]; and by interleaving ILP and CLP in our approach.

8.3 Reformulation

A strong motivation for reformulating ILP problems into simpler problems, e.g. in propositional form, is that propositional learners are good at dealing with numbers [8, 2, 26]. LINUS [8] achieves such transformation under several assumptions, which altogether ensure that one first-order example is transformed into *one* attribute-value example; this transformation thereby does not address the case of multiple structural matchings among examples. LINUS nicely uses the theory of the domain in order to introduce new variables and enrich the attribute-value representation of the examples.

Another approach is that of Zucker and Ganascia [26, 27], that focuses on restricting the set of predicates and substitutions relevant to a given level of induction. Simply put, moriological reformulations rely on a hierarchical description of the problem domain, where a morion of a given level can be decomposed into one or several morions of a lower level (e.g. the *car* morion involves the description of four *tire* morions). One may then restrict oneself to consider pattern matchings among examples, that preserve the structure (front tires, back tires). Such restrictions allow to drastically decrease the complexity of induction (which could benefit to ICP too); but the machine learning of such restrictions is still an open problem [26].

Note that [8] and [26] both map an induction problem into another simpler induction problem. In opposition, the mapping presented here enables a shift of paradigm: an induction problem is transformed into a constraint program, which can in turn be solved by an external tool.

8.4 Perspectives

This work opens several perspectives of research:

New variables (as in [8]) and new types of constraints could be considered. Ideally, language bias would be expressed via additional constraints (for instance, requiring the solution clauses to be connected could be expressed via additional constraints).

Also, the user could supply some optimality function in order to guide the selection of the admissible solutions. Selective discriminant induction could then be reformulated as a constrained optimization problem (finding the optimum of the objective function still satisfying the constraints).

But many promising tracks are opened by current experimental validations of this scheme [22].

Acknowledgments

This work has been partially supported by the ESPRIT BRA 6020 Inductive Logic Programming and by the ESPRIT LTR 20237 ILP^2.

References

1. F. Bergadano and A. Giordana. Guiding induction with domain theories. In Y. Kodratoff and R.S. Michalski, editors, *Machine Learning : an artificial intelligence approach*, volume 3, pages 474–492. Morgan Kaufmann, 1990.
2. S. Dzeroski, L. Todorovski, and T. Urbancic. Handling real numbers in ILP: a step towards better behavioral clones. In N. Lavrac and S. Wrobel, editors, *Proceedings of ECML-95, European Conference on Machine Learning*, pages 283–286. Springer Verlag, 1995.
3. A. Giordana, L. Saitta, and F. Zini. Learning disjunctive concepts by means of genetic algorithms. In Cohen W. and Hirsh H., editors, *Proceedings of ICML-94, International Conference on Machine Learning*, pages 96–104. Morgan Kaufmann, 1994.
4. ILOG. *Manuel SOLVER*. ILOG, Gentilly, France, 1995.
5. J. Jaffar and J. L. Lassez. Constraint logic programming. In *Proc. of the fourteenth ACM Symposium on the Principles of Programming Languages*, pages 111–119, 1987.
6. J. Jaffar and M.J. Maher. Constraint logic programming : a survey. *Journal of Logic Programming*, pages 503–581, 1994.
7. R.D. King, A. Srinivasan, and M.J.E. Sternberg. Relating chemical activity to structure: an examination of ILP successes. *New Gen. Comput.*, 13, 1995.
8. N. Lavrač and S. Džeroski. *Inductive Logic Programming: Techniques and Applications*. Ellis Horwood, 1994.
9. J.W. Lloyd. *Foundations of Logic Programming, second extended edition*. Springer Verlag, 1987.
10. R.S. Michalski. A theory and methodology of inductive learning. In R.S Michalski, J.G. Carbonell, and T.M. Mitchell, editors, *Machine Learning : an artificial intelligence approach*, volume 1, pages 83–134. Morgan Kaufmann, 1983.

11. T.M. Mitchell. Generalization as search. *Artificial Intelligence*, 18:203–226, 1982.
12. F. Mizoguchi and H. Ohwada. Constraint-directed generalizations for learning spatial relations. In *Proceedings of ILP-91, International Workshop on Inductive Logic Programming*, 1991.
13. S. Muggleton. Inverse entailment and PROGOL. *New Gen. Comput.*, 13:245–286, 1995.
14. S. Muggleton and L. De Raedt. Inductive logic programming: Theory and methods. *Journal of Logic Programming*, 19:629–679, 1994.
15. S. Muggleton and C. Feng. Efficient induction of logic programs. In *Proceedings of the 1st conference on algorithmic learning theory*. Ohmsha, Tokyo, Japan, 1990.
16. C. D. Page and A. M. Frisch. Generalization and learnability: A study of constrained atoms. In S. Muggleton, editor, *Proceedings of the first International Workshop on Inductive Logic Programming*, pages 29–61, 1991.
17. J.R. Quinlan. Learning logical definition from relations. *Machine Learning*, 5:239–266, 1990.
18. M. Sebag. A constraint-based induction algorithm in FOL. In W. Cohen and H. Hirsh, editors, *Proceedings of ICML-94, International Conference on Machine Learning*, pages 275–283. Morgan Kaufmann, July 1994.
19. M. Sebag. Delaying the choice of bias: A disjunctive version space approach. In L. Saitta, editor, *Proceedings of the 13th International Conference on Machine Learning*, pages 444–452. Morgan Kaufmann, 1996.
20. M. Sebag and C. Rouveirol. Induction of maximally general clauses compatible with integrity constraints. In S. Wrobel, editor, *Proceedings of ILP-94, International Workshop on Inductive Logic Programming*, 1994.
21. M. Sebag and C. Rouveirol. Constraint inductive logic programming. In L. de Raedt, editor, *Advances in ILP*, pages 277–294. IOS Press, 1996.
22. M. Sebag and C. Rouveirol. Tractable induction and classification in FOL. In *Proceedings of IJCAI-97*. Morgan Kaufmann, 1997.
23. A. Srinivasan and S. Muggleton. Comparing the use of background knowledge by two ILP systems. In L. de Raedt, editor, *Proceedings of ILP-95*. Katholieke Universiteit Leuven, 1995.
24. P. Van Hentenryck and Deville Y. Constraint Logic Programming. In *Proceedings of POPL'97*, 1987.
25. P. Van Hentenryck and Deville Y. Operational semantics of constraint logic programming over finite domains. In *Proceedings of PLILP'91*, 1991.
26. J.-D. Zucker and J.-G. Ganascia. Selective reformulation of examples in concept learning. In W. Cohen and H. Hirsh, editors, *Proc. of 11th International Conference on Machine Learning*, pages 352–360. Morgan Kaufmann, 1994.
27. J.-D. Zucker and J.-G. Ganascia. Representation changes for efficient learning in structural domains. In L. Saitta, editor, *Proceedings of the 13th International Conference on Machine Learning*, pages 543–551, 1996.

Belief Network Algorithms: A Study of Performance Based on Domain Characterisation

N. Jitnah and A. E. Nicholson

Department of Computer Science, Monash University, Clayton, VIC 3168, Australia,
{njitnah,annn}@cs.monash.edu.au

Topic indicator: Experimental studies of inference algorithms.

Abstract. In recent years belief networks have become a popular representation for reasoning with incomplete and changing information and are used in a wide variety of applications. There are a number of exact and approximate inference algorithms available for performing belief updating, however in general the task is NP-hard. Typically comparisons are made of only a few algorithms, and on a particular example network. We survey belief network algorithms and propose a system for domain characterisation as a basis for algorithm comparison. We present performance results using this framework from three sets of experiments: (1) on the Likelihood Weighting (LW) and Logic Sampling (LS) stochastic simulation algorithms; (2) on the performance of LW and Jensen's algorithms on state-space abstracted networks, (3) some comparisons of the time performance of LW, LS and the Jensen algorithm. Our results indicate that domain characterisation can be useful for predicting inference algorithm performance on a belief network for a new application domain.

1 Introduction

Belief, or Bayesian, networks (BNs) [23] have become a popular representation for reasoning with incomplete and changing information. They integrate a graphical representation of causal relationships with a sound Bayesian probabilistic foundation. Probabilities provide a quantitative way of modeling incompleteness by assigning a numerical value to each possible state of every variable in our problem domain. The values assigned represent our belief, which is uncertain, about variable states. Whenever new information is received, the change is entered as evidence into the BN by assigning new probabilities to variables affected by the change. Even if the information received is incomplete, i.e. if it does not totally capture changes in our problem domain, it can be handled by algorithms that correctly update the probabilities in the model. BNs have been used in a wide variety of applications which require reasoning under uncertainty and with changing information. These applications include medical diagnosis, model-based vision, robot-vehicle monitoring, traffic monitoring, and automated vehicle control.

Evidence of specific values of some nodes is incorporated into decision-making by belief updating of other nodes of interest, the query nodes. There are a number of exact and approximate inference algorithms available for belief updating.

In general, the complexity of exact inference for multiply-connected BNs is NP-hard [5]. Cooper [5] suggests that the complexity problem should be tackled by designing efficient special-case, average-case and approximation algorithms, rather than searching for a general, efficient exact inference algorithm. The approximation task is also NP-hard [6].

One class of approximate inference algorithms is based on stochastic simulation; a number of variations have been proposed. Another way to reduce the computational complexity is by approximating (i.e. simplifying) the model, for example by removing arcs [19], or abstracting the state space [29]. Other algorithms reduce the complexity by computing probability intervals rather than exact probabilities, or do not update beliefs for all nodes in the BN, only those of interest (e.g. [10]). When new belief updating algorithms, or variants on existing algorithms, are presented in the literature, usually a comparison is made only to one or two other algorithms, on one or two example BNs. This makes it difficult to compare the merits of the various algorithms for belief updating on a new BN model developed for a particular application domain. We propose a system for BN characterisation as the basis for algorithm comparison.

The paper is orgranised as follows. Sect. 2 gives an introduction to (BNs). In Sect. 3 we survey algorithms for updating beliefs, both exact and approximate. We survey methods for reducing the computational complexity by approximating the BN in Sect. 4. In Sect. 5 we describe a range of characteristics of BNs, including size, connectedness, the probability distributions, and number and location of evidence and query nodes. These characteristics are the basis for an experimental comparison on the performance of a number of inference algorithms and approximation techniques on a range of BNs, presented in Sect. 6.

2   Belief Networks

Belief networks are directed acyclic graphs, where nodes correspond to random variables, assumed to take discrete values (although in general they need not be discrete). A joint probability specifies the relationship between states of variables. The nodes in the BN are connected by directed arcs, which may be thought of as causal or influence links. The connections also specify independence assumptions between nodes, which allow the joint probability distribution of all the state variables to be specified by exponentially fewer probability values than the full joint distribution. Each node has an associated *conditional probability distribution* (CPD), which, for each combination of the variables of the parent nodes, gives a probability of each value of the node variable.

Observation of specific values for nodes is called *evidence*. Evidence can be specified about the state of any of the nodes in the BN — root nodes, leaf nodes or intermediate nodes. This evidence is then incorporated by computing posterior probability distributions for other nodes in the BNs, that is, updating beliefs. Any node whose posterior probabilities must be computed for decision-making is called a *query* node.

3 Algorithms for Updating Beliefs

Belief propagation for singly-connected networks, also called polytrees, can be done efficiently using a simple message passing procedure [23]. However, most interesting real-world problems involve multiply-connected BNs and then simple belief propagation is not possible; informally, this is because we can no longer be sure that evidence has not already been counted at a node having arrived via another route.

The two main techniques for exact updating of multiply-connected BNs are clustering and conditioning. **Clustering** is done by making compound variables such that the BN is transformed into a singly connected network of clusters. Rather than transforming the BN into a complex polytree, **Conditioning** algorithms transform the BN into many simpler subtrees; conditioning involves breaking the communication pathways along the loops by instantiating a select group of variables. The Jensen version of the Lauritzen and Spiegelhalter clustering algorithm [20] is the fastest exact clustering algorithm currently available. However, it is computationally intensive and sometimes impractical for evaluating large real-world BNs.

Stochastic simulation algorithms give an approximation of the exact evaluation by using the BN to generate many actual models of the domain that are consistent with the BN distribution. The general method involves "assigning each variable a definite value and having each processor inspect the current state of its neighbours, compute the belief distribution of its host variable, and select one value at random from the computed distribution. Beliefs are then computed by recording the percentage of times that each processor selects a given value." [23, p. 195]. Rather than using a percentage, the probabilities can also be estimated by counting the frequencies with which relevant events occur. Note that stochastic simulation is a special case of Gibbs Sampling as described in [14].

While stochastic simulation algorithms are quite effective if the BN contains no evidence [6], often events of interest occur only rarely, so when we have evidence for rare events, most simulation rounds have different values for the evidence variable and have to be discarded, as in the variant of stochastic simulation called **Logic Sampling** (LS) [12]. Thus the proportion of usable runs decreases exponentially with the number of evidence variables. The method of **Likelihood Weighting** (LW) [27, 3] overcomes this problem; the counts of each run are weighted according to how likely the evidence is, given the values generated for the parents of the evidence variables. Hence no samples are wasted. Pradham *et al.* [25] report that LW converges considerably faster than LS and can also handle very large BNs. There are a number of techniques for reducing the error that can be used with either LW or LS [26, 15]. LW and LS both belong to a class of stochastic simulation methods, called forward propagation, because values are first assigned to root nodes, then propagated towards the leaves along the direction of the arcs.

Evidence Reversal [4] is a technique in which evidence nodes are turned into root nodes by reversing any incoming arcs and recomputing the appropriate conditional probabilities. The advantage of this process is that it produces a version of the BN which is very suitable for forward propagation. Unfortunately, if the BN is highly connected, arc reversal is often too computationally intensive and hence has not been very popular.

It is well known that algorithm performance depends on network structure. For example, Kanazawa *et al.* [17] have looked at methods for stochastic simulation which take advantage of the specific structure of Dynamic Belief Networks, but their results were obtained using a very simple BN: a 50 time slice network, where each time slice contains a single state variable node, a single evidence node, and with all nodes having only 4 values. Note also, that with the simple structure within each time slice, the BN as a whole is in fact a tree, and hence performance results on this network may not be indicative of results on more complex structures.

Localized Partial Evaluation (LPE) [11, 10] computes interval bounds on the marginal probability of a specified query node by examining a subset of nodes in the entire BN. Basically, LPE ignores parts of the BN which are too far away from the query node to have much impact on its value. In [11] performance results compare LPE to LW, according to size (# of nodes) and connectivity (#arcs/node). In [10] performance results are given comparing exact and LPE evaluation of two example BNs: the ALARM network [2] a medical diagnosis network of 37 nodes (8 roots, 16 leaves and 13 intermediate nodes) and 46 arcs, where the nodes have between 2 and 4 states; and a subnetwork of CPCS-BN (364 nodes, 732 arcs) [25] called BN4 (245 nodes, 356 arcs), Other algorithms which, like LPE, evaluate only part of the problem and limit the potential effect of the rest include **Bounded Conditioning** [13], **Incremental SPI** [7] and Poole's search-based algorithms [24]; see [10] for a comparison to LPE.

Approximate evaluation based on conditioning can be done by evaluating only some of the polytrees generated. The approximation error is bounded by the total probability weight of the polytrees not yet evaluated; one obvious approach is to evaluate the most likely polytree first.

4 Model Approximation

In this section we describe techniques which attempt to reduce the computational complexity by approximating the model.

Chang and Fung [3] describe a method for abstracting the state space of a network by abstracting the state spaces of selected nodes. The resulting reduction in total state space size leads to faster evaluation of the BN. The overall joint probability distribution is approximated and the level of approximation depends upon the granularity of abstraction. Basically, nodes states are merged and the CPDs of the coarsened nodes and of their children are recomputed. For each state of a child of an abstracted node, the new conditional probability is assigned as an sum of the original conditional probabilities weighted by the prior probability of the abstracted states. No empirical performance results are given.

In [29, 21], Wellman and Liu use the same technique of state space abstraction, but instead they set the new conditional probabilities of children of an abstracted node as an average of the original conditional probabilities. This version of state space abstraction is tested on a set of example BNs and the relative error of the abstracted BN is shown to decrease as the granularity of abstraction is refined; by using successive refinements of granularity they produce an "anytime" algorithm [8]. The time to exactly evaluate (using the Jensen algorithm) one BN abstracted at different levels is also shown.

Kjaerulff [19] describes a method based on the removal of weak dependencies, that is arcs, in the join tree. The choice of arc to remove is based on reduction of the total state space; the Kullback-Leibler distance between the exact and the approximate clique potentials is determined, and preference is given to removing arcs with lower distance, with a measure of state space reduction used to break 'ties'. An upper bound is given on the absolute divergence in terms of the KL distance. This method is evaluated on a set of four example BNs and results are given in terms of the percentage reduction in the total state space. Kjaerulff discusses how link removal compares with a method for simplifying the computation by replacing small probabilities with zero, and using strategies for zero compression [16], and outlines cases in which each technique should be preferred.

Node removal, node merging and network pruning are some other ways of obtaining an approximate model, simpler than the original BN. These methods are described in [4].

5 Domain Characterisation

We characterise a problem by obtaining measurements for a set of features of the BN, individual nodes, the set of instantiated nodes (evidence) and the set of queried nodes (targets). These measurements are taken prior to each experiment and are used later for algorithm performance comparison. The most important ones are described here and we explain in what context these measures are significant.

5.1 Whole network characteristics

The first measures taken for the BN relate to size: the numbers of nodes (#nodes) and arcs (#arcs).

The total size of the state space ss-total is the product of the state space of each of the nodes in the envelope. We also include the size of state space of the largest node in the BN ss-max and the average state space size ss-avg. The size of a node's CPD is simply the product of the state space size of the parents, times its own state space size; we measure the maximum and average CPD size, cpd-max and cpd-avg. The connectedness, conn, can be calculated as simply #arcs/#nodes. We also include the maximum and average number of parents, #par-max and #par-avg. The performance of clustering algorithms is influenced by the state space size, the number of parents and the connectedness because these factors affect the complexity of the computation of clusters in the BN.

The maximum and average path length measures (pl-max, pl-avg) give the maximum and average path lengths between any two nodes in the BN; this gives an indication of how dispersed the BN is. Further topological information is given by the number of root and leaf nodes, #root, #leaf (all other nodes are classed as intermediate) and hence the maximum and average path lengths between any pair of root and leaf nodes in the BN are measured (rpl-max, rpl-avg). The width of the BN is also measured, it is the ratio #nodes/rpl-avg.

Path length considerations are important with respect to stochastic simulation algorithms. Generally, theses algorithms function by randomly assigning a specific value to a node and updating the values of its neighbours accordingly. This process is repeated throughout the BN until all nodes are updated. Hence a complete pass is achieved in time proportional to the length of the longest path. In forward simulation algorithms, such as LW and LS, nodes are updated by sending values from roots to leaves along the direction of the arcs. The time for one pass is thus proportional to the length of the longest root-leaf path.

In order to compare to the Jensen algorithm, we also record the **join-tree cost**, JTC, as proposed by Kanazawa [9] for assessing the computational expense of evaluating a belief network.

A measure of the skewness of the CPDs for each nodes is computed as follows. For a vector, $v = (v_1, ..., v_m)$, of conditional probabilities,

$$skv(v) = \frac{\sum_{i=1}^{m} |\frac{1}{m} - v_i|}{1 - \frac{1}{m} + \sum_{i=2}^{m} \frac{1}{m}}$$

where the denominator scales the skewness from 0 to 1. The skewness for the CPD of a node is the average of the skewness of the constituent vectors. We record the maximum and average node skewness, **skew-max** and **skew-avg**. It is a known fact that skewed distributions are slower to converge than uniform ones under stochastic simulation. In any given skewed node, the majority of states are very unlikely, so a large number of samples are needed to get a reasonable approximation of the frequency of each state.

5.2   Node characteristics

We generate a profile of the characteristics of each node, which is used in turn when describing the characteristics of evidence and target nodes. For each instantiated or queried node, we record: location (root, leaf or intermediate); the skewness of its CPD; the maximum and average distance of this node from all other nodes, root nodes and leaf nodes; the Jensen tree nodes to which it belongs.

5.3   Characteristics of an evaluation

The evidence nodes and query nodes involved in a particular evaluation of the BN has an effect on the performance of the inference algorithms. For each trial, we maintain a "map" of the query and evidence nodes.

For the set of queried nodes, we record: the size of the set as a proportion of the network size; the location and distribution of queries, the maximum and average skewness of the CPDs, and the total size of the query state space. Similarly, for the set of instantiated nodes, we record: the size of the set as a proportion of the network size; the location, distribution and probability of evidence; the maximum and average skewness of the CPDs; and the total size of the query state space. Evidence of low probability slows down the performance of simulation algorithms since it takes longer to generate samples which are consistent with the declared evidence. Evidence spread over numerous nodes has the same effect.

We also measure the maximum and average distance between instantiated and queried nodes. This is particularly relevant to the performance of algorithms which only evaluate the part of the BN where nodes of interest are located, such as LPE. Evidence and queries can be located in one or more of either leaf nodes, root nodes or intermediate nodes, or in combinations of these types of nodes. The distribution of evidence (or queries) is a measure of the average path-length between any two evidence (or queried) nodes with respect to the average path-length within the entire BN. When nodes closer to the roots are instantiated, forward simulation performs better because propagating evidence along the arc directions will lead to faster convergence of node values in the generated samples.

6 Results

The results given in this section were obtained using the Lisp-based IDEAL belief network development environment [28] on a GNU Common Lisp platform. The implementation is slow and hence for the purposes of algorithm comparison the results are given in terms of numbers of iterations rather than absolute performance times. Much faster computation speed and hence realistic computation time results would be obtained using a system such as the commercially available HUGIN [1].

See Table 1 for the profiles of each of the BNs used to produce our experimental results. Note that the L6 network is too large to evaluate by the Jensen algorithm hence we are unable to obtain its JTC. We do not calculate a JTC for S3 and DBN as they are both polytrees. A set of problems was then defined using these BNs and a range of evidence nodes.

In this paper, we present a selection of our results obtained using only the L6, ALARM and S6 networks. Results covering a larger set of networks and a wider range of domain characteristics are presented in [22].

The graphs shown in this section illustrate the reduction in the error as a function of the number of iterations of the LW (or LS) algorithm. The error measure used is the average Kullback-Leibler (KL) distance [23] of the approximate posteriors of the query nodes from their true posteriors. The KL distance between the true distribution P and the approximate distribution P' of a node

Network	ALARM	CANCER	M1	DBN	S3	S6	S6-var	S7	L6
#nodes	37	5	37	100	8	8	8	8	99
#arcs	44	5	44	99	7	10	10	10	131
conn	1.24	1.0	1.19	0.99	0.88	1.25	1.25	1.25	1.32
width	6.83	2.5	27.13	3.92	5.71	3.20	3.20	2.67	20.55
cpd-max	108	8	96	16	80	256	192	4096	7680
cpd-avg	20.32	4.4	16.13	15.88	19.38	55.0	55.25	666	210.06
pl-max	12	3	15	51	5	4	6	4	9
pl-avg	4.56	1.28	5.66	17.65	2.25	1.75	1.75	1.75	4.41
#root	12	1	12	1	3	2	2	2	29
#leaf	11	2	12	50	3	2	2	2	35
rpl-max	10	2	5	50	2	4	4	4	9
rpl-avg	4.02	2	1.36	25.5	1.40	2.5	2.5	3.0	4.82
#par-max	4	2	3	1	2	3	3	3	5
#par-avg	1.24	1.0	1.19	0.99	0.875	1.75	1.75	1.25	1.32
ss-total	1.73e16	32	1.73e16	1.61e60	1440	65536	23040	1.68e7	4.72e64
ss-max	4	2	4	4	8	4	8	8	8
ss-avg	2.84	2	2.84	4	4.63	4.0	4.625	8	4.83
JTC	2606	28	2550	-	-	704	576	7680	-
skew-max	0.98	0.75	0.98	0.87	0.58	0.73	0.38	0.28	0.77
skew-avg	0.84	0.61	0.84	0.66	0.32	0.06	0.28	0.25	0.30

Table 1. Characteristics of test networks

with states s, is given by:

$$KL(P, P') = \sum_s P(s) \log \frac{P(s)}{P'(s)}.$$

We compute the KL distance for each of the query nodes and plot the average; in this way we can compare results on BNs of different sizes and when there are different numbers of query nodes. The maximum number of iterations for each run was 2500. In some cases where the KL distance is clearly converging we plot fewer iterations.

For each trial instance, consisting of a set of evidence nodes and a set of query nodes for a given BN, we (sometimes randomly) assign the evidence values. In order to reduce the variation due to the particular evidence instantiations and the simulation algorithm, each trial shown in the graphs is the average over five runs of the same selected evidence.

The time for an iteration depends on the size of the BN, and we are presenting our results in terms of the number of iterations of the LW algorithm, so we do not make direct time comparisons between different sized BN. However, when relevant, we present the trial instance for two different BNs in adjacent graphs in the same figure so that the trends, at least, are apparent.

6.1 Performance of LW and LS Algorithms

In this part we present the results from the following large set of trial instances:

- Networks: ALARM, S6, S6-var, L6
- Evidence nodes: one root (1 1f), all roots (all rts), one intermediate (1 in), half the intermediate nodes (1/2 in), one leaf node (1 1f), all the leaf nodes (all lvs).
- Query nodes: same as for evidence nodes.
- Skewness: varied from 0.1 to 0.9 in increments of 0.1.

Skewness. The graph in Fig. 1 shows the effect of varying the skewness from 0.1 to 0.9 in increments of 0.2 for the S6 network (above) and ALARM (below) networks, for the particular evidence and query trial instances indicated in the figure captions. Clearly, in each evidence and query trial instance, the greater the skewness, the higher the initial error, and the slower the LW algorithm converges. Note that for the ALARM case, the error varies much more depending on the skewness, and the rate of convergence for higher skewness is much slower. Other factors do not seem to have much effect.

Evidence Nodes. The graph in Fig. 2 shows the effect of changing the number and location of evidence nodes for the S6 network (above, skew=0.8) and ALARM network (below, skew=0.8) for the all leaves being query nodes. We found that, generally, the LW algorithm converges to the true probabilities when the evidence is either a single root or all the roots, as we would expect given the LW algorithm, as a forward simulation algorithm. The error is higher and decreases more slowly when the evidence is in half the intermediate nodes and all the leaf nodes, partially because of the greater number of evidence nodes, and partially because of their location in the BN (i.e. away from the root nodes). This effect is greater in the larger ALARM network.

Query Nodes. The graph in Fig. 3 shows the effect of changing the number and location of query nodes for the S6 network (above, skew=0.8) and ALARM network (below, skew=0.8), for the evidence in all leaves. When the evidence is in the leaf nodes and the queries are further from the evidence nodes, the error tends to be larger and decrease more slowly. Note that in this case, when the evidence is *all* the leaves of the ALARM network, the LW algorithm does not converge; this may be due to inconsistencies in the randomly generated evidence instances.

LW and LS on a Large Network The graph in Figure 4 compares the performances of LW and LS for the L6 network which has 99 nodes. There is a significant difference in the convergence rates. The difference is even more pronounced when a leaf is instantiated and the roots are queried as shown. Since L6 is too large to be evaluated exactly by the Jensen algorithm, we could not obtain exact posteriors to use in the KL analysis. Instead, we ran LW and LS for 30,000 iterations and used the average of the posteriors thus obtained as "exact" values.

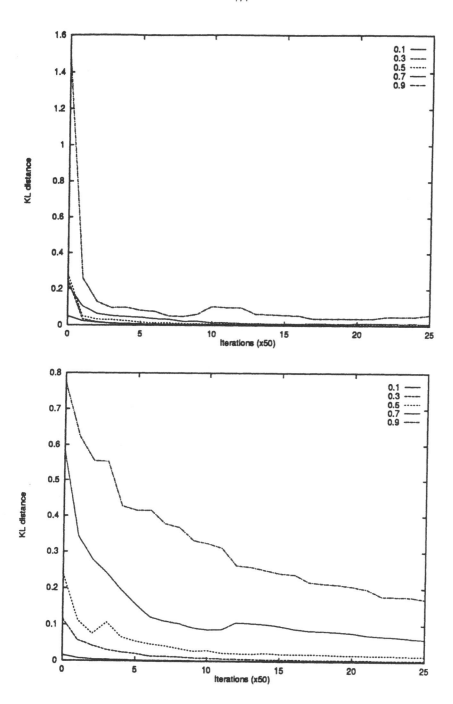

Fig. 1. Effect of varying the skewness: evidence all **lvs**; query all **rts**. S6 above, **ALARM** below.

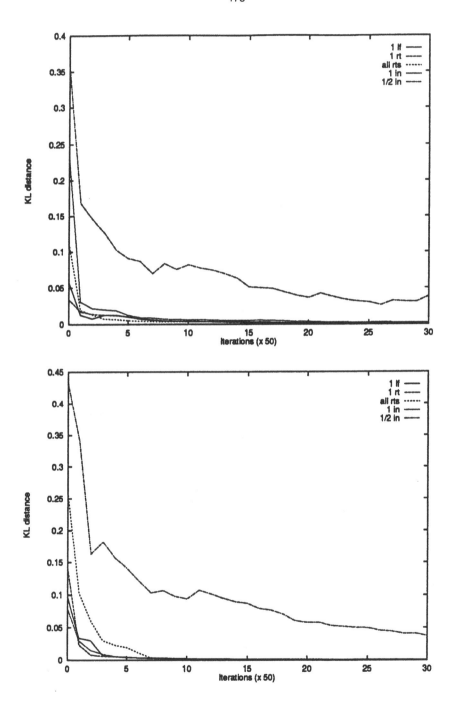

Fig. 2. Effect of varying the evidence nodes, query `all lvs`, `skew` = 0.8. S6 above, `ALARM` below.

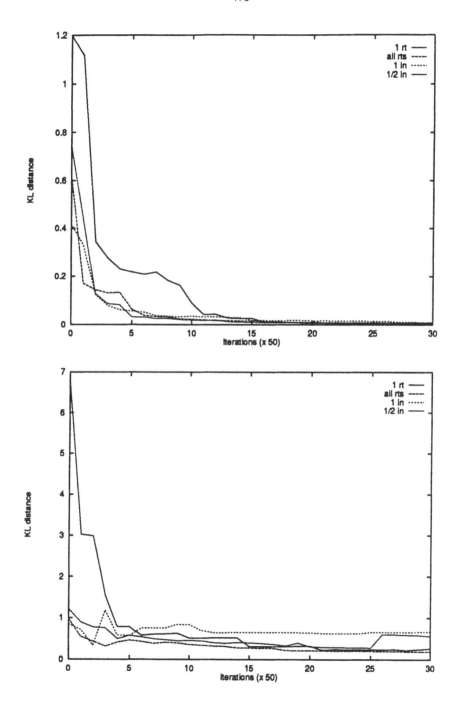

Fig. 3. Effect of varying the query nodes, evidence `all lvs`, `skew = 0.8`. S6 above, `ALARM` below.

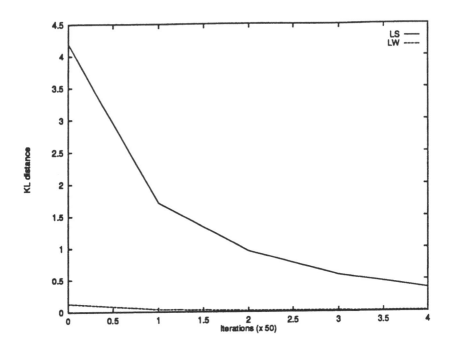

Fig. 4. Performances of LW and LS on the L6 network: evidence = 1 lf, query = all rts.

6.2 Network Abstraction

Here we present some results of our investigation of network abstraction. The graphs show the LW algorithm results for:

- the exact model (labelled **exact**);
- Wellman and Liu's abstraction algorithm (**WL**);
- Chang and Fung's (internal operation) abstraction algorithm (**CF**).

The BN used is the **ALARM** network, which has at most 4 values, which limits the variation in granularity of abstraction; we perform the LW inference on a single abstracted BN. We have implemented these abstraction algorithms by abstracting all the non-evidence and non-query nodes, which is of course somewhat arbitrary. Within a node, we simply merged adjacent states together. We do not include in the graphs the time to compute the abstracted BNs, which is done off-line. Note that Chang and Fung's abstraction method of weighting the conditional probabilities of the children takes longer.

Skewness. All the results in this section are obtained for the trial instance of evidence in all the leaf nodes (which is the real case for the **ALARM** network), and half the intermediate nodes being query nodes. This means that the root nodes and half the intermediate nodes are the nodes to be abstracted; since only nodes with 4 values are abstracted, only 9 of these nodes are abstracted. Fig. 5 shows the effect of varying the skewness for the exact ALARM network on the LW for the 3 cases described above. The skewness of the exact BN model, and the two abstractions (averaged over the various trials) are as follows:

exact ALARM	0.2	0.4	0.6	0.8
WL ALARM	0.25	0.39	0.55	0.70
CF ALARM	0.25	0.39	0.57	0.71

When the skewness is lower, the error from the LW algorithm on the two abstractions is very similar. As the skewness increases, the error for the exact BN is worse earlier, but decreases to be similar to the abstraction errors or slightly higher. The error is substantially larger and slower to decrease for all cases, as we would expect from the results in the previous section.

Evidence Nodes. The results in this section are obtained for the trial instance of $skew = 0.8$. 21 nodes are abstracted. In Fig. 6 (above), we can see that while the error is lower at the start for the two abstractions, the exact model fairly quickly produces more accurate results, as we would expect. However this trial instance is not a realistic one for the ALARM network, with the evidence being a single intermediate node. For the actual case where the evidence is in all the leaves, in the bottom graph, the 3 cases all have a larger error, which decrease at similar rates, but resulting in a larger error for the exact BN. This is particularly clear for the case of a single query node.

Changing the Level of Abstraction. The level of abstraction of a BN can be altered by varying the granularity at which nodes are coarsened. This is done by grouping different numbers of states together. A coarser granularity gives rise to the most abstracted BN, one whose overall state-space size is smaller. As the abstraction is coarsened, we expect a larger error on the posteriors of the queried nodes. For this experiment, we used the two randomly generated BNs, S6-var and S7. In S6-var the node state-space ranges from two to eight, whereas in S7 all nodes contain eight states. However, the two BNs have the same topological structure.

Table 2 shows the results of evaluating exact and coarsened versions of these BNs using the Jensen algorithm. Here we instantiated a root node and queried a leaf node in both BNs. The KL-distance column indicates how far the posteriors of the target node in a coarsened model are from the exact posteriors. We coarsened the nodes by merging their states in groups of two, three and four, as indicated in the second colum. For S7, we see that the least coarsened model provides the best approximation, which is what we expect since this model is closest to the original. We would expect that merging states in groups of three would be better that in groups of four, but the results indicate the opposite. This might be because of the particular conditional probabilities of the state.

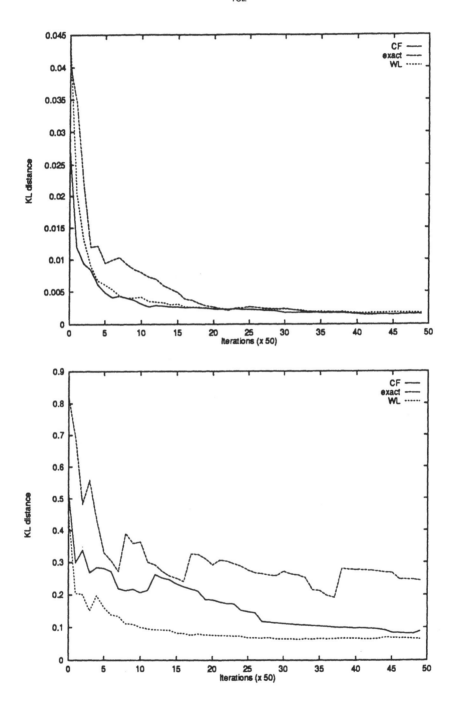

Fig. 5. Comparison of LW on abstractions and exact ne twork, evidence `all lvs`; query `1/2 in`. Above: `skew = 0.2`. Below: `skew = 0.6`.

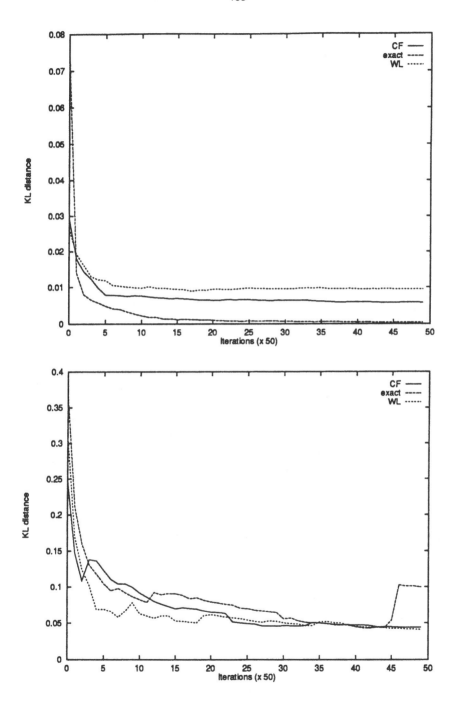

Fig. 6. Comparison of LW on abstractions and exact network, **skew** = 0.8. Above: evidence 1 in, query all rts. Below: evidence all lvs, query 1 rt.

Network	Coarsening Level	KL distance	JTC
S6-var	exact		576
	2	0.000054	118
	3	0.000005	76
	4	0.000005	72
S7	exact		7680
	2	0.000493	1344
	3	0.000809	675
	4	0.000627	264

Table 2. Performance of Jensen Algorithm on Abstracted Networks

6.3 Which States Should We Abstract?

In the experiments described above, we chose to coarsen a node simply by grouping adjacent states together. This is very arbitrary and only provides a gain in that the size of the state space is reduced. To attempt to preserve the overall form of the probability distribution of a node, it is better to try to coarsen "similar" states together.

We tested four ways of selecting states for coarsening:

- KL-abs: a measure of similarity is the KL distance between the probability vectors of states, given all parent combinations. This is the basis of our KL-abstraction procedure, where we choose to group states whose conditional probabilities are similarly distributed over all parent combinations.
- SS-abs: another way to select similar states is to chose those where the sums of the conditional probabilities are close since their overall likelihoods are most similar.
- DS-abs: we also tried grouping states where the sums differ the most; the idea here is that merging a more likely state with a less likely one would less significantly affect the overall likelihood of the former.
- RA-abs: in our last test, we randomly selected the states to be grouped. This was done only for comparative purposes.

The results are listed in Table 3 in order of performance. M1 and S7 were used, states were merged in pairs and the BNs were evaluated by the Jensen algorithm. AD-abs is simply the method of merging adjacent states. For both BNs, our KL-abs produces the best results and SS-abs the worst. The performance of AD-abs is average and the other two methods seem to depend upon the characteristics of the BN.

6.4 Performance Times

Table 4 shows timing information relating to the set of BNs used in our experiments. For LW and LS, the initialisation time is the time spent setting up the data structures necessary for the respective algorithms. The evaluation time is

Network	Abstraction	KL distance
S7	KL-abs	0.000298
	DS-abs	0.000430
	AD-abs	0.000493
	RA-abs	0.000900
	SS-abs	0.000900
M1	KL-abs	0.001081
	RA-abs	0.037236
	AD-abs	0.036752
	DS-abs	0.041936
	SS-abs	0.082767

Table 3. Effect of Different Abstraction Methods

given for 100 iterations. For the Jensen algorithm, the initialisation time corresponds to the time for constructing the Jensen Tree. The Jensen Tree Cost is also shown. Note that since L6 cannot be evaluated by the Jensen algorithm, we only show the time of LW and LS. The performance of the polytree algorithm is given for our two polytree networks DBN and S3. To obtain these performance times, the BNs were evaluated without evidence.

Network	DBN	S3	CANCER	S6	S6-var	S7	ALARM	M1	L6
#nodes	100	8	5	8	8	8	37	37	99
init LW			0.017	0.017	0.067	0.600	0.133	0.349	1.783
eval LW			0.200	0.400	1.150	0.700	2.783	2.883	13.900
init LS			0.017	0.033	0.050	0.383	0.383	0.333	2.650
eval LS			0.183	0.650	1.167	0.717	2.750	2.783	15.400
init Jensen			0.150	4.633	3.983	27.684	16.100	16.466	
eval Jensen			1.25	1.250	1.25	12.367	1.450	1.133	
JTC			28	704	576	7680	2465	2550	
init polytree	11.233	0.467							
eval polytree	9.517	0.883							

Table 4. Performance Times (seconds)

7 Discussion and Further Work

In this paper we have presented results on the performance of LW, LS, the polytree and the Jensen algorithms, investigating the effect of various domain characteristics as described in Sect. 5 and in Sect. 6.

We have shown results comparing the output of LW algorithm on exact and abstracted BNs, which indicate that using abstractions will be an improvement on using an approximate inference algorithm on the exact BN, provided that the time to do the abstraction is small, or if the abstraction can be done off-line. The Chang and Fung method for abstraction gives more accurate results, but weighting the conditional probabilities of the children takes longer, so the abstraction has to be done off-line to obtain the benefit. Obviously the performance of these types of abstraction algorithms depends on the method for choosing which nodes and states to abstract and further investigation needs to be done in this area. Our KL-abstraction method gives a preview of this issue.

We are currently gathering results for the abstraction algorithms, where we start off with the most coarsened BN abstraction and iteratively refine the abstraction. The problem is then that of deliberation scheduling, that is, how long to run the LW algorithm for each level of abstraction. We anticipate that it should be possible to use intermediate results of the stochastic simulation after changing the abstraction to give a better initial posterior.

The idea that classification of problems can provide an effective way to determine when a particular algorithm is appropriate for a given problem, is developed for planning systems in [18]. The particular characteristics of a BN affect the performance of belief updating algorithms. The domain characterisation presented in this paper gives a structured way to describe BN features and provide a framework for predicting algorithm performance. We hope that other researchers will provide these domain characteristics when they present algorithm performance results. Formalised domain characterisation and performance profiles will be of practical use, as the computational implications of any design choices can be taken into account during the development of a BN model for any new application domain.

Acknowledgements: Thanks to Mark Peot for electronic discussions and pointers to the literature and to Stuart Russell for providing us with a copy of the DBN used in [17].

References

1. S.K. Andersen, K.G. Olesen, F.V. Jensen, and F. Jensen. HUGIN — a shell for building Bayesian belief universes for expert systems. In *Proc. of IJCAI-89*, Detroit, MI, 1989.
2. I. Beinlich, H. Suermondt, R. Chavez, and G. Cooper. The alarm monitoring system: A case study with two probabilistic inference techniques for belief networks. In *Proc. of the 2nd European Conf. on AI in medicine*, pages 689–693, 1992.
3. K-C. Chang and R. Fung. Refinement and coarsening of bayesian networks. In *Proc. of UAI-90*, pages 475–482, 1990.
4. Homer L. Chin and Gregory F. Cooper. Bayesian belief network inference using simulation. In *Uncertainty in Artificial Intelligence 3*, pages 129–147, 1989.
5. G.F. Cooper. The computational complexity of probabilistic inference using bayesian belief networks. *Artificial Intelligence*, 42:393–405, 1990.
6. P. Dagum and M. Luby. Approximating probabilistic inference in belief networks is NP-hard. *Artificial Intelligence*, pages 141–153, 1993.
7. B. D'Ambrosio. Incremental probabilistic inference. In *Proc. of UAI-93*, pages 301–308, 1993.

8. T. Dean and M. Boddy. An analysis of time-dependent planning. In *Proceedings AAAI-88*, pages 49–54. AAAI, 1988.

9. T. Dean and M. P. Wellman. *Planning and control.* Morgan Kaufman Publishers, San Mateo, Ca., 1991.

10. D. Draper. *Localized Partial Evaluation of Belief Networks.* PhD thesis, Dept. of Computer Science, U. of Washington, 1995.

11. D. L. Draper and S. Hanks. Localized partial evaluation of a belief network. In *Proc. of UAI-94*, pages 170–177, 1994.

12. M. Henrion. Propagating uncertainty in bayesian networks by logic sampling. In J. Lemmer and L. Kanal, editors, *Proc. of UAI-88*, pages 149–163. North Holland, Amsterdam, 1988.

13. E.J. Horvitz, H.J. Suermondt, and G.F. Cooper. Bounded conditioning: Flexible inference for decisions under scarce resources. In *Proc. of UAI-89*, pages 182–193, 1989.

14. Thomas Hrycej. Gibbs sampling in bayesian networks. In *Artificial Intelligence*, pages 351–363, 1990.

15. M. Hulme. Improved sampling for diagnostic reasoning in bayesian networks. In *Proc. of UAI-95*, pages 315–322, 1995.

16. F. Jensen and S.K. Andersen. Approximations in Bayesian belief universes for knowledge based systems. In *Proc. of UAI-90*, 1990.

17. K. Kanazawa, D. Koller, and S. Russell. Stochastic simulation algorithms for dynamic probabilistic networks. In *Proc. of UAI-95*, pages 346–351, 1995.

18. J. Kirman. *Predicting real-time planner performance by domain characterization.* PhD thesis, Brown Univ., 1994.

19. U. Kjaerulff. Reduction of computation complexity in bayesian networks through removal of weak dependencies. In *Proc. of UAI-94*, pages 374–382, 1994.

20. S.L. Lauritzen and D.J. Spiegelhalter. Local computations with probabilities on graphical structures and their application to expert systems. *Journal of the Royal Statistical Society*, 50(2):157–224, 1988.

21. C. Liu and M. Wellman. On state-space abstraction for anytime evaluation of bayesian networks. In *IJCAI 95: Anytime Algorithms and Deliberation Scheduling Workshop*, pages 91–98, 1995.

22. A.E. Nicholson and N. Jitnah. Belief network algorithms: a study of performance using domain characterisation. Technical Report 96/249, Dept. of Computer Science, Monash University, 1996.

23. J. Pearl. *Probabilistic Reasoning in Intelligent Systems.* Morgan Kaufmann, 1988.

24. D. Poole. Average-case analysis of a search algorithm for estimating prior and posterior probabilities in bayesian networks with extreme probabilities. In *Proc. of IJCAI-93*, pages 606–612, 1993.

25. M. Pradham, G. Provan, B. Middleton, and M. Henrion. Knowledge engineering for large belief networks. In *Proc. of UAI-94*, pages 484–490, 1994.

26. R. Shachter and M. Peot. Evidential reasoning using likelihood weighting. *Personal Communication*, 1989.

27. R. Shachter and M. Peot. Simulation approaches to general probabilistic inference on belief networks. In *Proc. of UAI-89*, pages 311–318, 1989.

28. Sampath Srinivas and Jack Breese. Ideal: Influence diagram evaluation and analysis in lisp. Technical Report No. 23, Rockwell International Science Center, 1989.

29. Michael P. Wellman and Chao-Lin Liu. State-space abstraction for anytime evaluation of probabilistic networks. In *Proc. of UAI-94*, pages 567–574, 1994.

A Group Decision and Negotiation Support System for Argumentation Based Reasoning

Nikos Karacapilidis*   Dimitris Papadias**

* INRIA Sophia Antipolis, Action AID
2004 Route des Lucioles BP 93
06902 Sophia Antipolis Cedex, France
e-mail: nikos@sophia.inria.fr

** Dept. of Computer Science
The Hong Kong University of Science and Technology
Clear Water Bay, Kowloon, Hong Kong
e-mail: dimitris@cs.ust.hk

Abstract. This paper describes a Group Decision and Negotiation Support System for cooperative or non-cooperative argumentative discourses. The system provides agents means of expressing and weighing their individual arguments and preferences, the aim being the selection of a certain choice. It also supports defeasible and qualitative reasoning in the presence of ill-structured information. Argumentation is performed through a set of discourse acts which call a variety of procedures for the propagation of information in the corresponding discussion graph.

1 Introduction

Numerous researchers have dealt with argumentative discourse from different standpoints such as *philosophical* (where argumentation is considered as a way of theory formation [23]), *linguistic* (inspired by speech act theory and discourse analysis [17]), *rhetorical* (where argumentation is studied primarily as a form of manipulation through language [38]), and *psychological* (where the relationships between arguments and cognitive processes are explored [16]). Most approaches follow two main methodologies, namely, *formal* and *informal* logic (for an extensive survey see [12]).

According to the formal perspective, arguments are de-contextualized sets of sentences or symbols viewed in terms of their syntactic or semantic relationships. On the other hand, informal logic views arguments as pragmatic, i.e., their meaning is a function of their purposive context[1]. Most AI researchers have focused on formal models of argumentation based on various logics. For instance, Brewka [7] reconstructed Rescher's [30] theory of formal disputation, Prakken [27] used Reiter's default logic [29], while Gordon's work [15] was based on Geffner and

---

[1] The term informal logic was primarily used to denote an approach to argument interpretation and evaluation that is distinct from traditional, formal logic.

Pearl's concepts of conditional entailment [14]. An extensive discussion on the use of alternative logics in argumentative discourse appears in [28]. Based on these methodologies, several models of dialectical systems have been proposed [15], [28]. They basically consist of a set of abstract components, that specify the underlying logic, the speech acts allowed, and the protocol of rights and responsibilities of the participants.

Instead of proposing another argumentation theory, or presenting a new formal model, this paper describes a Group Decision Support System for argumentation based reasoning. The system is implemented in Java and can be run on the World Wide Web using any standard browser. Our primary goal was the implementation of an argumentation system, by which groups of natural or artificial agents can express their claims and judgements, aiming at informing or convincing, depending on the kind of the interaction. The system can be used in any kind of group decision making processes, and is able to handle inconsistent, qualitative and incomplete information in cases where one has to weigh reasons for and against the selection of a certain course of action.

Many problems involving argumentative discourse are very complex, requiring large amounts of information and collaboration of numerous participants from different contexts (e.g., resource managers, politicians, citizen groups, etc.). Part of our goals was to exploit information technology in order to meet three major practical requirements:

- the system must provide relatively inexpensive access to a broad public;
- it must have an intuitive interface in order to be easily usable by inexperienced users, and
- it must be available on all prominent operating systems and hardware platforms.

The above requirements are ideally met by the World Wide Web, and as a consequence, some systems have already been implemented on this platform (for an on-line survey see [40]). Current systems, however, merely provide threaded, hierarchical discussion forums, where a message can be posted specifically as a response to another message (such a system is Open Meeting, a highly structured conferencing system that supports on-line meetings with numerous participants [18]). On the contrary, our system includes reasoning mechanisms that monitor the discussion, constantly updating the status of argumentation. The system focuses on distributed, asynchronous collaboration, allowing agents to surpass the requirements of being in the same place and working at the same time.

The next section presents the argumentation elements of the system. Section 3 describes the proof standards, while Section 4 illustrates the discourse acts involved. The latter relate to a variety of procedures for the propagation of the information, such as consistency checking, aggregation of preferences, and labelling of the argumentation elements according to different standards. Section 5 discusses related work, focusing on the extraction of the pros and cons of our approach, and proposes directions for future work. Finally, Section 6 concludes the paper.

2 Elements of Argumentation

Our approach maps a multi-agent decision making process to a discussion graph with a tree-like structure. For the design of the model described in this paper, we have been inspired by the informal *Issue-Based Information System* (IBIS) model of argumentation (first introduced in [22], [32], later developed at MCC [39], [10]. Throughout this paper, we refer to a discussion example about the selection of a site for the location of a new airport in Southern France (there exist three alternative sites). The agents involved in the discussion bring up the necessary argumentation in order to express interests and perspectives of the affected parties, such as communities, related regional and federal Planning Departments, environmental protection groups, and industry. Our argumentation model has as elements *issues, alternatives, positions, arguments,* and *constraints* representing *preference relations*. IBIS used the concepts of *topic* (serving as a crude organization principle for denoting the foci of concern), *issue, position* and *question of fact* (requesting information which is not assumed to be controversial).

2.1 Issues, alternatives, positions and arguments

Issues correspond to decisions to be made, or goals to be achieved (e.g., issue I_1: "choose the most appropriate site for the new airport"). They are brought up by agents and are open to dispute. There is always an issue at the top (root) of the discussion tree. Issues consist of a set of *alternatives* that correspond to potential choices (e.g., alternative A_1 to I_1: "Select the Biot site", alternative A_2 to I_1: "Select the Grasse site"). Issues can be inside other issues in cases where some alternatives need to be grouped together. For instance, assume that there are two potential sites at the greater Biot area, namely, "Select the northern Grasse site" and "Select the southern Grasse site"). In this case, the last two alternatives should be grouped in an internal issue ("select the most appropriate site in Biot") and, after the related discourse, the selected (best) one will be compared to the alternatives A_2 and A_3 (alternative A_3 to I_1: "Select the Cagnes site"). Only one alternative of an issue is finally selected.

    Positions are asserted in order to advocate the selection of a specific course of action (alternative), or avert the agents' interest from it. For instance, position $P_{1.1}$: "alternative A_1 is a public land parcel" is asserted to support A_1, while position $P_{1.2}$: "alternative A_1 is an environmentally sensitive zone" expresses one's objection to A_1. Positions may also refer to some other position in order to provide additional information about it (e.g., positions $P_{1.1.1}$: "no purchase cost (if a site is a public land parcel)", and $P_{2.2.1}$: "local authority report (providing details about the owners of the land for the Grasse site)"). A position always *refers to* a single other position or alternative, while an alternative or issue is always *in* a single issue. This results to a tree-like argumentation structure. Figure 1 illustrates an instance of the discussion, where *refers to* is indicated by lines, alternatives and positions by ellipses, and issues by rectangles (actual graphs may have many more elements organized in multiple levels).

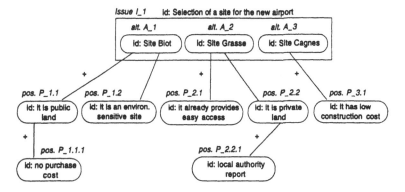

Fig. 1. An instance of the discussion graph for the airport example.

Numerous meanings and formalisms of the term *argument* have been proposed in the literature [28], in order to address various application areas [2]. For instance, in [9], an argument consists of a *support base*, that may contain formulas which speak for or against a certain position, and a *conclusion*. A similar notion of argument has been given in [3][2]. An argument in our system is a tuple of either the form (*position, link, position*) or (*position, link, alternative*). In other words, it links together a position with an alternative or another position belonging to a different issue. Agents put forward arguments to convince their opponents or to settle an issue via a formal decision procedure. We distinguish between *supporting arguments* and *counterarguments*. As in real life applications, two conflicting arguments can be simultaneously applied (see also [5], [6]).

In implementation terms, the elements of our system are illustrated in Figure 2 in the form of an Entity-Relationship diagram [1] (according to the E-R model, entities are represented as rectangles, attributes as ellipses, and relations as diamonds). The *Basic Element* consists of two attributes: an *Id* (primary key) and a *Url* that contains relevant information (sender of the argumentation element, submission date, comments, etc.). It is an abstract class that acts as a superclass for all the others. An *issue* is a basic element that contains other issues and alternatives. Each alternative has a *weight*, which is determined by its supporting and counter-arguments, an *activation label* indicating its status (it can be *active* or *inactive*), and a *proof standard* (discussed in the next section). In addition, each position has a boolean *link* that denotes whether it participates in a supporting (+), or a counter-argument (-).

Active alternatives correspond to "recommended" choices, i.e., choices that are the strongest among the alternatives in their issue. Active positions are considered "accepted" due to the discussion underneath (e.g., strong supporting arguments, no counter-arguments), while inactive positions are considered "rejected". The mechanisms for the calculation of activation labels are described in Section 3.

---

[2] Both are extensions of the one proposed in [34].

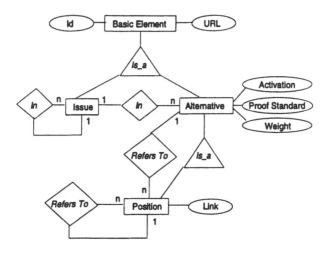

Fig. 2. Elements of the model.

2.2 Constraints

In many cases, we have to compare arguments in favor of the same conclusion, as well as arguments leading to contradictory conclusions. The subjects of priority relationships and preference orders between arguments have been mostly handled through quantitative approaches. For example, [25] and [33] have used the concepts of *penalty logic* (cost of not taking a premise into account) and *confidence factors*, respectively. Unfortunately, well defined utility and probability functions regarding properties or attributes of alternatives (used, for instance, in traditional OR approaches), as well as complete ordering of these properties are usually absent. On the other hand, non-monotonic formalisms have defined preference relations on subtheories in various ways (see for example the concepts of *preferred subtheories* [5], *conditional entailment* [14], *prioritized syntax-based entailment* [4]), and *Qualitative Value Logic* [8], [19].

Preference relations provide a qualitative way to weigh reasons for and against the selection of a certain course of action. In our system, a *constraint* is a tuple (*Position, Preference_Relation, Position*), where the preference relation can be ">", "=", "<" (">" is interpreted as *more important than* while "=" as *of equal importance as*)[3]. Constraints may attach various levels of importance to positions or alternatives. They may *refer to* another constraint, a position, or an issue. A constraint, like the other elements, is subject to discussion; therefore, it may be "linked" with positions supporting or challenging it, as well as other constraints that refer to it. Activation labels of constraints are calculated by the same proof standards used for positions. Figure 3 illustrates the E-R diagram for constraints.

---

[3] See also [20] introducing the following preference relations: *SMP (strongly more preferable), SLP (strongly less preferable), EQP (equally preferable), WMP (weakly more preferable)* and *WLP (weakly less preferable)*.

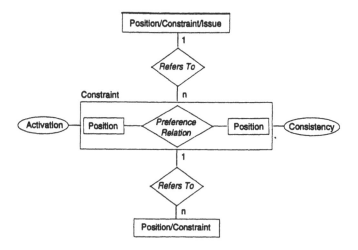

Fig. 3. E-R diagram for constraints.

Two types of preferences can be expressed by the system:

- *Local* preferences: when a constraint refers to a position, or another constraint, the positions that constitute the parts of the constraint must refer to the same element. Assume that in the example shown in Figure 1, there is also a position $P_{2.2.2}$:"Federal Government Map". Then, a preference of this type can be expressed by the constraint "$P_{2.2.1}$ (local report) is more important (accurate) than $P_{2.2.2}$ (federal map)". A constraint of the form "$P_{1.2}$ is more important than $P_{1.1.1}$" is not permitted.
- *Non-local* preferences: when a constraint refers to an issue, its parts must refer to alternatives (not necessarily the same one) of this issue (e.g., in Figure 1, "$P_{2.2}$ (the fact that Grasse site is a private land parcel) is less important than $P_{1.2}$ (Biot being an environmentally sensitive zone)"). Issues provide a way of grouping comparable elements together, since they permit the expression of preferences between positions attached to different alternatives.

These rules about the formation of constraints are preserved by the interface. When an agent wants to assert a constraint that refers to a position P_i, the related interface permits only a preference relation between the positions linked with P_i.

3 Proof Standards

Different elements of the argumentation, even in the same debate, do not necessarily need the same type of evidence. Quoting the well-used legal domain example, the arguments required to indict someone need not be as convincing as those needed to convict him [13]. Therefore, a generic argumentation system requires different *proof standards* (work on AI and Law uses the term *burdens of proof*). In the sequel, we describe the ones implemented in our system (the names have the same interpretation as in the legal domain). We do not claim that the list is exhaustive; other standards, that match specific application needs, can be easily incorporated to the system.

Scintilla of Evidence (SoE): according to this proof standard, a position is active if at least one active position is supporting it (linked with "+"):
$active(P_i) \Leftarrow \exists P_j \ni (active(P_j) \wedge link(P_j) \wedge Refers\_To(P_j, P_i))$.

Beyond Reasonable Doubt (BRD): according to *BRD*, a position is active if there are not any active positions that speak against it (linked with "-"):
$active(P_i) \Leftarrow \neg\exists P_j \ni (active(P_j) \wedge \neg link(P_j) \wedge Refers\_To(P_j, P_i))$.

In most cases the same proof standard is used for all positions in the argumentation graph in order to achieve fairness. However, when there is a reason, the system allows the discussion moderator to change the proof standard for individual positions.

Activation in our system is a recursive procedure; a change of the activation label of an element is propagated upwards, until the root of the discussion tree. Consider the two instances of the discussion illustrated in Figure 4, assuming that the proof standard is *BRD* for all elements (as discussed in the sequel, alternatives have another proof standard, namely Preponderance of Evidence; we assume here that A_2 has also the BRD standard to give a more illustrative example of the propagation performed). At the left hand side instance, $P_{2.2}$ is *active* (there is only a position supporting it), while A_2 is *inactive* (since $P_{2.2}$ is active). As shown in the right hand side instance, when $P_{2.2.2}$ is inserted, $P_{2.2}$ becomes *inactive*. This change is propagated upwards, making A_2 *active*. Note here that the leaf nodes of the tree (elements with no argumentation underneath) are always considered to be *active*[4].

When an alternative is affected during the discussion, the issue it belongs to should be updated because a new choice may be made. This brings us to the last proof standard, *Preponderance of Evidence (PoE)*, used for the selection of the best alternative (however, it can also be used for activation/inactivation of positions).

In the case of *PoE*, each position has a $weight = (max\_weight + min\_weight)/2$ while an alternative has $weight = min\_weight$. Max_weight and min_weight are initialized to some pre-defined values (for the following discussion we assume that initially $min\_weight = 0$ and $max\_weight = 10$; this may be changed by preference constraints). The *score* of an element E_i (position or alternative) is used to compute its *activation label* (score is calculated

---

[4] Similar ideas have been proposed in [11], viewing argumentation as a special form of logic programming. In this model, an argumentation model consists of two parts: an argument generation unit and an argument processing unit. The second one is a logic program consisting of the clauses `acc(x) ← ¬defeat(x)` (an argument is acceptable if it is not defeated) and `defeat(x) ← attack(y, x), acc(y)` (an argument is defeated if it is attacked by an acceptable argument).

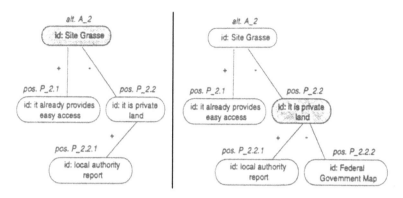

Fig. 4. Two instances of the discussion tree.

on-the-fly and is not stored in the database; therefore, it does not appear in the E-R diagram of Figure 2). If an element does not have any arguments, its score is equal to its weight; otherwise, the score is calculated from the weights of the active positions that refer to the element:

$$score(E_i) \;=\; \sum_{\substack{Refers\_To(P_j,P_i)\wedge \\ link(P_j)\wedge active(P_j)}} weight(P_j) \;-\; \sum_{\substack{Refers\_To(P_k,P_i)\wedge \\ \neg link(P_k)\wedge active(P_k)}} weight(P_k) \tag{1}$$

Preponderance of Evidence: According to this standard, a position is *active* when the active positions that support it outweigh those that speak against it: $active(P_i) \Leftarrow score(P_i) \geq 0$.
In case of alternatives, *PoE* will produce positive activation label (meaning that the alternative is a "recommended" choice) when there are no alternatives with larger score:
$active(A_i) \Leftarrow \forall A_j \; in issue(A_i), \; (score(A_j) \leq score(A_i))$.

The score of an element is used only for the calculation of its own activation label and does not propagate upwards. Before the insertion of $P_{2.2.2}$ in Figure 4, the scores are: $score(P_{2.1}) = score(P_{2.2.1}) = 5$, $score(P_{2.2}) = 5$, and $score(A_2) = 0$ (a counter-argument cancels a supporting one). When $P_{2.2.2}$ is inserted, the scores become: $score(P_{2.2}) = 0$, and $score(A_2) = 5$. In general, large positive scores indicate strong acceptance and large negative ones strong rebuttal of a claim (e.g., when another position that speaks against $P_{2.2}$ is inserted, it will be $score(P_{2.2}) = -5$).
Every time a constraint is inserted in the discussion graph, the system checks for *redundancy*. It actually checks if both positions of the new constraint exist in another, previously inserted, constraint. If this is the case, the new constraint is redundant (independently of its preference relation) and ignored. If not, its consistency is checked against previous active and consistent constraints referring to the same element and its consistency label is determined. This process is based on a polynomial ($O(N^3)$) *path consistency* algorithm [24]. Although path

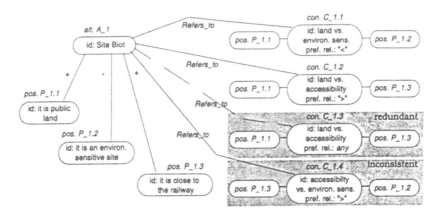

Fig. 5. Redundancy and inconsistency among constraints.

consistency, as most discourse acts described in the sequel, interacts with the database that stores the discussion graph, the algorithm is very efficient for local preferences, because in most cases N (the number of positions that refer to a single position, or constraint) is small. Even for non-local preferences involving issues with numerous alternatives and arguments, execution time is negligible compared to communication delay. In Figure 5, assume that constraints $C_{1.1}$ and $C_{1.2}$ have already been asserted. The new-coming constraint $C_{1.3}$ will be ignored as redundant, while $C_{1.4}$ will be labeled *inconsistent*.

The activation label of constraints can change due to two factors: the discussion underneath and the activation label of their consistuent positions. As shown in Figure 6 (which illustrates the discussion instance after that of Figure 5), the insertion of position $PC_{1.2.1}$ inactivates constraint $C_{1.2}$ (assume BRD as proof standard for all positions and constraints). In addition, position $P_{1.1.2}$ inactivates position $P_{1.1}$, which in turn inactivates constraint $C_{1.1}$ (we assume that $C_{1.2}$ is already *inactive*). $C_{1.4}$ remains active because it does not involve $P_{1.1}$. Notice that $C_{1.4}$ now becomes consistent (path consistency runs whenever there is a change to the activation status of a constraint), and is the only constraint taken into account by the scoring mechanism.

Active and consistent constraints participate in the weighting scheme. In order to demonstrate how the algorithm for altering weights works, we use the example of Figure 7. There exist five positions and four constraints that relate them as illustrated in Figure 7a. The arrowed lines correspond to ">" (e.g., $P_1 > P_2$) and the dotted line to "=" (e.g., $P_3 = P_4$). First path consistency explicates all ">" relations (Figure 7b). Then *topological sort* [21] is applied twice to compute the possible maximum and minimum weights for each position (Figure 7c). The *weight* is the average of the new *max_weight* and *min_weight*: $weight(P_1) = 6, weight(P_2) = 4.5, weight(P_3) = 5, weight(P_4) = 5$ and $weight(P_5) = 4$.

The basic idea behind the above scheme is that the weight of a position is increased every time the position is more important than another one (and

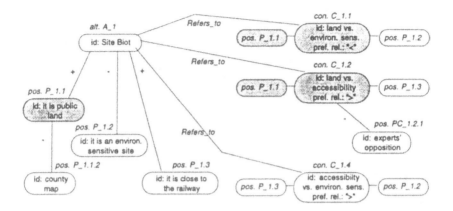

Fig. 6. Inactivation of constraints.

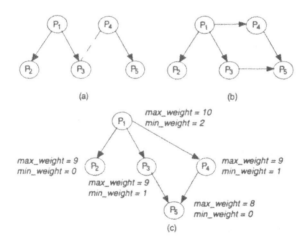

Fig. 7. The weighting scheme.

decreased when is less important), the aim being to extract a total order of alternatives. Since only partial information may be given, the choice of the initial maximum and minimum weights may affect the system's recommendation. Furthermore, this weighting scheme is not the only solution; alternative schemes, based on different algorithms, can be developed.

4 Discourse Acts

Argumentation in our framework is performed through a variety of *discourse acts*. These acts may have different functions and roles in the argumentative discourse. We classify them in three major categories: *agent acts, internal (system) acts* and *moderator acts*. Agent acts refer to user actions and correspond to functions directly supported by the user interface. Such functions include opening an issue, adding an alternative, etc. Below we present the pseudo-code for a few representative agent acts:

add_Alternative_to_Issue(*alternative A, issue I*) {
   $\ln(A)=I$;   /* *A is made a part of I* */
   update(I); }   /* *I is updated* */

add_Alternative_to_Alternative(*alternative A_i, alternative A_j*) {
   $I_j=\ln(A_j)$;
   create new issue I_i;
   $\ln(I_i)=I_j$;
   $\ln(A_j)=\ln(A_i)=I_i$;
   update(I_i); }

When an alternative A_i is added to another A_j (and not to the issue I_j where A_j belongs) a new issue I_i is created inside I_j. Both A_i and A_j are now put inside the new issue and compared through update(I_i). update(I_j) will be called from update(I_i) and the recommended choice between A_i and A_j will be compared against the other alternatives of the external (original) issue.

add_Constraint_to_Position(*constraint C, position P*) {
   RefersTo(C)=P;
   if (redundant(C)) *exit*;
   if (contains_Inactive(C)) ¬active(C);
      else {
      active(C);
      if (¬consistent_with_Previous(C))
         ¬*consistent*(C);
      else
      { *consistent*(C);
         update(P); }}}

Contains_Inactive(C) checks whether one or both positions related by C are *inactive*, in which case C becomes *inactive*. The justification is that it does not make sense to argue about the relevant importance of positions that are rejected (C will be activated automatically when the compared positions get activated - see activate(*position P*)). If C does not contain_Inactive, then it is checked for consistency. Only if it is found consistent, the position that it refers to is updated, since inconsistent constraints do not participate in the weighting scheme.

Other agent acts involve addition of constraints to issues, insertion of supporting and counter-arguments to positions, constraints and alternatives, etc. There is also a second type of agents acts, which is not immediately connected to the discussion forum, but allows agents to ask the database queries of the form "give me all messages by a *specific user* on an issue" or "what was the recommended solution on a *given date*".

Internal acts are functions performed by the system in order to check consistency, update the discussion status and recommend solutions. These functions are called mainly by the agent or moderator acts and are hidden from the end user. For instance, consistent_with_Previous(C), called by add_Constraint_to_Position, constructs a graph (similar to Figure 7) from the arguments of the position where C refers to and applies path consistency. Some other representative internal acts are:

```
boolean compute_activation(position P) {
boolean ¬ status_changed, old_activation=activation(P);
switch Proof_Standard(P) {
      case Scintilla of Evidence {
              ¬activation(P);
              for all positions Pⱼ that refer to P
                      if (active(Pⱼ) ∧ link(Pⱼ))
                      {      activation(P);
                             break; }}
      case Beyond Reasonable Doubt {
              activation(P);
              for all positions Pⱼ that refer to P
                      if (active(Pⱼ) ∧ ¬link(Pⱼ))
                      {      ¬activation(P);
                             break; }}
      case Preponderance of Evidence {
              score(P)=0;
              calculate_weights(P);
              for all positions Pⱼ that refer to P
                      if (active(Pⱼ) ∧ link(Pⱼ))
                              score(P) += weight(Pⱼ);
                      else if (active(Pⱼ)∧ ¬link(Pⱼ))
                              score(P) -= weight(Pⱼ);
              if (score(P) ≥ 0) activation(P);
                      else ¬activation(P) }}
if (¬ old_activation==activation(P)) status_changed;
return status_changed; }
```

Compute_activation returns *status_changed*, which is *true* if the activation label of the position changed. Activation is calculated according to the proof standard used. Proof standards are a straightforward implementation of the definitions in Section 3. In case of *PoE*, calculate_weights(P) calls topological sort to compute the weights of the supporting and counter-arguments of P.

```
update(position P) {
if (compute_activation(P)) {
    if (active(P)) activate(P);
        else inactivate(P);
    update(RefersTo(P)); }}        /*Propagate upwards */
```

update calls compute_activation to check whether activation label has changed. If this is the case, activate (see below) or inactivate are called and the change is propagated upwards.

```
activate(position P) {
Pj=RefersTo(P);
for all constraints Cj that refer to Pj
    if (¬active(Cj) ∧ Cj has a preference relation on P)
        if (compute_Activation(Cj)) {
            if (consistent_with_Previous(Cj)
                consistent(Cj);
            else ¬consistent(Cj); }}
```

Activation of positions involves finding the potential constraints where the position appears (these constraints must refer to the same position as P) and checking whether they can now become *active* and *consistent*.

Inactivation of positions is similar, in the sense that when a position becomes inactive, the system searches for the constraints where the position appears in a preference relation and inactivates them as well. This may cause some other inconsistent constraints to become consistent, so consistency check is performed again for the related constraints. A number of additional internal acts were implemented for the activation-inactivation of constraints, update of issues (in which case there is only *PoE*), etc.

Moderator acts are invoked by the discussion mediator and may involve the assignment of *access rights* (or *importance weights*) to agents, change of the proof standard, etc. The procedures described in this section, although only a subset of the whole set of functions performed by the system, give an indication of its dynamic structure. A single insertion in the discussion graph may update a large portion of the tree. Every time there is a change, the status of the argumentation elements is recorded in the database that keeps track of the discourse.

5   Related and future work

In this section we focus on previous, well-tried concepts and theories, attempting to account for how humans combine various types of reasoning during argumentative discourse. We aim at extracting the pros and cons of our approach, and motivation for further work.

Toulmin's argumentation theory [37] identified six components in the construction of an argument: *datum* (i.e., a fact or data), *warrant* (i.e., inference rule), *backing* (i.e., support of the warrant), *claim* (i.e., conclusion of the argument), *rebuttal* (i.e., objection or exception) and *qualifier* (similar to *score* in our system). Figure 8 illustrates how Toulmin's structure of arguments can be mapped onto ours. We view any component as a position (claims may also be alternatives) with the appropriate role in the discussion graph. Main weaknesses of Toulmin's theory are the lack of the appropriate formalism for addressing multiple issues and ordering competing arguments, and its orientation towards only cooperative-type argumentation. Instead, our framework is applicable to adversarial or cooperative group decision making, and provides a means of ordering positions and alternatives in an issue.

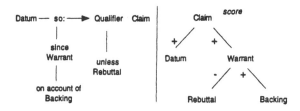

Fig. 8. Structure of an argument according to Toulmin's (left) and the proposed (right) model.

Pollock's OSCAR model of defeasible reasoning [26] was one of the first attempts to base defeasible reasoning on arguments, influencing later work (see for example [34], [14]). His model does not deal with resolving disputes, but with prescribing the set of beliefs a single rational agent should hold, under certain simplifying assumptions. According to him, the initial *epistemic basis* of an agent consists of a set of positions, either supported by perception or recalled from memory, a set of defeasible and a set of nondefeasible *inference rules*. Belief on positions stands until defeated by new reasons, disregarding the original ones. Pollock also distinguishes between *warranted* and *justified belief*; we deal with these issues using proof standards. A weakness of OSCAR, addressed in our framework, is that there are no reasoning schemata provided for the validity of inference rules, or their relative weight and priority.

Rescher, in his theory of *formal disputation* [30], considers disputation to be a three-party game, taking place with a *proponent*, asserting a certain position, an *opponent*, able to challenge the proponent's position, and a *determiner* which decides whether the proponent's position was successfully defended or not. Our model plays the last role, mediating the discussion among multiple agents. A more formal reconstruction of Rescher's theory has been presented by Brewka [7], based on Reiter's Default Logic [29]. His work clarifies Rescher's concepts and goes ahead defining *elementary* and *legal moves* during a dispute, as well as *winning situations*. Nevertheless, both approaches are limited in that the "players" have no chance to disagree about defaults.

Approaches to reasoning in the presence of inconsistency can be divided into those based on the notion of *maximal consistent subbase*, where coherence is restored by selecting consistent subbases, and those based on *argumentation principles*, where inconsistency is "accepted" by providing arguments for each conclusion [9]. Non-monotonic inference relations are basically used in the first category, defined by methods of generating *preferred belief subbases* and classical inference [5]. The second category, inspired from work done on AI and Law, views the validity and priority of belief bases as subject to debate. Throughout this paper, we have taken into account belief bases that have been explicitly stated by an agent.

In the kind of discussions our system addresses, domain theories are usually weak, i.e., rules and concepts may have not been expressed and, if there are, they often suffer from definitional flaws. To remedy this, future work directions include incorporation of an agent's *viewpoint* in the system, and integration of *Case-Based Reasoning (CBR)* methods. Viewpoints will model each agent's agenda, aiming at making clear (from the beginning) his interpretation of the issue under discussion. They will include desired attributes that each alternative should possess in order to "win" the issue, and the preference relations between them. Viewpoints will explicitly map the interests of each participant, and may evolve during the discourse. Integration of our system with CBR methods will increase its efficiency, by reusing previous instances (*cases*) of similar discussions [36], [35]. One will contrast precedent cases with the current one, reason about the similarities and differences with it, and finally argue why a previous interpretation can (or cannot) be applied. Issues involved are *case indexing, retrieval of relevant cases* from the case base, *selection of the most promising cases* to reason with, *adaptation of case* (construction of a solution or interpretation for the new case), and *update* of case base adjusting relevant indices (see also [31]).

Moreover, we need to implement norms or protocols about the rights and duties of the different types of agents that participate in a discussion. Ideas from similar structures in formalized public activities should be exploited together with approaches from AI and Law (i.e., Deontic Logic, Argumentation Theory) and Distributed AI. Protocols should take into account the roles of participants and the evolution of the decision making procedure.

6 Conclusion

The argumentation system is a part of a larger project that attempts to link argumentation with *collaboration* services in the context of Group Decision Making Applications. Collaboration services include a *shared workspace*, where agents can put any type of files (e.g. text, images) related to the argumentation, *navigation mechanisms* and appropriate *visualization tools*. In addition the system includes *information services* which facilitate information retrieval from internal (e.g., shared workspace) and external (e.g., the World Wide Web) resources. Several interesting problems (beyond the scope of this paper) related to the project, include *authentication* and *access rights*, *concurrency control* (in some cases, users may need to simultaneously modify different parts of the same object) and *data conversion* and *integration* issues.

Use of information technology may assist multi-agent decision making in various ways. An important goal is to provide easy access to the current knowledge, at any time. This would be greatly facilitated if all relevant data and documents are made available and maintained in electronic form, in a well-structured and organized way. Our system's primary task is to provide direct computer support for the argumentation, negotiation and mediation process in these environments. A computer network can be used as a medium for such a process, in which documents are indexed according to their role and function, using the presented model of argumentation. The system presented in this paper combines concepts from various well-established areas such as Decision Theory, Non-Monotonic Reasoning, Constraint Satisfaction and Cognitive Modeling. We intend it to act as an assistant and advisor, by recommending solutions and leaving the final enforcement of decisions and actions to agents.

Acknowledgements: The authors thank Gerhard Brewka, Tom Gordon, Brigitte Trousse and Hans Voss for helpful discussions on various topics of this paper. Nikos Karacapilidis is financed by the Commission of the European Communities through the ERCIM Fellowship Programme. Dimitris Papadias is supported by a DAG grant from Hong Kong RGC.

References

1. Batini, C., Ceri, S., Navathe, S.B.: *Conceptual Database Design: An Entity-Relationship Approach*. Benjamin/Cummings Publishing, 1992.
2. Bench-Capon, Tr.: Argument in Artificial Intelligence and Law. In J.C. Hage, T.J.M. Bench-Capon, M.J. Cohen and H.J. van den Herik (eds.), *Legal knowledge based systems - Telecommunication and AI & Law*, Koninklijke Vermande BV, Lelystad, 1995, pp. 5-14.
3. Benferhat, S., Dubois, D., Prade, H.: How to infer from inconsistent beliefs without revising? In *Proceedings of the 14th IJCAI*, Montreal, 1995, pp. 1449-1455.
4. Benferhat, S., Cayrol, C., Dubois, D., Lang, J., Prade, H.: Inconsistency Management and Prioritized Syntax-Based Entailment. In *Proceedings of the 13th IJCAI*, Chambery, 1993, pp. 640-645.
5. Brewka, G.: Preferred Subtheories: An extended logical framework for default reasoning. In *Proceedings of the 11th IJCAI*, Detroit, 1989, pp. 1043-1048.
6. Brewka, G.: Reasoning about Priorities in Default Logic. In *Proceedings of the 12th AAAI*, Seattle, 1994, pp. 940-945.
7. Brewka, G.: A Reconstruction of Rescher's Theory of Formal Disputation Based on Default Logic. In *Working Notes of the 12th AAAI Workshop on Computational Dialectics*, Seattle, 1994, pp. 15-27.
8. Brewka, G., Gordon, T.: How to Buy a Porsche: An Approach to Defeasible Decision Making. In *Working Notes of the 12th AAAI Workshop on Computational Dialectics*, Seattle, 1994, pp. 28-38.

9. Cayrol, C.: On the Relation between Argumentation and Non-monotonic Coherence-Based Entailment. In *Proceedings of the 14th IJCAI*, Montreal, 1995, pp. 1443-1448.
10. Conklin, E.J.: Capturing Organizational Memory. In D. Coleman (ed.) *Groupware '92*, 1992, pp. 133-137.
11. Dung, P.M.: On the acceptability of arguments and its fundamental role in non-monotonic reasoning and logic programming. In *Proceedings of the 13th IJCAI*, Chambery, 1993, pp. 852-857.
12. Eemeren, F.H. van, Grootendorst, R., Snoeck Henkemans, F.: *Fundamentals of Argumentation Theory: A Handbook of Historical Backgrounds and Contemporary Developments*. Lawrence Erblaum Associates, Mahwah, New Jersey, 1996.
13. Farley, A.M., Freeman, K.: Burden of Proof in Legal Argumentation. In *Proceedings of the 5th Int. Conference on AI and Law*, 1995, pp. 156-164.
14. Geffner, H., Pearl, J.: Conditional Entailment: Bridging two Approaches to Default Reasoning. *Artificial Intelligence* 53 (2-3), 1992, pp. 209-244.
15. Gordon, T.: *The Pleadings Game: An Artificial Intelligence Model of Procedural Justice*. Kluwer, 1995.
16. Green, D.W.: Arguments and Mental Models. In *Proceedings of the Int. Conference on Formal and Applied Practical Reasoning*, 1996.
17. Heidrich. C.H.: Montague-grammars for Argumentative Dialogues. In Barth & Martens (Eds.) *Argumentation: Approaches to Theory Formation*. John Benjamins, Amsterdam, 1982.
18. Hurwitz, R., Mallery, J.C.: The Open Meeting: A Web-Based System for Conferencing and Collaboration. In *Proceedings of the 4th Int. WWW Conference*, 1995.
19. Karacapilidis, N.I.: Planning under Uncertainty: A Qualitative Approach. In C. Pinto-Ferreira and N.J. Mamede (eds.), *Progress in Artificial Intelligence*, LNAI 990, Springer-Verlag, 1995, pp. 285-296.
20. Karacapilidis, N.I., Papadias, D., Gordon, T.: An Argumentation Based Framework for Defeasible and Qualitative Reasoning. *Advances in Arificial Intelligence*, LNAI 1159, Springer-Verlag, Berlin, 1996, pp. 1-10.
21. Knuth, D. E.: *Fundamental Algorithms*, Art of Computer Programming, Vol.1, Addison-Wesley, Second Edition, 1973.
22. Kunz, W., Rittel, H.W.J.: Issues as Elements of Information Systems. Working Paper 131, Universität Stuttgart, Institut für Grundlagen der Plannung, 1970.
23. Lueken, G-L.: Incommensurability, Rules of Argumentation and Anticipation. In *Proceedings of the 2nd Int. Conference of Argumentation*, 1991.
24. Mackworth, A., Freuder, E.: The Complexity of some Polynomial Network Consistency Algorithms for Constraint Satisfaction Problems, *Artificial Intelligence* 25, 1985, pp. 65-74.
25. Pinkas, G.: Propositional Non-Monotonic Reasoning and Inconsistency in Symmetric Neural Networks. In *Proceedings of the 12th IJCAI*, Sydney, 1991, pp. 525-530.
26. Pollock, J.: Defeasible Reasoning. *Cognitive Science* 11, 1988, pp. 481-518.
27. Prakken, H.: Logical tools for modelling legal argument. Ph.D. Dissertation, Free University of Amsterdam, 1993.
28. Prakken, H.: From Logic to Dialectics in Legal Argument. In *Proceedings of the 5th International Conference on AI and Law*, ACM Press, 1995, pp. 165-174.
29. Reiter, R.: A Logic for Default Reasoning. *Artificial Intelligence* 13, 1980, pp. 81-132.
30. Rescher, N.: *Dialectics: A Controversy-Oriented Approach to the Theory of Knowledge*. State University of New York Press, Albany, 1977.

31. Rissland, E.L., Skalak, D.B.: CABARET: rule interpretation in a hybrid architecture. *Int. Journal of Man-Machine Studies* 34, 1991, pp. 839-88.

32. Rittel, H.W.J., Webber, M.M.: Dilemmas in a General Theory of Planning. *Policy Sciences* 4, 1973, pp. 155-169.

33. Sian, S.S.: Adaptation based on cooperative learning in multi-agent systems. In Y. Demazeau and J.P. Müller (eds.), *Decentralized AI 2*, Elsevier Science Publishers B.V., 1991, pp. 257-272.

34. Simari, G.R., Loui, R.P.: A Mathematical Treatment of Defeasible Reasoning and its Implementation. *Artificial Intelligence* 53 (2-3), 1992, pp. 125-157.

35. Sycara, K.: Resolving Goal Conflicts via Negotiation. In *Proceedings of the 7th AAAI*, Saint Paul, Minnesota, 1988, pp. 245-250.

36. Sycara, K.: Resolving Adversarial Conflicts: An Approach Integrating Case-Based and Analytic Methods. Ph.D. diss., School of Information and Computer Science, Georgia Institute of Technology, 1987.

37. Toulmin, S.E.: *The Uses of Argument*. Cambridge University Press, 1958.

38. Valesio, P.: *Novantiqua: Rhetorics as a Contemporary Theory*. Indiana University Press, 1980.

39. Yakemovic, K.C.B., Conklin, E.J.: Report on a Development Project Use of an Issue-Based Information System. In F. Halasz (ed.), *Proceedings of CSCW 90*, LA, 1990, pp. 105-118.

40. http://union.ncsa.uiuc.edu/HyperNews/get/www/collab/conferencing.html.

From Belief Revision to Design Revision: Applying Theory Change to Changing Requirements

C K MacNish
Department of Computer Science
The University of Western Australia
Nedlands, WA 6907, Australia
kym@cs.uwa.edu.au

M-A Williams
Department of Management
The University of Newcastle
Newcastle, NSW 2308, Australia
maryanne@frey.newcastle.edu.au

Abstract

The ability to correctly analyse the impact of changes to system designs is an important goal in software engineering. A framework for addressing this problem has been proposed in which logical descriptions are developed alongside traditional representations. While changes to the resulting design have been considered, no formal framework for design change has been offered.

This paper proposes such a framework using techniques from the field of belief revision. It is shown that under a particular strategy for belief revision, called a maxi-adjustment, design revisions can be modelled using standard revision operators.

As such, the paper also offers a new area of application for belief revision. Previous attempts to apply belief revision theory have suffered from the criticism that deduced information is held on to more strongly than the facts from which it is derived. This criticism does not apply to the present application because we are concerned with *goal decomposition* rather than reasoning from facts, and it makes sense that goals should be held onto more strongly than the decompositions designed to achieve them.

1 Introduction

The ability to correctly analyse the impact of changes to system designs is an important goal in software engineering. It has been estimated [9] that in safety-critical systems such as those found in the aerospace industry, as much as 80% of software development costs are consumed in modifications rather than initial development. Without automated assistance, the complexity of these systems make it difficult to assess the effects of changes in advance.

In [3] Duffy *et al* propose a framework called *Goal-structured Analysis* (GSA) which addresses this problem. The framework promotes the development of logical representations of requirements and design decisions alongside traditional representations, providing a semantic link between requirements. This link can be used to support automated analysis. The use of natural language processing tools to help in the development of these logical expressions is considered in [7].

From a technical point of view the main result of [3] is the formalisation of conditions under which goals are *supported* by the underlying model, and more particularly the conditions for *local support* which enable a goal structure to be built up incrementally. The latter requires a partial order on sentences, which we will call a *support order*, in which goals must be entailed by statements that strictly precede them. Duffy *et al* briefly discuss changes to goal structures by way of an example involving aircraft landing control but do not provide any formal machinery for changing the structure.

In this paper we investigate the use of the AGM paradigm for *belief revision* [1] as a way of providing a formal mechanism for the revision of top-down designs and, in particular, goal structures. In doing so we also provide a pragmatic application for the AGM paradigm, which has received a largely theoretical treatment in the literature.

The AGM paradigm, which is discussed in more detail in Section 2, proposes a number of postulates for the evolution of a corpus of logical information, called a *belief set* or *theory*, based on the Principle of Minimal Change. These postulates do not prescribe a particular operation for revising information, but rather specify properties that any such operation should obey. Particular revision operators are obtained by augmenting belief sets with preference relations [1, 4, 5, 6, 8].

Perhaps the most commonly encountered preference relation, called an *epistemic entrenchment* [4], is a relative ranking on sentences subject to a number of conditions which ensure that revisions satisfy the AGM postulates. One such condition requires that a sentence never precede any sentences that entail it — roughly the converse of the support order described above. In Section 3 we show that, by modifying the partial order on goals to give "causal rules" a special status, the two orderings become compatible. The goal structure can then be constructed, in a top-down fashion, according to an epistemic entrenchment.

In order to iteratively modify a belief set, each revision needs to adjust the preference order on the set as well as the information represented in the set. This is achieved in [11] by defining a *partial entrenchment ranking* which maps sentences to ordinals, and a *transmutation* which adjusts the ranking with each revision. This ranking is used in [14] to propose a formal characterisation of one sentence being a *reason* for another. By appealing to the notion of *reason* a particular transmutation, called a *maxi-adjustment*, was introduced in [12]. Maxi-adjustments modify a partial entrenchment ranking as little as possible whilst incorporating the new information. In particular, when new information is inconsistent with the current ranking, then only information that is either a *reason* for the negation of the new information, or *spurious* (information derivable from the negation of the new information) is removed. In Section 4 we argue that maxi-adjustments can be used to perform the three most common types of design revision. The application of standard revision operators can thus be considered to provide a formal mechanism for modeling changing user requirements.

In providing a model for design change, the paper also offers a new area of application for belief revision. Previous attempts to apply belief revision theory have suffered from the criticism that deduced information is held on to more strongly than the facts from which it is derived, prompting a preference for truth maintenance systems [2] and the like. This criticism does not apply to the present application because we are concerned with *goal decomposition* rather than reasoning from facts, and it makes sense that goals should be held onto more strongly than the decompositions designed to achieve them. Putting it another way, there can be no confusion in the present application between entrenchment and "strength" of belief. Rather, levels of entrenchment reflect the importance attached to statements and the order in which they are generated.

2 Belief Revision and Partial Entrenchment Rankings

The AGM paradigm is a standard theoretical framework for modeling changes to repositories of information. Its change operators can be constructed from various forms of preference relations. Intuitively, these preference relations encapsulate the information *content* of a system, the system's *commitment* to this information, and the relative importance of information with respect to *change*.

Partial entrenchment rankings can be used as a finite representation of an epistemic entrenchment ordering; a popular preference relation from which contraction and revision operators can be defined.

Partial entrenchment rankings grade information by mapping sentences to ordinals. Intuitively, the higher the ordinal assigned to a sentence, the more resistant it is to change. More formally we have the following definition. Note that $\mathcal{O}_{\max}$ is chosen to be sufficiently large for the purpose of the discussion.

Definition 2.1 A partial entrenchment ranking is a function **B** from a set of sentences into the class of ordinals such that the following condition is satisfied for all $a \in \text{dom}(\mathbf{B})$:

(PER1) If $\nvdash a$ then $\{b \in \text{dom}(\mathbf{B}) : \mathbf{B}(a) < \mathbf{B}(b)\} \nvdash a$.

(PER2) If $\vdash \neg a$ then $B(a) = 0$.

(PER3) $B(a) = \mathcal{O}_{\max}$ if and only if $\vdash a$.

According to this definition, sentences which are assigned ordinals higher than an arbitrary sentence a cannot entail a, inconsistent information is assigned zero, and the tautologies are assigned the highest rank.

We refer to $B(a)$ as the degree of acceptance of a. The intended interpretation of a partial entrenchment ranking is that sentences with a degree of acceptance greater than zero represent the *explicit* beliefs of the system, and their logical closure represents its *implicit* beliefs.

Definition 2.2 Define the *explicit information content* of a partial entrenchment ranking B to be $\{a \in \text{dom}(B) : B(a) > 0\}$, and denote it by $\exp(B)$. Similarly, define the *implicit information content* of B, denoted content(B), to be $\text{Cn}(\exp(B))$, where Cn denotes logical closure (or "consequences").

Intuitively, a partial entrenchment ranking represents a system's incomplete preferences concerning information about the world from which a complete entrenchment ranking can be generated. The function *degree*, defined below, derives the minimum possible degree of acceptance for implicit information as specified by a partial entrenchment ranking [10].

Definition 2.3 Let a be a nontautological sentence. If B is finite, then

$$
\text{degree}(B, a) = \begin{cases} \text{the largest } j \text{ such that} \\ \quad \{b \in \exp(B) : B(b) \geq j\} \vdash a & \text{if } a \in \text{content}(B) \\ 0 & \text{otherwise.} \end{cases}
$$

The process of changing partial entrenchment rankings is a *transmutation*. We briefly describe a particular transmutation schema called *maxi-adjustment* [12]. Maxi-adjustments change a partial entrenchment ranking under *maximal inertia* in accordance with the Principle of Minimal Change. In other words, maxi-adjustments modify a ranking in a minimal way while maintaining as much of the content of the original ranking as possible. Maxi-adjustments assume by default that revisions to one piece of information do not effect another unless dependence is derivable from the explicitly specified information.

The system designer specifies all the known information dependencies using the notion of a sentence being the *reason* for another sentence, and a maxi-adjustment uses these explicit dependencies to determine the information to be retracted. Essentially, for a and b in content(B), a is a reason for b with respect to B whenever degree$(B, b) <$ degree$(B, a \rightarrow b)$.

A maxi-adjustment involves the absolute minimal change of a partial entrenchment ranking that is required to incorporate the desired new sentence such that currently held information is retained unless there is an explicit reason to retract it. The maxi-adjustment of B defined below is suitable for modeling changes to finite knowledge bases where the systems designer specifies all the dependencies, and independence is then assumed otherwise. It involves successive calls to the function degree for each sentence in the domain of **B**. In Section 4 we illustrate maxi-adjustment with a simple example.

Definition 2.4 Let **B** be a finite partial entrenchment ranking. We enumerate the range of **B** in ascending order as $j_0, j_1, \ldots, j_{\mathcal{O}_{\max}}$. Let a be a contingent sentence, $j_m = \text{degree}(\mathbf{B}, a)$ and $0 \le i < \mathcal{O}_{\max}$. Then the (a, i)-maxi-adjustment of **B** is $\mathbf{B}^\star(a, i)$ defined by:

$$\mathbf{B}^\star(a, i) = \begin{cases} \mathbf{B}^-(a, i) & \text{if } i \le \text{degree}(\mathbf{B}, a) \\ (\mathbf{B}^-(\neg a, 0))^+(a, i) & \text{otherwise} \end{cases}$$

where for all $b \in \text{dom}(\mathbf{B})$, we define $\mathbf{B}^-(a, i)$ as follows:

1. For b with $\mathbf{B}(b) > j_m$ we have $\mathbf{B}^-(a, i)(b) = \mathbf{B}(b)$.

2. For b with $i < \mathbf{B}(b) \le j_m$, suppose we have defined $\mathbf{B}^-(a, i)(b)$ for b with $\mathbf{B}(b) \ge j_{m-k}$ for $k = -1, 0, 1, 2, \ldots, n-1$, then for b with $\mathbf{B}(b) = j_{m-n}$ we have

$$\mathbf{B}^-(a, i)(b) = \begin{cases} i & \text{if } a \equiv b \text{ and } b \in \Gamma \\ & \text{where } \Gamma \text{ is a minimal subset of} \\ & \{\gamma : \mathbf{B}(b) = j_{m-n}\} \text{ such that} \\ & \{\gamma : \mathbf{B}^-(a, i)(b) > j_{m-n}\} \cup \Gamma \vdash a \\ \mathbf{B}(b) & \text{otherwise.} \end{cases}$$

3. For b with $\mathbf{B}(b) \le i$ we have $\mathbf{B}^-(a, i)(b) = \mathbf{B}(b)$.

and for all $b \in \text{dom}(\mathbf{B}) \cup \{a\}$ we define $\mathbf{B}^+(a, i)$ as follows:

$$\mathbf{B}^+(a, i)(b) = \begin{cases} \mathbf{B}(b) & \text{if } \mathbf{B}(b) > i \\ i & \text{if } a \equiv b \text{ or} \\ & \mathbf{B}(b) \le i < \text{degree}(\mathbf{B}, a \to b) \\ \text{degree}(\mathbf{B}, a \to b) & \text{otherwise.} \end{cases}$$

A (a, i)-maxi-adjustment changes the ranking such that a is assigned rank i. Its definition is discussed further in [12] where several examples can be found. A procedural description of maxi-adjustment, and a discussion of its complexity is given in [13]. It turns out that if i is greater than zero then content$(\mathbf{B}^\star(a, i))$ satisfies the postulates for revision, and similarly content$(\mathbf{B}^\star(a, 0))$ satisfies all bar the recovery postulate for contraction. Maxi-adjustment also provides subsumption removal as an optional facility.

The following lemma states that when we retract a sentence from a ranking we retain all sentences with higher epistemic ranking.

Lemma 2.5 Let $\text{cut}_<(\mathbf{B}, a) = \{b \in \exp(\mathbf{B}) : \text{degree}(\mathbf{B}, a) < \mathbf{B}(b)\}$. Then $\text{cut}_<(\mathbf{B}, a) \subseteq \text{content}(\mathbf{B}^\star(a, 0))$

Thus, when considering the desirable behaviour of contractions and revisions (more precisely transmutations) in the design process, we only need to consider the effects on sentences at an equal or lower rank than the retracted sentence.

3 Goal-structured Analysis and Epistemic Entrenchments

Maxi-adjustments provide a way of revising information based on a partial entrenchment ranking. In this section we specify a suitable entrenchment ranking for goal structures. In the following section we show that the resulting revision operators are suitable for design revision. First we must introduce some of the basic concepts of goal-structured analysis.

3.1 Introduction to Goal-structured Analysis

Goal-structured analysis (GSA) is a design and analysis methodology based on goal decomposition. In order to give our presentation of goal structures we will require some terminology from [3]. However, we will have space here only to briefly introduce some aspects of the framework that are pertinent to the present discussion: for a fuller motivation and discussion the reader is referred to [3].

A goal structure consists of a directed acyclic graph (DAG) of *frames*, each of which contains a number of fields of information. This will include a principal *assertion* or statement, and may include additional information such as the system to which the assertion refers, stakeholders in the assertion, a decomposition of the assertion and so on. As well as information expressed in natural language, the frame will contain corresponding fields which express some of the information as logical sentences, and it is this representation that will interest us in this paper.

There are four different classes of frames and corresponding logical assertions:

goals are statements of what the system should achieve, and can be decomposed into subgoals that will bring about their achievement.

effects are similar to goals, and identical from a logical point of view — the difference is that although they still require decomposition, they may be undesirable.

facts are statements that require no further decomposition — they may for example be always true, be trivially implementable, or be passed as goals to the design team of a different subsystem.

conditions are like facts in that they form the "leaves" of the structure, however, they may be true in some scenarios and false in others, representing, for example, environmental conditions. A *scenario* is a set of conditions.

In a complete structure the satisfaction of a goal (or effect) should follow from just facts and conditions. In this case the goal is said to be *(globally) supported*. During the process of top-down decomposition, however, there is no way of knowing whether a goal will eventually be globally supported. One of the aims of [3] is to identify constraints on incremental development which, if followed by the designer, will ensure global support in the final structure. Goals satisfying these constraints are said to be *locally supported.*

One of the main results in [3] is a proof that local support leads to global support. In order to achieve this, a partial order on goals, $\prec_G$, is developed in order to prevent support "loops". For a goal to be locally supported, it must be entailed by assertions lower in the partial order.

3.2 Development of a Goal Structure

Each stage in the development of a goal structure consists of the decomposition of a goal or effect into goals, effects, facts or conditions which are strictly lower in the partial order. This is illustrated by the following two examples taken from [3]. They relate to a design problem, developed throughout the remainer of this paper, which is derived from accounts of an actual incident in which an aircraft over-ran a runway when landing in poor conditions. The strategies outlined below are simplifications of alternative strategies that have been used in passenger-carrying aircraft.

In the first example, the strategy for satisfying the goal is based on existing facts which the designer has no control over. For example, assume our goal is to bring an aircraft to a stop within 1000m. We know from information about the dynamics of the aircraft, or perhaps tests on previous models of similar weight, that applying the wheel brakes is sufficient provided that the speed of the aircraft is less than 154km/h. This is embodied in the following fact:

Fact	
Label	Fact1
System	Aircraft dynamics
Assertion	The aircraft will stop within 1000m if wheel brakes are applied when speed $\leq$ 154km/h.
Assertion*	$(speed \leq 154) \wedge applied(wheel.brakes) \rightarrow (stop.length < 1000)$
Rationale	Engineering tests

The logical assertion in this frame (marked by an asterix) represents a *causal rule.*

On the basis of this we can develop a goal frame such as the following:

Goal	
Label	Goal1
System	Landing control
Assertion	Stop aircraft within 1000m
Assertion*	$stop.length < 1000$
Selection	Apply wheel brakes when speed $\leq$ 154 km/h
Rationale	Based on Fact1

The 'selection' field refers to a selected strategy — this, in conjunction with the fact F1, ensures that the goal is satisfied. The selection will in turn be treated as a goal and decomposed.

In the second example the designer of the control system has more scope — it is up to them to decide under what conditions the reverse thrusters will fire. Two alternatives are shown:

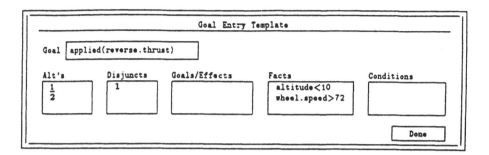

Figure 1: A template for entering goals and strategies for their decomposition.

Goal	
Label	Goal2
Assertion*	applied(reverse.thrust)
Alternatives	wheel.loads > 12; (altitude < 10) ∧ (wheel.speed > 72)
Selection	wheel.loads > 12

The selection will be implemented and therefore lead to the following causal rule:

Fact	
Label	Fact2
Assertion*	(wheel.loads > 12) → applied(reverse.thrust)

Notice that both of the above examples include a causal rule which makes explicit the relationship between assertions and selected strategies in the goals. This will always be the case, and is in fact necessary from a deductive point of view. In [3] a causal rule is not treated differently to any other fact. In our treatment it will be necessary to treat causal rules as a special case. We argue, however, that this is a natural thing to do. Causal rules do clearly perform a different, more "implicit", role to other facts.

From a practical point of view we do not want to think explicitly about the causal rules at all. Rather we would like to enter alternative strategies through a template such as that illustrated in Figure 1, and automatically generate appropriate causal rules.

3.3 Redefining Support using an Entrenchment Ranking

As discussed above, local support is defined in [3] with respect to a partial order $\prec_G$ on assertions. This partial order is, in general, at odds with an entrenchment ranking, since it will violate PER1. As a simple example, the ordering

$$a \prec_G (a \to b) \prec_G b$$

is suitable for local support, but cannot correspond to an entrenchment ranking since $b \models a \to b$. (An inverse ranking is also impossible since $\{a, a \to b\} \models b$.)

If as discussed above, however, we are prepared to give a special status to causal rules, then an alternative ranking can be quite naturally applied. In the following, $\mathcal{O}_c$, $\mathcal{O}_f$ and $\mathcal{O}_r$ represent arbitrary ordinals such that

$$0 < \mathcal{O}_c < \mathcal{O}_f < \mathcal{O}_r < \mathcal{O}_{max}.$$

We will insist that conditions are ranked in the interval $(0, \mathcal{O}_c]$, facts are ranked in the interval $(\mathcal{O}_c, \mathcal{O}_f]$, goals and effects are ranked in the interval $(\mathcal{O}_f, \mathcal{O}_r)$, and causal rules are ranked in the interval $[\mathcal{O}_r, \mathcal{O}_{max})$.

Definition 3.1 (global support) Let **B** be a partial entrenchment ranking. An assertion g is *globally supported* (with respect to a scenario) iff there exists a set of assertions $S = \{s_1, \ldots, s_m\}$ such that:

GS1 For each $s_i \in S$, either $0 < \text{degree}(\mathbf{B}, s_i) \leq \mathcal{O}_f$ or $\text{degree}(\mathbf{B}, s_i) \geq \mathcal{O}_r$.

GS2 $S \models g$.

We say that g is globally supported by the set S. Of course a goal or effect may be supported by more than one set of assertions.

Definition 3.2 (local support) Let **B** be a partial entrenchment ranking. An assertion g is *locally supported* (in a scenario) iff there exists a set of assertions $S = \{s_1, \ldots, s_m\}$ such that:

LS1 For each s_i, either $0 < \text{degree}(\mathbf{B}, s_i) < \text{degree}(\mathbf{B}, g)$ or $\text{degree}(\mathbf{B}, s_i) \geq \mathcal{O}_r$.

LS2 $S \models g$.

We say that g is locally supported by the set S.

In [3] it is proven that local support implies global support. This can be recast in the current context as follows:

Theorem 3.3 *If all goals and effects (that is, assertions g where $\mathcal{O}_f < g < \mathcal{O}_r$) are locally supported (w.r.t. a scenario), then they are also globally supported.*

Proof. Assume all goals and effects are locally supported. The proof is by induction on the ordinals.

Base case There can be no goals/effects with rank $\mathcal{O}_f$ (or lower), so the result follows trivially.

Inductive step Assume all goals/effects at rank $n-1$ are globally supported. For each goal/effect g with rank n, there exists $S = \{s_1, \ldots, s_m\}$ satisfying LS1 and LS2. Let $S' = \{s_j, \ldots, s_k\} \subseteq S$ be the set of assertions from S with rank greater than $\mathcal{O}_f$ and less than $\mathcal{O}_r$. From LS1 all assertions in S' have rank less than n. Therefore from the inductive assumption each assertion in S' is globally supported. Form the set S'' by replacing each assertion in S' with a set which globally supports it. Then from LS2 and the fact that for any sentences a and b, and sets A and A', we have $\{a\} \cup A \models b$ and $A' \models a$ only if $A' \cup A \models b$, $(S - S') \cup S'' \models g$ and g is globally supported. $\square$

In fact Theorem 3.3 is stronger than we need. In general we do not require that all goals are (locally or globally) supported in a particular scenario, but rather that there is a "tree" of support for certain high-level goals.

3.4 Syntactic Characterisations of Support

From a practical vantage, we would like a simple syntactic characterisation of support. That is, we would like to be able to decompose goals in an intuitive way — by coming up with alternative strategies, selecting one, and placing its component assertions in designated positions in the entrenchment ranking — without the need to show entailment. This would allow us to develop tools which aid in the decomposition process, that avoid the computational complexity normally associated with theorem proving.

The structure we have in place allows us to do this in a very straightforward way if we are willing to place tighter constraints on the form of causal rules. Given the above intuition — that we would like to form alternative strategies and select one — a natural constraint is to require that the antecedents of causal rules are expressed in disjunctive normal form. That is, our causal rules will be of the form

$$\text{alternative } 1 \vee \cdots \vee \text{alternative } n \rightarrow \text{goal}$$

where each alternative is a conjunction of literals. Conditions for goal support can then be defined syntactically as follows.

Definition 3.4 (causal support) An assertion g is *causally supported* in a partial entrenchment ranking $\mathbf{B}$ iff there exists a dnf sentence $d = c_1 \vee \cdots \vee c_m$ such that:

CS1 $d \rightarrow g$ is asserted as a causal rule — therefore $\mathcal{O}_r \leq \text{degree}(\mathbf{B}, d \rightarrow g)$.

CS2 For some disjunct $c_i = s_1 \wedge \cdots \wedge s_l$ appearing in d, each s_j appearing in c_i is asserted such that $0 < \text{degree}(\mathbf{B}, s_j) < \text{degree}(\mathbf{B}, g)$.

We say that the goal or effect g is causally supported by the set $\{s_1, \ldots, s_l, d \rightarrow g\}$. As is the case for local support, an assertion may be causally supported by more than one set.

It is a simple matter to show that these conditions are sufficient to guarantee local support and hence global support:

Theorem 3.5 *If g is causally supported in $\mathbf{B}$ then g is locally supported.*

Proof. We adopt the notation of Definition 3.4 and show that g is locally supported by the set $\{s_1, \ldots, s_l, d \rightarrow g\}$. This set satisfies LS1 since $\mathcal{O}_r \leq \text{degree}(\mathbf{B}, d \rightarrow g)$ from CS1 and for each s_j, $\text{degree}(\mathbf{B}, s(j)) < \text{degree}(\mathbf{B}, g)$ from CS2. LS2 is satisfied since $\{s_1, \ldots, s_l\} \models d \rightarrow g$ and hence $\{s_1, \ldots, s_l, d \rightarrow g\} \models g$. $\qquad \square$

$\mathcal{O}_{max}$

Causal Rules	
speed $\leq$ 154 $\wedge$ applied(wheel.brakes) $\rightarrow$ stop.length < 1000	R1
154 < speed $\leq$ 170 $\wedge$ applied(wheel.brakes) $\wedge$ applied(reverse.thrust) $\rightarrow$ stop.length < 1000	R2
wheel.loads > 12 $\rightarrow$ applied(reverse.thrust)	R3
wheel.loads > 12 $\vee$ altitude < 10 $\wedge$ wheel.speed > 72 $\rightarrow$ applied(wheel.brakes)	R4
cross.wind $\wedge$ banked $\rightarrow$ wheel.loads > 12	R5
tail.wind $\wedge$ level $\rightarrow$ wheel.loads > 12	R6
cross.wind $\wedge$ throttle(high) $\rightarrow$ speed $\leq$ 154	R7
tail.wind $\wedge$ throttle(high) $\rightarrow$ 154 < speed $\leq$ 170	R8

$\mathcal{O}_r$

Goals and Effects	
stop.length < 1000	G1
applied(reverse.thrust)	G2
applied(wheel.brakes)	G3
speed $\leq$ 154	G4
154 < speed $\leq$ 170	G5
wheel.loads > 12	G6

$\mathcal{O}_f$

Facts	
altitude < 10	F1
wheel.speed > 72	F2

$\mathcal{O}_c$

Conditions	
cross.wind	C1
banked	C2
throttle(high)	C3

0

Figure 2: A partial entrenchment ranking for the landing control system.

Note that the converse of Theorem 3.5 does not hold.

Finally, although it is not necessary for the above arguments, it is convenient to separate conditions from facts by placing them lower in the ranking. This has pragmatic advantages since the conditions are regularly changed when examining different scenarios. It also accords with the original notion of epistemic entrenchment, in which the least entrenched sentences are those that we are most willing to give up.

3.5 An Example of an Entrenchment Ranking

Figure 2 shows a partial entrenchment ranking for the landing control example in [3]. It is easy to see that goal G1 is locally supported under the conditions shown, since it is causally supported by R1, G3 and G4. Similarly G3 is supported by R4, F1 and F2; and G4 is supported by R7, C1 and C3. G1 is therefore globally supported according to theorem's 3.5 and 3.3. G5 on the other hand is not causally supported under these conditions.

Note that it is only the relative ranking of sentences that is important. The absolute values of $\mathcal{O}_c$, $\mathcal{O}_f$ and so on are unimportant, and the assertions between any pair of horizontal lines may be equally ranked or ordered arbitrarily.

Having replaced the partial order on assertions with an entrenchment ranking, we now turn to design revision and show that the entrenchment ranking supports revision using transmutations.

4 Revision

In Section 2 we saw that when adjustments retract a sentence b they also retract sentences a that are *reasons* for b: that is, those such that degree$(\mathbf{B}, b) <$ degree$(\mathbf{B}, a \to b)$. This is reflected in Definition 2.4. We also saw in Lemma 2.5 that retracting sentences leaves intact those that are higher in the entrenchment ranking.

In this section we illustrate that these properties make adjustments appropriate for revision of top-down designs, where these are constructed according the conventions discussed in the previous section. We consider three types of revisions: testing alternative scenarios, revising goals and effects, and retracting causal rules.

4.1 Testing Alternative Scenarios

The most common, and simplest, change to a goal structure results from a "what if?" analysis — testing different scenarios to see whether goals are still supported. This can be illustrated by the landing control example from [3].

In this (simplified) account, the pilot is informed of a cross-wind and takes the appropriate action of banking the aircraft and increasing throttle, thus giving the conditions shown in Figure 2. As we saw in Section 3, the main goal, that the aircraft stop within 1000m, is supported under these conditions.

Just as the aircraft is making its approach, however, the wind swings around to a tail wind. In terms of the content of the ranking, condition C1 is retracted (given rank 0) and tail.wind is asserted. This causes a coincidence of two things. First, the tail wind and high throttle lead to a greater speed (R8), which in turn means that reverse thrusters are required (R2). Secondly, because the aircraft is banked without a cross-wind, the weight is skewed and one of the wheels does not register a weight of 12 tonnes. As a result, the reverse thrusters are not applied (R3).

From a belief revision point of view, the conditions are revised by performing maxiadjustments $\mathbf{B}^*(a, i)$, where a is a condition and $0 \le i \le \mathcal{O}_c$. In the above example, for instance, we are making the adjustments

$$[\mathbf{B}^*(\text{cross.wind}, 0)]^*(\text{tail.wind}, \mathcal{O}_c).$$

To show that the maxiadjustment transmutation is appropriate, we need to show that varying the conditions does not affect the rest of the design: that is, the causal rules, goals, effects or facts. This follows directly from Lemma 2.5. Moreover, information ranked equally or less than the information to be revised will be retracted *only if* it is a reason for the information to be revised. Thus other unrelated conditions will not be affected.

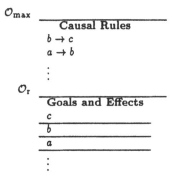

Figure 3: A simple example of "transitivity" in retraction of goals.

4.2 Revising Goals and Effects

The second type of revision we consider is the retraction of goals and effects. This will occur when part of a design is considered to be inadequate and an alternative top-down decomposition path is sought.

A typical example would be where a causal rule with disjunctive antecedents has been used (such as rule R4 in Figure 2), the decomposition from treating one of the disjuncts as a goal has proved unsuccessful, and an alternative disjunct is to be treated as a goal.

Retracting the old goal should satisfy two constraints. First, neither the causal rule in which it appears as an antecedent, nor the goal representing the consequent of that rule, should be retracted. This follows once again from Lemma 2.5 along with conditions CS1 and CS2, respectively, from Definition 3.4. This ensures that the retracted assertion appears lower in the entrenchment ranking than either the causal rule or its consequent.

Second, we would like to retract that part of the design (if any) which resulted from decomposing the disjunct. In the simplest case this is handled automatically by the maxi-adjustments. This is illustrated in Figure 3, where goal c has been decomposed to a subgoal b, which in turn is decomposed to a. If c is retracted, then b is also eliminated since degree$(\mathbf{B}, c) <$ degree$(\mathbf{B}, b \to c)$. Although $a \to c$ is not in exp$(\mathbf{B})$, it follows from PER1 in definition 2.1, along with the fact that $\{a \to b, b \to c\} \models a \to c$, that it must be ranked at least as highly as $a \to b$. Therefore a is eliminated also. This "transitive" behaviour will continue so that the subtree in the design rooted at goal c is retracted. Note that this transitive behaviour does not necessarily occur with other transmutation strategies.

The case where the retracted goal is the consequent of a causal rule with disjunctive antecedents will not upset this transitivity, since that causal rule will be equivalent to the conjunction of two or more rules with just the individual disjuncts as antecedents. Again PER1 will ensure that these new rules rank at least as highly as the original causal rule.

There are two cases, however, which do require further development of the maxi-adjustment strategy. First, in the case where the retracted goal is the consequent of a causal rule with conjunctive antecedents, the maxi-adjustment strategy is not sufficient on its own. The maxi-adjustment ensures only that the subtree rooted at *at least one* of the conjuncts is retracted. Secondly, since the design is strictly speaking a directed acyclic graph rather than a tree, we need to consider what happens when assertions are shared by multiple design "trees".

4.3   Retracting Causal Rules

Returning to the landing example used earlier, Duffy *et al* go on to show that an alternative choice of strategy for the reverse thrust goal (see Goal2 in Section 3) re-supports the top level goal. In particular, the coincidence of events leading to failure can be traced back to the fact that the reverse thrusters did not fire when required. This in turn was caused by the choice of wheel loads as the impetus for making the reverse thrusters fire. The designers may wish to examine the alternative strategy of firing on the basis of altitude and wheel speed.

   Choosing an alternative strategy requires the retraction of a causal rule, followed by expansion with respect to a new causal rule. Typically no further goals or facts will be retracted with a causal rule, since this would require a further implication at a higher rank than the causal rule. Since only tautologies are ranked higher this would indicate redundancy in the design. The designer has the option of removing the subtree related to the causal rule, however, simply by retracting the consequent (goal or effect) as described above prior to retracting the causal rule.

5   Conclusion

In this paper we have demonstrated that:

1. Entrenchment rankings can be used to provide a suitable partial order for supporting top-down design using the goal-structured approach. We have described a set of conventions for developing the partial order.

2. Under the above conventions, maxi-adjustment transmutations can be used to provide a suitable framework for design revision.

This has two benefits. First, it provides a formal framework for describing and implementing top-down design revision. Secondly, it offers an important application for belief revision theory.

   There is a great deal more work to be done in this area. In particular, variations on maxi-adjustment may need to be developed that deal with conjunctive preconditions and overlapping design trees in an appropriate way. What is appropriate must in turn be determined from applying the techniques to larger design examples. We are currently working on an implementation of a revision tool using maxi-adjustments which will help in this task.

References

[1] C. Alchourron, P. Gärdenfors, and D. Makinson. Partial meet contraction and revision functions. *J. Symbolic Logic*, 50:510–530, 1985.

[2] J. Doyle. A truth maintenance system. *Artificial Intelligence*, 12:231–272, 1979.

[3] D. Duffy, C. MacNish, J. McDermid, and P. Morris. A framework for requirements analysis using automated reasoning. In J. Iivari, K. Lyytinen, and M. Rossi, editors, *Advanced Information Systems Engineering: Proc. Seventh International Conference*, volume LNCS-932, pages 61–81. Springer-Verlag, 1995.

[4] P. Gärdenfors and D. Makinson. Revisions of knowledge systems using epistemic entrenchment. In *Second Conference on Theoretical Aspects of Reasoning about Knowledge*, pages 822 – 830, 1988.

[5] A. Grove. Two modellings for theory change. *Journal of Philosophical Logic*, 17:157 – 170, 1988.

[6] H. Katsuno and A. Mendelzon. On the difference between updating a knowledge base and revising it. In P. Gärdenfors, editor, *Belief Revision*, pages 183 – 203. Cambridge University Press, 1992.

[7] M. Osborne and C. K. MacNish. Processing natural language software requirement specifications. In *Proc. ICRE'96: 2nd IEEE International Conference on Requirements Engineering*, pages 229–236. IEEE Press, 1996.

[8] P. Peppas and M.-A. Williams. Constructive modelings for theory change. *Notre Dame Journal of Formal Logic*, 36(1):120 – 133, 1995.

[9] E. Williams. 1st DTI/SERC Proteus Project Workshop: Understanding Changing Requirements. Address from industrial participants, 1993.

[10] M.-A. Williams. Two operators for theory bases. In *Proc. Australian Joint Artificial Intelligence Conference*, pages 259 – 265. World Scientific, 1992.

[11] M.-A. Williams. Iterated theory base change: A computational model. In *Proc. Fourteenth International Joint Conference on Artificial Intelligence*, pages 1541 – 1550. Morgan Kaufmann, 1995.

[12] M.-A. Williams. Towards a practical approach to belief revision: Reason-based change. In *Proc. Fifth International Conference on Principles of Knowledge Representation and Reasoning*. Morgan Kaufmann, 1996.

[13] M.-A. Williams. Anytime belief revision. In *Proc. Fifteenth International Joint Conference on Artificial Intelligence*. Morgan Kaufmann, 1997 (in press).

[14] M.-A. Williams, M. Pagnucco, N. Foo, and B. Sims. Determining explanations using transmutations. In *Proc. Fourteenth International Joint Conference on Artificial Intelligence*, pages 822 – 830. Morgan Kaufmann, 1995.

Using Histories to Model Observations in Theories of Action

Javier A. Pinto*

Departamento de Ciencia de la Computación, Escuela de Ingeniería, Pontificia
Universidad Católica de Chile, Casilla 306, Santiago, CHILE
jpinto@ing.puc.cl

Abstract. In this article we present an approach to integrate observations in theories of action written in the Situation Calculus, a state–based, branching temporal language. In our approach, observations are added as dynamic constraints on *valid histories*. We describe two applications of these dynamic constraints, namely the representation of observations of action occurrences as well as observations of truth values of fluents.

An important novelty of our proposal is that we do not need to make unnecessary assumptions regarding the occurrence or non-occurrence of events. Furthermore, by virtue of exploiting the branching nature of time in the Situation Calculus, we can reason, within the logic, about all possible ways in which the world can evolve; i.e., without having to appeal to meta-theoretic constructs.

1 Introduction

The Situation Calculus is a logical language designed to represent theories of action and change. One of its most salient features is that time is viewed as a branching structure. Indeed, in the Situation Calculus, there is a distinguished initial situation, S_0, and there are infinitely many other situations that result from the different actions that might be performed. The structure of situations forms a tree rooted at S_0. Any sequence of actions defines a branch that starts in the initial situation. A situation is considered to be legal, if all the actions that lead to it starting in S_0 obey precondition constraints that might be specified.

The theories of action written in the Situation Calculus include specifications of knowledge about the initial situation, plus the specification of *causal laws* that may be written as *effect axioms*. These effect axioms describe how change arises as actions are performed in the world. In order to deal with the *frame problem*, we use Reiter's monotonic approach [10]. Thus, we make completion assumptions, which, together with the effect axioms, lead to the *successor state axioms*. A successor state axiom

---

*This work has been partly funded by Fondecyt under grants 195-0885 and 197-1304

establishes, for each fluent[1] in the domain, necessary and sufficient conditions for the fluent to be true after an action is performed.

There has been a great deal of work to extend the language of the Situation Calculus in the context of Reiter's solution to the frame problem [13, 6, 9, 12]. In the same spirit, this article seeks to extend the language of the Situation Calculus in order to add the ability to incorporate observations regarding action occurrences and the status of fluents into the logical theories. This problem has been addressed by Shanahan and Miller [4], and by Pinto and Reiter [8]. Both approaches select one possible development, or branch, in the Situation Calculus as the actual development. Any observation is regarded as a constraint on this single actual development. A related approach is used by Baral, Gelfond, and Provetti [1] in the context of the $\mathcal{A}$ language. An important difference is that the Situation Calculus based approaches are axiomatic and rely on standard Tarskian semantics, whereas the $\mathcal{A}$ language relies on a special definition of an entailment relation in order to model reasoning about change [2].

In this paper we present a Situation Calculus in which observations are specified as constraints on the *legal* world developments or *partial histories*. For instance, assume that we state that some action A occurs at a certain time point T. Under these circumstances, we consider that any development that does not include the occurrence of A at time T is illegal. Our approach to representing observations, regarding action occurrences or fluent values, allows us to accept those observations without over-committing to some notion of preferred development. For instance, if the only observation available is that action A occurs, we do not make the assumption that A is the only action that occurs. Rather, we assume that the information is inherently incomplete and that all possible developments that include A are possible. In fact, we show that our axiomatization does not preclude one from considering action occurrences that are not entailed by the theory. This feature allows one to interpret statements about action occurrences as incomplete information about the development of the world. In certain applications, it might be necessary to make assumptions regarding the actions that occur in the world. For instance, one might want to introduce notions of *likely* or *preferred developments*. How this can be done is matter for future research.

The structure of the paper is as follows. In section 2, we present the theoretical framework on which the rest of the paper is based. We also present the basic constructs that allow us to represent observations. In section 3, we introduce the notion of situation legality. Also in section 3, we show how observations can be represented as constraints on the legality of situations. Finally, in section 4 we present our conclusions and discuss our ongoing research.

2 Theoretical Framework

The basic language and axiomatization are based on extensions to the Situation Calculus that have been proposed in [6, 12]. Of particular interest to us is the definition of a basic language over which different kinds of observations can be specified. As mentioned in the introduction, observations are taken as incomplete information regarding the evolution of the world.

---

[1] A fluent is a dynamic property of the world.

The Situation Calculus is a sorted first order language extended with some second order features. We distinguish the sorts $\mathcal{A}$, $\mathcal{C}$, $\mathcal{S}$, $\mathcal{F}$, and $\mathcal{T}$ for primitive actions, concurrent actions, situations, fluents, and time. We also use a sort $\mathcal{D}$ for other objects. The sort $\mathcal{T}$ ranges over the real numbers. We use the convention that all variable symbols start with lower case letters, whereas constant symbols start with upper case letters. Also, we use the Greek letter φ as a second order predicate variable, which is only used in the specification of the induction axiom given in the next subsection. The sort of the variables and constants should be obvious from the context. In formulas, we assume that all free variables are universally quantified. The sort $\mathcal{C}$ corresponds to sets of simple actions. We take the standard interpretation for sets and don't axiomatize them.

Function and Predicate Symbols

- $start : \mathcal{S} \to \mathcal{T}$. If s is a situation term, then $start(s)$ denotes the time at which that situation starts.
- $do : \mathcal{C} \times \mathcal{S} \to \mathcal{S}$. If c denotes a concurrent action and s denotes a situation, then $do(c,s)$ denotes the situation that results from performing c in s.
- $\in \subseteq \mathcal{A} \times \mathcal{C}$. This is the standard membership operator for sets. Thus, if a denotes a primitive action and c denotes a *concurrent* action, then $a \in c$ would be true if a was part of the concurrent action c.
- $holds \subseteq \mathcal{F} \times \mathcal{S}$. If f denotes some fluent and s denotes a situation. Then $holds(f,s)$ is intended to mean that fluent f is true in situation s.
- $not : \mathcal{F} \to \mathcal{F}$. If f denotes some dynamic property or fluent, $not(f)$ denotes its negation.
- $hasOccurred \subseteq (\mathcal{C} \cup \mathcal{A}) \times \mathcal{T} \times \mathcal{S}$. $hasOccurred(a,t,s)$ would be true if action a occurred at time t on the path that leads from S_0 to s. The first argument of $hasOccurred$ can be either a concurrent action or a primitive action.
- $\prec \subseteq \mathcal{S} \times \mathcal{S}$. If s_1 and s_2 denote situations, then $s_1 \prec s_2$ is true if some sequence of concurrent actions leads from s_1 to s_2. We use the abbreviation $s_1 \preceq s_2 \equiv s_1 \prec s_2 \vee s_1 = s_2$.
- $Poss \subseteq (\mathcal{A} \cup \mathcal{C}) \times \mathcal{S}$. If c is a concurrent action and s a situation, then $Poss(c,s)$ is true if the concurrent action c is possible in s (i.e., if the action preconditions are satisfied in the situation denoted by s).
- $< \subseteq \mathcal{T} \times \mathcal{T}$. Standard comparison operator for reals (the abbreviation $\leq$ is also used).
- $legal_{poss}, legal \subseteq \mathcal{S}$. These are the legality predicates that we need to model observations (observations of action occurrences and observations of fluent values). As will be discussed later, a situation is *legal* if the set of situations that lead to it is faithful to the observations.
- $proper \subseteq \mathcal{S}$. Is an auxiliary predicate used to define *legal* situations.
- $Sit \subseteq \mathcal{T} \times \mathcal{S} \times \mathcal{S}$. If t is denotes a time point, and s and s_h denote situations, then the literal $Sit(t,s,s_h)$ should be true if t falls in the situation s in the path that leads from S_0 to s_h.

- $occurs_T \subseteq \mathcal{A} \times \mathcal{T}$. Is used to represent observations of action occurrences. Thus, if a and t denote an action and a time point, then $occurs_T(a,t)$ represents the observation that a occurs at time t.
- $holds_T \subseteq \mathcal{F} \times \mathcal{T}$. Is used to represent observations of fluent values. Thus, if f and t denote a fluent and a time point, then $holds_T(f,t)$ represents the observation that f holds at time t.

In this paper, we consider a Situation Calculus in which actions are considered to be instantaneous. As discussed elsewhere (e.g., [5]), this restriction does not limit the representational power of the language. Also, we ignore precondition interactions and concurrent effects or cancellations. These problems are addressed in [5, 6].

The issues discussed in this paper are orthogonal to those mentioned above. Therefore, any approach to deal with precondition interactions and concurrent effects or cancellation of effects, should integrate well with the theory presented in this paper.

2.1 Basic Situation Calculus Axiomatization

In the Situation Calculus that we present here, there is an initial situation, denoted by the special constant symbol S_0. Given an arbitrary situation s, a new situation is obtained by performing some concurrent action c in s. Following Reiter [10], we use an induction axiom in order to force the set of situations to form a tree rooted at S_0. Thus, an arbitrary situation s identifies a unique sequence of concurrent actions that leads from S_0 to s. Each situation s in the tree has a unique starting time [8]; this time corresponds to the time of the last action in the sequence leading to s. On the other hand, there is no unique ending time for a situation. In fact, in [8], Pinto and Reiter define an *end* predicate that takes an action and a situation as arguments. In that approach, the end of a situation s, with respect to an action c, corresponds to the start time of the situation $do(c,s)$. Therefore, each situation has one ending time associated to each possible concurrent action. These multiple ending times arise from the fact that, in the Situation Calculus, the future branches.

The basic axioms for situations are:

$$(\forall \varphi).[\varphi(S_0) \wedge (\forall s,c) (\varphi(s) \supset \varphi(do(c,s)))] \supset (\forall s) \varphi(s), \qquad (1)$$

$$do(c_1,s_1) = do(c_2,s_2) \supset c_1 = c_2, \qquad (2)$$

$$s_1 \prec do(c,s_2) \equiv s_1 \preceq s_2, \qquad (3)$$

$$s_1 \prec s_2 \supset \neg s_2 \prec s_1, \qquad (4)$$

$$Poss(c,s) \equiv (\forall a)[a \in c \supset Poss(a,s)], \qquad (5)$$

$$Poss(c,s) \supset start(s) < start(do(c,s)). \qquad (6)$$

Axiom (1) states that the only situations that exist are S_0, the initial situation, and all the situations that are reachable from S_0 by performing sequences of actions starting in S_0. Axiom (2) ensures that the structure of situations forms a tree. Axioms (3) and (4) define the relation $\preceq$. The literal $S_1 \prec S_2$ is true if there is a path from S_1 to S_2 in the Situation Calculus tree; i.e., S_2 is reached by performing a sequence of actions starting from S_1. Axiom (5) states that a concurrent action is possible iff all its constituent actions are individually possible. We assume that the predicate *Poss* for simple actions is completely specified by domain axioms.

As mentioned before, the function *start* denotes the starting time of a situation. Axiom (6) ensures that the situations along a path are chronologically ordered. This ordering is only enforced for situations that are obtained when performing actions that are possible.

In the Situation Calculus we use in this paper, we treat fluents at the object level. An alternative, that we used in [7], is to regard fluents as predicates in the language. The *reification* of fluents is due to the fact that we want to be able to observe them. Furthermore, we need to be able to specify how the branches of the Situation Calculus tree are constrained given the observation that some arbitrary fluent is observed to hold. The reification is done by using the predicate *holds* and a function symbol *not*, along with the following axioms:

$$holds(not(f),s) \equiv \neg holds(f,s), \tag{7}$$

$$not(not(f)) = f. \tag{8}$$

Also, we require *unique names axioms* for fluent and action terms[2]. We omit these axioms (the interested reader may consult [6] for a similar use of these unique names axioms).

2.2 Situation Legality

In the previous sub-section, we presented the basic axiomatization that defines the universe of situations S in terms of the initial situation S_0 and the set of concurrent actions C. Notice that this universe of situations is defined without taking into consideration whether or not the situations were actually possible. Our objective is to specify which situations in the Situation Calculus tree can be regarded as viable or *legal* given knowledge regarding action preconditions, laws of physics, occurrence statements, etc. In [11], Reiter defines a first notion of legality which basically says that a situation s is legal if it can be reached by performing actions in S_0 and all the actions leading to s are performed in situations in which their preconditions are met. This motivates the following:

Definition 2.1 *A situation s is considered legal with respect to the action preconditions, denoted legal$_{poss}$, if all the actions that lead from S_0 to s have been performed in situations in which they are possible. Thus, legal$_{poss}$ is defined as:*

$$legal_{poss}(s) \equiv [s = S_0 \vee (\forall c, s')\, do(c, s') \preceq s \supset Poss(c, s').] \tag{9}$$

As illustrated by the legality predicate *legal$_{poss}$*, we can constrain the tree of situations by refining the notion of legality. Legal situations form a subtree of the original tree structure of situations. Given an observation, many branches in the Situation Calculus tree can be pruned. This is the approach taken in section 3, where all the branches that do not comply with the given observations are regarded as not *legal*.

---

[2]These unique names axioms exclude nesting of the *not* fluent function symbol.

2.3 Histories or Paths

The notion of a history, within the Situation Calculus, corresponds to the sequence of actions that leads to a situation starting from S_0. Also, we refer to this as a *partial path* within the Situation Calculus tree[3]. Any situation s identifies a unique partial path that starts at S_0 and ends with s. In fact, any situation in the domain S is fully identified with a sequence of actions. For instance, the sequence $c_1, c_2, \ldots, c_n$ uniquely identifies the situation S_n, where:

$$S_n = do(c_n, do(\ldots, do(c_1, S_0) \ldots)),$$

which can also be abbreviated as $do([c_1, \ldots, c_n], S_0)$. Thus, all the actions $c_1, \ldots, c_n$ can be said to belong to or have occurred before S_n, and they correspond to the history of situation $do([c_1, \ldots, c_n], S_0)$. It turns out that one essential feature of the Situation Calculus, not available in linear time languages, is that there are terms denoting situations, which also denote histories. Thus, a situation s corresponds to a single history or linear time description of one possible evolution of the world starting from S_0. A situation s' is said to appear or belong to a history s iff $s' \prec s$. Thus, S_0 belongs to all histories (except to the empty history, which corresponds to S_0). Notice that the notion of history comes for free in the Situation Calculus, and no added machinery is necessary to introduce them in the language.

The branching nature of time in the Situation Calculus makes it difficult to impose a unique ending time on situations (they do have a unique start time, since time in the Situation Calculus is left linear). On the other hand, in a given history, any situation has a unique starting and a unique ending time. If s and $do(c, s)$ belong to some history s', then $start(s)$ and $start(do(c, s))$ correspond to the starting and ending times of s along the history s'.

In this paper, we exploit the notion of histories to define occurrences. We do so by defining the notion of a concurrent action c occurring within a history, partial path or situation:

Definition 2.2 *We say that a concurrent action c has occurred at time t along the history of a situation s with the predicate hasOccurred as follows:*

$$hasOccurred(c, t, s) \equiv (\exists s') \, do(c, s') \preceq s \wedge start(do(c, s')) = t. \tag{10}$$

This can be extended for primitive actions as:

$$hasOccurred(a, t, s) \equiv (\exists c) \, a \in c \wedge hasOccurred(c, t, s). \tag{11}$$

Finally, we introduce the following:

Definition 2.3 *We say that $Sit(t, s, s_h)$ is true whenever s corresponds to the situation in the history s_h which includes time t (thus t is between the start of s and the end of s along the history s_h). Formally,*

$$Sit(t, s, s_h) \equiv (\exists c) \, do(c, s) \preceq s_h \wedge start(s) < t \wedge t \leq start(do(c, s)). \tag{12}$$

---

[3] A *path* in the Situation Calculus tree corresponds to an infinite sequence of situations that start in S_0, a partial path is a prefix of infinitely many paths.

Using these definitions we have:

Observation 2.1 *From axioms (1) to (12) it follows that:*

$$Sit(start(do(c,s)),s,do(c,s)),$$
$$Sit(t,s_1,s_h) \land Sit(t,s_2,s_h) \supset s_1 = s_2.$$

As we show in the next section, the predicates *hasOccurred* and *Sit* allow us to express *dynamic state constraints* to represent observations within the language of the situation calculus. One key idea, is that in the Situation Calculus, situation objects denote histories. Therefore, one can quantify over histories by quantifying over situations.

3 Formalizing Observations

3.1 Situation Legality

Observations – i.e. observations of action occurrences or observation of the status of fluents – are considered to be primitive statements that constrain the paths in the Situation Calculus tree that can be regarded as legal. Legality is introduced in the language with the predicate *legal* $\subseteq S$, which in turn is defined using the notion of a *proper history* which is introduced with the predicate *proper* $\subseteq S$. A situation *s* is considered to be a proper history if the sequence of actions that lead to *s* is consistent with all the observations that might have been introduced. *proper* is a predicate defined in terms of occurrences and the *legal_{poss}* legality predicate. However, for presentation purposes, the specification of *proper* will be given as a set of implications or necessary conditions. In the end, the definition of *proper* is taken to be the completion of these necessary conditions.

The first necessary condition for a situation to represent a proper partial path is:

$$proper(s) \supset legal_{poss}(s). \tag{13}$$

All other constraints on *proper* will be introduced in the context of the occurrence predicates that are introduced later.

The predicate *legal* should be taken as a refinement of the legality notion introduced with the *legal_{poss}* predicate. In fact, if a situation is *legal*, then it is also *legal_{poss}*. We say that a situation is *legal* if it obeys all constraints, related to action preconditions and *occurrence* sentences. The definition of *legal* is done in terms of the *proper* predicate. The definition of *legal* is:

Definition 3.1 *A situation or history s is considered to be legal with respect to the action preconditions and observation statements if every time after its start there is a proper future history that contains s. This is formalized as:*

$$legal(s) \equiv ((\forall t)\ start(s) < t \supset (\exists s')\ s \prec s' \land t < start(s') \land proper(s')) \tag{14}$$

Notice that according to (14) for a situation to be legal, at any time *t* after its start, some action must always be possible some time *t'* after *t*. This precludes one from writing theories in which infinitely many actions arise within a history. Thus, axiomatizing Zeno's paradox in this context would yield a contradiction. It should be noted here that the notion of a history or partial path, which is formally equivalent to a situation, is essential for the representation of observations. In fact, the basic language introduced in the previous section might be considered as the foundational layer that allows one to introduce observations. The set of axioms (1)-(14) constitute the background axioms that will be used to express dynamic constraints and to represent observations.

3.2 Observing Values of Fluents

As mentioned in the introduction, in a Situation Calculus theory we normally specify observations regarding the values of fluents in the initial situation, S_0. However, oftentimes we have knowledge regarding time points other than the initial one. This is particularly true when we try to formalize narratives that might include direct observations. As a simple example, consider the narrative:

> Yolanda leaves home for work 7:30 in the morning while her husband Raoul is at home. She arrives at her office and calls home at 8 a.m.; her son, Art, tells her that dad, Raoul, is not there.

This simple narrative will allow us to exemplify our approach to handling observations. We use the constants *Yolanda, Raoul,* and *Art,* to denote three individuals. We also use location constants *Home* and *Office*. We assume that all domain terms are conveniently sorted.

We will have two types of actions. First, the action *leaves* by which an individual leaves a certain location; the action has two arguments, so that *leaves(Yolanda,Home)* denotes the action of Yolanda leaving her home. The other action is *arrives* which also has two arguments, so that *arrives(Yolanda,Office)* denotes the action of Yolanda arriving at her office.

Finally, in this domain we have the fluent *at* which takes two arguments, an *individual* and a *location*. Thus the fluent term *at(Yolanda,Home)* would hold in those situations in which Yolanda is at home. We also have the fluent *commuting* with one argument, such that *commuting(Yolanda)* would hold in situations in which *Yolanda* is traveling.

The axiomatization of this example in the language of the Situation Calculus includes the following action precondition axioms:

$$Poss(leaves(ind,loc),s) \supset holds(at(ind,loc),s), \tag{15}$$

$$Poss(arrives(ind,loc),s) \supset holds(commuting(ind),s), \tag{16}$$

There are gross simplifications regarding axiom (16), since the conditions for arrival are much more complex. However, a more precise axiomatization of this domain would not contribute to the issue that concerns ourselves in this article.

Since we are using Reiter's monotonic approach to the frame problem, we proceed to specify, for each fluent function, with the sole exception of the fluent function *not*, a *successor state axiom.* In the example, we only have fluent function *at*. Thus, we write:

$$Poss(a,s) \supset holds(at(ind,loc),do(a,s)) \equiv$$
$$holds(at(ind,loc),s) \wedge a \neq leaves(ind,loc) \vee$$
$$a = arrives(ind,loc).$$

Finally, we specify the values of fluents in the initial situation.

$$holds(at(Yolanda,Home),S_0),$$
$$holds(at(Raoul,Home),S_0),$$
$$start(S_0) < 730.$$

As mentioned before, in a standard theory of change in the Situation Calculus we are able to specify the dynamics of the world. The theory includes successor state and precondition axioms. Also, we include a specification of the initial situation (which does not need to be complete). Such a theory allows us to wonder about the outcome of all possible sequences of actions that might be started at S_0. For instance, in the example, we can ask what the world looks like in the situation:

$$S_2 = do(arrives(Yolanda,Office),do(leaves(Yolanda,Home),S_0)).$$

or in the situation:

$$S_4 = do(arrives(Yolanda,Office),$$
$$do(leaves(Raoul,Home),do(leaves(Yolanda,Home),S_0))).$$

Are these situations legal? Since we have not yet introduced observations, we can take *proper* to be the completion of (13), namely:

$$proper(s) \equiv legal_{poss}(s).$$

Therefore, the situations S_2 and S_4 are both legal, since the actions obey the precondition axioms (15) and (16). In order to incorporate the *observation* that Raoul is not home at eight o'clock, we add the literal:

$$\neg holds_T(at(Raoul,Home),800). \tag{17}$$

By modeling the acquisition of information in this manner, we are glossing over several important open issues. For instance, in order to properly model the communication between Art and Yolanda, we should introduce communication actions. Also, communication among individuals should have no effect on the environment. Instead, communication actions should change the epistemic state of the individuals [13]. These issues are left for further research.

Now, how should we interpret assertions like (17). Our proposal is to *prune* the subtree of legal situations. This is done by providing further axioms about the legality of situations. Thus, with respect to the example, we want an axiomatization in which a situation is considered legal if and only if it has some possible future in which Raoul is not at home at eight o'clock. Furthermore, a situation cannot be legal if it starts after eight o'clock and is part of a history in which Raoul is at home at eight o'clock. This notion of legality is achieved by using axiom (14) and by providing further constraint on the definition of *proper*. Thus, we have (13) and the following:

$$proper(s) \supset [holds_T(f,t) \wedge t < start(s) \wedge Sit(t,s',s) \supset holds(f,s')]. \quad (18)$$

Therefore, in our particular example, any situation that represents a proper history, and that starts after eight o'clock, must be part of a history in which $at(Raoul, Home)$ does not hold at eight o'clock.

If we take *proper* as the completion of (13) and (18), we obtain:

$$proper(s) \equiv legal_{poss}(s) \wedge \\ [holds_T(f,t) \wedge t < start(s) \wedge Sit(t,s',s) \supset holds(f,s')]. \quad (19)$$

From where it follows that the situation:

$$S_2 = do(arrives(Yolanda, Office), do(leaves(Yolanda, Home), S_0)),$$

where

$$start(do(arrives(Yolanda, Office), do(leaves(Yolanda, Home), S_0))) = 800,$$

cannot be legal. In fact, the successor state axiom for the fluent *at*, along with the specification for the initial state S_0, allow us to infer that in situation S_2, the fluent $at(Raoul, Home)$ holds, independently of the time assignment for the situations in the history of S_2. Thus, S_2 violates the observation (17).

On the other hand, the situation:

$$do(arrives(Yolanda, Office), do(leaves(Raoul, Home), do(leaves(Yolanda, Home), S_0))$$

is legal, as long as it has a starting time earlier than 800.

In general, we have:

Theorem 3.1 *From axioms (1)-(12), (14) and (19), it follows that:*

$$holds_T(f,t) \wedge legal(s) \wedge t < start(s) \wedge Sit(t,s',s) \supset holds(f,s') \quad (20)$$

Thus, if fluent f is observed to hold at time t, then all legal histories that include time t, must make f true at time t.

3.3 Observing Action Occurrences

In the narrative of the previous subsection, we have references to different actions that occur. For instance, Yolanda's leaving home for work and her arrival to the office. The axiomatization that we presented does not, in any sensible manner, establish that these actions must occur. Indeed, if there were other ways in which Yolanda could have shown up at work, they would act as alternative explanations.

We need some way of explicitly stating that certain actions occur. In the example, we want to say that at some time before eight o'clock, Yolanda leaves home, and that she arrives at eight o'clock. For simplicity, we don't refer to the phone call as an explicit event. In order to specify the occurrences, we use the predicate *occurs* which takes an action and a time as arguments. Therefore, we may write:

$$occurs(leaves(Yolanda, Home), 730),$$
$$occurs(arrives(Yolanda, Office), 800).$$

The occurring statements should also constrain the legal situations. Thus, if we state that the event *arrives(Yolanda, Office)* occurs at eight o'clock, then we do not want to have any legal situation that starts at eight o'clock or after and that does not have a history in which the occurrence is present. To formalize this constraint, we add a new axiom for *proper*. Thus, along (13) and (18), we now have:

$$proper(s) \supset [occurs(a,t) \wedge t < start(s) \supset hasOccurred(a,t,s)]. \tag{21}$$

So far, we have introduced three axioms that establish necessary conditions for a situation to be *proper*. If we consider that these necessary conditions are also sufficient conditions, then we may replace (13), (18) and (21), with the axiom:

$$proper(s) \equiv legal_{poss}(s) \wedge$$
$$[holds_T(f,t) \wedge t < start(s) \wedge Sit(t,s',s) \supset holds(f,s')] \wedge \tag{22}$$
$$[occurs(a,t) \wedge t < start(s) \supset hasOccurred(a,t,s)].$$

The following theorem establishes essential conditions to deal with narratives. In fact, as discussed in [7], a simple narrative can be described in terms of these occurrences (which are called *non-preventable*) and this theorem ensures that all legal situation include the events mentioned in the narrative:

Theorem 3.2 *From axioms (1)-(12), (14) and (22) it follows that:*

$$occurs(a,t) \wedge legal(s) \wedge t < start(s) \supset hasOccurred(a,t,s).$$

Thus, in our example, for a situation to be considered a proper history, it has to fulfill the following conditions:

1. The sequence of actions leading to the situation have to obey the action preconditions. Thus, if a *leaves* action is performed, then it has to have been performed in a situation satisfying axiom (15).
2. The history of the situation must comply with all fluent value observations made before the situation's starting time.
3. All action occurrences that are observed before the starting time of the situation must belong to the history of the situation.

The occurrence constraints introduced with the *occurs* predicate have several features that are fairly restrictive. Indeed, in order for a model to satisfy a literal *occurs(A, T)* every legal history must have the occurrence of A at the same time. However, we might want to allow for the action to occur at different time points in different histories. In order to express this, we need to introduce another type of occurrence. For instance, we might write $occurs'(A, T)$ to mean that action A must occur in every valid history before time T. This frees us from having to give A a fixed time of occurrence. In the same vein, there are many other kinds of dynamic constraints that can be expressed as occurrence of different kinds. In [7], we explore these issues and apply this approach to several problems. For instance, we show how to model some forms of *triggers* using these dynamic constraints.

4 Concluding Remarks

In this article we have presented a novel approach to representing observations of fluent values and action occurrences in the Situation Calculus as dynamic constraints on valid histories. This approach allows one to reason about hypothetical developments which obey all constraints imposed by observation literals (i.e., $holds_T$ and $occurs$ literals). One interesting feature of the approach presented is that the constraints allow one to *prune* the tree of situations, keeping *all* the histories that are consistent with the observations. This is a feature that must be present in any language used to represent incomplete knowledge about the evolution of dynamic domains. One important departure of our contribution from other related research [1, 4, 8], is that we consider observations to be constraints on all possible developments, as opposed to constraints on one preferred *actual* development.

There are several important extensions to this work that we would like to pursue. For instance, we would like to consider occurrence statements involving complex actions (actions that involve conditionals, loops, etc.). Also, we are interested in investigating our approach to specifying theories of action and the approach based on the GOLOG language being developed at the Cognitive Robotics group in the University of Toronto [3].

Another interesting issue is the study of the computational aspects of reasoning with our theory. It is likely that tasks like *plan verification* will be difficult. In particular, non-preventable occurrences may introduce difficulties to prove legality of situations. The reason is that one might be forced to think about the future of a situation in order to determine its legality. This difficulty does not always arise, and we would like to characterize classes of theories for which this reasoning is easy.

We are interested in studying planning in the presence of exogenous events, probably formalized using occurrence statements. For instance, we would like to be able to come up with a plan for an agent to go to the airport, knowing that the bus to the airport leaves for the airport every hour on the hour. However, we should not be able to prove that the plan is successful, unless we assume that the bus does not run into trouble. To do this, we can have likelihood predicates and plan for likely situations.

References

1. C. Baral, M. Gelfond, and A. Provetti. Representing Actions: Laws, Observations and Hypotheses. *Journal of Logic Programming*, 31:201–244, 1997.
2. Michael Gelfond and Vladimir Lifschitz. Representing Action and Change by Logic Programs. *The Journal of Logic Programming*, 17:301–322, 1993.
3. Hector J. Levesque, Raymond Reiter, Yves Lespérance, Fangzhen Lin, and Richard B. Scherl. GOLOG: A Logic Programming Language for Dynamic Domains. *The Journal of Logic Programming*, 31:59–84, 1997.
4. Rob Miller and Murray Shanahan. Narratives in the Situation Calculus. *The Journal of Logic and Computation*, 4(5):513–530, 1994.
5. Javier Pinto. Concurrent Events: Synergy and Cancellation of Effects. In *European Conference on Artificial Intelligence, Workshop on Logic and Change*, pages 105–110, 1994. URL = ftp://lyrcc.ing.puc.cl/pub/jpinto/ecai.ps.gz.
6. Javier Pinto. *Temporal Reasoning in the Situation Calculus*. PhD thesis, Department of Computer Science, University of Toronto, Toronto, Ontario, Canada, February 1994. URL = ftp://ftp.cs.toronto.edu/~cogrob/jpThesis.ps.Z.
7. Javier Pinto. Occurrences and Narratives as Constraints in the Branching Structure of the Situation Calculus. *Journal of Logic and Computation*, 1998. To appear.
8. Javier Pinto and Raymond Reiter. Reasoning about Time in the Situation Calculus. *Annals of Mathematics and Artificial Intelligence*, 14(2-4):251–268, September 1995.
9. Javier A. Pinto. On the Existence and Formalization of Natural Events. In *Proceedings of the IJCAI Workshop on Nonmonotonic Reasoning, Action and Change.*, August 1995. URL = ftp://lyrcc.ing.puc.cl/pub/jpinto/ijcwrk.ps.gz.
10. Raymond Reiter. *The Frame Problem in the Situation Calculus: A Simple Solution (sometimes) and a completeness result for goal regression*, pages 359–380. Artificial Intelligence and Mathematical Theory of Computation: Papers in Honor of John McCarthy. Academic Press, San Diego, CA, 1991.
11. Raymond Reiter. Proving Properties of States in the Situation Calculus. *Artificial Intelligence*, 64(2):337–351, December 1993.
12. Raymond Reiter. Natural Actions, Concurrency and Continuous Time in the Situation Calculus. In *Principles of Knowledge Representation and Reasoning: Proceedings of the Fifth International Conference(KR'96)*, Cambridge, Massachussetts, U.S.A., November 1996. Morgan Kaufmann.
13. Richard Scherl and Hector Levesque. The Frame Problem and Knowledge Producing Actions. In *Proceedings AAAI-93*, pages 689–695, Washington, D.C., July 1993. AAAI.

Modelling Inertia in Action Languages (Extended Report)

Mikhail Prokopenko[1] and Pavlos Peppas[2]

[1] CSIRO Mathematical and Information Sciences
Locked Bag 17, North Ryde, NSW 2113, AUSTRALIA
Email: mikhail.prokopenko@cmis.csiro.au
[2] Knowledge Systems Group
Department of Computing, School of MPCE
Macquarie University, NSW 2109, AUSTRALIA
Email: pavlos@mpce.mq.edu.au

Abstract. Logic-based approaches to reasoning about actions, change and causality, highlight efficient representation and processing of domain background knowledge as an important task. Action theories recently developed in the framework of action languages with inertia and ramifications [20,14] not only adopt the principle of minimal change reinforced with the policy of categorisation (assigning different degrees of inertia to language elements) but also try to incorporate background causal knowledge. In this paper we aim to trace the evolution of action languages and to explore interactions between ontological characteristics of action domains such as inertia and causality. Such an analysis should clarify how possible solutions to the frame and the ramification problems are affected by applying the policy of categorisation to causal domains. We first attempt to identify conditions (more precisely, restrictions) which preserve the meaning of domain descriptions when moving among various analysed languages. Relaxing such restrictions can help in evaluating the role of the frame concept (and policy of categorisation, in general) in an action language with fluent-triggered causality.

1 Introduction

Various investigations of the ramification problem have demonstrated that in order to deduce the indirect effects of actions it is necessary to *efficiently* represent background domain knowledge. The notion of efficiency is usually based on the idea of a compact and concise representation and dates back at least as far as Occam's Razor: other things being equal, simple theories are to be preferred to complex ones. For instance, in the framework of first-order logic and its nonmonotonic extensions, representation of background knowledge in the form of domain constraints [6] is more economical than explicit description of actions consequences (such as in STRIPS [3]) because it avoids exponential difficulties usually associated with the latter[1]. Appropriately represented knowledge at the

---

[1] It is not trivial to find a set of domain constraints always producing desirable inferences in the domain, and the complexity of this task sometimes is comparable

same time has to be *efficiently* "readable" and "processable" by an underlying reasoning mechanism. Such a reasoning system[2] should be capable of inferring both direct and indirect consequences of a performed action (an occurred event) as well as preserve inertial properties of a domain (solve the frame problem [16]).

Action theories recently developed in the framework of action languages with inertia and ramifications [11,7,10,8] use the idea of minimising change to deduce the set of possible next states (successor states). The notion of minimal change is usually defined by set inclusion and incorporates the concept of frame, assigning different degrees of inertia to language elements (fluents, literals, formulas, etc.). For example, in [7] it is noted that "if F is not a frame fluent then it is not expected to keep its old value after performing an action, so that the change in its value is disregarded". In addition, some action theories try to represent domain knowledge in a way that not only provides a solution to the frame and the ramification problems but also embodies background information in the form of "causal laws" of a domain. Moreover, it was successfully argued in many publications [2,12,15,20] that, in general, propositions embracing causal dependencies are "more expressive than traditional state constraints" [20]. Following recent approaches to representing causal information, we do not intend here to investigate philosophical aspects of the phenomenon – probably discovering, understanding, and formalising an elusive nature of the cause - effect relation will by itself mark a significant improvement on the way to engineer artificial intelligence. However, we shall try to highlight possible areas of interaction between ontological characteristics of action domains such as inertia and causality and to address the following questions:

- under what conditions do we gain by dividing fluents on inertial and non-inertial ones in the framework of an action language with fluent-triggered causality[3] (fact causality) and
- how does it affect possible solutions to the ramification problem.

We believe that the best way to proceed towards this goal is to trace the evolution of action languages.

2 Evolution of Action Languages

As mentioned in [14], the original idea behind introducing action languages was to present a methodology allowing for translation from a specialised action language to a general-purpose formalism, such as a nonmonotonic reasoning system based on first-order logic. A domain described in the first action language $\mathcal{A}$ [5], for instance, can be translated [9] into a logic programming language or into the circumscriptive approach of Baker [1]. Similarly in [11] there is a translation

---

with that of maintaining satisfactory descriptions of the actions in an explicit consequences approach [18].

[2] The term "reasoning system" is used to refer to "any formal system that produces inferences about the effects of events" [17].

[3] The terms action- and fluent-triggered causality are due to Lin [12].

from $\mathcal{AR_O}$, another action language, into the formalism of nested abnormalities theories [13]. In addition, subsequent research has shown that strict syntax and clear semantics of action languages makes them a useful tool for understanding the different aspects of reasoning about action. Hence "defining action languages, comparing them and studying their properties" [14] can help in "capturing our commonsense intuitions about the whole family of action domains expressible in the language" [20].

2.1 $\mathcal{AR}$ Languages

Consider the oldest and better developed branch of the action languages' "evolutionary tree" that can be represented as follows:

$$\mathcal{A} \longrightarrow \mathcal{AR}^- \longrightarrow \mathcal{AR_O} \longrightarrow \mathcal{AR} \longrightarrow \mathcal{ARD}.$$

The possibility of ramifications is the main feature [11] of all "$\mathcal{AR}$"-dialects of $\mathcal{A}$. Despite the fact that the $\mathcal{AR}^-$ language [9] appeared chronologically later than the $\mathcal{AR_O}$ [11] we treat the former as evolutionary predecessor of the latter. Syntactically, $\mathcal{AR}^-$ is a subset of $\mathcal{AR_O}$. But more important, the class of domains expressible in $\mathcal{AR}^-$ is contained in the class of domains expressible in $\mathcal{AR_O}$. The notions of expanding the expressibilitiy of action languages and classes of domains are central to ordering the languages and constructing the tree. All mentioned above languages are capable of describing domains with deterministic actions, truth-valued fluents, inertia, and action-triggered causality. In addition, they evolve by expanding the domains properties as shown in the following table:

	$\mathcal{A}$	$\mathcal{AR}^-$	$\mathcal{AR_O}$	$\mathcal{AR}$	$\mathcal{ARD}$
dependent fluents					*
non-truth valued fluents				*	*
non-deterministic actions			*	*	*
inertial (frame) fluents		*	*	*	*
state constraints		*	*	*	*

One can expect that general-purpose formalisms to which action languages are translated, increase in complexity as well. A detailed investigation of such a parallel evolution lies, however, beyond the scope of this paper.

On the other hand, relationships among classes of domains covered by evolving action languages are of major interest. The expanding expressibility of the languages does not guarantee, by itself, enlargement of the corresponding classes of domains. Nevertheless, in the analysed evolutionary branch one can observe that such a process is at least non-diminishing:

- $\mathcal{AR}^-$ adds inertial (frame) fluents and domains constraints to $\mathcal{A}$; ie., "$\mathcal{A}$ domains can be thought of as a special case of deterministic $\mathcal{AR}^-$ domains where there are no constraints" [10];

- $\mathcal{AR_O}$ broadens the classes of deterministic and temporal projection action domains expressible in $\mathcal{AR}^-$ by allowing simple forms of non-determinism;
- $\mathcal{AR}$ [7] introduces new language elements (non-propositional fluents) but "preserves the meaning" [7] of a domain description thus guaranteeing that classes of action domain did not reduce[4];
- the contribution of $\mathcal{ARD}$ [8] is not only in showing how to represent "non-persistent ramifications" but also in introducing "a history" in the language semantics - opening a way to formalise some of the action domains with "hypothetical reasoning".

2.2 $\mathcal{AC}$ Languages

The $\mathcal{AR}$-languages are characterised by the use of state constraints to represent background knowledge - constraints usually restrict the set of possible states and produce indirect effects of actions. All $\mathcal{AC}$-languages (named after the language $\mathcal{AC}$ introduced by Turner [20]) feature fluent-triggered (fact) causality in both these roles.

The $\mathcal{AC}$ follows the approach of representing causal background knowledge that was proposed by McCain and Turner in [15] and was not formalised as an action language. Nevertheless, it is straight-forward to describe an action language, called, let us say, $\mathcal{AC_O}$, based on the approach constructed in [15] that can serve as an origin of the $\mathcal{AC}$-languages branch[5].

As an action language, $\mathcal{AC}$ is modelled after a propositional version of the language $\mathcal{AR}$ and hence incorporates the idea of inertial fluents and the notion of non-determinism. In this paper we propose to augment the basic language $\mathcal{AC_O}$ incrementally: firstly, by adding the concept of a frame, and secondly, by extending it to non-deterministic action domains. In other words, we propose to consider yet another subset of $\mathcal{AC}$: the language $\mathcal{AC}^-$ that takes the intermediate place between the $\mathcal{AC_O}$ and the $\mathcal{AC}$. This suggestion has a dual purpose - to present the evolution in a more systematic way and to answer the questions regarding the role of the frame concept.

The evolution along the $\mathcal{AC}$-line can be represented then in the following table:

	$\mathcal{AC_O}$	$\mathcal{AC}^-$	$\mathcal{AC}$
non-deterministic actions			*
inertial (frame) fluents		*	*
fluent-triggered causality	*	*	*

---

[4] Influence propositions of $\mathcal{AR}$ are supposed to correct $\mathcal{AR_O}$'s handling of non-deterministic actions.

[5] See the next section for the formal description of $\mathcal{AC_O}$.

The action languages' evolutionary tree is shown in Fig. 1. Since the propositional version of $\mathcal{AR}$ differs from $\mathcal{AR_O}$ (different semantics of "release" / "possibly changes" propositions), the "propositional $\mathcal{AR}$" has been identified as a missing link of evolution that improves handling of non-deterministic actions compared to $\mathcal{AR_O}$.

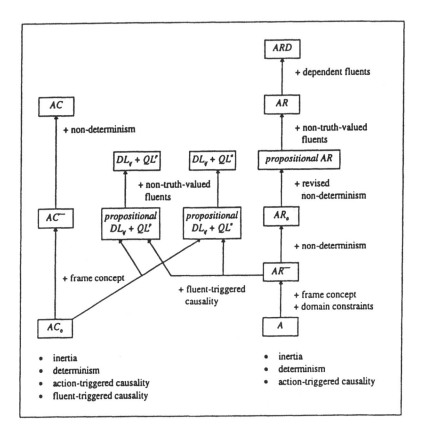

Fig. 1. Evolutionary tree of action languages.

In addition, the tree includes a family of languages with the frame concept and fact causality introduced by Lifschitz in [14]. The languages describe deterministic action domains: the "$DL_{if} + QL^p$" language is aimed at temporal projection problems and the "$DL_{if} + QL^a$" language - at temporal explanation problems. Although these two languages allow to represent non-propositional fluents from the moment of their appearance it is quite natural to assume that the evolutionary tree might include their propositional counterparts as well.

3   A Comparison between $\mathcal{AC_O}$ and $\mathcal{AC^-}$

3.1   The $\mathcal{AC_O}$ Language

Following [15,20], we can define an $\mathcal{AC_O}$ language by

- a non-empty set of symbols Φ, that are called fluent names, or fluents and
- a non-empty set of symbols Ω, that are called action names, or actions.

In other words, an $\mathcal{AC_O}$ language is defined by its signature $< \Phi, \Omega >$. A formula is a propositional combination of fluents. A fluent literal is an expression F or ¬F, where F is a fluent name. An $\mathcal{AC_O}$ domain description consists of

- value propositions

$$\varphi \textbf{ after } \Lambda,$$

where φ is a fluent formula and Λ is a string of actions. If Λ is the empty string, value proposition is abbreviated as

$$\textbf{initially } \varphi;$$

- sufficiency propositions

$$\varphi \textbf{ suffices for } \psi$$

where φ and ψ are fluent formulas[6];

$$\textbf{always } \varphi$$

is an abbreviation for

$$\text{True } \textbf{suffices for } \varphi,$$

- effect propositions

$$\text{A } \textbf{causes } \varphi \textbf{ if } \psi,$$

where A is an action, and φ and ψ are fluent formulas.

Detailed description of the $\mathcal{AC_O}$ semantics can be easily obtained from the corresponding description of the $\mathcal{AC}$ semantics [20]. For our purposes it is sufficient to remark that

- D is an $\mathcal{AC}$ domain description (ie., a set of propositions);
- R is the set of all sufficiency propositions φ/ψ contained in D;
- for a set Γ of formulas and a set R of sufficiency propositions we define the closure of a set Γ under R, denoted $Cn_R(\Gamma)$, to be the smallest set of formulas such that:
  a) $Cn_R(\Gamma)$ contains Γ;
  b) $Cn_R(\Gamma)$ is logically closed;

---

[6] A sufficiency proposition sometimes is abbreviated as φ/ψ.

c) for all $\varphi/\psi \in R$, if $\varphi \in Cn_R(\Gamma)$ then $\psi \in Cn_R(\Gamma)$;

we write $\Gamma \vdash_R \varphi$ to denote that $\varphi \in Cn_R(\Gamma)$;

- an interpretation S of the fluent atoms is a state if Cn(S) is closed under R: $Cn(S) = Cn_R(S)$;
- E(A, S) is the set of fluent formulas φ for which there is an effect proposition

$$A \text{ causes } \varphi \text{ if } \psi$$

in D such that S satisfies ψ.

For simplicity, we do not use executability propositions and say that an action A is prohibited in a state S if there is an effect proposition

$$A \text{ causes False if } \psi$$

in D such that S satisfies ψ. Consequently, a set $E = E(A, S)$ is an explicit effect of A at S if A is not prohibited in S.

Finally, a state S' may result from doing A in S if there is an explicit effect E of A in S such that

$$Cn(S') = Cn_R[(S \cap S') \cup E] \tag{1}$$

It is easy to see that this fixpoint definition is equivalent to definition 4 for $Res_R(E, S)$ in [15], where R is the set of inference rules, and allows us to obtain the same possible next states as the latter. Since there is no "frame/non-frame distinction", all fluents are subject to inertia. The language DL_{if} was introduced in [14] to overcome this particular limitation. However, it does not appear to be such a restriction.

3.2 The AC^- Language

Following the described process of the evolution (Fig. 1), in order to introduce AC^- we need to augment AC_O with the concept of a frame and appropriately change the fixpoint condition (1).

To do that we designate the elements of a certain subset, Φ_{frame}, of the set Φ as inertial. The set Φ_{frame} is called a frame designation for a domain description D if it is not empty, and is included in the augmented language signature $< \Phi, \Phi_{frame}, \Omega >$. The signature $< \Phi, \Omega >$ of the AC_O language is subsumed by the signature of the AC^- language and can be considered as $< \Phi, \emptyset, \Omega >$.

Let L_f denote the set of inertial fluent literals[7]. Then the following fixpoint condition defines a state S' that may result according to the AC^- semantics from applying A at S,

$$Cn(S') = Cn_R[(S \cap S' \cap L_f) \cup E] \tag{2}$$

where E is an explicit effect of A in S as before. It is interesting to compare at this point, condition (2) with the following similar condition

$$S' \cap L_f = Cn_R[(S \cap S' \cap L_f) \cup E] \cap L_f, \tag{3}$$

---

[7] A literal is inertial if the fluent name F occuring in it is inertial [14].

which basically defines the transition system of the language DL_{if} [14]. It is clear that these two conditions become equivalent if we require that an AC^- domain description includes an explicit definition

$$\textbf{always } F \equiv \varphi$$

where φ is an inertial fluent formula[8], for each non-inertial fluent F. Without this requirement condition (3) defines possible next states that, in general, do not necessarily satisfy condition (2). On the other hand, a state S' satisfying (2) should, obviously, satisfy (3). In [20] Turner indicated that under the requirement of explicitly defining every non-inertial fluent in a domain, a domain description D becomes both an AC and a propositional AR domain description, and the AC models of D are exactly the propositional AR models of D. In other words, the AR Theorem [20] establishes a "horizontal" connection between different branches of the evolutionary tree. In this paper an attempt is made to identify conditions (more precisely, restrictions) which preserve the meaning of domain descriptions produced in the AC_O language when moving "vertically" to the AC^- language and employing the frame concept. Relaxing such restrictions will demonstrate what we gain by dividing fluents on inertial and non-inertial ones in the framework of an action language with fluent-triggered causality (fact causality).

3.3 A Connection between AC_O and AC^- Language

As mentioned in [7] domain constraints in the AR language "play two different roles: they determine the set of states, and they also determine the indirect effects of actions". Like the DL_{if} language, the AC^- language does not impose the requirement to explicitly define every non-inertial fluent on its domain descriptions. This leaves some of non-inertial fluents less supported as far as indirect effects are concerned. In other words, the "ramification constraints" [15,20] expressed in the form of sufficiency propositions "φ **suffices for** ψ" become the only source for updating the truth values of not explicitly defined non-inertial fluents when an action is performed. There is, however, a way to introduce an analogue, albeit not a straight-forward one, for an explicit definition adopted in the AR and the AC languages.

Definition 1. A fluent F of an AC^- (AC) domain description D is called an effect-complete fluent if there exists an inertial formula φ such that

$$\varphi \textbf{ suffices for } F \in D,$$

$$\neg \varphi \textbf{ suffices for } \neg F \in D.$$

We will denote the set of all effect-complete fluents as Φ_{ec}.

The following proposition establishes a connection between the languages AC_O and AC^-.

---

[8] An inertial fluent formula is a formula whose atoms are inertial fluents.

Proposition 2. *Let D^- be an $\mathcal{AC}^-$ domain description such that each non-inertial fluent is an effect-complete fluent:*

$$\Phi \setminus \Phi_{frame} \subseteq \Phi_{ec}.$$

Then $D_0 = D^-$ defined in the signature $< \Phi, \emptyset, \Omega >$ by abandoning the frame designation Φ_{frame} is an $\mathcal{AC}_O$ domain description, and the $\mathcal{AC}_O$ models of D_0 are exactly the $\mathcal{AC}^-$ models of D^-.

The proof is sketched in the appendix.

The following example enhances the Two-Switches example [11,15,20] and illustrates the differences among $\mathcal{AC}_O$, $\mathcal{AC}^-$, and DL_{if} dependent on the type of relation between the sets Φ_{ec} and $\Phi \setminus \Phi_{frame}$.

Example. There are two switches, a light, and shadows. The light is on only when both switches are on. Light "causes" shadows to appear or, in other words, light is "sufficient" for the appearance of shadows. The $\mathcal{AC}_O$ domain can be described using four propositional fluent names:

$$\Phi = \{\text{Switch1, Switch2, Light, Shadows}\}.$$

There are two action names:

$$\Omega = \{\text{Toggle1, Toggle2}\}.$$

The propositions are:

$$\text{Toggle1 \textbf{causes} } \neg\text{Switch1 \textbf{if} Switch1,} \tag{4}$$

$$\text{Toggle1 \textbf{causes} Switch1 \textbf{if} } \neg\text{Switch1,} \tag{5}$$

$$\text{Toggle2 \textbf{causes} } \neg\text{Switch2 \textbf{if} Switch2,} \tag{6}$$

$$\text{Toggle2 \textbf{causes} Switch2 \textbf{if} } \neg\text{Switch2,} \tag{7}$$

$$\text{Switch1} \wedge \text{Switch2 \textbf{suffices for} Light,} \tag{8}$$

$$\neg\text{Switch1} \vee \neg\text{Switch2 \textbf{suffices for} } \neg\text{Light,} \tag{9}$$

$$\text{Light \textbf{suffices for} Shadows,} \tag{10}$$

$$\textbf{initially } \neg\text{Switch1,} \tag{11}$$

$$\textbf{initially } \neg\text{Switch2,} \tag{12}$$

$$\textbf{initially } \neg\text{Light,} \tag{13}$$

$$\textbf{initially } \neg\text{Shadows.} \tag{14}$$

Consider the action Toggle2 performed in the initial state $S = \{\neg \text{Switch1}, \neg \text{Switch2}, \neg \text{Light}, \neg \text{Shadows}\}$. It is easy to check that the only possible next state satisfying (1) is $S' = \{\neg \text{Switch1}, \text{Switch2}, \neg \text{Light}, \neg \text{Shadows}\}$ and this, indeed, is the intuitive choice. Now let us consider the $\mathcal{AC}^-$ domain description based on (4)-(14) with at least one not effect-complete non-inertial fluent. The frame designation

$$\Phi_{frame} = \{\text{Switch1, Switch2}\} \tag{15}$$

leaves the fluent Shadows non-inertial, and propositions (4)-(14) do not define it as effect-complete, unlike the fluent Light which is non-inertial but effect-complete.

It is worth noting that the $\mathcal{AC}^-$ domain description (4)-(15) is not an $\mathcal{AC}$ domain description because the non-inertial fluent Shadows is not explicitly defined in terms of inertial fluents. However, this description is a "legal" one in the $DL_{if} + QL^p$ language (if we use proper propositions for axioms: **now** φ instead of **initially** φ).

Again consider the action Toggle2 performed in the initial state S. It turns out that there are no interpretations satisfying condition (2). The "task" to derive value of the non-inertial fluent Shadows fails because this fluent is neither effect-complete nor explicitly defined in terms of inertial fluents. In other words, semantics of the $\mathcal{AC}^-$ language produces no models for the action.

The $DL_{if} + QL^p$ domain description (4)-(15), however, treats two next states as possible - both

$$S_1' = \{\neg \text{ Switch1, Switch2, } \neg \text{ Light, } \neg \text{ Shadows}\}$$
$$S_2' = \{\neg \text{ Switch1, Switch2, } \neg \text{ Light, Shadows}\}$$

satisfy condition (3). In other words, the semantics of the DL_{if} language can not decide on the value of the non-inertial fluent Shadows, disregarding the corresponding change.

3.4 Discussion

Disagreement among models obtained by the $\mathcal{AC}_\mathcal{O}$, the $\mathcal{AC}^-$ and the DL_{if} languages can be avoided either by a better frame designation of the domain description including the not effect-complete fluent Shadows in the frame, or by the introduction of a "cause" effecting the disappearance of "shadows", eg.

$$\neg \text{ Light } \textbf{suffices for } \neg \text{ Shadows.}$$

Consider the first way (a better frame designation) for our example. Let

$$\Phi_{frame} = \{\text{Switch1, Switch2, Shadows}\} \tag{16}$$

be the new frame designation. Then the domain description (4)-(14), (16) entails S_1' as the unique successor state in both the $\mathcal{AC}^-$ and the DL_{if} semantics.

However, attachment of the not effect-complete fluent Shadows to the frame (for not well conceived reasons in the first place) does not make reasoning about domain actions more intuitive - as shows, for instance, the case when the action Toggle2 is performed in the state S = {Switch1, Switch2, Light, Shadows}. Now all three languages ($\mathcal{AC}_\mathcal{O}$, $\mathcal{AC}^-$ and DL_{if}) agree that the only next possible state must be

$$S'_1 = \{\text{Switch1}, \neg \text{Switch2}, \neg \text{Light}, \text{Shadows}\}.$$

The fluent Shadows is in the frame and keeps its value through the change. That should not contradict our intuition - since no one indicated a sufficient reason for "shadows" to disappear, it behaves like a persistent ramification. However, the designation of the fluent Shadows as a non-inertial one would be, perhaps, more intuitive. In any case, the necessity to attach this fluent to the frame arbitrarily seems to be a concern.

The latter way (introduction of a "cause" effecting the disappearance of "shadows") is not always available because, in general, an agent performs reasoning about action in the absence of complete information. Besides, if we necessarily require from each non-inertial fluent to be effect-complete (or explicitly defined, for that matter) then the provided solution to the ramification problem does not look like a principal one.

Instead, one may be tempted to refine the state transition system and consider yet another action language. Let us define an $\mathcal{AC}^*$ language exactly as $\mathcal{AC}^-$, except that the state transition system is given by the following resultant function mapping a current state S and an explicit effect E to a set of possible next states

$$Res(E, S) = \{S' \in Res^*(E, S) : S' \cap (L \backslash L_f) = Cn_R[(S \cap S') \cup E] \cap (L \backslash L_f)\}, \tag{17}$$

where

$$Res^*(E, S) = \{S' : S' \cap L_f = Cn_R[(S \cap S' \cap L_f) \cup E] \cap L_f\}, \tag{18}$$

and L is a set of all domains fluent literals. In other words, the state transition system (17)-(18) works in two steps: firstly, it selects the states satisfying the fixpoint condition (3) - thus agreeing with the semantics of the DL_{if} language and minimising changes only in inertial fluents L_f; secondly, among states selected on the first step, it minimises changes in non-inertial fluents $(L \setminus L_f)$. It is easy to see that

$$Res(E, S) \subseteq Res^*(E, S),$$

so the semantics of the $\mathcal{AC}^*$ language would never prefer more states than the semantics of the DL_{if} language. For instance, in the considered example if the action Toggle2 is again performed in the initial state S then the state

$$S'_1 = \{\text{Switch1}, \neg \text{Switch2}, \neg \text{Light}, \text{Shadows}\}$$

is the only member of $Res(E, S)$ being "shortlisted" from $Res^*(E, S) = \{S'_1, S'_2\}$ as the state with less changes in non-inertial fluents.

However, this approach does not seem to be promising enough. It is not evident that more complex domains will not require more "layers" of minimisation applied to fluents with varied degrees of inertia. Moreover, in some domains it can be difficult to properly categorise fluents. For instance, it has been shown (the Relay example) [19] that it does not appear possible to select only intended resulting states according to semantics of the $\mathcal{AR_O}$ language for any division of fluents on inertial and non-inertial ones. It is worth noting, however, that considered languages with fluent-triggered causality and frame concept (the $\mathcal{AC}^-$, the DL_{if} and the $\mathcal{AC}^*$) handle the Relay example as intended provided that all non-inertial fluents are chosen from effect-complete ones. But so does the $\mathcal{AC_O}$ language - without employing fluents categorisation.

4 Conclusion

Employment of the frame concept (the policy of categorisation) in an action language operating with causal background knowledge might have helped to advance us towards a better (a simpler) solution to the Frame and the Ramification problems. Unfortunately, such a solution imposes, from our point of view, too severe restrictions on a domain description: each non-inertial fluent has to be defined in terms of inertial fluents - either through an explicit definition, or as an effect-complete fluent. This demand decreases the value of the frame concept in a framework of languages with fluent-triggered causality - at least in the considered branch of the evolutionary tree. Probably, further development of action languages will clarify what role should the policy of categorisation (and the frame concept, in particular) play in logic-based approaches to reasoning about actions, change and causality.

4.1 Appendix. Proof of proposition 2.

By construction $D_0 = D^-$. Consider now the set $Cn_R [(S \cap S' \cap L_f) \cup E]$. It is clear that

$$Cn_R[(S \cap S' \cap L_f) \cup E] \subseteq Cn_R[(S \cap S') \cup E] \qquad (19)$$

Let L be a set of domain's fluent literals, and L_{ec} be a set of domain's effect-complete fluent literals. Then

$$Cn_R [(S \cap S') \cup E] = Cn_R [(S \cap S' \cap L) \cup E] =$$
$$Cn_R [\{S \cap S' \cap (L_f \cup L\backslash L_f)\} \cup E] =$$
$$Cn_R [(S \cap S' \cap L_f) \cup \{S \cap S' \cap (L\backslash L_f)\} \cup E].$$

Since $L\backslash L_f \subseteq L_{ec}$, we have

$$Cn_R [(S \cap S') \cup E] \subseteq Cn_R [(S \cap S' \cap L_f) \cup (S \cap S' \cap L_{ec}) \cup E].$$

Lemma. $\forall \varphi$, if $S \cap S' \cap L_{ec} \vdash_R \varphi$, then $S \cap S' \cap L_f \vdash_R \varphi$. The proof is trivial.

Using the lemma,

$$Cn_R[(S \cap S') \cup E] \subseteq Cn_R[(S \cap S' \cap L_f) \cup E] \qquad (20)$$

Relationships (19) and (20) together establish that

$$Cn_R [(S \cap S' \cap L_f) \cup E] = Cn_R [(S \cap S') \cup E]$$

Therefore the set of states Res(A,S) that may result from doing A at S is the same for the $\mathcal{AC}_O$ and the $\mathcal{AC}^-$ semantics:

$$Res_0(A,S) = Res^-(A,S).$$

Consequently, the $\mathcal{AC}_O$ models of D_0 are exactly the $\mathcal{AC}^-$ models of D^- (see the definition of a model in [20]).

5 Acknowledgements

The authors are thankful to members of the Sydney Knowledge Systems Group for fruitful discussions on different paradigms of Reasoning about Action.

References

1. Baker, A.B.: Nonmonotonic reasoning in the framework of situation calculus. Artificial Intelligence **49** (1991) 5–23
2. Brewka, G., Hertzberg, J.: How to do things with worlds: on formalizing actions and plans. J. Logic Computat. Vol. 3, **5** (1993) 517–532
3. Fikes, R., Nilsson, N.J.: STRIPS: A new approach to the application of theorem proving to problem solving. Artificial Intelligence **2** (1971) 189 – 208
4. Finger, J.J.: Exploiting constraints in design synthesis. PhD Thesis. Stanford University, Stanford, CA (1987)
5. Gelfond, M., Lifschitz, V.: Representing action and change by logic programs. The Journal of Logic Programming **17** (1993) 301 - 322
6. Ginsberg, M.L., Smith, D.E.: Reasoning about action I: A possible worlds approach. Artificial Intelligence **35** (1988) 165 – 195
7. Giunchiglia E., Kartha, G.N., Lifschitz, V.: Actions with indirect effects (Extended abstract). In Working Notes of the AAAI Spring Symposium on Extending Theories of Action (1995) 80 – 85
8. Giunchiglia, E., Lifschitz, V.: Dependent fluents. In Proceedings of International Joint Conference on Artificial Intelligence, Montreal (1995) 1964 – 1969
9. Kartha, G.N.: Soundness and completeness theorems for three formalizations of action. In Proceedings of International Joint Conference on Artificial Intelligence, Montreal (1993) 724 – 729
10. Kartha, G.N.: On the range of applicability of Baker's approach to the frame problem. In Proceedings of the Third Symposium on Logical Formalizations of Commonsense Reasoning (1996)
11. Kartha, G.N., Lifschitz, V.: Actions with indirect effects (Preliminary report). In Proceedings of the Fourth International Conference on Principles of Knowledge Representation and Reasoning, Bonn (1994) 341 – 350
12. Lin, F.: Embracing causality in specifying the indirect effects of actions. In Proceedings of International Joint Conference on Artificial Intelligence, Montreal (1995) 1985 – 1991
13. Lifschitz, V.: Nested abnormality theories. Artificial Intelligence **74** (1995) 351 – 365

14. Lifschitz, V.: Two components of an action language. In Proceedings of the Third Symposium on Logical Formalizations of Commonsense Reasoning, Stanford (1996)
15. McCain, N., Turner, H.: A causal theory of ramifications and qualifications. In Proceedings of International Joint Conference on Artificial Intelligence, Montreal (1995) 1978 – 1984
16. McCarthy, J., Hayes, P.: Some philosophical problems from the standpoint of artificial intelligence. In Machine Intelligence IV, edited by B. Meltzer and D. Michie (1969) 463 – 502
17. Peppas, P.: Belief change and reasoning about action. An axiomatic approach to modelling inert dynamic worlds and the connection to the logic of theory change. PhD thesis. Dept. of Computer Science, University of Sydney (1993)
18. Prokopenko, M., Lindley, C., Kumar, V.R.: The application of reasoning about action techniques to dispatch management. In Proceedings of the AI'95 First Australian Workshop on Commonsense Reasoning, Canberra (1995) 74 – 88
19. Thielscher, M.: Computing ramification by postprocessing. In Proceedings of International Joint Conference on Artificial Intelligence, (1995) 1994 – 2000
20. Turner, H.: Representing actions in default logic: a situation calculus approach. In Proceedings of the Third Symposium on Logical Formalizations of Commonsense Reasoning, Stanford (1996)

Combinatorial Interpretation
of Uncertainty and Conditioning

Arthur Ramer
Knowledge Systems Group
Computer Science, UNSW
Sydney, Australia 2052
ramer@cse.unsw.edu.au

1 Introduction

Various concepts of probabilistic conditioning [6, 8] can be linked to the properties of information measures through use of generating functions [14]. The basic
approach is to interpret various objects resulting from the conditioning process
and their parameters through analytic operations on the space of suitable generating functions [13, 16]. These are generalized Dirichlet sums [9], usually finite,
based on probability values both as coefficients and the bases of the exponents.

For evidence and possibility theory a similar approach is available. Now the
appropriate Dirichlet sums are formed from the belief values of atomic formulae
used as the bases of the exponents. In these theories one deals with uncertainty,
rather than information, measures. This leads to interpreting a large variety
of uncertainty measures as linear functionals of the analytic functions defined
by these Dirichlet sums. This connection is the reason for the term *uncertainty
generating* function.

The method originated indepently in two papers. In 1966 Golomb [4, 5]
observed that, for a discrete probability distribution p_i, the first derivative of

$$f(u) = \sum_i p_i^u$$

corresponds to Shannon entropy; moreover, these functions behave in a natural fashion when joint distributions are formed. He proposed term *information
generating* for the discrete case, with an obvious modification for continuous
densities and Boltzmann entropy. In 1987 Ramer [17] linked *nonspecificity* of an
evidence assignment to a standard Dirichlet sum, with weights of the basic assignment as coefficients. Both these approaches can be combined and extended,
to cover a great majority of standard uncertainty measures, entropies, and information distances.

To illustrate of the effectiveness of this approach, we show a 'one-line' proof
of Lewis' classical triviality result for the probabilistic conditionals [11, 8, 3].
Applications to Markov and Bayesian networks [12, 20] are possible, simplifying
reasoning about dependencies and belief propagation.

2   Probabilistic generating functions

With every probability distribution

$$\{p_i = P(x_i) : \ x_i \in X\}$$

we associate a generating function of Dirichlet type [9]

$$f(u) = \sum_i p_i^{1-u};$$

it is a modification of Golomb's information generating function [4, 5], and also closely related to the evidential uncertainty function [17]. This form enjoys two advantages, minor one being the avoidance of various sign changes in entropy evaluation. As the major advantage we have

$$f(u) = \sum_i \frac{p_i}{p_i^u},$$

which form permits several important extensions and generalizations.

For subsets $A \subset X$, the corresponding sums are

$$f_A(u) = \sum_{i:x_i \in A} p_i^{1-u}.$$

Each such function would fully characterize the probability distribution on the respective subset (up to a permutation). In particular

- $P(A) = f_A(0)$
  probability

- $H(X) = F'(0)$
  Shannon entropy

- $H(A) = (\log f_A)'(0) + H(f_A(0)^{-1})$
  conditional entropy

In addition, the product of two such functions, defined for independent domains X and Y equals the generating function for the cartesian product

$$f_X(u) \cdot f_Y(u) = f_{X \times Y}(u).$$

The basic conditioning formula

$$P(A \cap B) = P(A|B) \cdot P(B)$$

now suggests a possible generating function 'identity'

$$f_{A \cap B}(u) = f_{A|B}(u) \cdot f_B(u).$$

Here the function $f_{A|B}$ for the 'conditional object' $A|B$ is not yet been defined, but the reqired division is permissible for the generating functions.

If we would need primarily the probability values, we could only consider

$$f_{A|B}(0) = \frac{f_{A\cap B}(0)}{f_B(0)} = \frac{f_{A\cap B}(0)}{1 - f_{\bar{B}}(0)}$$

where $\bar{B} = X \setminus B$ - the complement of B. The last function can be expanded into a formal power series

$$f_{A|B}(0) = f_{A\cap B}(0) \cdot (1 + f_{\bar{B}}(0) + f_{\bar{B}}^2(0) + \ldots)$$

Presence of a power $f_{\bar{B}}^k(0)$ suggests using a k-fold product of X with itself. This leads immediately to the geometric structure of the infinitely dimensional product

$$\mathcal{X} = \prod_{i=1}^{\infty} X_i, \qquad X_i \sim X.$$

as the locum of conditional probabilities and conditional evidence assignments.

Such structure was first proposed by van Fraasen [18], and then extensively analysed by Goodman and Nguyen [7]. The conditionals residing 'inside' $\mathcal{X}$ are not perfect - while they represent conditioning in X, they cannot be conditioned on each other. The use of generating functions shows the direct reason - the compromise of replacing f_B with $1 - f_{\bar{B}}$ instead of $f_X - f_B$. The ideal solution is unattainable, due to the Lewis' *triviality theorem* [1, 11].

As k goes to infinity, each $f_{\bar{B}}^k$ corresponds to cylinder

$$\prod_{i=1}^{k} \bar{B} \times \prod_{i=k+1}^{\infty} X,$$

with a similar cylinder over (one time) $A \cap B$. For the low values of k we can visualize each such structure as a union of rectangular subsets of X_{k+1}. The full subset represents the conditional object $A|B$. As $\prod_1^{\infty} X_i$ carries a probability measure from X, $P(A|B)$ is well defined.

The computations on conditionals correspond to forming unions, intersections, and complements of such sets. The evaluation of probability of a conditional object of any order, is represented by evaluation of various power series.

3   Trivial proof of triviality theorem

The theorem in question asserts that the conditional objects $A|B$ cannot be modeled as boolean functions, ie. one cannot construct $C = f(A, B) \subset X$, such that $P(C) = P(A|B)$ for all possible $P(.)$. In fact, it can be done only for some very special cases of A and B or certain particular probability distributions. This theorem, and many of its subsequent generalizations can be given a 'one-line' proof (which we present here in two lines).

Were it possible to construct $A|B$ it would hold for an arbitrary P

$$P(A \cap B) = P(A|B) \cdot P(B)$$
$$\sum_{A \cap B} p_i = \sum_{A|B} p_i \cdot \sum_{B} p_i$$

Replacing $p_i \mapsto p_i^x$
and normalizing $p_i^x / \sum p_i^x$

$$\sum_{A \cap B} p_i^x \cdot \sum_{X} p_i^x = \sum_{A|B} p_i^x \cdot \sum_{B} p_i^x$$

This is no longer an equality between numbers. Rather, it is equality between two products ot two functions each. An this means that the terms on the left and on the right must be pairwise identical. In particular, it gives the only three situations when $A|B$ exists

$-\ A \cap B = B \Rightarrow A \supset B \Rightarrow A|B := X$

$-\ B = X \Rightarrow A|B := X$

$-\ A \cap B = \emptyset \Rightarrow A|B := \emptyset$

4 Entropies and change of belief

We used generating functions to discus uncertainty formalisms based on Shannon entropy. There have been proposed several other entropies and entropic distances in the literature [10] (and references therein). Most of them have a straightforward interpretation as various functionals on the space of Dirichlet sums. Moreover, this interpretation makes various relations among those entropies quite explicit.

We list here a few, beginning with the best known - Renyi's entropy. This one obtains as the linear (difference) approximation to the logarithmic derivative at 0 (which represents Shannon entropy)

$$l'(0) \approx \frac{l(\alpha) - l(0)}{\alpha} = \frac{1}{\alpha} \log \sum p_i^{1-\alpha}.$$

If, instead, we use a simple derivative, the resulting entropy is one of Havrada-Charvat

$$h'(0) \approx \frac{h(\alpha) - h(0)}{\alpha} = \frac{1}{\alpha} (\sum_i p_i^{1-\alpha} - 1).$$

Linear averaging in an interval $[a, b]$ gives Kapur entropy

$$fracl(\beta) - l(\alpha)\beta - \alpha = \frac{1}{\beta - \alpha} \log \frac{\sum p_i^\alpha}{\sum p_i^\beta}$$

or Sharma-Mittal function

$$\frac{h(\beta) - h(\alpha)}{\beta - \alpha} = \frac{1}{\beta \cdot} \frac{}{\alpha} (\sum p_i^\alpha - \sum p_i^\beta).$$

Analysis of the information distance (termed 'cross-entropy' by Kullback and Leibler, and 'I-divergence' by Csiszar) suggests an attractive *change of belief* interpretation.

The distance $I(\mathbf{p}, \mathbf{r})$ (between two probability distributions $\mathbf{p}, \mathbf{r}$ on the same domain) is obtained by changing the type (in Hardy-Riesz terminology) of the Dirichlet series. We construct

$$f(x) = \sum \frac{p_i}{p_i^x}, \quad g(x) = \sum \frac{p_i}{r_i^x}$$

and then define

$$I(\mathbf{p}, \mathbf{r}) = (\log f)' - (\log g)'|_0.$$

This change of type could be viewed as a change of belief (or belief base), hence the distance would measure change in our perception. Regardless of any such interpretation, this method can be applied to several (not necessarily probabilistic) models of belief; in particular, it applies to the general evidence model, and to the possibilistic one. We discuss it in the next two sections.

5   Evidential generating functions

We refer to the classic monograph [19] and some new collected papers [6, ?] for the relevant definitions. We take m_A as the basic assignment of evidence on a finite domain of discourse X. It serves to define such notions as belief *Bel*, plausibility *Pl*, and commonality *Q*.

Basic *belief generating function* can be taken as

$$g(x) = \sum \frac{m_A}{Bel(A)^x}$$

or its logarithm $\log g(x)$.

Change of belief can be reflected by changing the *type of series*

$$g(x) = \sum \frac{m_A}{Bel^{(m)}(A)^x}$$

$$h(x) = \sum \frac{m_A}{Bel^{(n)}(A)^x}$$

suggesting as *quantitative distance*

$$d(\mu, \nu) = (\log g)' - (\log h)'|_0.$$

Similar constructions can be based on plausibility and commonality

$$j(x) = \sum \frac{m_A}{Pl(A)^x}$$

$$k(x) = \sum \frac{m_A}{Q(A)^x}$$

Another consideration, of interest in relation to Dempster rule of combination, is the use of Hadamard product

$$\sum \frac{m_A}{\varphi(A)^x} \star \sum \frac{n_A}{\varphi(A)^x} = \sum \frac{m_A n_A}{\varphi(A)^x}.$$

When arbitrary sets are permitted (within the domain of discourse), it is natural to consider the assignment of beliefs $Bel(A)$, $A \subset X$ as primary and initially given. Then the basic weights m_A can be retrieved through Möbius transform [2]. This last approach can be used in possibility. Under the interpretation of nested sets, beliefs are the possibilities $p_1 \geq p_2 \geq \ldots$ themselves; their Möbius transform consists of the differences

$$r_i = p_i - p_{i+1}.$$

This 'explains' the structure of the possibilistic information measure

$$\sum_i (p_i - p_{i+1}) \log i.$$

It obtains from the *possibility generating function*

$$f(u) = \sum_i (p_i - p_{i+1}) i^u.$$

6   Possibility generating fuction

Usefulness of Dirichlet sums in probability and in evidence models was predicated on the multiplicative structure of the weights of joint beliefs. To carry this program to possibility theory, a suitable 'multiplicative' concept must be found [15]. While the possibility values themselves are not appropriate (they combine using *min* and *max* operations), the α-cuts and their cardinalities have the required properties.

For a domain of discourse $V = \{v_i\}$, with a *possibility* assignment $p_i = \pi(v_i)$, we define its α-cuts

$$C_\alpha(V) = \{v_i : p_i \geq \alpha\}$$
$$C_\alpha(W) = \{v_i \in W : p_i \geq \alpha\}$$
$$c_a(V) = |C_\alpha(V)|$$
$$c_a(W) = |C_\alpha(W)|$$

By abuse of notation, we discuss simply the cuts of the possibility assignment itself

$$C_\alpha(\pi) = \{p_i \geq \alpha\}$$
$$c_a(\pi) = i : p_i \geq \alpha, p_{i+1} < \alpha$$

Assume two noninteracting domains of discourse, with two independent possibility assignments $\pi = \{p_i\}$ and $\varpi = \{q_i\}$. Then the following multiplicative property of cuts holds

$$\mathcal{C}_\alpha(\pi \otimes \varpi) = \mathcal{C}_\alpha(\pi) \times \mathcal{C}_\alpha(\varpi)$$
$$c_a(\pi \otimes \varpi) = c_a(\pi)c_a(\varpi)$$

we can define *possibility generating function*

$$h(u) = \int_0^1 c_\alpha^z d\alpha$$
$$= \sum (p_i - p_{i+1})i^u \;.$$

As expected, the uncertainy is simply the derivative at 0

$$h'(0) = (\log h)'|_0.$$

7 Concluding remarks

The relationship between the belief values, which define the type of a series, and the coefficients, which are often their Möbius transform, suggests that a similar approach might be possible for the belief structures based on more general lattices. Arguably, evidence theory is constructed on a lattice of subsets of a finite domain, possibility corresponds to linearly ordered set, and probability could be viewed as defined on a 'flat' partial order.

In the analysis of causation through use of Bayesian networks [12, 20] several formulae of decopmposition and conditioning of probability values have been established. Without much effort, several of them can be extended to equalities for Dirichlet sums, based on those probability values. Then the evaluation of some linear functionals (derivatives and like) would permit assigning information parameters to the networks of inference. Study of such properties is proposed for the future research.

References

1. Adams, E.W., *On the logic of high probability*. J. Phil. Logic 15(1986), 225–279.
2. Aigner, M., Combinatorial Theory. Springer-Verlag, New York 1979.
3. Eells, E., Skyrms, B., (eds.) Probability and Conditionals, Cambridge University Press, New York 1994.
4. Golomb, S.W., *The information generating function of a probability distribution*. IEEE Trans. IT 12(1966), 75–77.
5. Golomb, S.W., Peile, R.E., Scholtz, R.A. Basic Concepts in Information Theory and Coding. Plenum Press, New York 1994.
6. Goodman, I.R. et al. (eds.) Conditional Logic in Expert Systems, North-Holland, New York 1991.

7. Goodman, I.R., Nguyen, H.T. *Mathematical foundations of conditionals and probabilistic assignments.* Tech. Rep. US Navy R&D.

8. Goodman, I.R., Nguyen, H.T., Walker, E.A. Conditional Inference and Logic for Intelligent Systems, North-Holland, New York 1991.

9. Hardy, G.H., Riesz, M. The General Theory of Dirichlet's Series Cambridge University Press,

10. Kapur, J.N., Kesavan, H.K. Entropy Optimization Principles with Applications, Academic Press, San Diego 1992.

11. Lewis, D., *Probabilities of conditionals and conditional probabilities*, Phil. Review 85(1976), 297–315.

12. Pearl, J. Probabilistic Reasoning in Intelligent Systems: Networks of Plausible Inference. Morgan Kaufmann, San Mateo, CA 1988.

13. Ramer, A., *Uncertainty generating functions*, FAPT'95 - Foundations and Applications of Possibility Theory, Ghent, Belgium, December 1995.

14. Ramer, A., *Uncertainty reasoning with generating functions*, PRICAI'96 Reasoning with Incomplete Information Workshop, Cairns, Australia, August 1996.

15. Ramer, A., *Conditioning in Possibility Theory*, Int. Joint Conf. CFSA/IFIS/SOFT'95, Taiwan, December 1995.

16. Ramer, A., *Existence of possibilistic conditional objects*, EUFIT'95 - 3rd European Congress on Intelligent Techniques and Soft Computing, Aachen, Germany, August 1995.

17. Ramer, A., *Uniqueness of information measure in the theory of evidence*, Fuzzy Sets Syst., 24(1987), 2:183–196.

18. van Fraasen, B.C., *Probabilities of conditionals*. Foundations of Probability Theory, Statistical Inference and Statistical Theories of Science I. D. Reidel Publ., Dordrecht, Holland 1976, 261–308.

19. Shafer, G. A Mathematical Theory of Evidence. Princeton University Press, Princeton 1976.

20. Spirtes, P., Glymour, C., Scheines, R. Causation, Prediction, and Search. Lecture Notes in Statistics 81, Springer-Verlag, New York 1988.

Probabilistic Diagnosis as an Update Problem

Angelo C. Restificar
Department of Computer Science
Assumption University
Huamark, Bangkok 10240, Thailand
Email : angelo@science.s-t.au.ac.th

Abstract
Incompleteness is addressed by using a framework that allows expression of probability. An update procedure is given to handle nonmonotonic change of knowledge. We point out the relationship between probabilistic diagnosis and probabilistic deductive database updates, and present a coincidence theorem which formally establishes it. An implication of the result allows us to treat diagnostic problems naturally within a probabilistic deductive database framework using the same procedure to insert and diagnose.

1. Introduction

Incomplete and uncertain knowledge can be captured in frameworks that allow expression of probabilities. We use Ng & Subrahmanian's framework presented in [8] to define a probabilistic deductive database. As new information is received, currently-held beliefs in the database may need to be revised. This process is nonmonotonic, i.e., the addition of new information could lead to deletion of existing ones. We outline an update procedure presented in [12] to handle the change of knowledge that may need to be effected in the database. The procedure handles deletion and insertion, and ensures the consistency of the database.

Many domains are modeled more accurately if incompleteness and uncertainty can be expressed in the underlying framework used to represent them. One such domain is diagnosis, where logical formulas in fault-models may be expressed quantitatively. Probabilistic information could also be used to help cut down the number of explanation by choosing only the most probable ones.

We illustrate how a diagnostic problem could be represented in our framework. Moreover, we show that a solution to a probabilistic update query for insertion coincides with generating probable explanations of a given observation. The result allows us to treat a diagnostic problem naturally within the framework of a probabilistic deductive database. We can invoke the same procedure to find both most probable explanations and first-best minimal transactions.

2. An Overview of the Probabilistic Framework

We present the framework in [8] where we base our update procedure. Let L be a language generated by finitely many constant and predicate symbols without ordinary function symbols. For c,d such that $0 \leq c,d \leq 1$, let a closed interval[c,d] be the set $\{x \mid c \leq x \leq d\}$. If $C[0,1]$ denotes the set of all closed sub-intervals of the unit interval $[0,1]$ then an *annotation function* f of arity n is a total function $(C[0,1])^n \rightarrow C[0,1]$.

L contains *object variables*, which is the normal variables in first order logic and the *annotation variables* whose values only range between 0 and 1 and which appear only in annotation terms. The term $[\rho_1,\rho_2]$ is called an annotation term ρ_i ($i = 1,2$) if (1) it is either a constant in $[0,1]$ or an annotation variable in L, or (2) is of the form $f(\mu_1,...,\mu_n)$, where f is an annotation function of arity n and $\mu_1,...,\mu_n$ are annotation terms. A ground annotation is called *c-annotation*, otherwise it is called *v-annotation*. The Herbrand base of L, B_L is finite since it does contain function symbols.

A *basic formula*, not necessarily ground, is either a conjunction or a disjunction of atoms. A disjunction and conjunction cannot occur simultaneously in one basic formula. Let $bf(B_L) = \{ A_1 \wedge \ldots \wedge A_n \mid n \geq 1$ and $A_1,...,A_n \in B_L$ and for all $1 \leq i,j \leq n, i \neq j \rightarrow A_i \neq A_j\} \cup \{ A_1 \vee \ldots \vee A_n \mid n \geq 1$ and $A_1,...,A_n \in B_L$ and for all $1 \leq i,j \leq n, i \neq j \rightarrow A_i \neq A_j \}$, where all A_i's are all ground atoms. If $F_0,...,F_n$ are basic formulas, and $\mu_0,...,\mu_n$ are annotations such that all the annotation variables that appear in μ_0, if any, also appear in at least one of $\mu_1,...,\mu_n$, then the clause $F_0:\mu_0 \leftarrow F_1:\mu_1 \wedge \ldots \wedge F_n:\mu_n$ is called a *pf-clause*. A probabilistic logic program, *pf-program*, with annotated formulas is a finite set of pf-clauses.

Intuitively, $F:[c_1,c_2]$ where $[c_1,c_2]$ is a c-annotation means : "the probability of the basic formula F must lie in the interval $[c_1,c_2]$". The notion of world probability density function relates a formula function and a probabilistic interpretation. The concept of worlds and world probability functions here are similar in essence to the "possible worlds" of [10]. Suppose world W is a Herbrand Interpretation. A *World Probability Density Function* $WP : 2^{B_L} \rightarrow [0,1]$ assigns to each world $W_j \in 2^{B_L}$ a probability $WP(W_j)$ such that for all $W_j \in 2^{B_L}$, $WP(W_j) \geq 0$ and $\sum_{W_j \in 2^{B_L}} WP(W_j) = 1$.

To simplify the notation, we use p_j instead of $WP(W_j)$.

Let h be formula function which is a mapping h: $bf(B_L) \rightarrow C[0,1]$. A set of linear constraints denoted by LC(h) is defined as follows. For all $F_i \in bf(B_L)$, if $h(F_i) = [c_i,d_i]$, then the inequality $c_i \leq \sum_{W_j \models F and W_j \in 2^{B_L}} p_j \leq d_i$ is in LC(h). In addition, LC(h) contains the following 2 constraints: (1) $\sum_{W_j \in 2^{B_L}} p_j = 1$ and (2) $\forall W_j \in 2^{BL}$, $p_j \geq 0$.

Let WP(h) denote the solution set of LC(h). Note that each solution $WP \in WP(h)$ is a world probability density function.

To compute the probabilistic truth value of a formula F, the probabilities of all possible worlds in which F is true is added. A probabilistic interpretation $I_{WP} : bf(B_L) \rightarrow [0,1]$ is defined as follows: $I_{WP}(F) = \sum_{W_j \models F and W_j \in 2^{B_L}} p_j$ for all basic formulas $F \in$

bf(B_L). Let I be a probabilistic interpretation and let $F_0,...,F_n$ be in bf(B_L), and $[c_0,d_0],...,[c_n,d_n]$ be closed sub-intervals of [0,1]. Furthermore, let C be a pf-clause, and let x and V denote an object and annotation variable, respectively.

> 1) $I \models_p F_1 :[c_1,d_1]$ iff $I(F_1) \in [c_1,d_1]$;
> 2) $I \models_p (F_1:[c_1,d_1] \wedge ... \wedge F_n:[c_n,d_n])$ iff for all $1 \le j \le n$, $I \models_p F_j:[c_j,d_j]$;
> 3) $I \models_p F_0:[c_0,d_0] \leftarrow F_1:[c_1,d_1] \wedge ... \wedge F_n:[c_n,d_n]$ iff $I \models_p F_0:[c_0,d_0]$;
>   or $I \not\models_p (F_1:[c_1,d_1] \wedge ... \wedge F_n:[c_n,d_n])$;
> 4) $I \models_p (\exists x)(C)$ iff $I \models_p (C(x/t))$ for some ground term t, where C(x/t) denotes the replacement of all free occurrences of x in C by t;
> 5) $I \models_p (\forall x)(C)$ iff $I \models_p (C(x/t))$ for all ground terms t;
> 6) $I \models_p (\exists V)(C)$ iff $I \models_p (C(V/c))$ for some $c \in [0,1]$; and
> 7) $I \models_p (\forall V(C))$ iff $I \models_p (C(V/c))$ for all $c \in [0,1]$ such that $\mu(V/c) \ne \emptyset$, where V occurs in annotation term μ.

A program P probabilistically entails a formula F iff $I \models_p F$ for all probabilistic interpretation I that satisfies each clause in P. A ground instance of a pf-clause C is a clause obtained by replacing the object variables in C by members of the Herbrand Universe. Let *grd*(P) denote the ground instances of the clauses in a program P.

Next, we present the notion of query processing in this framework. Let θ be a unifier of $(A_1 \wedge ... \wedge A_n):\mu_1$ and $(B_1 \wedge ... \wedge B_m):\mu_2$ iff $\{A_i\theta| 1 \le i \le n\} = \{B_i\theta| 1 \le i \le m\}$. Similarly, θ unifies of $(A_1 \vee ... \vee A_n):\mu_1$ and $(B_1 \vee ... \vee B_m):\mu_2$ iff $\{A_i\theta| 1 \le i \le n\} = \{B_i\theta| 1 \le i \le m\}$. Given θ a unifier of C_1,C_2, let $[\theta]$ denote $\{\gamma| \theta \le \gamma$ and $\gamma \le \theta$ and γ unifies $C_1,C_2\}$. We say that $[\theta_1] \le [\theta_2]$ iff there exists γ such that $[\theta_1] = [\theta_2\gamma]$, and that $[\theta_1] < [\theta_2]$ iff $[\theta_1] \le [\theta_2]$ and $[\theta_1] \ne [\theta_2]$. Furthermore, θ is a max-gu (maximally general unifier) of C_1 and C_2 iff θ is a unifier of C_1,C_2 and there does not exist another unifier θ_1 such that $[\theta] < [\theta_1]$.

Suppose P is a finite but non-empty set of ground clauses, i.e. $P=\{C_1,...,C_n\}$, where for all $1 \le i \le k$, C_i is of the form $F_i:[\delta_i,\rho_i] \leftarrow Body_i$. (1)Define a set LP(P) of linear constraints in the following way. For all $1 \le i \le k$, the inequality $\delta_i \le$

$$\sum_{W_j \models F and W_j \in 2^{B_L}} p_j \le \rho_i \text{ is in LP(P)}.$$

In addition, LP(P) contains the 2 constraints: (1)

$$\sum_{W_j \in 2^{B_L}} p_j = 1 \text{ and (2) } \forall W_j \in 2^{B_L}, p_j \ge 0.$$

(2) Define the closure of P, denoted by cl(P), as follows. Let cl(P) = P $\cup$ {$F:[\delta_F,\rho_F] \leftarrow Body_1 \wedge ... \wedge Body_k \wedge Con_{sol}$ | F $\in$ bf(B_L), $\delta_F = \min_{LP(P)} \sum_{W_j \models F and W_j \in 2^{B_L}} p_j$ and $\rho_F = \max_{LP(P)} \sum_{W_j \models F and W_j \in 2^{B_L}} p_j$ and Con_{sol} denotes the conjunction of constraints on the annotation terms for LP(P) to have solutions.}Furthermore, define (1) *redun*(P) = {F:[0,1] $\leftarrow$ | F $\in$ bf(B_L)} and the compiled version of P, *com*(P) = $\cup$ cl(Q) for each subset Q of *redun*(P) $\cup$ *grd*(P).

A *query* is a formula of the form $\exists(F_1:\mu_1 \wedge \ldots \wedge F_n:\mu_n)$ such that for all $1 \leq i \leq n$, F_i is a basic formula not necessarily ground, and $\mu_i = [\delta_i, \rho_i]$ where δ_i, ρ_i are either constants in $[0,1]$ or annotation variables in L. A *constrained query* Q is of the form $\exists(F_1:\mu_1 \wedge \ldots \wedge F_n:\mu_n \wedge Con_Q)$ where the query part of Q is $F_1:\mu_1 \wedge \ldots \wedge F_n:\mu_n$ and the constraint part Con_Q is a conjunction of constraints on the annotation terms. Hence, an *SLDp-deduction* of a constrained query Q_1 from a pf-program P is a sequence $<Q_1,C_1, \theta_1>, \ldots <Q_r,C_r, \theta_r>, \ldots$, where for all $i \geq 1$, C_i is a renamed version of a clause in *com*(P) and Q_{i+1} is an SLDp-resolvent of Q_i and C_i via a maximally general unifier θ_i. An SLDp-refutation is a finite SLDp-deduction where the query part is empty and the constraint part is satisfiable.

If the linear constraints in P does not have a solution then it does not have a probabilistic model hence inconsistent. A pf-compact program is a set of pf-clauses such that $\forall F \in bf(B_L) \exists$ an integer $k < \omega$ such that $\forall F\ lfp(T_p)(F) = T_p \uparrow k(F)$. Our update procedure assumes that P is pf-compact.

3. The Update Procedure

We now define our deductive database and outline its update procedure[12]. Consider a pf-program pf-ddb. The pf-clauses in pf-ddb can be partitioned into two classes: The *pf-extensional database definition* (pf-edb) and the *pf-intensional database definition* (pf-idb). The head of a pf-clause with a non-empty body is called a *pf-intensional database predicate*. All predicates in pf-ddb that are not pf-intensional database predicates are called *pf-extensional database predicates*. A collection of pf-clauses having the same pf-intensional database predicate is called a *view definition* which is associated with a set of nonempty clauses with possibly nonground annotations defining it.

We restrict pf-edb to contain only ground unit clauses whose annotations are constant and whose interval assignment is unique, i.e., for all base predicates b_i there is only one interval to which b_i is mapped. Note that **pf-edb $\cup$ pf-idb = pf-ddb**. An update translation T, chosen to satisfy an update request, only contains elements of the pf-edb. Suppose D is a pf-ddb and U(pf-ddb) denotes an updated pf-ddb, after a deletion update on fact F, U(pf-ddb) $\not\models_p$ F and after an insertion update, U(pf-ddb) $\models_p$ F. A *valid* translation is a set of updates applied to the deductive database that satisfy an update request.

To reduce the number of valid translations we use the notion of *Δ-factor* and *measures of ignorance*. If b:[d,r] is an annotated base predicate, the *measure of ignorance* of the base predicate b, denoted as $m_{ig}(b)$, is equal to the absolute value of the difference of d and r, i.e. $m_{ig}(b_j) = |d_j - r_j|$. The measure of ignorance for a set S of base predicates, denoted as $m_{ig}(S)$, is the sum of all $m_{ig}(b_i)$ for each $b_i \in S$. Moreover, if L is the total number of view dependencies on the pf-edb predicates in pf-idb then the *Δ-factor* of a pf-edb predicate B, denoted as $\Delta(B)$, is the ratio of the number of views that depend on B to L. Hence $\Delta(B) = n / L$, where n is the number of views dependent on a base predicate. If k is the number of base predicates in the pf-idb then $\Sigma \; \Delta(B_i) = 1$ for all i = 1, . . ., k.

When a unique probability range is assigned to each base predicate in the pf-edb, the notion of minimality w.r.t. set inclusion [3][4] can be generalized to the level of probabilistic satisfiability. For example, { b_1:[0.5,1], b_2:[1,1]} $\models_p$ { b_1:[0.5,1] } generalizes { b_1 } $\subseteq$ { b_1, b_2}. Hence, given update translations T and T', T' > T iff T' $\models_p$ T. If $T_1,...,T_m$ is a finite sequence of translations s.t. $\forall i \; (T_i > T_{i+1})$, then the translation T_m is defined to be a *minimal translation.*

We only need to consider those elements of the pf-edb, called *support set for deletion (SSD)*, such that these elements appear as input clauses in a successful branch of a derivation tree rooted at the update request.

Preference Criteria For Deletion (resp. Insertion)
Let T be a translation of an update request. Choose the minimal sets and order the elements of T in the following manner: (1) The smaller (higher) the sum of *Δ-factor* the higher the preference; (2) Among equal values in (1), the larger (smaller) the sum of $m_{ig}(b)$ of base predicate(s) the higher the preference.

We assume that an external system be forced to choose from among the possible translations if criterion (2) still yield equal values. We abuse the word "best" to mean the first element of the queue (T_b).

Procedure For Finding A Translation For Deletion
Let k be the number of SSDs in an SLDp derivation tree rooted at the delete request. An element e of SSD_i is redundant iff $\exists \; e' \in SSD_i, e,e' \in T_b$.

STEP1: Let **CSD** be the $\cap \; SSD_i$
        IF **CSD** $\neq \varnothing$ then
            begin
              order(**CSD**)
              $T_b = first(\textbf{CSD})$
              return T_b
            end
      ELSE
STEP2: *order*(SSD_i) i = 1,..,k
        $T_b := $ { collection of all first elements of each SSD_i s.t.
              no element is redundant }

The function *first* returns the first element in the ordered set **CSD** while the procedure *order* arranges the entire set according to the preference criteria.

Example 1:   Consider the following probabilistic deductive database:

pf-idb: $a(X):[V_1,V_2] \leftarrow b_1(X):[V_1,V_2], h(X):[1,1]$
          $a(X):[1,1] \leftarrow b_3(X):[1,1], q(X,X):[0,0], b_2(X):[0.70,0.70]$
          $q(X,Y):[0.60,0.70] \leftarrow b_1(X):[1,1], b_3(Y):[1,1]$
          $h(X):[0.75,0.75] \leftarrow b_3(X):[0,0]$
pf-edb: $\emptyset$

The following table shows the *Δ-factor* of each of the base predicates:

base predicate	dependent views	*Δ-factor*
$b_1(X)$	$a(X), q(X,Y)$	0.33
$b_2(X)$	$a(X)$	0.17
$b_3(X)$	$q(X,Y), a(X), h(X)$	0.50
TOTAL	$L = 6$	1.00

Clearly, the preferred base predicate is the base predicate $b_2(X)$.

On the other hand, the insertion of a view into the database is the process by which we make the SLDp-tree succeed, making at least one branch succeed. This process is *nonmonotonic*. [1] argues that it is not always possible to find the best translation.

The procedure traverses the tree by expanding a set in the queue with the highest precedence and adds into the ordered set of generated translations the translations generated at each level. This is an analogue to SLD-BF in [11] which is applied to a non-probabilistic framework. *The threshold for the measure of ignorance and that of the Δ-factor may be set to a user-satisfiable value which can be used to prune the tree.* In cases where a variable needs to be grounded or a probability range needs to be provided, which may happen during the insertion procedure, we assume that the data is provided by an external system separate from our update procedure.

While traversing the tree, candidate translations which contain a pf-idb predicate or a nonground pf-edb predicate are queued up in the *partial priority translation queue* (**PTQ**) according to the *Preference Criteria For Insertion*. If all the elements of a candidate translation are already ground pf-edb predicates then they are placed into the *full priority translation queue*. A ground base predicate $b:[d_1,r_1]$ is *preferred* to $b:[d_2,r_2]$ iff $b:[d_1,r_1] \models_p b:[d_2,r_2]$, i.e., $b:[d_1,r_1]$ is preferred to $b:[d_2,r_2]$ iff $[d_1,r_1] \subseteq [d_2,r_2]$.

Procedure For Finding First-Best Minimal Translation For Insertion

Let $(A:[V_1,V_2])\theta$ be a ground basic formula whose annotations are variables, $(A:[k_1,k_2])\theta$ be a strictly ground formula and $\textbf{INSERT}(A:[k_1,k_2])\theta$ be an insert request.. Let elements of FTQ and PTQ be sets of the form $<p_1,...p_n>$ where each p_i is a basic formula.

STEP1: { View Consistency Checking }
    begin
      construct derivation tree for $(A:[V_1,V_2])\theta$
      INC_VIEWS := $\varnothing$
      IF $(A:[V_1,V_2])\theta\sigma$ succeeds with annotation instantiation σ **THEN**
          begin
            FOR each σ s.t. $[k_1,k_2] \not\subseteq ([V_1,V_2])\sigma$ **DO**
                INC_VIEWS := { $(A:[V_1,V_2])\theta\sigma$ } $\cup$ **INC_VIEWS**
            IF INC_VIEWS $\neq \varnothing$ **THEN**
              begin
                query the user. Q = (Yes/No). {Proceed to insert ?}
                IF Q = Yes **THEN**
                  begin
                      FOR each $F \in$ **INC_VIEWS DO**
                        DELETE(F) {invoke our deletion procedure}
                end
                ELSE *terminate* { maintain current view }
            end
            ELSE
                INSERT $(A:[k_1,k_2])\theta$ { **STEP2** executes this }
          ELSE { no inconsistency }
             INSERT$(A:[k_1,k_2])\theta$ { **STEP2** executes this }
      end
STEP2: { Insertion of the View }
      PTQ := { $<A:[k_1,k_2]\theta>$ }
      FTQ:= $\varnothing$
      WHILE PTQ $\neq \varnothing$ **DO**
        begin
        choose *first*(PTQ)
        { a condition for user-satisfiable threshold values can be placed here }
        Let $<p_1,...,p_i,...,p_n> \in$ PTQ
        FOR each pf-clause $(a:[l,r] \leftarrow D)$ s.t. max-gu$(a,p_i)=\theta$ **DO**
          begin
            PTQ := $(<p_1,...,p_{i-1},D,p_{i+1}...,p_n>)\theta \cup$ **PTQ**
            let t,t' be candidate translations
            CASE1: **IF** t is already the set of strictly ground pf-extensional
              database predicates and $\exists$ t' s.t. t $\not\models_p$ t' **THEN FTQ** := t $\cup$ **FTQ**
            CASE2: **IF** t is already the set of strictly ground pf-extensional
              database predicates and $\exists$ t' s.t. t' $\models_p$ t **THEN FTQ**:=t $\cup${**FTQ**\ t'}

```
       order(FTQ)
       FLAG := true;
       WHILE (Flag and FTQ ≠ Ø) DO
           begin
               T_temp := first(FTQ)
               IF good(T_temp)¹ THEN
                   begin
                       T_fb := T_temp
                       FLAG:= false
                   end
               ELSE FTQ := { FTQ\T_temp }²
           end
       end
       order(PTQ)
   end
```

STEP3: Upon inserting each element in the pf-edb insert the preferred element only

¹The predicate good(T_{temp}) is true iff for all elements e:[l,r] ∈ T_{temp}, ∄ e':[l',r'] ∈ pf-edb s.t. [l,r] ∩ [l',r'] = Ø. ²To force T_{temp} to be a solution we must delete all pf-edb elements that would cause inconsistency when T_{temp} is inserted.

4. Probabilistic Abductive Diagnosis and Updates

The relationship between diagnosis and deductive database updates lies in abduction. Given a set of formulae T, an observation obs and a set of hypotheses H, D ⊆ H is a diagnosis iff (1) D ∪ T |= Obs and (2) D ∪ T is consistent. Extending the concept to our framework, an abductive diagnostic problem is a triple <pf-ddb,obs,T>, where a diagnosis T is a set of ground pf-edb predicates satisfying (1) pf-ddb ∪ T |=$_p$ obs and (2) pf-ddb ∪ T is consistent.

Example 2 : Suppose that we observe that a person is sneezing and according to an empirical data, the probability that a person sneezes (symptom s) given that he has colds (disease d) is 0.8 (the 0.2 account for the unknown cause other than colds) and the chances that a person has colds if he sneezes is 0.5. We can express the above statements with the following representation of the Bayes rule:

s(sneezes):[(0.8*V)/0.5,(0.8*V)/0.5] ← d(colds):[V,V], p(colds|sneezes):[0.5,0.5]

Given an observation, obs = s(sneezes):[1,1], i.e., we certainly observed that person P sneezes, an explanation d(colds):[0.625,0.625] could be abduced. Note that although the connective "|" is not defined in L it could be syntactically provided.

We represent causal rules so that no hypothesis appear as pf-intensional predicate. We assume that the atoms representing conditional probability, e.g. A|B for A given

B, have both object and annotation variables as ground. This reflects representation of specific empirical data.

The set of ground hypotheses clearly maps to pf-edb predicates. Hence, given an abductive problem <pf-ddb,insert(A:[c,d]),T>, for a probabilistic deductive database pf-ddb and an insert request A:[c,d]θ, a translation T is a set of pf-edb predicates such that (1) pf-ddb ∪ T |=$_p$ A:[c,d]θ and (2) pf-ddb ∪ T is consistent. By applying our insert procedure which uses the derivation tree, we can find the possible minimal translations to satisfy the update request. Since our update procedure ensures consistency, condition (2) is also satisfied. Analogously, applying our insert procedure to the abductive diagnostic problem <pf-ddb,obs,T> with obs = A:[c,d]θ we can find the minimal explanations T that will probabilistically imply the current observation obs.

Example 3. Suppose we are to insert the view p(e):[1,1]. The update problem is to find a minimal translation to satisfy the insert update request. Analogously, suppose that p(e) is observed to occur, the diagnostic problem is to find a minimal explanation for this observation.

pf-idb: p(X):[1,1] ← t(X):[1,1], υ(X):[0.5,1]
       p(e):[(0.8*V)/0.5,(0.8*V)/0.5] ← δ(a):[V,V] ∧ q(a|e):[0.5,0.5]
       t(X):[1,1] ← μ(X):[0.3,1]
pf-edb: Ø

If we insert the view p(e):[1,1] the insertion procedure generates the following **PTQ**(Partial Priority Translation Queue):
t_1) { <t(X):[1,1], υ(X):[0.5,1]> , <δ(a):[0.625,0.625]> }
t_2) { <μ(X):[0.3,1],υ(X):[0.5,1]> }
t_3) Ø

FTQ(Full Priority Translation Queue) will contain
t_1) Ø
t_2) {<δ(a):[0.625,0.625]> }
t_3) {<δ(a):[0.625,0.625]>, <μ(e):[0.3,1],υ(e):[0.5,1]> }

Using our preference criteria for insertion we choose that translation for which the sum of 'our ignorance' is zero. Accordingly, the best explanation is δ(a):[0.625,0.625].

By using the insertion procedure it is possible to both satisfy the update insert request and explain an observation. The deletion procedure is invoked when an inconsistency would be caused by the insertion request. In the diagnostic problem, this corresponds to withdrawal of a hypothesis.

To formally establish these ideas we present the following theorem:

Coincidence Theorem
Given an abductive probabilistic diagnostic problem <pf-ddb,obs,T>, s.t. obs = A:[c,d]θ, the set T is a diagnosis iff T is a solution to the insertion update problem <pf-ddb, insert(A:[c,d] θ),T>.

Abduction provides the framework for characterizing a probabilistic diagnostic problem as an insert update request. In a related work for non-probabilistic framework Inoue and Sakama in [14] proposed a method for nonmonotonic theory change using abduction. Kakas and Mancarella [6] emphasized database updates and has not discussed formal characterization of updates and diagnosis. Recently, Ngo and Haddawy [9] proposed a method to represent probabilistic logic programs by assigning a probabilistic value to the entire logical sentence. However, this representation can also be done in the framework used here.

5. Conclusion
We have outlined the insertion update procedure which could be used to generate both minimal translations and explanations. Both deletion and insertion procedure provides a method to handle nonmonotonic revision. The coincidence theorem formally establishes the relation between probabilistic database updates and diagnosis.

Acknowledgments. I wish to thank Phan Minh Dung for his valuable comments and encouragement. The communications with Raymond Ng and V.S. Subrahmanian have benefited this work.

References

1.   Tom Bylander, Dean Allemang, Michael C. Tanner and John R. Josephson, The computational complexity of abduction. *Artificial Intelligence*, 49, 1991, pp. 25-60.
2.   Console, L., Theseider Dupre, D., and Torasso, P.. A Theory of Diagnosis for Incomplete Causal Models in : *Proceedings of the 11th International Joint Conference in Artificial Intelligence*, 1989, pp. 1311-1317.
3.   Hendrik Decker. Drawing Updates From Derivations in: *Proceedings of the International Conference on Database Theory*, 1990, pp. 437-451.
4.   R. Fagin, G.M. Kuper, J.D. Ullman, M.Y. Vardi. Updating Logical Databases. *Advances in Computing Research*, Vol. 3, JAI Press, 1986.
5.   A. Guessoum and J. W. Lloyd. Updating Knowledge Bases II. TR-90-13, Univ. Bristol, Comp. Sc., 1990.
6.   A.C. Kakas and P. Mancarella. Database Updates through Abduction in: *Proceedings of the 16th International Conference on Very Large Databases*, 1990, pp. 650-661.

7.   Michael Kifer and V.S. Subrahmanian. Theory of Generalized Annotated Logic Programming and its Applications. *J. of Logic Programming*, Vol. 12, 1992, pp. 335-367.

8.   Raymond T. Ng and V.S. Subrahmanian. A Semantical Framework for Supporting Subjective and Conditional Probabilities in Deductive Databases in: *Proceedings of the 8th International Conference in Logic Programming*, 1991, pp. 565-580.

9.   L. Ngo and P. Haddawy. Probabilistic Logic Programming and Bayesian Network in: *Proceedings of the 1995 Asian Computing Science Conference*, 1995, pp. 286-300.

10. N. Nilsson. Probabilistic Logic. *Artificial Intelligence*, 28, pp. 71-87.

11. D. Poole. Logic Programming, Abduction and Probability in: *Proceedings of the International Conference on Fifth Generation Computer Systems*,1992, pp. 530-538

12. A. Restificar. An Update Procedure for A Probabilistic Deductive Database in: *Proceedings of the 4th Pacific Rim International Conference on Artificial Intelligence*, 1996, pp. 144-156.

13. Anthony Tomasic. A View Update Translation via Deduction and Annotation in: *Proceedings of the 2nd International Conference on Database Theory*, 1988, pp. 338 - 352.

14. K. Inoue and C. Sakama. Abductive Framework for Nonmonotonic Theory Change in: *Proceedings of the 14th International Joint Conference in Artificial Intelligence*, 1995, pp. 204-210.

Cooperative Combination of Default Logic and Autoepistemic Logic

Choh Man Teng
teng@cs.rochester.edu

Department of Computer Science, University of Rochester, Rochester NY 14627, USA

Abstract. When we work with information from multiple sources, the formats of the knowledge bases may not be uniform. It is desirable to be able to combine a knowledge base of default rules with one containing autoepistemic formulas. "Cooperative combination" refers to the integration of knowledge bases in different formats, in a way that retains as much of the individual characteristics of the component formalisms as possible. Previous work on relating default logic and autoepistemic logic mostly imposes some constraints on autoepistemic logic, and thus is not suitable for combining the two logics. We first present a fixed point formulation of autoepistemic logic analogous to that of default logic. Then we introduce a possible world framework with a partition structure, which corresponds to our intuitive notion of accessibility as linking alternate "possible" worlds. We show that both default logic and autoepistemic logic can be characterized using this common framework, which is important for developing a semantics applicable to the two logics, both separately and combined. We show one way of cooperatively integrating the two logics, and provide both a syntactic fixed point and a semantic possible partition sequence characterization.

1   Introduction

Default logic [Rei80] and autoepistemic logic [Moo85] are two major approaches to non-monotonic reasoning. Each of the logics is characterized with the use of a fixed point, but the two fixed point formulations are not comparable straightforwardly. When we work with information from multiple sources, the formats of the knowledge bases may not be uniform. It is desirable to be able to combine a knowledge base of default rules with one containing autoepistemic formulas. In order to do so, we need to first cast the two logics into a common framework, so that they can be compared and manipulated in a uniform fashion.

Most of the efforts in relating the two logics focus on the syntactic transformation of default rules to embed default logic into autoepistemic logic using some particular translation schema and modal system [Kon88, MT90, Tru91b, Tru91a]. However, most of these efforts impose additional constraints on autoepistemic logic, such as requiring stronger groundedness or using different base modal systems. Thus, although default logic can be translated into some variants of autoepistemic logic, the two logics cannot be easily combined using these translation schemes. Gottlob [Got93] gave a translation for embedding default logic into unrestricted autoepistemic logic, by first translating a default theory into a theory in the modal system N (modal system with the rule of necessitation but no axioms) [MT90, Tru91a], and then adding a "grounding formula" which picks out the N-expansions from among the standard autoepistemic expansions. This translation works with unrestricted autoepistemic logic, but it is not obvious how it can be extended to incorporate additional autoepistemic formulas *not* coming from the default theory.

We address the syntactic and semantic relationship between default logic and autoepistemic logic from a different perspective. First, we present a fixed point formulation of autoepistemic logic analogous to that of default logic. Then we introduce a possible world framework with a partition structure, which corresponds to our intuitive notion of accessibility as linking alternate "possible" worlds. We show that both default logic and autoepistemic logic can be characterized using this possible partition framework, and the constraints imposed on the partition structures correspond to the requirements for the fixed point operators. Casting both default logic and autoepistemic logic in a common framework is important for developing a semantics applicable to the two logics, both separately and combined. We show one way of cooperatively integrating the two logics, aiming at retaining as much as possible the individual characteristics of the component formalisms while incorporating the information available from both sources. We provide a fixed point formulation and a corresponding semantic characterization in terms of possible partition sequences for the combination.

The rest of this paper is organized as follows. Section 2 gives an overview of default logic and autoepistemic logic, and presents a fixed point formulation of autoepistemic logic similar to that of default logic. Section 3 describes some of the previous work in relating the two logics. Section 4 introduces the "possible" accessibility relation and the corresponding possible partition sequence, and shows how they can be used to characterize default logic and autoepistemic logic. Section 5 discusses a cooperative combination of the two logics, and provides both a fixed point formulation and a possible partition sequence characterization. Section 6 concludes the discussion. Proofs of the theorems can be found in the Appendix.

2 Syntactic Characterization

Let us first briefly review the preliminary terminology and machinery of default logic and autoepistemic logic. Let $\mathcal{L}$ be a standard propositional language, $\mathcal{ML}$ be a standard propositional modal language, with $\Box$ and $\Diamond$ being the necessity and possibility operators, and let $\mathcal{P}$ be the finite set of propositional constants in $\mathcal{L}$ and $\mathcal{ML}$. We denote the provability operator by $\vdash$. For any set of well formed formulas $S \subseteq \mathcal{L}$, we denote by $\mathbf{Th}(S)$ the set of well formed formulas provable from S by propositional logic; that is, $\mathbf{Th}(S) = \{\phi : S \vdash \phi\}$.

2.1 Default Logic

Definition 1. A *default rule* is an expression of the form $\frac{\alpha : M\beta_1, \ldots, M\beta_n}{\gamma}$, where α (prerequisite), $\beta_1, \ldots, \beta_n$ (justifications) and γ (consequent) are well formed formulas of $\mathcal{L}$. A *default theory* Δ is an ordered pair $\langle D, F \rangle$, where D is a set of default rules and F is a set of well formed formulas (facts) of $\mathcal{L}$.

Intuitively, a default rule $\frac{\alpha : M\beta_1, \ldots, M\beta_n}{\gamma}$ represents that if α is provable, and $\neg\beta_1, \ldots, \neg\beta_n$ is each not provable, then we by default assert that γ is true. For a default theory $\Delta = \langle D, F \rangle$, the known facts about the world constitute F, and a theory extended from F by applying the default rules in D is known as an *extension* of Δ, defined as follows.

Definition 2. Let $\Delta = \langle D, F \rangle$ be a default theory over the language $\mathcal{L}$, and E be a subset of $\mathcal{L}$. $\Gamma(E)$ is the smallest set of formulas satisfying the following three properties. [1] $F \subseteq \Gamma(E)$, [2] $\Gamma(E) = \mathbf{Th}(\Gamma(E))$, and [3] for every default rule $\frac{\alpha : M\beta_1, \ldots, M\beta_n}{\gamma} \in D$, if $\alpha \in \Gamma(E)$, and $\neg\beta_1, \ldots, \neg\beta_n \notin E$, then $\gamma \in \Gamma(E)$.

E is an *extension* for Δ iff E is a fixed point of the operator Γ, that is, $E = \Gamma(E)$.

2.2 Autoepistemic Logic

Given a set of premises $A \subseteq \mathcal{ML}$, an *autoepistemic theory* $T \subseteq \mathcal{ML}$ is a set of modal formulas representing a set of beliefs of an agent when reflecting upon A. The principal modal operator of autoepistemic logic is $\mathbf{L}$, where $\mathbf{L}\phi$ is interpreted to mean that ϕ is believed. The following two syntactic properties, *groundedness* and *stability*, are used in characterizing autoepistemic theories that represent ideal belief sets.

Definition 3. An autoepistemic theory T is *grounded* in a set of premises A iff every formula of T is included in the tautological consequences of $A \cup \{\mathbf{L}\alpha : \alpha \in T\} \cup \{\neg\mathbf{L}\alpha : \alpha \notin T\}$.

Definition 4. An autoepistemic theory T is *stable [Sta80]* iff it satisfies the following three conditions. [1] If $\alpha_1, \ldots, \alpha_n \in T$, and $\alpha_1, \ldots, \alpha_n \vdash \beta$, then $\beta \in T$, [2] If $\alpha \in T$, then $\mathbf{L}\alpha \in T$, and [3] If $\alpha \notin T$, then $\neg\mathbf{L}\alpha \in T$.

One useful property of stability is that each stable autoepistemic theory is uniquely determined by its *kernel*, the set of non-modal formulas in the theory. Thus, we only need to specify the kernel when we refer to stable theories.

An ideal rational belief set based on a premise set A contains the set A itself, and is stable and grounded in A. Such autoepistemic theories are called *stable expansions* of A.

Konolige [Kon88, Kon89] showed that in the modal system **K45**, every well formed formula of $\mathcal{ML}$ is equivalent to a formula of the *normal form* $\neg\mathbf{L}\alpha \vee \mathbf{L}\beta_1 \vee \ldots \vee \mathbf{L}\beta_n \vee \gamma$, where $\alpha, \beta_1, \ldots, \beta_n, \gamma$ are all non-modal formulas, and any of the formulas $\alpha, \beta_1, \ldots, \beta_n$ may be absent.[1] For the rest of the paper, we assume that autoepistemic formulas are given in an equivalent normal form $L\alpha \wedge \neg L\beta_1 \wedge \ldots \wedge \neg L\beta_n \rightarrow \gamma$.

2.3 Fixed Point Formulation of Autoepistemic Logic

Both default logic and autoepistemic logic are characterized via a fixed point. The definition of an extension E (in the case of default logic) or a stable expansion T (in the case of autoepistemic logic) each refers to E or T itself, so that the definition is "circular". An extension is characterized using the operator Γ such that a set of formulas E is an extension of a default theory Δ if and only if it is a fixed point of Γ, that is, $E = \Gamma(E)$. A stable expansion T requires the properties of groundedness and stability, both of which make reference to T itself in their definitions.

Although both logics make use of fixed points, the two fixed points have different forms, and are not comparable straightforwardly. In this section, we characterize stable expansions of autoepistemic logic in a way analogous to the fixed point formulation of extensions in default logic.

Theorem 5. *Let $A \subseteq \mathcal{ML}$ be a set of formulas (premises) in normal form and T be a consistent subset of $\mathcal{ML}$. $\Omega(T)$ is the set with the smallest kernel satisfying the following two properties. [1] $\Omega(T)$ is stable, and [2] for every formula $L\alpha \wedge \neg L\beta_1 \wedge \ldots \wedge \neg L\beta_n \rightarrow \gamma \in A$, if $\alpha \in T$, and $\beta_1, \ldots, \beta_n \notin T$, then $\gamma \in \Omega(T)$.*

T is a stable expansion of A iff T is a fixed point of the operator Ω, that is, $T = \Omega(T)$.

Note that this fixed point formulation for stable expansions of autoepistemic logic is laid out in a way very similar to that specified for extensions of default logic in Definition 2. The "smallest" requirement is imposed on the kernel of the set of formulas constituting $\Omega(T)$ for autoepistemic logic rather than on the whole set as in $\Gamma(E)$ of default logic, since a consistent stable set cannot have a proper stable subset. Note that knowing the kernel is sufficient to recover the modal components of a stable set. The first property of Theorem 5 is also similar to the second property of Definition 2. The stability condition for autoepistemic logic corresponds to the requirement that a default extension be deductively closed.

The first property of Definition 2 does not have a counterpart in Theorem 5, since in autoepistemic logic "facts" (formulas with no modal components) are not formally distinguished. A more significant difference between the two formulations is that in Theorem 5, we have $\alpha \in T$ instead of $\alpha \in \Omega(T)$ in the antecedent of the conditional in the second property, while the corresponding specification for a default extension calls for $\Gamma(E)$ and not E. The difference between using T and $\Omega(T)$ in the formulation can be demonstrated in the following example.

---

[1] Note that the non-modal disjunct γ has to be present, and thus the normal form of the formula $L\alpha$ is $L\alpha \vee \perp$, where $\perp$ is the contradiction symbol.

Example 1. Let Ω_1 be defined the same way as Ω, except that the second property requires $\alpha \in \Omega_1(T)$ instead of $\alpha \in T$. Consider the premise set $A = \{Lp \rightarrow p\}$. The stable set T with kernel $\{p\}$ is a stable expansion of A. It is easy to check that $T = \Omega(T)$, while $\Omega_1(T)$ has an empty kernel, and thus T is not a fixed point of Ω_1.

The two similar yet different fixed point formulations indicate that default logic and autoepistemic logic are closely related, though with some subtle differences. We can think of E as a hypothesized extension, and the Γ operator is used to verify whether E is indeed an extension. The set of formulas $\Gamma(E)$ represents those formulas that can be inferred from the facts by permissible rules in default logic, and we can conclude that E is an extension if and only if it matches $\Gamma(E)$. The mechanism for verifying stable expansions in autoepistemic logic is similar to the one for default logic, except that $\Omega(T)$ is constructed using slightly different rules. These rules can be seen as the characterizing properties of the two logics.

In particular, α is evaluated against T in the second condition of Theorem 5, while α is evaluated against $\Gamma(E)$ in the third condition of Definition 2. This suggests that stable expansions are more "liberal", as the condition that is checked against the "verifier" $\Gamma(E)$ in default logic is only checked against the hypothesized stable expansion T, which may include formulas without a sound justification ("not sufficiently grounded" in autoepistemic terms).

3   Syntactic Translations between the Two Logics

Most work in relating default logic and autoepistemic logic concentrates on translating default theories into some autoepistemic modal formulas, and then showing that each extension of the default theory corresponds to the kernel of an expansion of the translated autoepistemic premises in some modal system. Each transformation differs in terms of the choice of modal systems and the choice of translations.

One common characteristic for many of these approaches is that autoepistemic logic needs to be somewhat modified to exclude the stable expansions that do not correspond to default extensions. For example, Konolige [Kon88, Kon89] required extra groundedness conditions to select the appropriate stable expansions. These strongly grounded expansions are sensitive to the syntactic representation of the formulas. Marek and Truszczyński [MT90, Tru91b, Tru91a] showed that default logic can be translated using various schemes into modal systems ranging from **N** (modal system with the rule of necessitation but no axioms) to **S4F** [Seg71] (S4 plus F: $\phi \wedge \neg L\neg L\psi \rightarrow L(\neg L\neg \phi \wedge \psi)$). Notably, however, the applicable modal systems do not include **K45**, the modal system which has been shown to correspond to full fledged autoepistemic logic [Shv90].

The choice of translations also differs from system to system. However, it is not clear why, for example, a justification of a default rule should be translated as $\neg L\neg \beta_i$ in one system [Kon88] and $L\neg L\neg \beta_i$ in another [Tru91b]: should it be that

$\neg\beta_i$ is not believed, or that $\neg\beta_i$ is *believed to be* not believed? Konolige [Kon92] observed that since nested modal atoms at different depths are propositionally distinct, that is, p, Lp, $L(p \wedge p)$, and LLp are all considered to be different atoms in propositional logic, there is a simple schema for translating default theories such that there is a one-to-one correspondence between extensions of the original default theory and strongly grounded stable expansions of the translated theory: we just need to keep the different components of a default rule propositionally distinct (for example, by placing them at different modal depths), with the basic pattern being $L\alpha \wedge \neg L\neg\beta_1 \wedge \ldots \wedge \neg L\neg\beta_n \rightarrow \gamma$. The prerequisite terms then cannot interact with the justification terms unexpectedly. The translation schemes used in [MT90, Tru91b, Kon92] all fall into this category. This suggests that the specific syntactic form of the translation is not crucial, since we can choose from a whole family of translations as long as they adhere to the schema outlined above.

Gottlob [Got93] proposed a transformation of default logic into standard autoepistemic logic by first translating a default theory into a theory in the modal system **N**, and then adding a "grounding formula" to restrict the admissible stable expansions. This transformation does not place any restrictions on autoepistemic logic, but it is not obvious how it can be extended to incorporate additional autoepistemic formulas coming from sources other than the default theory itself.

All of the above approaches related the two logics by applying a syntactic transformation on the default theory. In the following section, we take a different approach and view the task from the semantic perspective.

4 Possible Partition Sequence

Here we forgo the syntactic issues and instead motivate the mechanisms of the two logics from a semantic point of view. We construct a possible world framework in which the accessibility relation has an intuitive correspondence with what we think of as "possible". This accessibility relation can be characterized by imposing an ordering on classes of possible worlds, so that the order reflects the dynamics of the inference process. By casting both default logic and autoepistemic logic in this common framework, we can compare the constraints imposed by the two logics on the underlying semantic structure, and also establish a semantics which allows the mixed use of the two logics.

Our approach is similar to that of Lin and Shoham's logic of **GK** [LS90], in that we provide a common framework in which both default logic and autoepistemic logic can be expressed. **GK** employs two independent modal operators, **K** and **A**, and thus there are two accessibility relations. We employ the traditional one-modal operator framework, and impose a partition structure on the possible worlds.

4.1 Basic Framework

In a possible world structure, each possible world corresponds to a possible scenario of the actual world. There is only one real world, but due to insufficient information, we cannot determine exactly which world it is. Thus we have a set of worlds, each of which satisfies all the constraints and knowledge we have of the real world. In this framework, it seems reasonable to think of the accessibility relation as a link to all those worlds that are possible, or accessible, at the current state. In other words, each world has access to all those worlds indistinguishable from itself according to the currently available information, and thus are just as likely as itself to be a candidate for the actual world. As we draw new conclusions, either monotonically when new information is acquired, or non-monotonically by means of some non-deductive rule of inference, we successively eliminate some of the worlds that are not possible any more in light of the newly obtained conclusions. We introduce below the formal notations.

Definition 6. Given a set of elements W, a *partition sequence* of W is a tuple $\langle W_0, \ldots, W_l \rangle$, $l \geq 1$, such that the sets $\{W_i : W_i \neq \emptyset\}$ form a partition[2] of W.

Definition 7. Given a set of elements W, a binary relation $R \subseteq W \times W$ is a *possible order* of W iff there is a partition sequence $\langle W_0, \ldots, W_l \rangle$ of W, such that for all $w_i \in W_i$ and $w_j \in W_j$, $R(w_i, w_j)$ iff $i \leq j$. The tuple $\langle W_0, \ldots W_l \rangle$ constitutes a *possible partition sequence* of W with respect to R.

We will use partition sequences to define possible interpretations and possible models. In this context, R is the accessibility relation which imposes a possible order on a set of possible worlds W. If $R(w_i, w_j)$, we say that w_j is accessible from w_i, or informally, w_i cannot distinguish w_j from itself as far as the information at hand is concerned.

We can think of a possible partition sequence as a hierarchy of sets of worlds, with W_0 being the highest and W_l being the lowest level. Each world in a level can access worlds in the same level as well as those at lower levels, but worlds at a lower level cannot access elements at a higher level. The inference process can then be seen as traveling down the levels of worlds. At first, the "inference pointer" is at the topmost level (W_0), where all the worlds are accessible. When we incorporate new information, some worlds are deemed impossible, and the repertoire of worlds gets smaller as those impossible worlds are eliminated from the set of candidates for the real world. These impossible worlds are grouped at a certain level i of the hierarchy, and the inference pointer moves down to level $i + 1$, from which the worlds at level i are no longer accessible.

Thus, the worlds that are accessible from the worlds at level i, that is, the worlds in $W_i, \ldots, W_l$, are the worlds that are consistent with the knowledge base *before* the new piece of information is incorporated. On the other hand, the worlds that are accessible from the worlds at level $i + 1$ are all the worlds

---

[2] A partition of a set S is a set of *non-empty* sets $S_1, \ldots, S_l$, such that $\bigcup_i S_i = S$, and $S_i \cap S_j = \emptyset$ for $i \neq j$.

that are accessible from level i *except* those residing at level i. These worlds in $W_{i+1}, \ldots, W_l$ are the worlds that are still consistent with the revised knowledge base *after* the new information has been added. The set of worlds W_l at the lowest level of the inference hierarchy represents the set of candidate worlds that are still consistent with the information and rules we have considered during the l inference steps.

Definition 8. A *possible interpretation* is an ordered pair $I = \langle \langle W_0, \ldots, W_l \rangle, m \rangle$, where $W = \bigcup_i W_i$ is an exhaustive set of possible worlds, each of which corresponds to a different interpretation of the propositional constants in $\mathcal{P}$. The tuple $\langle W_0, \ldots, W_l \rangle$ constitutes a possible partition sequence of W with respect to some possible order R. The truth assignment function m is a function from $\mathcal{P} \times W$ into the truth values $\{0, 1\}$.

Note that the accessibility relation R can be derived from the partition sequence $\langle W_0, \ldots, W_l \rangle$. The valuation function V_I of a possible interpretation $I = \langle \langle W_0, \ldots, W_l \rangle, m \rangle$ is defined to be the same as that for the interpretation $I' = \langle \bigcup_i W_i, R, m \rangle$ in standard propositional modal logic, where R is the corresponding possible order implicit in the partition sequence. As a shorthand notation in examples, each world w is denoted by the set of propositional constants or their negations that are true in that world. For example, $\{p, \neg q\}$ represents a world in which p is true and q is false.

Now we are ready to present possible models for default logic and autoepistemic logic.

4.2 Default Possible Models

Definition 9. A possible interpretation $M = \langle \langle W_0, \ldots, W_l \rangle, m \rangle$ is a *default possible model* for a default theory $\Delta = \langle D, F \rangle$ iff it satisfies the following properties.

1. $W_0 = \{w \in \bigcup_i W_i : V_M(F, w) = 0\}$.[3]
2. For each W_i, $0 < i < l$, there exists a default rule $\frac{\alpha : M\beta_1, \ldots, M\beta_n}{\gamma} \in D$, such that [1] $V_M(\Box \alpha, w) = 1$ for some $w \in W_i$, [2] $V_M(\Diamond \beta_1 \wedge \ldots \wedge \Diamond \beta_n, w) = 1$ for some $w \in W_l$, and [3] $W_i = \{w \notin W_0, \ldots, W_{i-1} : V_M(\gamma, w) = 0\}$.
3. For all default rules $\frac{\alpha : M\beta_1, \ldots, M\beta_n}{\gamma} \in D$, if $V_M(\Box \alpha \wedge \Diamond \beta_1 \wedge \ldots \wedge \Diamond \beta_n, w) = 1$ for some $w \in W_l$, then $V_M(\gamma, w) = 1$ for all $w \in W_l$.

Theorem 10. *A set of formulas E is an extension of a default theory $\Delta = \langle D, F \rangle$ iff there is a default possible model $M = \langle \langle W_0, \ldots, W_l \rangle, m \rangle$ for Δ, such that E is the set of non-modal formulas $\{\phi : V_M(\phi, w) = 1, \forall w \in W_l\}$.*

A default possible model captures the successive restriction of the set of possible worlds as more default rules are applied to the theory. The first set W_0 in the partition sequence consists of all those worlds that are not consistent with

---

[3] We assume here that the set of formulas $F = \{f_1, f_2, \ldots\}$ is equivalent to the single formula $F = f_1 \wedge f_2 \wedge \ldots$

the given facts F. These worlds are pruned before any default rule is considered. At each level $0 < i < l$ of the hierarchy, an applicable default rule is chosen, and the worlds that cannot be possible anymore after that default rule is used are grouped at level i. These are the worlds in which the consequent γ of the default rule is false, and they are excluded from consideration in future computations as they are not accessible from worlds further down in the hierarchy. Thus, the set of worlds $\bigcup_{i+1\le k\le l} W_k$, or the set of worlds that are accessible from the worlds in W_{i+1}, is the set of worlds that are still "possible" after i default rules have been applied, and the final level W_l consists of all the possible worlds of the extension.

Note that there can be more than one default possible model for each extension, depending on, for example, the order in which the default rules are applied when there are multiple applicable rules at some stage. Two different default models characterize the same extension if the last sets W_l in the two models are the same.

The following examples illustrate the correspondence between extensions of a default theory and their default possible models.

Example 2. $\Delta = \langle D, F\rangle$, where $D = \{\frac{:Mp}{p}, \frac{:M\neg p}{\neg p}, \frac{p:Mq}{q}\}$ and $F = \emptyset$.
There are two extensions, $E_1 = \mathbf{Th}(\{\neg p\})$, and $E_2 = \mathbf{Th}(\{p, q\})$. A default possible model corresponding to E_1 has the partition sequence $\langle W_{10}, W_{11}, W_{12}\rangle$, as follows:

$$W_{10} = \emptyset, \quad W_{11} = \{\{p, q\}, \{p, \neg q\}\}, \quad W_{12} = \{\{\neg p, q\}, \{\neg p, \neg q\}\},$$

where only the default rule $\frac{:M\neg p}{\neg p}$ is applied. A default possible model corresponding to E_2 has the partition sequence $\langle W_{20}, W_{21}, W_{22}, W_{23}\rangle$, as follows:

$$W_{20} = \emptyset, \quad W_{21} = \{\{\neg p, q\}, \{\neg p, \neg q\}\}, \quad W_{22} = \{\{p, \neg q\}\}, \quad W_{23} = \{\{p, q\}\},$$

where $\frac{:Mp}{p}$ is used for the transition from W_{21} to W_{22}, and $\frac{p:Mq}{q}$ is used for the transition from W_{22} to W_{23}.

Example 3. $\Delta = \langle D, F\rangle$, where $D = \{\frac{:Mp}{\neg p}\}$ and $F = \emptyset$.
This default theory has no extension. To construct any default possible model, W_0 has to be $\emptyset$, since there is no world where F, which is empty, is not true. There are four possible candidates for W_l. [1] $W_l = \emptyset$. Then there has to be some intermediate level(s) to place the two worlds $\{p\}$ and $\{\neg p\}$ in. However, condition 2 of Definition 9 is not satisfied by the only default rule in D. [2] $W_l = \{\{p\}\}$. Then $\neg p$ has to be true in all the worlds in W_l according to condition 3, a contradiction. [3] $W_l = \{\{\neg p\}\}$. But there is no default rule that will allow us to allocate the world $\{p\}$ to an intermediate level. [4] $W_l = \{\{p\}, \{\neg p\}\}$. Same problem as case [2]. Thus, we cannot construct a default possible model for Δ.

4.3 Autoepistemic Possible Models

Moore has developed a possible world semantics [Moo84] for autoepistemic logic. Given the similarity between the fixed point formulations of default logic and autoepistemic logic as discussed in Section 2.3, we can specify a possible model for an autoepistemic stable expansion using the possible partition framework.

Definition 11. A possible interpretation $M = \langle\langle W_0, \ldots, W_l \rangle, m\rangle$ is an *autoepistemic possible model* for an autoepistemic premise set A iff it satisfies the following properties.[4]

1. $W_0 = \emptyset$.[5]
2. For each W_i, $0 < i < l$, there exists a formula $L\alpha \wedge \neg L\beta_1 \wedge \ldots \wedge \neg L\beta_n \to \gamma \in A$ such that [1] $V_M(\Box\alpha, w) = 1$ for some $w \in W_l$, [2] $V_M(\Diamond\neg\beta_1 \wedge \ldots \wedge \Diamond\neg\beta_n, w) = 1$ for some $w \in W_l$, and [3] $W_i = \{w \notin W_0, \ldots, W_{i-1} : V_M(\gamma, w) = 0\}$.
3. For all formulas $L\alpha \wedge \neg L\beta_1 \wedge \ldots \wedge \neg L\beta_n \to \gamma \in A$, if $V_M(\Box\alpha \wedge \Diamond\neg\beta_1 \wedge \ldots \wedge \Diamond\neg\beta_n, w) = 1$ for some $w \in W_l$, then $V_M(\gamma, w) = 1$ for all $w \in W_l$.

Theorem 12. *T is a consistent stable expansion of a set of premises A iff there is an autoepistemic possible model $M = \langle\langle W_0, \ldots, W_l \rangle, m\rangle$ for A, such that $W_l \neq \emptyset$ and T is the set of formulas $\{\phi : V_M(\phi, w) = 1, \forall w \in W_l\}$.*

The definition of an autoepistemic possible model is very similar to that of a default possible model, with differences parallel to those occurring in their fixed point formulations. Specifically, in condition 2.[1] of Definition 11, $\Box\alpha$ is evaluated against worlds in the last element W_l, while the corresponding condition in Definition 9 is evaluated against worlds in W_i.

Another difference particular to possible models is that a default extension is characterized by only the non-modal formulas that are true in all the worlds in W_l of a default possible model, while an autoepistemic stable expansion is characterized by the set of all formulas, modal and non-modal, that are true in all the worlds in W_l of an autoepistemic possible model. The set of non-modal formulas in the autoepistemic case corresponds to the kernel of the stable expansion, and for stable sets, the modal formulas are exactly those derivable in S5 from the set of worlds representing the kernel.

Note that the last element W_l of the autoepistemic possible model is the same as the complete S5 structure in Moore's formulation of possible world semantics [Moo84]. Our formulation however highlights the similarity of autoepistemic logic and default logic, and it provides a foundation for combining the two logics in Section 5.

Example 4. $A = \{Lp \to p, \neg Lp \to q\}$.
The premise set A has two stable expansions, T_1 with the kernel $\{p\}$, and T_2 with the kernel $\{q\}$. An autoepistemic possible model corresponding to T_1 has the partition sequence $\langle W_{10}, W_{11}, W_{12} \rangle$, as follows:

$$W_{10} = \emptyset, \quad W_{11} = \{\{\neg p, q\}, \{\neg p, \neg q\}\}, \quad W_{12} = \{\{p, q\}, \{p, \neg q\}\},$$

---

[4] We identify the modal operator $\Box$ with the operator L in autoepistemic logic.
[5] This condition is not strictly necessary. It is included here to stress the similarity of the structure of autoepistemic and default possible models.

where the formula $\mathbf{L}p \rightarrow p$ is used for the partition. An autoepistemic possible model corresponding to T_2 has the partition sequence $\langle W_{20}, W_{21}, W_{22} \rangle$, as follows:

$$W_{20} = \emptyset, \quad W_{21} = \{\{p, \neg q\}, \{\neg p, \neg q\}\}, \quad W_{22} = \{\{p, q\}, \{\neg p, q\}\},$$

where the formula $\neg \mathbf{L}p \rightarrow q$ is used for the partition.

Example 5. $A = \{\neg \mathbf{L}p \rightarrow q, \neg q\}$.

A has no consistent stable expansion.[6] To construct any autoepistemic possible model, W_l can only contain one or both of the worlds $\{p, \neg q\}$ and $\{\neg p, \neg q\}$, since $\neg q \in A$ and therefore by condition 3 needs to be true in all the worlds in W_l. If $W_l = \{\{p, \neg q\}\}$, then $\neg \mathbf{L}p \rightarrow q$ does not satisfy condition 2.[2], and there is no formula that can be used to put the other world $\{\neg p, \neg q\}$ into a different class. If $W_l = \{\{\neg p, \neg q\}\}$ or $W_l = \{\{p, \neg q\}, \{\neg p, \neg q\}\}$, then by $\neg \mathbf{L}p \rightarrow q$ and condition 3 we need to have q in all the worlds in W_l, a contradiction. Thus, we cannot construct an appropriate autoepistemic possible model for A.

5 Combining the Two Logics

When we work with information from multiple sources, the formats of the knowledge bases may not be uniform. In this section, we show how the fixed point formulations and possible partition sequence semantics can be extended easily to cooperatively combine a default theory with an autoepistemic theory.

5.1 Cooperative Combination

First let us consider briefly how knowledge bases of different formats can be combined. By *cooperative combination* we mean the formulation of a reasoning process that makes use of the different sources of information in a way that reflects the spirit of the individual formalisms. The resulting system incorporates the component formalisms in a cooperative way, retaining the characteristics of each component as much as possible. Cooperative combination allows us to combine and extract maximal information from different sources, keeping close to their original intended interpretations. The components are able to interact in a constructive way, so that the result is more than just the sum of the components stacked together. This is particularly useful when we need to reason about already existing information from diverse sources.

Given a default theory and an autoepistemic theory, one strategy is to combine the "end results" of the two theories, that is, an extension of the default theory is merged with a stable expansion of the autoepistemic knowledge base. Another strategy is to combine the default rules and autoepistemic formulas at "intermediate levels"; the default rules and autoepistemic formulas are interleaved to generate a combined extension. We take the latter approach, and define a *default-autoepistemic logic* as follows.

---

[6] It has no inconsistent stable expansion either.

5.2 Default-Autoepistemic Logic

First we provide a fixed point definition of the combined extension.

Definition 13. A *default-autoepistemic theory* is a tuple $\langle F, D, A \rangle$, where $F \subseteq \mathcal{L}$ is consistent, D is a set of default rules, and $A \subseteq \mathcal{ML}$. Given a default-autoepistemic theory $\langle F, D, A \rangle$ and a set of consistent formulas $E \subseteq \mathcal{ML}$, $\Lambda(E)$ is the set with the smallest kernel satisfying the following properties. [1] $F \subseteq \Lambda(E)$, [2] $\Lambda(E)$ is stable, [3] For every default rule $\frac{\alpha:M\beta_1,\ldots,M\beta_n}{\gamma} \in D$, if $\alpha \in \Lambda(E)$, and $\neg\beta_1, \ldots, \neg\beta_n \notin E$, then $\gamma \in \Lambda(E)$. [4] For every formula $L\alpha \wedge \neg L\beta_1 \wedge \ldots \wedge \neg L\beta_n \to \gamma \in A$, if $\alpha \in E$, and $\beta_1, \ldots, \beta_n \notin E$, then $\gamma \in \Lambda(E)$.

E is a *default-autoepistemic extension* of $\langle F, D, A \rangle$ iff E is a fixed point of the operator Λ, that is, $E = \Lambda(E)$.

A default-autoepistemic theory $\langle F, D, A \rangle$ is derived from two components, a default theory $\langle D, F \rangle$, and an autoepistemic premise set A. The definition of a default-autoepistemic extension combines the fixed point conditions of the two component logics as specified in Definition 2 and Theorem 5. Condition 1 is adopted from Definition 2. Condition 2 applies to both components. The stability condition, which is required of autoepistemic stable expansions, implies the deductive closure condition required of default extensions. Conditions 3 and 4 are analogous to the final conditions of Definition 2 and Theorem 5 respectively.

Note that if the autoepistemic A (default D and F) component of a default-autoepistemic theory is absent, any default-autoepistemic extension is equivalent to a default extension of $\langle D, F \rangle$ (autoepistemic stable expansion of A), provided we only consider non-modal formulas when A is absent. This conforms to our notion of being "cooperative": the behavior of each component formalism is unaltered when it is the sole formalism in the combined system.

Note also that a default-autoepistemic extension is a stable autoepistemic theory, and thus can be uniquely determined by its kernel. Now we give the corresponding possible partition sequence characterization.

Definition 14. A possible interpretation $M = \langle \langle W_0, \ldots, W_l \rangle, m \rangle$ is a *default-autoepistemic possible model* for a default-autoepistemic theory $\langle F, D, A \rangle$ iff it satisfies the following properties.

1. $W_0 = \{w \in \bigcup_i W_i : V_M(F, w) = 0\}$.
2. For each W_i, $0 < i < l$, there exists either
   (a) $\frac{\alpha:M\beta_1,\ldots,M\beta_n}{\gamma} \in D$, such that [1] $V_M(\Box\alpha, w) = 1$ for some $w \in W_i$, [2] $V_M(\Diamond\beta_1 \wedge \ldots \wedge \Diamond\beta_n, w) = 1$ for some $w \in W_l$, and [3] $W_i = \{w \notin W_0, \ldots, W_{i-1} : V_M(\gamma, w) = 0\}$, or
   (b) $L\alpha \wedge \neg L\beta_1 \wedge \ldots \wedge \neg L\beta_n \to \gamma \in A$, such that [1] $V_M(\Box\alpha, w) = 1$ for some $w \in W_l$, [2] $V_M(\Diamond\neg\beta_1 \wedge \ldots \wedge \Diamond\neg\beta_n, w) = 1$ for some $w \in W_l$, and [3] $W_i = \{w \notin W_0, \ldots, W_{i-1} : V_M(\gamma, w) = 0\}$.
3. For all default rules $\frac{\alpha:M\beta_1,\ldots,M\beta_n}{\gamma} \in D$, if $V_M(\Box\alpha \wedge \Diamond\beta_1 \wedge \ldots \wedge \Diamond\beta_n, w) = 1$ for some $w \in W_l$, then $V_M(\gamma, w) = 1$ for all $w \in W_l$.

4. For all formulas $L\alpha \wedge \neg L\beta_1 \wedge \ldots \wedge \neg L\beta_n \to \gamma \in A$, if $V_M(\Box\alpha \wedge \Diamond\neg\beta_1 \wedge \ldots \wedge \Diamond\neg\beta_n, w) = 1$ for some $w \in W_l$, then $V_M(\gamma, w) = 1$ for all $w \in W_l$.

Theorem 15. *A set of consistent formulas $E \subseteq \mathcal{ML}$ is a default-autoepistemic extension of $\langle F, D, A \rangle$ iff there is a default-autoepistemic possible model $M = \langle\langle W_0, \ldots, W_l \rangle, m \rangle$ for $\langle F, D, A \rangle$, such that $W_l \neq \emptyset$ and E is the set of formulas $\{\phi : V_M(\phi, w) = 1, \forall w \in W_l\}$.*

Again the default-autoepistemic possible model combines the properties of the two component possible models. Properties 1, 3, and 4 correspond directly to the first and last properties in Definitions 9 and 11. Property 2 corresponds to the second conditions in both definitions, specifying that default rules and autoepistemic formulas can be applied interleavingly to partition the possible worlds.

Here is an example to illustrate the interaction between the default and autoepistemic components.

Example 6. Consider the default-autoepistemic theory $\langle F, D, A \rangle$, where $F = \emptyset$, $D = \{\frac{:Mp}{p}, \frac{q:Mr}{r}\}$, and $A = \{Lp \to q\}$.
Taking the default component alone, the default theory $\langle D, F \rangle$ has a single extension $\mathbf{Th}(p)$. Taking the autoepistemic component A alone gives rise to a single stable expansion with an empty kernel. Now consider the default-autoepistemic theory $\langle F, D, A \rangle$. There is a default-autoepistemic extension with the kernel $\{p, q, r\}$. The default conclusion p from the first default rule makes it possible for the autoepistemic formula to be used to infer q, which is in turn used to satisfy the prerequisite condition of the second default rule. The corresponding default-autoepistemic possible model $\langle W_0, W_1, W_2, W_3, W_4 \rangle$ is as follows.

$$W_0 = \emptyset, \quad W_1 = \{\{\neg p, q, r\}, \{\neg p, q, \neg r\}, \{\neg p, \neg q, r\}, \{\neg p, \neg q, \neg r\}\},$$
$$W_2 = \{\{p, \neg q, r\}, \{p, \neg q, \neg r\}\}, \quad W_3 = \{\{p, q, \neg r\}\}, \quad W_4 = \{\{p, q, r\}\}.$$

The default $\frac{:Mp}{p}$ is used to generate W_1, the autoepistemic formula $Lp \to q$ is used to generate W_2, and the default $\frac{q:Mr}{r}$ is used to generate W_3. The cooperative default-autoepistemic extension gives us more information than a simple union of the conclusions of the two theories.

6 Conclusion

This concludes our discussion of fixed points and possible partition sequences of default logic and autoepistemic logic. We presented both a syntactic and a semantic way to relate the two logics. First, a default logic style fixed point characterization was formulated for autoepistemic logic. The main difference between the two fixed points is in how the prerequisite (antecedent) of a default rule (autoepistemic formula) is evaluated. In default logic, the prerequisite of a default rule is checked against $\Gamma(E)$, while in autoepistemic logic, the positive modal term in the antecedent of a formula is checked against the "less grounded" theory T itself. Second, we presented an intuitively reasonable description of the accessibility relation in modal systems in terms of a partition sequence of possible world equivalence classes. We utilized the fixed point formulations to characterize default extensions and autoepistemic stable expansions in this framework. This helps to establish a common semantics when we need to combine information from different sources involving both default logic and autoepistemic logic. We constructed a cooperative combination of the two logics, and provided both a syntactic fixed point and a semantic possible partition sequence characterization for the resultant logic.

Acknowledgements

Special thanks to Henry Kyburg, not only for his insightful comments on the infinite versions of this paper, but also for his patience during the long and hard evolutionary process. This work was supported by National Science Foundation grant IRI-9411267.

References

[Got93] Georg Gottlob. The power of beliefs or translating default logic into standard autoepistemic logic. In *Proceedings of the Thirteenth International Joint Conference on Artificial Intelligence*, pages 570–575, 1993.

[Kon88] Kurt Konolige. On the relation between default and autoepistemic logic. *Artificial Intelligence*, 35:343–382, 1988.

[Kon89] Kurt Konolige. On the relation between default and autoepistemic logic. *Artificial Intelligence*, 41:115, 1989. Errata.

[Kon92] Kurt Konolige. Ideal introspective belief. In *Proceedings of the Tenth National Conference on Artificial Intelligence*, pages 635–641, 1992.

[Kon94] Kurt Konolige. Autoepistemic logic. In Dov M. Gabbay, C. J. Hogger, and J. A. Robinson, editors, *Handbook of Logic in Artificial Intelligence and Logic Programming*, volume 3: Nonmonotonic Reasoning and Uncertain Reasoning. Clarendon Press, 1994.

[LS90] Fangzhen Lin and Yoav Shoham. Epistemic semantics for fixed-point nonmonotonic logics. In *Proceedings of the Third Conference on Theoretical Aspects of Reasoning about Knowledge*, pages 111–120, 1990.

[Moo84] Robert C. Moore. Possible-world semantics for autoepistemic logic. In *Proceedings of AAAI Non-monotonic Reasoning Workshop*, pages 344–354, 1984.

[Moo85] Robert C. Moore. Semantical considerations on nonmonotonic logic. *Artificial Intelligence*, 25:75–94, 1985.

[MT90] Wiktor Marek and Miroslaw Truszczyński. Modal logic for default reasoning. *Annals of Mathematics and Artificial Intelligence*, 1:275–302, 1990.

[Poo94] David Poole. Default logic. In Dov M. Gabbay, C. J. Hogger, and J. A. Robinson, editors, *Handbook of Logic in Artificial Intelligence and Logic Programming*, volume 3: Nonmonotonic Reasoning and Uncertain Reasoning. Clarendon Press, 1994.

[Rei80] R. Reiter. A logic for default reasoning. *Artificial Intelligence*, 13:81–132, 1980.

[Seg71] K. Segerberg. An essay in classical modal logic, 1971. Filosofiska Studier, Uppsala University, 13.

[Shv90] Grigori Shvarts. Autoepistemic modal logics. In *Proceedings of the Third Conference on Theoretical Aspects of Reasoning about Knowledge*, pages 97–109, 1990.

[Sta80] R. Stalnaker. A note on non-monotonic modal logic. Department of Philosophy, Cornell University, Ithaca, New York, U.S.A., 1980. Unpublished manuscript.

[Tru91a] Mirosław Truszczyński. Embedding default logics into modal nonmonotonic logics. In *Proceedings of the First International Workshop on Logic Programming and Non-monotonic Reasoning*, pages 151–165, 1991.

[Tru91b] Mirosław Truszczyński. Modal interpretations of default logic. In *Proceedings of the Twelfth International Joint Conference on Artificial Intelligence*, pages 393–398, 1991.

Appendix: Proofs of Theorems

We append here proof sketches of the theorems presented in this paper.

Theorem 5. *Let $A \subseteq \mathcal{ML}$ be a set of formulas (premises) in normal form and T be a consistent subset of $\mathcal{ML}$. $\Omega(T)$ is the set with the smallest kernel satisfying the following two properties. [1] $\Omega(T)$ is stable, and [2] for every formula $L\alpha \wedge \neg L\beta_1 \wedge \ldots \wedge \neg L\beta_n \to \gamma \in A$, if $\alpha \in T$, and $\beta_1, \ldots, \beta_n \notin T$, then $\gamma \in \Omega(T)$.*

T is a stable expansion of A iff T is a fixed point of the operator Ω, that is, $T = \Omega(T)$.

Proof. ($\Longrightarrow$) Suppose T is a consistent stable expansion of A. We need to show $T = \Omega(T)$.

First we show the kernel of $\Omega(T)$ is a subset of the kernel of T. Observe that T is a candidate for $\Omega(T)$ since T satisfies the two conditions in the theorem: [1] T is stable, and [2] For every formula $L\alpha \wedge \neg L\beta_1 \wedge \ldots \wedge \neg L\beta_n \to \gamma \in A$, if $\alpha \in T$, and $\beta_1, \ldots, \beta_n \notin T$, then $\gamma \in T$ since T is stable and $A \subseteq T$. $\Omega(T)$ is the set with the *smallest* kernel that satisfies these conditions, and so the kernel of $\Omega(T)$ is a subset of the kernel of T.

Now we show that there cannot be a non-modal formula in T that is not in $\Omega(T)$. For any non-modal formula p in T, since T is grounded in A, p is a tautological consequence of $A \cup \{L\alpha : \alpha \in T\} \cup \{\neg L\alpha : \alpha \notin T\}$. Thus, p has to be derivable from the consequents of those formulas in A whose antecedents are true in T. Since T is a consistent stable set, for any formula $L\alpha \wedge \neg L\beta_1 \wedge \ldots \wedge \neg L\beta_n \to \gamma$ in A, we have [a] $L\alpha \in T \Longrightarrow \alpha \in T$, and [b] $\neg L\beta_i \in T \Longrightarrow \beta_i \notin T$. Together with condition [2] in the theorem, any consequent γ that is in T is also in $\Omega(T)$, and thus p has to be in $\Omega(T)$ as well.

Thus, the kernel of T and the kernel of $\Omega(T)$ are the same, and since the kernel uniquely characterizes a stable set, we have $T = \Omega(T)$.

($\Longleftarrow$) Suppose $T = \Omega(T)$ for some consistent $T \subseteq \mathcal{ML}$. We need to show that T is a stable expansion of A.

T is a stable expansion iff it satisfies the following three conditions: [a] $A \subseteq T$, [b] T is stable, and [c] T is grounded in A. For condition [a], since T is stable and consistent, for every formula $\mathbf{L}\alpha \wedge \neg \mathbf{L}\beta_1 \wedge \ldots \wedge \neg \mathbf{L}\beta_n \to \gamma \in A$, we have $\mathbf{L}\alpha \in T \Longrightarrow \alpha \in T$, and $\neg \mathbf{L}\beta_i \in T \Longrightarrow \beta_i \notin T$. Thus, by condition [2] of the theorem, if the antecedent of a formula in A is satisfied in T, then the consequent is in $\Omega(T)$ (and therefore T). Condition [b] is the same as condition [1] of the theorem. For condition [c], we need to show that every formula in T is included in $B = \mathbf{Th}(A \cup \{\mathbf{L}\alpha : \alpha \in T\} \cup \{\neg \mathbf{L}\alpha : \alpha \notin T\})$. Since the kernel of $\Omega(T)$ is the smallest among those satisfying the two conditions of the theorem, it is exactly the set $\{\gamma \mid \mathbf{L}\alpha \wedge \neg \mathbf{L}\beta_1 \wedge \ldots \wedge \neg \mathbf{L}\beta_n \to \gamma \in A, \alpha \in T, \beta_1, \ldots, \beta_n \notin T\}$, which is clearly included in B. Since $\Omega(T)$ is stable and consistent (and $T = \Omega(T)$), it follows that all the formulas in $\Omega(T)$ that are *not* non-modal are included in the $\{\mathbf{L}\alpha : \alpha \in T\} \cup \{\neg \mathbf{L}\alpha : \alpha \notin T\}$ part of B as well. This shows that T is grounded in A. □

Theorem 10. *A set of formulas E is an extension of a default theory $\Delta = \langle D, F \rangle$ iff there is a default possible model $M = \langle \langle W_0, \ldots, W_l \rangle, m \rangle$ for Δ, such that E is the set of non-modal formulas $\{\phi : V_M(\phi, w) = 1, \forall w \in W_l\}$.*

Proof. ($\Longrightarrow$) Suppose E is an extension of a default theory $\Delta = \langle D, F \rangle$, that is, $E = \Gamma(E)$. We need to show that there is a default possible model $M = \langle \langle W_0, \ldots, W_l \rangle, m \rangle$ for Δ, such that E is the set of non-modal formulas $\{\phi : V_M(\phi, w) = 1, \forall w \in W_l\}$.

We can always construct W_0 according to condition 1 in Definition 9. Let W_l be the set of all possible worlds in which E is true. Now we order the worlds not in W_0 into a sequence $\langle W_1, \ldots, W_m \rangle$ according to condition 2 of Definition 9, until W_m cannot be further partitioned. We need to show that $W_m = W_l$. We proceed in two steps.

Note that W_0 and W_l are disjoint since $F \subseteq E$. For each subsequent level W_i, if $V_M(\Box\alpha, w) = 1$ for some $w \in W_i$, then $V_M(\alpha, w) = 1$ for all $w \in W_l$, and $\alpha \in E = \Gamma(E)$. Similarly, if $V_M(\Diamond\beta_1 \wedge \ldots \wedge \Diamond\beta_n, w) = 1$ for some $w \in W_l$, then $\neg\beta_1, \ldots, \neg\beta_n \notin E$. Together with condition 3 of Definition 2, these two conditions ensure that $\gamma \in \Gamma(E) = E$ and $V_M(\gamma, w) = 1$ for all $w \in W_l$. Therefore none of the worlds in W_l can be grouped into any of the W_i's, $i < m$, and thus $W_l \subseteq W_m$.

Now we show that it is not the case that $W_l \subset W_m$. Assume the contrary. Let $E' = \{\phi : V_M(\phi, w) = 1, \forall w \in W_m\}$. Recall that W_l is a maximal set for E, and the additional worlds in W_m makes $E' \subset E$. E' also satisfies the three conditions in Definition 2 as a candidate for $\Gamma(E)$, which contradicts the assumption that E is an extension and thus the *smallest* such candidate. Thus, $W_m = W_l$.

Lastly, condition 3 of Definition 9 is satisfied by W_l as a consequence of condition 3 of Definition 2.

($\Longleftarrow$) Suppose there is a default possible model $M = \langle \langle W_0, \ldots, W_l \rangle, m \rangle$ for $\Delta = \langle D, F \rangle$. We need to show that the set E of non-modal formulas $\{\phi : V_M(\phi, w) = 1, \forall w \in W_l\}$ is an extension of Δ, that is, $E = \Gamma(E)$.

E satisfies the three conditions in Definition 2, and thus $\Gamma(E) \subseteq E$. Now let $E_i = \{\phi : V_M(\Box\phi, w) = 1, \forall w \in W_i\}$. We show $E_i \subseteq \Gamma(E)$ for $i > 0$. $E_1 = \mathbf{Th}(F) \subseteq \Gamma(E)$. Now assume $E_i \subseteq \Gamma(E)$. $E_{i+1} = \mathbf{Th}(E_i \cup \{\gamma\})$, where there is a default rule $\frac{\alpha:M\beta_1,\ldots,M\beta_n}{\gamma} \in D$, such that [1] $V_M(\Box\alpha, w) = 1$ for some $w \in W_i$, and [2] $V_M(\Diamond\beta_1 \wedge \ldots \wedge \Diamond\beta_n, w) = 1$ for some $w \in W_l$. From [1] we have $\alpha \in \Gamma(E)$, and from [2] $\neg\beta_1, \ldots, \neg\beta_n \notin E$. Thus, $\gamma \in \Gamma(E)$ according to condition 3 of Definition 2, and $E_{i+1} \subseteq \Gamma(E)$. In particular, $E = E_l \subseteq \Gamma(E)$. $\Box$

Theorem 12. *T is a consistent stable expansion of a set of premises A iff there is an autoepistemic possible model $M = \langle\langle W_0, \ldots, W_l\rangle, m\rangle$ for A, such that $W_l \neq \emptyset$ and T is the set of formulas $\{\phi : V_M(\phi, w) = 1, \forall w \in W_l\}$.*

Proof. The proof follows closely the one for Theorem 10, with obvious modifications. We can draw a correspondence between the fixed point formulation we developed in Theorem 5 and autoepistemic possible models along the same lines as the correspondence between Definition 2 and Theorem 10 for default logic. The differences between the two models are discussed in Section 4.3. $\Box$

Theorem 15. *A set of consistent formulas $E \subseteq \mathcal{ML}$ is a default-autoepistemic extension of $\langle F, D, A\rangle$ iff there is a default-autoepistemic possible model $M = \langle\langle W_0, \ldots, W_l\rangle, m\rangle$ for $\langle F, D, A\rangle$, such that $W_l \neq \emptyset$ and E is the set of formulas $\{\phi : V_M(\phi, w) = 1, \forall w \in W_l\}$.*

Proof. This theorem follows from Theorems 10 and 12. $\Box$

Lecture Notes in Artificial Intelligence (LNAI)

Lecture Notes in Computer Science